THE NEW MEDIA WRITER

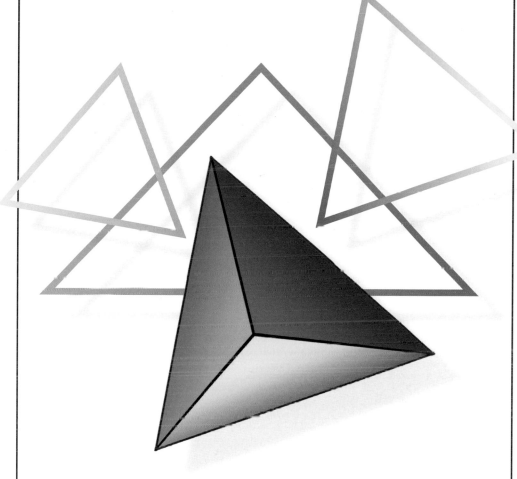

Sean Morey

FOUNTAINHEAD
PRESS

Our green initiatives include:

Electronic Products
We deliver products in non-paper form whenever possible. This includes pdf downloadables, flash drives, & CDs.

Electronic Samples
We use Xample, a new electronic sampling system. Instructor samples are sent via a personalized web page that links to pdf downloads.

FSC Certified Printers
All of our printers are certified by the Forest Service Council which promotes environmentally and socially responsible management of the world's forests. This program allows consumer groups, individual consumers, and businesses to work together hand-in-hand to promote responsible use of the world's forests as a renewable and sustainable resource.

Recycled Paper
Most of our products are printed on a minimum of 30% post-consumer waste recycled paper.

Support of Green Causes
When we do print, we donate a portion of our revenue to green causes. Listed below are a few of the organizations that have received donations from Fountainhead Press. We welcome your feedback and suggestions for contributions, as we are always searching for worthy initiatives.
Rainforest 2 Reef
Environmental Working Group

This one's for Sofia.

ACKNOWLEDGEMENTS

This book began with a lunch conversation with Felix Frazier about the state of the academic publishing industry, and how to teach new media in a way that also used new media, incorporating the technology into the design of the pedagogical materials. Rather than simply produce an e-book made up of scanned pages with a few annotated tools, Felix had the vision and foresight to push this project and think bigger. I offer Felix my sincere and deepest gratitude for this and for his faith and diligence in working through this project, helping me keep aim of the larger goal, and for believing in this project from that first conversation.

This book is also very much a product of the ideas that it espouses, and one of those is certainly the collaborative nature of writing. Although this book's cover displays only one name, it's more accurate to say that it was composed by many writers, some of which will never read the book and only know that they granted an image and signed a permission form. Some nonhuman (and human) contributors will read this book not knowing they helped write it. Of course, others contributed consciously and painstakingly, especially Susan Moore, Amy Salisbury, Shelley Smith, and the rest of the Fountainhead Press production team. Without their expertise, guidance, and thoughtful comments this book would never have reached production. I also want to thank Scott Timian for his patience working through this project and his steadfast determination in seeing this book's development from start to finish. A big thanks to everyone at Fountainhead Press for their enthusiasm and encouragement. Thanks also to Clay Arnold who helped germinate some of the original ideas for this project.

Thanks to all my students who show me new things, give me fresh perspective, and constantly make me grow as a teacher.

Finally, I want to thank friends and family. Of friends, John Tinnell and Caroline Stone have helped me rethink what writing with new media technologies can mean and the effects it can produce. Many thanks go to Greg Ulmer—even though this book may not completely execute an electrate logic, it breathes with an electrate spirit. And especially, I thank Sid Dobrin, who has given me invaluable advice about writing books and let me steal some of his ideas (ok, all of them). Of family, you have become too numerous to list, but you know who you are—I thank all of you. Most importantly, though, my deepest gratitude goes to Aubrey and Sofia, for hanging in there with me and making this project worthwhile.

HOW TO USE THIS BOOK

While this textbook may look like any other printed book, it includes special features to provide you with a more interactive learning experience, making use of new media to actually teach new media. As you read through the book's pages, several hypertext features allow you to easily reference online components that provide examples, tutorials, articles, and other content.

Quick Reference Codes

Quick Reference (QR) codes appear throughout the book that link to other online content, such as articles, audio, or Web pages. This book becomes a node within the larger new media environment, allowing you to quickly connect with other media and sources of information. While Google Goggles can be used to scan QR codes, you can also use dedicated QR code reader applications, with many versions available for free.

The following QR code readers and QR code scanners work on most major smartphones and at the time of this printing were free

- NeoReader
- TapMedia's QR Reader
- i-nigma

Video Tutorials

Since many assignments require you to use different kinds of software, such as video and image editors, the book also contains QR codes to video tutorials that walk you through the basics.

Multiple Platforms

In addition to a printed book, *The New Media Writer* is available in many electronic platforms, such as tablets, smart phones, computers, and other e-readers. Using the book with these other devices enhances the interactivity and multimodality of the text and images. This turn to electronic versions also supports Fountainhead Press's continued and conscientious effort to embrace the "green" initiatives inherent in *The New Media Writer*.

Companion website

While all the URLs listed in the book will be accessible with a device with Google Goggles or a QR code app, they will also be listed on a companion web site (http://www.fountainheadpress.com/newmediawriter/). This website will also contain updated example banks to use in class or for your own analysis.

TABLE OF CONTENTS

PREFACE TO INSTRUCTORS

When I first began teaching, I was fortunate to be in a graduate program that stressed not only the analysis of new media texts but also their production. In other words, I learned that we as writing teachers—broadly construed— shouldn't just teach students how to interpret film, websites, online video, blogs, brand marks, and other visual media, but we should also teach them how to *make* such media, so they can become producers of visually based new media texts and not just consumers of media.

Such is the impetus for this book. *The New Media Writer* is an attempt to combine both the hermeneutical strengths found in other books on new media and visual studies as well as the pedagogical instruction to teach students how to make these texts for themselves. While students using this text probably won't receive recognition at a film festival or become the latest blogging sensation, they will begin to understand how to interpret, plan, compose, revise, and disseminate new media texts that can solve problems in their daily lives, whether it's standing out on a job search by creating a video resume, making flyers to help find their lost pet, or creating an "iReport" for CNN to bring attention to an important cause in their community. While they will certainly be able to use these skills toward other writing courses in their university careers, this book looks beyond the university, to where students engage with media outside of the classroom.

Both inside and outside the classroom, the definition of "writing" continues to expand to include non-alphabetic print modalities. Both inside and outside the academic curriculum, students need to know how to manipulate images in a photo editor, edit video, mix text and image, and choose the best online media for a rhetorical situation. Most of the time, students already compose these texts through tweets, wall posts, e-mails, and YouTube. However, they don't always write these rhetorically, according to a thorough reading of

1

audience and the rhetorical environment. They don't always choose the best genre, medium, and design to fit this environment. This book addresses a rhetorical process for creating and reading new media texts, walking students through the process from traditional rhetorical questions, to ones specific for new media.

Many classes that teach new media do so in a very narrow sense, and worse, sometimes create a dichotomy between "writing" and making texts with visuals, which itself is just another kind of writing. Often, writing with new technologies focuses mainly on either the technology, or reading new media texts produced by the technology. However, few classes, and even fewer textbooks, focus on both analyzing new media works *and* producing them. Producing works of new media, or writing through media (which also includes alphabetic print), is of central importance for today's students who must be able to read the visuals they see around them every day, make sense of what they see, and relate them to their own lives. However, to be truly rhetorical and participate in a democratic society, students must also be able to produce such visuals; they need a visual rhetoric in addition to a literate one. They need to be able to write and think in images and not just in words.

This textbook separates new media (and closely related, visual rhetoric) from literacy because, stemming from the work of Gregory L. Ulmer, the typical new media texts that a student will encounter do not operate (wholly) based on a literate logic, but on what Ulmer calls *electracy*, a post-literate language apparatus that is emerging in the current multimedia saturated environment. Succinctly, Ulmer states that "electracy is to the digital Internet what literacy is to print." Electracy is different than literacy because it incorporates the chief psychological component that alphabetic text is unequipped to handle—emotion. Part of the critical analysis that the visual rhetoric of new media texts should attend to is the emotional response (and what that entails for community interpretation and action) that a visual evokes. Except for *Internet Invention*, Ulmer's textbook designed for upper-division hypermedia courses, no other new media textbook exists that teaches from an electrate perspective.

However, there are traditional design elements that a new media text should address. *The New Media Writer* covers these different design principles but does so in a culturally responsible way that looks at the rhetorical reasons for why such design principles should be used and how they should be used ethically. Students learn to read common new media texts that exist in the public sphere, what these texts try to argue, and how students can make use of such design principles for their own rhetorical purposes.

To accomplish all of this, *The New Media Writer* incorporates some specific features to help both you and the student create and study new media texts; they are described next.

THE RHETORICAL TETRAHEDRON

One of the traditional models used to help students think through the parts of a rhetorical interaction has been the rhetorical triangle. The triangle has traditionally been composed of writer/reader/text, or *logos/pathos/ethos*, depending if one focuses on the actors at play, or the appeals of persuasion. However, since new media writing extends beyond the printed essay, other rhetorical choices become as important to the writing process, such as creating a design, choosing a genre, and specifying a medium. Given these six domains of rhetorical choice, as well as *ethos, pathos, logos*, and *kairos*—the relation of time to rhetoric—this book offers the rhetorical triangle made up of six lines and four planes, no longer a triangle but a tetrahedron. In addition, by labeling the *sides* of the tetrahedron—and not the points—the tetrahedron more accurately models the rhetorical options that lie across a continuum of possibilities, such as:

- multiple audiences (that may be unknown, unwarranted, or unaccounted for)
- multiple designs
- multiple genres
- multiple mediums
- multiple authors (in the forms of author collaboration, remixing, blogging comments, or peer responses)

This change in orientation allows your students to move along the continuum from the singularity of one to the infinite possibilities of the many in a new media world without sacrificing authentication. The rhetorical tetrahedron becomes a more sophisticated way to display the various elements at play in a rhetorical situation, and because it exists in three-dimensional space, it is in constant motion, allowing you and your students to discuss the ever-shifting problem of a rhetorical situation. The rhetorical tetrahedron is integrated into every chapter, and it's recommended that you use it as discussed in the introduction, for such simplicity makes it more pedagogically useful. You can, of course, take the tetrahedron, relabel it, and use it however you feel is most effective for your particular class.

FOCUS ON MEDIA AS WRITING

Many textbooks will attempt to fit new media into a print-based paradigm. However, doing so can be reductive, limiting how students understand and compose new media texts. For example, a video résumé is not just a reading of a list of accomplishments to a video camera. Instead, it is a genre that uses the logic of video editing, such as cuts, montage, lighting, and other elements not found in a print resume. By taking a terminological approach that breaks teaching new media out of a traditional writing frame while still situating it within a tradition of writing, *The New Media Writer* helps students create and engage with new media more creatively. For example, although much of the terminology in Chapter 4 might be new to students—such as ekphrasis, montage, or puncept—terms such as these help students focus on writing practices specific to media other than alphabetic writing and provide them more tools when producing texts in different media.

VIDEO TUTORIALS

Several of the assignments in *The New Media Writer* are best completed by using media production software such as photo and video editors. To help you better understand how to use and teach these platforms, this book includes links to video tutorials that show the basics and some advanced techniques toward making the texts required of the various assignments. You can also share these links with your students, providing them with ready-made pedagogical aids. In addition, this book also offers a list of common programs found on most computer systems, as well as a list of software available for free online.

IN-DEPTH ANALYSIS

Although *The New Media Writer* stresses media production, it also walks students through examples and case studies on which they can model their own texts. Such analysis includes how the text might be composed, how it functions rhetorically, or larger social impacts that might concern its production or reception. You can also use these examples as models for the analysis of similar examples, helping students learn to read new media texts before attempting to write their own. For example, Chapter 6 provides a thorough look at the Waste Isolation Pilot Plant and how it account for audiences that may not exist for 10,000 years. While students probably won't have to consider this kind of audience, this in-depth analysis helps them to think through those audiences that will read their documents.

FRESH (AND CLASSIC) EXAMPLES

The New Media Writer uses contemporary examples of photographs, advertisements, videos, artwork, and other visuals to appeal to students (such as the use of memes or music videos as examples). However, the book also injects some classic examples from time to time, but avoids the overused iconic images found in many visual readers. When such images do appear, they do so to offer a new perspective or history of the image not found in other textbooks (such as the case study of the "Crying Indian" in Chapter 7). Moreover, the examples are selected to be interesting, edgy, and sometimes humorous to students, helping them engage more aesthetically, emotionally, creatively, and critically.

HYPERLINKED EXAMPLES

Most of the examples in *The New Media Writer* include an online component made accessible through a Quick Reference code or a hyperlink. Using a smartphone, tablet, or a computer with Internet connection, students can "click" on a photo, podcast, or video still and view (or listen) to the example. This feature makes the print book more interactive, and allows you to teach new media *with* new media, even if your classroom isn't equipped with computers for every student.

ADAPTABLE ASSIGNMENTS

Since there might be some technologies or software that you or your students don't have access to, most of the assignments in *The New Media Writer* can be adapted as traditional writing assignments, composed with traditional writing technologies (pencil and paper), or written with a word processor. For example, a video résumé can be adapted to a visual résumé, or an iReport can be scripted as a more traditional, written research report. Even if you don't have all the new media tools discussed in this text, your students can still analyze new media texts, write about them, and learn how to compose them in other modalities.

PREFACE TO STUDENTS

Imagine living during a time when the only people who wrote were the sons of kings or pharaohs. Or, imagine living in a society that had just learned of the alphabet and was coming to terms with how to use it in their daily lives. You probably don't often think about how alien a technology writing can seem, for Western cultural traditions have incorporated, developed, and improved upon writing for more than 2,500 years. However, writing was once a strange, magical technology, made more natural to us over time by its evolution, most notably from the ancient Greeks who gave the alphabet vowels and started to invent practices for writing, such as concepts, proofs, or definitions (before writing, there were no definitions, at least not the kind found in a dictionary).

Writing is no longer just the domain and privilege of the highest classes of a society; you probably write on a daily basis and were taught to read and write as soon as you were able (although, unfortunately, not everyone is taught to read and write). Yet, a writer today finds herself in another time of transition with strange writings that go beyond the alphabet. Never before have so many writing technologies been invented and introduced in such a short span of time. While the Greeks inherited the alphabet from the Phoenicians, and used a few basic writing tools to make letters, the past few years have seen an amazing proliferation in the ways that writers communicate and make not only letters but all kinds of meaning with all kinds of marks.

Writers make and upload millions of hours of videos to YouTube, a service only started in 2005. Writers unleash a barrage of tweets on Twitter, launched in 2006. Facebook, only slightly older, appeared in 2004. And Google, which seems to be everywhere, offering every kind of service including writing platforms like Blogger, first searched the Internet in 1998. The most recent of Google's projects, Google Glass, affords a method to write and read "in the air" as it provides a mobile augmented reality platform, so that as one goes about his or her daily activities, one can instantly write texts, send tweets, snap photos, or shoot video from a pair of wearable glasses. And speaking of devices, Apple's iPhone, already released in multiple generations, first became available only in 2007.

Whenever a new writing technology comes along, a society has to invent how to use it. Although you probably take alphabetic writing for granted, Aristotle—an ancient Greek philosopher—lived when the technology of the alphabet was still new and tried to determine the rules for how writing should work, developing theories that eventually produced mathematics, science, and literature. In short, Aristotle helped develop *literacy*. Gregory L. Ulmer, a modern-day media scholar, has identified the current era of new media writing as *electracy*, a word that combines the shared component of writing across media—*electricity*—and the word *trace*, a term for the marks an author leaves as he or she writes with new media technologies (electricity + trace = electracy). As Ulmer writes, "electracy is to the digital Internet what literacy is to print." If an author writes letters to make words, he or she writes with electricity to make hypertext, images, video, and all the other kinds of texts made with computers, smartphones, video cameras, and other devices.

As modern-day Aristotles living among new writing technologies, Ulmer believes that we need to investigate and write new media. Given all the technologies that allow us to compose new media texts—texts that use images, videos, hyperlinks, and other forms of writing in addition to the alphabet—we must develop and learn how writing in this new communication environment is different from writing with the written word. Today's writers live in an era unlike any other, and what it means "to write" is changing on a daily basis.

Although writing nearly 50 years ago, the educational advice from another media scholar, Marshall McLuhan, still rings true:

> Would it not seem natural and necessary that the young be provided with at least as much training of perception in this graphic and photographic world as they get in the typographic? In fact, they need more training in graphics… (*Understanding Media*, 230)

While writing with new media in an age of electracy is more than just simply learning the tools, *The New Media Writer* starts (or continues) you down the path of how to write with new media technologies and logics, realizing that the path continues to shift. This text may be difficult at times, asking you to engage with new writing tools and terminology that you might not have encountered before. However, by the end of the book, you'll be able to produce your own new media texts, to write both graphically and typographically, and to know the reasons and logic behind your compositions. As culture continues to shift from literacy to electracy, you'll find that knowing how to make these kinds of texts and knowing how to contend with new writing technologies will be essential, for every day holds the potential that writing will never again be the same.

CHAPTER DESCRIPTIONS

Chapter 1: Making Connections

Chapter 1 provides some of the background you'll need as you progress through the text. Ultimately, no matter which specific outputs you make, all of these assignments will require you to make a variety of connections between different parts of images, between text and image, between image and environment, and between different kinds of media.

Chapter 2: Visual Rhetoric

While new media has its own kind of rhetoric, many traditional rhetorical techniques can still be useful when reading and writing in images. This chapter will provide an overview of some basics of classical and modern rhetoric, but will repurpose their concepts for use in the rest of the text. As just one example, this chapter will go into more detail about the rhetorical triangle, and how these become more useful as the rhetorical tetrahedron. The chapter will cover the rhetorical appeals of *logos*, *pathos*, *ethos*, and *kairos*, and will examine and illustrate each appeal using both print and image-based examples. While you may have learned these terms in other writing classes, this chapter will both refresh your memory and refresh your understanding within a visual context.

Chapter 3: Reading Visual Arguments

As stated above, this text's primary goal is to have you making your own images for your own purposes. However, an understanding of how to "read" or view other images in a rhetorical context can help make you a better designer and producer of new media texts. Chapter 3 will look at a variety of different kinds of new media texts and provide tools for how to approach their analysis, looking for the argumentative features in each. While the chapter is not an exhaustive rehearsal of all the possible readings an image may have, it will help you think rhetorically about different kinds of arguments based in visual media.

Chapter 4: Media Convergence

One definition of media convergence describes the way that multiple forms of media converge into one another, so that what you see on television converges with what you see on the Web, and vice versa. While this is certainly one aspect of media convergence, the practices of producing media also converge. This chapter will look at these practices—specifically, rhetorical practices—that most visual media share in one way or another. This chapter moves away from forms of traditional modes of rhetoric covered in Chapter 2 and focuses specifically on rhetorical techniques that appear in new media texts that diminish (though do not eliminate) the reliance on alphabetic text.

Chapter 5: Scouting Media Environments and Ecologies

Before filming a movie, the director or assistant directors will usually scout locations where filming might take place. The director does not only look for the places themselves for scenery, but also the overall logistics that a location can offer, such as proximity to lodging, food, casting extras, and other elements. When writing in the visual, you must often consider the entire environment in which a visual will appear. Using this film practice of scouting as a metaphor, this chapter asks you to consider the "scene" of writing as a larger environment, or what Lloyd Bitzer terms the "Rhetorical Situation." When a media composition is placed at a location with other media, then these media create relationships that may not be advantageous to your argument. This chapter will help you begin to consider these variables and use them to maximize your rhetorical effectiveness.

Chapter 6: Screening Audiences and Actors

Most of the decisions you make when writing will revolve around your understanding of what your audience wants, expects, likes, dislikes, and will find persuasive. Determining these preferences requires a careful analysis of your audience, and you must screen them before writing. However, especially with new media texts, audiences can also be actors who interact with your texts. Moreover, the ultimate goal of any rhetorical communication is to get your audience to act (or not act) in a particular way. However, in new media, your audience may not even be human, such as search engine robots that scour the Web on behalf of search engines such as Google or Bing. This chapter will offer instruction on how to research and analyze your multiple audiences, and how to design different media to maximize their activity during and after engaging with new media.

Chapter 7: Pre-production (Research)

While you've probably conducted research to write a paper for another composition class, other kinds of research are often necessary when composing a piece of new media. In addition to reviewing traditional research methods, this chapter will explain some other research practices you'll need to consider in the preproduction phase of your writing. This research might include investigating the history of a particular visual element you want to include in a design, the best software to complete a particular effect, or who holds the copyright on a piece of media you want to integrate into a video project. This chapter will cover some basics for you to consider before fully launching into design and production.

Chapter 8: Story Development (Argument)

Even though you'll be working with images, video, sound, and delivery technologies other than a traditional word processor, these media can still be used to craft arguments that most writers usually associate with traditional essays. However, such arguments don't need to be explicit but can be crafted in a way so that their arguments are implicit within a narrative and not overtly stated. This chapter will analyze both kinds of arguments as they occur in visual media, and discuss the strategies for crafting an argument within a visual discourse.

Chapter 9: Scripts (Writing)

While much of your projects in this book will involve final outputs in new media, you'll still need to do a lot of alphabetic writing during the planning, research, and revising process. Such writing comes in a variety of forms, such as outlines, scripts, camera directions, and collaboration materials to help you communicate with other students you might be working with. This chapter covers the writing necessary to produce the new media artifacts presented in this text, writing that may range from a traditional research report, a simple timeline, a list of equipment, or other written documents that help you finish a project. Writing in words has always been an important tool to write in images, and this chapter will cover the ways that traditional writing can transfer to final outputs that may not even contain words.

Chapter 10: Design

This chapter covers all of the design techniques that you'll need to complete your visuals, including basic strategies concerning color and typography, as well as how to achieve perspective and variety. While this chapter will cover *how* to implement these design practices into your compositions, it will also explain *why*; that is, the rhetorical impact that a particular design element will have and how such an element might further your rhetorical goals for making a visual composition in the first place.

Chapter 11: Editing

One of the most important parts in the process of any piece of writing is the step of editing and revising. This chapter will cover techniques that will help during the revision process for image and video, as well as traditional writing, since all of these media are intertwined during the production process. While new media require their own set of specific practices when revising, some basic underlying principles govern all types of revision, and here you'll learn both.

Chapter 12: Delivery

The Greek orator Demosthenes once claimed that delivery was the most important aspect of rhetoric. How you say something can be as important as what you say, and this chapter explains different considerations for how to deliver your new media productions, whether it is as simple as where to post a flyer in the community, different places to upload videos for particular audiences, or even something as complex as search engine optimization for blogs so that audiences can more easily find them.

1

INTRODUCTION

MAKING CONNECTIONS

What is new media writing? While this chapter will explore this question, some simple definitions will help you answer it.

You might say that *new media* writing is digital writing; that is, writing that occurs with digital technologies. New media writing uses a variety of writing technologies, from images, video, audio, hypertext, Web coding, Web apps, print, digital storage, and other technologies that go beyond the pencil, paper, and word processor (Figure 1.1).

This may be one way to think about writing in new media. However, new media writing can also appear in analogue (non-digital) forms. Although you might design a document on a computer, this document could eventually be printed and posted in a

Figure 1.1
New media writing technologies have significantly changed the way you read and write.

space where it regularly gets rained on, touched by people, buffeted by wind, or undergoes other physical changes.

New media writing is material. Even though you might not typically think of digital messages [or writing] as something you can hold, the Internet itself is constructed with millions of miles of cable, millions of servers, individual computers and smart phones, and other technologies (Figure 1.2). If you've ever lost a flash drive, you know how material such writing can be. Even writing in the Internet cloud is subject to erasure.

Credit: The National Archives (UK)

Figure 1.2
The National Archives in the United Kingdom holds more than paper documents, but this new digital material is still "material."

Because of this materiality, the new media writer must pay attention to the physical attributes of a text, such as its medium, design, and genre. These elements of new media writing become more important than in traditional writing where such choices become more restricted.

The new media writer also has to consider audience like never before. Although the digital version of a term paper could find its way to an inbox in China, few recipients care to circulate what you write for an English class. However, when composing in images and video, you might encounter audiences who are much more interested in viewing and sharing your work, making it go viral. The whole world instantly becomes a potential audience.

New media writing, then, uses digital technologies, requires new rhetorical strategies, has a new concern for audience awareness, and acquires a material presence in the world (for electricity itself takes up space and is affected if it

Credit: Nobuyuki Kayahara; Procreo Flash Design Laboratory

Figure 1.3
Which way do you see the dancer twirl?

http://www.youtube.com/
watch?v=nwsGDfzDEOA

mixes with water). However, new media texts also change how you view, use, and interact with them in ways much different than traditional writing that you're more familiar with. Such changes include not only how you make new media writing, but also how others respond to it.

Look at this animation of a twirling dancer (Figure 1.3). Which way do you see her spinning? Clockwise? Counter-clockwise? Just by looking, can you make her turn in the opposite direction?

Some argue that your perspective changes, depending on which half of the brain is most used at the time (however, you always use both sides of the brain). That is, if you see the dancer turning clockwise, you're processing the image mostly with the right hemisphere of your brain. If you see the image turning counter-clockwise, then the left hemisphere of the brain is at work. If you can flip the image, then you're able to alternate between the two hemispheres at any given moment.

This animation, of course, is an optical illusion, and can be seen as turning clockwise, counter-clockwise, or either direction by the individual viewer. Neuroscientists have indicated that this spinning dancer does not really indicate which side of the brain you're using, but it does make viewers reflect upon their brain and how they process images.

Neuroscientists have shown that different areas of the brain have specific roles for different kinds of thinking. As you can see in Figure 1.4, the left brain hemisphere is responsible for analytic thought, a kind of thinking humans use in subjects such as logic, language, science, and math. The major functions of the right hemisphere of the brain include holistic thought, intuition, creativity, art, music, and thinking in images.

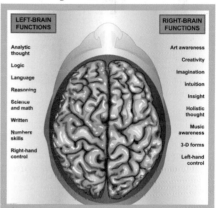

Here's another "test." Look at the video in Figure 1.5.

What did you first see? The letter Ds? Or did you see the L-shape that the Ds composed? If you saw the letter Ds, then you used the left hemisphere to process the image. This is because your brain was dissecting the larger image into smaller pieces rather than looking at the larger picture. If, however, you saw the L-shape, then your right brain was scanning the image for the whole, trying to synthesize all the pieces and fit them together.

Figure 1.4
The two hemispheres of the brain contribute differently toward different tasks.

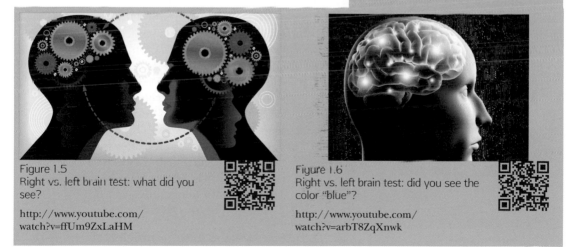

Figure 1.5
Right vs. left brain test: what did you see?

http://www.youtube.com/watch?v=ffUm9ZxLaHM

Figure 1.6
Right vs. left brain test: did you see the color "blue"?

http://www.youtube.com/watch?v=arbT8ZqXnwk

Here's one last test. When you view the video in Figure 1.6, look for the color "blue."

Now, did you first notice the *color* blue or the *word* "blue"? If you noticed the color, then your right brain was looking for the color rather than the word. It was focusing on the visual rather than the verbal. If you noticed the word, your left brain's language bias was trying to find the written representation of blue rather than the actual color.

Why does this matter? In this TED talk (Figure 1.7), Sir Ken Robinson argues that traditional models and practices of education consistently teach students "out" of creativity, primarily by focusing instruction on tasks mostly performed by the left side of the brain: that is, the side focused on analysis, logic, reading, mathematics, and the sciences. Instead, he argues that teachers need to revolutionize education so that aspects of creativity housed in the right brain can be more developed, allowing students to solve problems in new situations and in jobs that probably haven't even been invented yet.

Credit: Ted.com

Figure 1.7
Sir Ken Robinson argues that teachers must change education.

http://www.youtube.com/watch?v=iG9CE55wbtY

Credit: Matt H. Wade at Wikipedia Commons

Figure 1.8
How many images can you count and identify in this one photo?

So what does all this have to do with writing in new media? Neurologists have scanned human brains and discovered that if you read a book, your left brain is highly active, but your right brain is mostly dormant. However, when subjects shift their glance from the book to a television screen, the reverse occurs; the left brain shuts down, and the right brain activity skyrockets. The right brain is mostly responsible for reading images, but if educators don't teach students how to think with this part of the brain, then students won't be able to "read" images as well as they read words. In a culture heavily saturated with images, this can be a problem (Figure 1.8).

So why is this image saturation a problem? Some new media scholars have a pessimistic outlook that so many images—with their circulation increased by the technology of the Internet—

destroy rational thinking and make it impossible for a democracy to succeed. From some of its earliest forms, a functioning democracy has depended on the ability of its citizens to make informed decisions and vote for candidates and ballot measures that are in their best interests.

The image, because it is initially processed by the right brain, bypasses critical thinking centers and triggers an emotional response, sometimes causing the viewer to make bad choices if she doesn't stop and analyze exactly what images are attempting to argue. But sometimes, even when an image can be rationalized, it still influences the viewer on a physical and emotional level.

The more optimistic perspective, one advocated by this text, is that the problem is not one of medium per se, but developing a system by which one can "think" with the image as well as one does with written words. That is, borrowing from Robinson's argument, the education system needs to start educating citizens on how images are made, how they're designed, and how to make images for themselves.

One goal of this text is to help make the connections between the two halves of the brain, to help the right side catch up, so to speak, so that you're thinking and writing with a more "whole" brain instead of just one side. This text doesn't necessarily have exercises that a neurological therapist might prescribe but it does discuss how and why images make meaning and how to connect those methods to your own writing, writing that includes these new media genres that circulate all around you.

If you can't get the twirling figure to spin in both directions, that's okay. But try again when you're finished with this book and see what you see or what you can make yourself see.

FROM LITERACY TO ELECTRACY: MAKING CONNECTIONS ACROSS WRITING TECHNOLOGIES

When you think about writing, you probably imagine sitting at a desk with paper and pencil, typing a document on your computer for class, or writing in your blog. You might also envision the different situations in which you write. You probably write notes for class, scribble a list for the store, jot down a phone number, or post a message for a roommate. You write in a variety of contexts every day, whether within formal academic settings or for informal, everyday tasks.

And while all these situations call for writing, do you ever use images to supplement or replace writing? Do you create shopping lists with images of what you plan to buy, or jot a diagram to help you remember a concept from class? Do you take a picture of a new contact when you add the person to your phone's address book?

In some respect, the first question posed above is misleading. You always use images when you write, for that's what writing is: images used as representations for aural words. In essence, this is what the alphabet is—a set of images for the basic sounds you use to say those words. The "words" you're reading right now are not "words" exactly, but images of words. Whenever you write, you write with images.

Writing with the images of the alphabet—what this book will call alphabetic writing—has existed for roughly 2,500 years in various incarnations of alphabets. However, its logic system, how you use these systems of images, has been slowly evolving during that time. Many cite the ancient Greeks as the first culture that really analyzed how writing could be used and developed, especially Socrates, Plato, and Aristotle (Figures 1.9-1.11).

Credit: Bhickey

Credit: Marie-Lan Nguyen

Marie-Lan Nguyen/ Ludovisi Collection/

Figure 1.9
Bust of Socrates

Figure 1.10
Bust of Plato

Figure 1.11
Bust of Aristotle

For example, the concept of giving an object a "definition" didn't always exist and had to be invented as a literate practice. The ability to write the essence of a thing (its definition), and commit it to image, provided one of the first early inventions of what writing could create. Eventually, dividing the "things" of the world into particular definitions produced the natural sciences. Even though natural historians still argue about how to divide animals, plants, rocks, or planets into different categories, they still use definitions to accomplish their work.

In general, the term "*literacy*" refers to the ability to use alphabetic writing, which denotes mastery in both reading and writing with letters. This ability includes not only skill at making the letters, but understanding the logic and practices that make them work to build words, sentences, paragraphs, pages, books, as well as arguments, proofs, concepts, and definitions. Reading or writing a book is certainly one aspect of literacy, but a literate person can also use inductive or deductive logic, make and break apart an argument, understand a fallacy, or organize information into a logical system.

Writing, however, continues to evolve and society is moving into a post-literate age that uses other kinds of writing tools, practices, and logics. Since the invention of photography in the 1800s (Figure 1.12), the image has come into prominence as a mode of recording experience, prompting scholars such as W. J. T. Mitchell to call the current age the "pictorial turn."

However, composing an image doesn't stop once you "take" a picture. These photographs are often incorporated into other media, and new images are composed. Taking a photograph, as Roland Barthes (1978) describes, is not simply an act of "recording" what's in front of the lens, but a rhetorical process. The photographer chooses what elements of a photo should remain in frame, what elements receive the focus or most prominence, how the people or object should be positioned, or whether the person or object should even be aware the photograph is being taken (Figure 1.13).

Credit: Frank Gosebruch

Figure 1.12
Although photography was invented in the 1800s, new ways to use it are still being developed.

Many of your own photos probably end up on social media sites. In this way, you compose images and then compose with images, just as you compose with images of words when you write a paper. And after you take a picture, you often revise it, using a photo editor to remove distortions or crop a photo to focus on a particular element.

While this textbook is partly constructed with alphabetic writing, and at times discusses alphabetic writing, it is mostly focused on writing with the image, both the skills and logics necessary to do so. Such skill sets are not inherently literate, but what Gregory L. Ulmer refers to as "electrate," the skill sets needed to effectively communicate within a digital media environment. As a supplement to the literate skills you've already developed, this text looks at *electracy* (sometimes referred to as "digital literacy" or "media literacy").

Credit: Mack Male

Figure 1.13
There's a lot happening behind the camera lens that the viewer never sees.

Such logic and skill sets don't just appear from nothing but have to be invented. While someone invented the automobile (or horseless carriage) and probably had the idea that it would be used for transportation, many other practices and purposes for the car were invented since the invention of the actual technology. You don't just use automobiles for transportation, but also for fun, relaxation, or sport. The rules for driving had to be invented, as well as making sure people knew the rules (thus, driver's licenses) and mechanics for making sure cars kept working (changing the oil, checking tire pressure, filling it with fuel). Being "literate" in the automobile entails more than just building a car and more than just driving one.

The same process occurred with writing. But just as the ancient Greeks began the invention process for literacy, someone needs to invent the logic and practices of electracy. Who are currently developing electrate skill sets (Figure 1.14)? To the extent that people as individuals have adopted new media technologies, all users of these technologies invent new practices and uses every day, whether or not these practices catch on and become used by everyone else. At this point, such practices become institutionalized and their use becomes widespread. Regarding these practices, another question arises: What are the institutions that have spread the most used practices of an emerging electracy?

Ulmer cites the institution of "entertainment" as the dominant producer of electrate practices, which can be widely understood as the products of Hollywood movies, but also to the smaller units of media entertainment, from video games, graphic novels, and photography. In addition, advertising and marketing adopt the logic of cinema and make advertisements entertaining, humorous, sad, ironic, and give them other narrative techniques to hook a viewer and make them part of a product's "story."

Credit: Antonio Zugaldia

Figure 1.14
Emerging technologies, such as Google Glass, will require that wearers invent ways to use them.

Credit: Mr3641

Figure 1.15
Emerging writing technologies such as Augmented Reality allow authors to "write in the air," augmenting physical spaces with invisible text.

The underlying principle of these entertainment practices is that they don't necessarily appeal to a person's conscious, literate logic of analysis, but to their emotions. Such logic is based in aesthetics, or what the viewer likes. If a viewer doesn't like the "look" of a design, then chances are he will have a negative reaction to whatever the design is trying to argue, whether or not he agrees with the "literate" message the design is trying to communicate.

The electrate skill set that this text will present, then, is one of design and aesthetics, how these aspects of writing can be used toward rhetorical goals in a new media environment. This text will present general design aesthetics that most beginning arts classes might teach, such as courses in photography, painting, or Web design. However, this text will place these practices in the larger umbrella of "writing," because these are all ways to produce a mark, to create visible (and sometimes audible) ways of communicating through the digital Internet, even if some of those visuals become printed and distributed in hard copy (Figure 1.15).

Electracy, although post-literate, is also parallel to literacy. Literacy is useful and will always exist alongside electracy (just as people still use oral modes such as the church recital, theatrical plays, and political debates). Part of learning electrate skillsets is also learning how alphabetic writing adapts, integrates, and supports certain practices of visual communication. Throughout the examples and assignments in this text, you will still need to rely on literate modes of analysis and composition and apply them to understanding and creating more electrate modes of writing. Authors will use the practices that they're best at as a way to build and develop new ones.

THE RHETORICAL TETRAHEDRON: MAKING CONNECTIONS ACROSS RHETORIC

At some point in learning about writing and rhetoric, you may have been taught the "rhetorical triangle," a diagram meant to help students learn about the different rhetorical elements at play when communicating with an audience.

Figure 1.16 offers one version of the rhetorical triangle that focuses on the different people involved when communicating. The three vertices represent the writer, audience, and message. Together, these three elements make up the major parts of any rhetorical exchange.

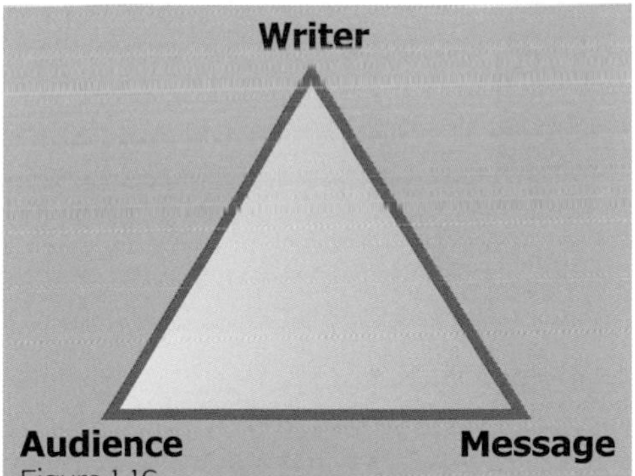

The point labeled "writer" represents not simply the person writing, but those aspects of the person that affect her or his rhetorical appeal, such as her character, credibility as a speaker, eloquence in delivery, style of writing, choice of examples, and other rhetorical choices she might make.

The "audience" makes up another point. The audience has its own beliefs, values, expectations, and experiences that the author must consider when crafting an argument.

Figure 1.16
The rhetorical triangle showing writer, audience, and message.

The last point represents the actual "message," including its information, claims, style, examples, evidence, and structure.

As the triangle shows, each point affects the others, and as the writer sees how the audience responds, she can adjust the message until the audience finds it convincing.

While this triangle can be useful for thinking about how different rhetorical elements interact when communicating, it provides a very static way of understanding how communication works. The act of making an argument doesn't occur in a two-dimensional world, but one in which people, things, events, and time all effect the larger situation. The argument you might make at one point in time could completely change five minutes later. The simplicity of the rhetorical triangle can't take this complexity into account.

As an alternative, this book adopts a three-dimensional version called the *rhetorical tetrahedron* (Figure 1.17). A tetrahedron is a three-dimensional shape made up of four triangles. This model incorporates the traditional labels of writer, audience, and message, but also adds three other elements that are important to writing in new media, a kind of writing that goes beyond writing on paper. These elements are medium, design, and genre.

© Fountainhead Press

Figure 1.17
The rhetorical tetrahedron
http://youtu.be/0Gwym9h1ccE

For writing traditional essays, the questions of medium, design, and genre are usually pretty simple. Most often, the medium is 8.5"x11" white paper, the design consists of double-spaced 12 pt Times New Roman font, and the genre is a five-paragraph essay, short response, or term paper.

When writing in new media, the number of choices you have for each of these explodes. For a medium, should you choose paper? Video? A website? A podcast? A blog? How will the design of your website, video, or blog look when you're not simply limited to font selection and margin size? And should you present your work as an essay? A short documentary? The tetrahedron represents these aspects of writing, helping you remember to take them into account as you compose in new media.

As the old cliché states, "it's not what you say, but how you say it." This *how* relates to these three aspects. As already discussed, the aesthetic plays an important aspect in rhetoric. If an audience *likes* what it sees or hears, then this audience is more inclined to act in the way that the writer is requesting. The design of a composition (and this includes something as *literate* as an essay for class) can be as important as the content of its message. Instead of separating the design (form) from content, consider them integral and always interrelated.

As part of the design, the genre plays an important role in how the piece communicates to an audience. Should you create the design as a flyer or brochure, or make it interactive as a website or online video? Does the audience expect that the information will appear in a certain form, such as an e-mail, memo, or letter? If so, these expectations limit the choices you have. The genre you choose will influence how you design the visual composition and your ideas for a design will likewise influence what genres you feel will best fit your overall message.

The design and genre come together in the medium that you choose. The proposal genre can appear in the medium of paper, but it can also appear via a website or video. An essay can also appear in a different medium than you're probably used to, and your instructor may have you complete the video essay assignment in Chapter 11. Much of your choice in medium will depend upon your audience's expectations about standard pairings of genre and medium, or limitations your audience may have in using different media. While you should be creative in thinking about new ways to mix the two, if your audience does not have the resources to play a video proposal sent to them on DVD, they'll never see your design nor receive your message. Whenever you're considering design, genre, and medium, you often have to consider all of them together simultaneously, just as you do writer, audience, and message.

As you can see in Figure 1.17, instead of placing these six aspects on the points of the tetrahedron, this book places them on the edges. A point only represents a single number, while the edge can represent a continuum. Rather than considering just a single audience, the edge labeled audience suggests that you consider all the possible audiences that might read a particular work, for in a world with Facebook and Twitter, documents can quickly circulate beyond your intended audience. Rarely does a document find a single audience, and often an author must consider everyone that will encounter the document. This includes not only human audiences, but also nonhuman ones, such as search engine robots, bits of code that search the Web on behalf of search engines like Google or Bing, and categorize this information to optimize a user's search results. You may never directly encounter these invisible audiences, but if you post a document online, these audiences will eventually find it.

Moreover, many texts are not written by a single writer, but instead have many collaborators that contribute to finish a piece of writing, whether a simple memo or something more complex like a website. Rather than a single point, the sliding continuum along the edge of the tetrahedron allows you to visualize the flux of possibilities that may exist when you're working on a document with others. Likewise, a range of mediums, designs, and genres may be selected from, and this diverse range is ignored by a single point.

As a three-dimensional object, the tetrahedron also moves in space and time to represent the shifting nature of a rhetorical situation. In Chapter 2, you'll learn about *kairos*, the timing of rhetoric, an often neglected component that helps you to think about the "right" moment for speaking or writing. *Kairos* is an important element that the traditional, two-dimensional rhetorical triangles leave out. Furthermore, *kairos* is especially important in new media since the digital Internet allows the delivery of a document at a moment's whim, and as Figure 1.18 demonstrates, once a document is on the Web, there are no "take backs."

Credit: Ad Council

THE DECISION'S OUT OF YOUR HANDS NOW.

Figure 1.18
Remember to "think before you post" images or other documents to the Internet, because once you hit send, it's "out of your hands."

http://www.youtube.com/watch?v=cBkZkf2Vmdw

Of course, the rhetorical tetrahedron also helps you analyze other works of new media. You can use the same six elements to ask questions of the message itself, of the writer of the work, its intended audience, why a particular medium was chosen, how it was designed, and why a particular genre was selected. These questions can help you understand new media texts as you encounter them on a daily basis.

THE MEDIUM IS THE MESSAGE: MAKING CONNECTIONS ACROSS MEDIA

Credit: John Reeves

Figure 1.19
Marshall McLuhan argues that "the medium is the message."

"The medium is the message." (McLuhan 7) This famous quote from media scholar Marshall McLuhan suggests that the medium becomes a message in itself, no matter what the content (Figure 1.19). One of his examples for this was the light bulb (a different kind of medium than you're probably used to thinking about). By itself, the light bulb emits light, and it doesn't matter what that light is used for; this light can be used to do anything from working on your car or watching a football game at night. The important feature is not what you do with the light bulb, but that the light bulb allows you to alter how you conduct your life. The important message is that you can do anything at night because of the medium of the light bulb and not the particular activity (content) you choose.

Beyond the light bulb, McLuhan was interested in how all media affect human lives, from print to television. Given the new devices being released every day in your own time, you might consider other media, from smartphones to tablets, as media that have their own messages no matter what content the user is viewing or interacting with. The fact that the user can interact with what they see on a touchscreen has become a message in its own right, but one often masked by the content.

The choice of medium, then, becomes an important part of an author's ethos and reflects on their character. What if Steve Jobs, when talking to us about the latest computer innovation, were giving his presentation using a slide projector rather than the latest Apple presentation software? You would probably ask why the leader of one of the biggest computer companies and one of the leading computer innovators is using technology that is nearly fifty years old. Doesn't he have something better available, and doesn't he know how to use it? In fact, he does, and he used the latest high-res graphics and animations in his presentation when he launched the new iPad (Figure 1.20).

Credit: Matt Buchanan

Figure 1.20
Steve Jobs unveils the iPad.

FOCUS ON PRODUCTION: MAKING CONNECTIONS BETWEEN THEORY AND PRAXIS

This text will analyze—and ask you to analyze—a variety of new media compositions to reveal how they function rhetorically. These analytical dissections can help you recognize persuasive elements in the texts you see around you every day. However, this analysis is mainly focused toward the production of your own texts. While it is important to know how to "read" an image, this text's ultimate goal is that you are able to produce your own new media compositions for a variety of purposes, audiences, contexts, and rhetorical situations.

As you encounter sections in the text that analyze an image or video, the analysis will suggest ways that you can use similar techniques within your own works. Use these examples as relays or models to construct your new media compositions. Remember, however, that yours will be much different given that you will have a different rhetorical situation. The basic principles in the example, however, will be applicable to all of your works.

FOCUS ON ENVIRONMENT: MAKING CONNECTIONS BETWEEN IMAGES AND THE OUTSIDE WORLD

When this text discusses "environment," it's referring to more than just the natural environment. For instance, this text will often discuss the environmental effects of using different kinds of media. However, "environment" also refers to the larger rhetorical environment in which you might see, make, or place an image. This larger visual environment will most likely contain many other images, whether this is a public bulletin board where you might place a flyer, or a website that has a variety of images, videos, and texts (Figure 1.21). Each chapter will consider some of these environmental aspects you should be aware of when taking a particular step in the production process (Figure 1.22).

Credit: Andrew Booher/FEMA

Figure 1.21
After Hurricane Katrina struck New Orleans, many residents of the city temporarily moved to Houston for shelter. During the natural disaster, many families were separated, and bulletin boards such as this one provided a location to place notes. This bulletin board provides just one example of how environment, in many senses of the word, influences writing.

Credit: AvWijk

Figure 1.22
Unlike more "natural" writing technologies such as paper and pencils, electronic writing tools can poison the environment if not disposed of properly. However, they are usually just tossed into landfills without thinking about the toxic effects.

KEY TERMS

electracy	*new media*
literacy	*rhetorical tetrahedron*

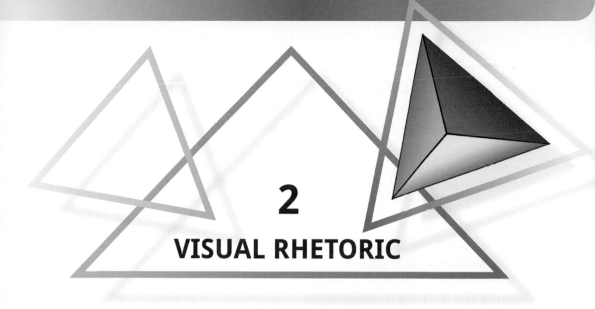

2

VISUAL RHETORIC

Most of what you'll create and analyze from this text can be considered *visual rhetoric*, a branch of rhetoric that refers to how a writer creates arguments and persuades audiences through the use of images, graphics, video, and other visual media.

For instance, something as commonplace as a commercial or advertisement can be considered a visual argument and employs visual rhetoric to make that argument. Examples that market a product are probably the most overt, since the audience knows that a company is trying to persuade it to buy something.

Of course, everyday images also contain rhetorical elements that persuade or influence the audience more subtly. How a press photograph is framed, cropped, or color-corrected are choices made by the photographer or editor that affect how one reads and responds to the photo. This image might not be trying to get someone to buy something at the store, but it might be trying to persuade the reader to take some other kind of action, such as getting involved in a political issue, participating in a charity event, or changing an unhealthy habit (Chapter 3 will devote more space to reading images).

However, while new media has its own kind of rhetoric, many traditional rhetorical techniques can still be useful when reading and writing through images. This chapter will provide an overview of basic rhetorical techniques but reframe their concepts for use in the rest of the text.

Of course, you've probably heard the term "rhetoric" used pejoratively, as in, "he's just full of empty rhetoric." Consider the "defense" of rhetoric in Figure 2.1 that helps explain why rhetoric is a tool for communication and not simply a means of manipulation.

THE RHETORICAL TETRAHEDRON: LOGOS, ETHOS, PATHOS, KAIROS

Chapter 1 described the rhetorical tetrahedron as presenting six rhetorical elements that you should consider as a rhetorician: writer, audience, message, design, medium, and genre. These elements were labeled along the six edges of the tetrahedron.

Credit: Department of English, Clemson University

Figure 2.1
A defense of rhetoric.

http://www.youtube.com/
watch?v=BYMUCz9bHAs

© Fountainhead Press

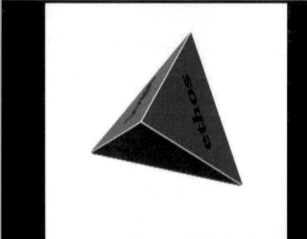

Figure 2.2
The Rhetorical Tetrahedron with a focus on the appeals of *logos, ethos, pathos,* and *kairos.*
http://youtu.be/0Gwym9h1ccE

In addition to this configuration, you can also label the four faces of the tetrahedron with the four basic appeals of rhetoric: *logos, ethos, pathos,* and *kairos* (Figure 2.2). These appeals represent rhetorical choices you can make, choices that change as the rhetorical situation changes. Just as the rhetorical tetrahedron exists in three dimensions (including movement in time), a rhetorical situation unfolds in space and time, always moving, always dynamic. The following rhetorical elements will help you think about how to make different kinds of rhetorical appeals, as well as how to avoid some pitfalls that might hurt the content and delivery of your message.

Logos

Logos is a term from Greek that translates to "word" and is usually understood as the "logic" of your argument. For instance, when writing a research paper, you would most likely include definitions, evidence, deductive or inductive reasoning, or examples to support your points.

These elements typically provide the logical reasons

why a reader should accept your perspective. This kind of logic is usually based on facts, precedence, descriptions, empirical observations, computation, and other evidence not necessarily based on emotion. *Logos* is the persuasionary tactic of Spock in *Star Trek*. Spock argues with logical appeals, but can also be convinced with logical appeals (Figure 2.3).

The graph in Figure 2.4 shows the relationship between shark attacks and population in the state of Florida. The trend indicates that as human population increases, so do the occurrences of shark attacks. The logical relationship that the graph attempts to show is that sharks aren't attacking more swimmers because they're aggressive and out to eat people, but as more people enter the water and encounter sharks, more possibilities exist for human and shark interaction.

The organization that produced this graphic—the International Shark Attack File—also points out that your chance of being killed from a shark attack is 1 in 3,748,067. Comparatively, your chance of dying from a car accident is 1 in 84. These graphs and statistics attempt to persuade viewers of the site though logical, scientific means. As Spock might say, the fear of being killed by a shark is . . . illogical.

Logos also includes the arrangement, organization, and internal consistency of a document. For example, if you were

Figure 2.3
Spock is always logical.

- creating a documentary about a historical event, the retelling would be much more logical if you followed a chronological sequence.
- designing a video tutorial to teach someone how to edit a video in Apple's iMovie, then placing each step in sequential order would be important, otherwise the tutorial would be worthless.

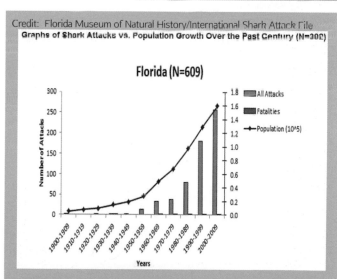

Credit: Florida Museum of Natural History/International Shark Attack File

Figure 2.4
Graph comparing shark attacks with population growth over the past century.

■ writing a legal brief to a judge about your client who is accused of armed robbery, instead of using synonyms such as weapon, handgun, gun, or pistol, the brief would make more logical sense if you refer to the weapon consistently, using only one term.

Credit: Six Flags over Texas

Besides using words logically, images can be used logically to show *logos* as well. Figure 2.5 depicts the Six Flags over Texas theme park map that you might use if you visited Six Flags. Note how similar information is clustered together based on the theme of each different area so that the audience can easily find popular rides and locations. Also, notice how the map uses color in a logical way: each theme has a different color so that it can be more easily located on the map. If you look at other kinds of maps, such as a road atlas or political map, you'll notice a logical use of color.

Figure 2.5
This map of Six Flags over Texas clusters information by theme and use of color.

On the home page for Clemson University (Figure 2.6), information is arranged logically by audience. Each major link on the navigation menu provides further links to information that is relevant to particular readers. It wouldn't make much sense to include information on how to donate money (in the alumni section) within the perspective students' section. On a sports news site like ESPN.com, you wouldn't expect to find hockey scores in the football section; this would defy audience expectations. Consider carefully not only the particular evidence you use to create an argument, but also how you arrange and present that evidence.

Figure 2.6
Clemson University's homepage organizes its information by audience.

MAKING CONNECTIONS

AS A CLASS

View a short documentary movie or television program. Together, identify how the film uses *logos* to make its argument. For example, what evidence does it provide for its claims? Is this evidence logical? How does the film arrange its argument? What visual aspects does it use to create logical cohesion?

IN A GROUP

Look at television commercials from cell phone providers (such as Sprint, Verizon, AT&T, T-Mobile, or Alltel). What's the thesis of the commercial? How does each commercial use *logos* to create its argument and support this thesis? Do the commercials use statistics? Do they use comparison and contrast? Do they use color to create organization or associations within the commercial? For each provider, list as many strategies as you can and provide your findings to the class.

ON YOUR OWN

The use of color is often considered to be subjective, but sometimes there are good reasons for selecting certain colors. For instance, in most Western cultures, "red" symbolically represents something dangerous, so writers use that color for important warnings such as "Stop" signs (see more on color in Chapter 10). Research your college's or university's colors and determine why these colors were chosen. Was the choice based on purely aesthetic tastes, or does the background information you find provide logical reasons why certain colors were chosen over others?

Ethos

Ethos refers to the audience's trust in the author of a document. An audience typically believes an author—or has trust in his or her argument—when he or she has some expertise or special knowledge about a subject.

For instance, if you had a question about how to build a house, you would probably trust the information given to you by an architect or construction contractor rather than an English professor. The contractor has expert knowledge and experience to suggest that her advice will help you complete the project successfully.

If you want to know the weather forecast, you would trust a meteorologist more than a cardiologist. On the other hand, you would trust the cardiologist to diagnose your heart health over the meteorologist. When creating your own texts, you should use sources that you feel will persuade the audience—sources the audience will trust. You've probably used such sources in other research papers. These same principles of *ethos* apply to new media texts as well.

Ethos might be present from the outset, or reveal itself during the unfolding of a piece of writing, video, or other kind of communicative event. If you've watched the weather segment of the local television news station, you'll often hear or see that the channel's meteorologist has some sort of certification or approval from a national organization (Figure 2.7). This statement is an attempt to give credentials to the meteorologist so that the viewer knows she can trust the forecaster.

Credit: American Meteorological Service

Figure 2.7
According to the American Meteorological Service, "The AMS Seal of Approval was launched in 1957 as a way to recognize on-air meteorologists for their sound delivery of weather information to the general public. Among radio and television meteorologists, the AMS Seal of Approval is sought as a mark of distinction." Having the seal can enhance a meteorologist's *ethos*.

Audiences also tend to trust information from those who are impartial and having nothing to gain from an argument. For instance, if a city investigated whether a new football stadium for the local NFL team would raise money for the community, the city would probably trust independent experts in city planning and economics rather than the owner of the team who has a clear vested interest in building the stadium. While the owner may care whether the whole community benefits or not, the audience knows he will personally benefit. The meteorologist wants to create an accurate forecast to keep her job, but she gains nothing if the weather consists of sun or snow.

However, sometimes this kind of information isn't given up front. Perhaps through conversations with your English professor, you learn that he has built his own house, and has lots of advice to give you, advice that a professional contractor might not think of. While you would still trust someone in building construction more, the fact that your professor is also a do-it-yourselfer might convince you that he has unique insights that an expert might not. In this case, the speaker's *ethos* develops and persuades you despite your initial hesitation at taking his advice. Of course, the presence of *ethos* doesn't necessarily mean that an audience will agree with the author's perspective, but *ethos* makes it more likely that the audience will believe what the author communicates and take him or her more seriously.

One common means of creating *ethos* is through the use of celebrity endorsements. If one wants a good basketball shoe, what better shoe than that of a famous basketball player like Michael Jordan? His credibility is so high that other famous basketball players wear his shoes, such as Dwyane Wade, even though Jordan has been retired for many years. This endorsement from current players further increases the credibility of Jordan and his shoes.

Figure 2.8 explains how Nike designed Jordan shoes for Dwyane Wade, Carmelo Anthony, and Chris Paul. While the video uses a lot of logical arguments about foot movement, materials, and athlete needs, it also relies on Wade, Anthony, and Paul as the users of the product to attest to its benefits. Because the audience knows that these players are great—that they have proven their *ethos* on the court—it's more inclined to trust them.

Logically, the audience might know that these celebrities are paid a lot of money to endorse and use these products, but it can still be influenced by who delivers the message. In order to provide balance to the players' voices, the video also interviews the shoe designers themselves. These designers do not use the shoes as the players do, but because they are most likely material engineers of some sort, they provide a different kind of credibility (mostly based on arguments of *logos*) and why they should be trusted by the audience.

© Nike, inc.

Figure 2.8
New Team Jordan Signature Shoes: celebrities and designers add their credibility to Nike's discussion of these shoes
http://www.youtube.com/watch?v=grGSpZoGaRg

Finally, a writer loses credibility if their writing contains grammatical errors or factual mistakes. When establishing your own *ethos*, it's critical that you check your sources, proofread your writing, and polish your documents as much as possible. This advice pertains to written texts and also to images, video, and any new media texts you might produce.

MAKING CONNECTIONS

AS A CLASS

Revisit the documentary you watched for the *Logos* section above (Making Connections, Prompt #1). How does the film attempt to create *ethos*—how does it attempt to gain your trust? Does it use expert testimony to provide evidence and credibility for its claims? Does it include a variety of perspectives so that its argument seems more fair and balanced?

IN A GROUP

Many commercials on financial planning, banking, or real estate mention the notion of trust. With a partner, view commercials from institutions involved in these businesses and notice how they attempt to gain the viewer's trust. Consider how respected you think the company might be already (doing research if you need to) and note how the advertisement either capitalizes on that trust, or tries to reestablish trust they might have lost. Write up your findings in a short report and share them with the class.

ON YOUR OWN

At home, watch any evening news broadcast. During the program, pay attention to how the program creates *ethos*, attempting to convince the viewer that the station or network producing the program is a credible news source, that the people interviewed deserve your trust. Keep a list as you notice these appeals toward *ethos*, and share them at the next class meeting.

Pathos

Often, someone's state of mind, or mood, plays an important role in how he or she receives a particular message. If you're angry, you often respond to information differently than if you're calm. If you lost your dog and needed help convincing an audience to help you find her, you would have a much better chance if you were able to elicit the emotions of sorrow or panic, helping the audience to share your own emotions. This would help place the audience in a sympathetic state of mind that would make them more receptive, increasing the likelihood that they would help you search the neighborhood. *Pathos* names this emotional appeal made within a text and it can be a very powerful rhetorical tool to help your reader understand your point of view.

Pathos is also an appeal to one's identity, in which most people have an emotional investment. Typically, politicians use the language of patriotism as a way to appeal to a collective sense of what it means to be a member of a certain country, and that language plays to an emotional connection *with* the country. Patriotic language often uses code words or phrases that many people identify with and feel identifies them. For example, Americans are "hard working" or "independent." Within this discourse, the speaker places herself within the group she is addressing so that the audience identifies her as "one of us" and are more likely to accept her message.

In addition, the politician is also trying to flatter the audience, making them more like the speaker, perhaps by saying that as Americans they must be "hardworking" and "independent" so that they identify with and believe these descriptions about themselves. The audience develops a more positive reaction to the politician who makes the compliment.

Pathos might also be directed at the audience's self-interests (which is a kind of identity). If you were trying to persuade someone to donate money to help Haiti after its earthquake, you might cite another disaster that your audience has more directly experienced (such as a hurricane or tornado), evoking a shared sense of pity or fear between the people of Haiti and themselves. As another example, consider the following speech from Dr. Martin Luther King, Jr. (Figure 2.9):

Figure 2.9
Martin Luther King Jr. addresses a crowd from the steps of the Lincoln Memorial. During the speech, he uses *pathos* to appeal to the audience.

Here, Dr. King describes the shared struggles of his audience and their self-interest in obtaining civil rights. He creates an image of "trials and tribulations" to remind his audience of the emotional pain they've undergone to reach this point, creating an emotional connection that he uses to rally them to keep fighting. Note how he also flatters his audience, calling them the "veterans of creative suffering."

Pathos can also be used to induce the audience to feel an emotion toward a

I am not unmindful that some of you have come here out of great trials and tribulations. Some of you have come fresh from narrow jail cells. And some of you have come from areas where your quest—quest for freedom left you battered by the storms of persecution and staggered by the winds of police brutality. You have been the veterans of creative suffering. Continue to work with the faith that unearned suffering is redemptive. Go back to Mississippi, go back to Alabama, go back to South Carolina, go back to Georgia, go back to Louisiana, go back to the slums and ghettos of our northern cities, knowing that somehow this situation can and will be changed.

—*I Have a Dream* by Martin Luther King, Jr.
August 28, 1963.

particular person or group. However, you should do this, strangely enough, logically. For instance, certain categories are typically associated with certain emotions. "Predators" might make us fearful, while "prey" evokes sympathy, making the audience feel sorry for the animal being hunted (Figure 2.10). The categories are logical constructions, but you can use them in this way to create emotion.

For example, if you want to create positive emotions about a new park that the city wants to build, you might describe the project by depicting a scene of children playing in the park rather than simply telling the audience, "You should be happy about this park" (Figure 2.11). Since most people typically

Figure 2.10
Although these fish logically fall into the categories of "predator" and "prey," emotionally, audiences usually root for the "little guy," or in this case, the "little fish."

Figure 2.11
While a detailed plan of a park can make a logical appeal, you'd more effectively create *pathos* if you used an image that helped to show how the audience's children might play and enjoy the park once it's built.

dislike bullies, the writer might frame an adversary as being a bully, providing a clear category with which the audience can be angry. Most of *pathos* involves using a story or image that taps into the values of the audience, making the audience imagine the author's emotion as their own. Use creative images to create a scene that summons these emotions.

Advertisements often use *pathos* to appeal to emotions. Figure 2.12 shows a commercial for the American Society for the Prevention of Cruelty to Animals (ASPCA). This commercial makes use of images of wounded animals to elicit two emotional reactions: sympathy for the abused animals and anger toward those who would commit such acts. In addition to the images, the commercial uses the popular yet somber song "Angel" by Sarah McLachlan to connect the animals with the positive connotations the audience might usually associate with angels. The ad also uses an appeal from Sarah McLachlan herself, providing a celebrity spokesperson to help persuade the audience that they should support the ASPCA.

However, as indicated by the meme in Figure 2.13, sometimes an appeal can be too good and turn people away. Many view the ASPCA commercials as too sad, making them want to turn the commercials off rather than watch them.

Cigarette advertisements have used many appeals throughout the decades. If you conduct an image search for "vintage Camel ads" (or scan the QR code in figure 2.14), you'll find vintage Camel cigarette ads that make an appeal to ethos by using a doctor as a spokesperson. The main tagline probably says something like "More Doctors smoke Camels than any other cigarette," encouraging the viewer to believe that one should trust the doctor regarding the best brand of cigarette to smoke.

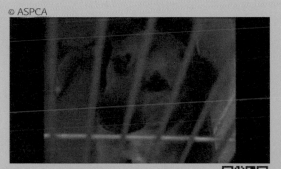

Figure 2.12
This public service announcement uses a song to elicit *pathos*, and a celebrity to create *ethos*.

http://www.youtube.com/watch?v=YliPZ0p0SNQ

Figure 2.13
Sometimes, an appeal can be too strong for a viewer to take.

Figure 2.14
QR code for an image search of vintage Camel ads.

Figure 2.15
This cigarette ad attempts to evoke the mood of "cool," and changing the "c" to a "k" isn't fooling anyone.

Of course, more recent Camel ads have used emotional appeals, specifically in the guise of "Joe Camel," the cigarette-smoking camel developed by the tobacco company R. J. Reynolds. Joe Camel is depicted in a variety of leisure activities, from playing pool to riding motorcycles, appearing cool and "smooth." These ads do not make a logical appeal, but an emotional one, attempting to coerce the viewer into buying not only a cigarette but also the state of mind. This state of mind varies depending on the ad, but Joe Camel and other cigarette ads mostly promote the mood of "cool" (Figure 2.15).

To counter the "cool" mood of tobacco use, the United States Food and Drug Administration (FDA) attempted to create a counter mood in a set of new warning labels to be placed on cigarette packaging. Rather than the standard "Surgeon General's Warning" (Figure 2.16), the new packaging displays more graphic examples of what can happen to those who smoke. Figure 2.17, an example of one of these ads, compares a healthy set of lungs with those exhibiting damage from smoking cigarettes. The FDA (Figure 2.18) hopes that these ads strike a more emotional appeal (*pathos*) than the current warning, which simply states the facts about the damage smoking can cause (*logos*).

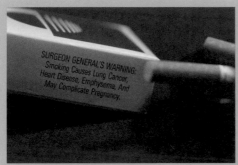

Figure 2.16
The Surgeons General's Cigarette Warning uses facts to appeal to its audience.

Credit: fda.gov

Figure 2.17
New cigarette ads try to appeal to *pathos* (emotion) more than *logos* (reason).

Like the ASPCA public service announcements, many viewers feel that these new anti-smoking warnings are too sad or grotesque, especially the television commercials that are a part of this public service announcement campaign (Figure 2.19). You should consider if your own appeals will grab your audience's attention or shock them so much that they tune out your argument.

Credit: fda.gov

Credit: Anti-Smoking PSA/CDC

Figure 2.18
FDA announcement unveiling the new cigarette warning ads.

http://www.youtube.com/watch?v=ps0ASyGjXXo

Figure 2.19
Testimonies from former smokers are effective, but are they too effective?

http://www.youtube.com/watch?v=EyVLKHEqTu0

Of course, the point of *pathos* isn't to solely illicit emotions in your audience. You don't want your audience acting on emotion alone, but in conjunction with *logos* and *ethos*: all three should be directed toward some desired outcome, the reason for your writing.

MAKING CONNECTIONS

AS A CLASS

Revisit the documentary you watched for the *Logos* section above (Making Connections, Prompt #1). How does the film attempt to create *pathos*? How does it attempt to appeal to your emotions? Does it use graphic or moving images? How does it use music? What state of mind does it attempt to create? Of the three rhetorical appeals, which is more prominent?

IN A GROUP

View the video about the new cigarette warning labels in Figure 2.18. How do the officials who are interviewed talk about the new labels? In other words, how do they frame the selection of the images in terms of *pathos, logos*, or *ethos*? Why do you think they discuss the new labels as they do? Research opposition to the new ads, and analyze how this opposition makes its own arguments as well. Report your findings to the class.

ON YOUR OWN

Collect a series of ads (other than cigarette ads) promoting a particular kind of product, such as soft drinks. How do these ads attempt to use *pathos* to persuade the audience? Like cigarette ads, do they attempt to place the viewer in a particular state of mind, such as "coolness"? Try to create a list of these moods and present your findings to the class.

Kairos

The Ancient Greeks used two words to denote two different kinds of time. The word chronos refers to chronological time (the word "chronological" comes from chronos). This kind of time describes sequential happenings, annual and daily cycles often recognized as making up "time."

However, they also used the word *kairos*, which refers to a particular moment in time that has some special significance. While chronos can be measured quantitatively by a watch, *kairos* is more qualitative, measured not by a device but by intuition and foresight (Figure 2.20).

As an analogy, if a football team is in position to win a game with a field goal, the players on the field will often wait to score in order to run as much time off the clock as possible. Usually, the coach will call a time out with only a few seconds left so that the other team will not have time to get the ball back and score. Here, the coach is choosing the best, most effective moment to call a time out to help win the game. The kicker might miss the field goal, but if he makes it, the other team won't have a chance to win (Figure 2.21).

Figure 2.20
This fresco painting by Francesco Salviati depicts the idea of *kairos* as a mythical figure. What do you think his physical attributes say about the concept of *kairos*?

Within rhetoric, *kairos* signifies the best, most strategic moment in which one should communicate. If one communicates too early, before an audience is prepared to hear an argument, or too late, when the argument is no longer necessary or valid, then the rhetor has not utilized the kairotic moment to make the best case.

In a political campaign, for instance, a candidate might wait until the week before the election to present his or her most effective evidence against his or her opponent. Waiting to reveal this evidence allows the politician to make it fresh in voters' minds as they enter the voting booths. This opportune moment would give the candidate being attacked less time to respond, and not enough time could elapse before voting day to help voters forget.

Figure 2.21
Navy waited until four seconds left to kick this field goal, winning the game against Air Force.

Many politicians called for gun reform after the mass shootings at Sandy Hook Elementary School in 2012 (Figure 2.22). This terrible tragedy put the issue of gun availability in the country's mind. The period after the shootings was the most kairotic moment in which to advocate gun control, right after the event showed everyone what could happen if the wrong person got a gun. If politicians had advanced gun control before the shooting, the issue would not have received much media coverage as other issues were more pressing. However, if too much time passed after this event, then the pain and heartache would fade from memory, making the issue feel less important than during the immediate aftermath. In other words, the mood would have changed. *Kairos*, then is partly about capturing the audience during a particular emotion.

As related to new media, *kairos* can become even more important, as many interactions are in real-time and require precise timing to connect with the audience.

It wouldn't make much rhetorical sense for Google to offer a tour a year after the user started the account, nor would it make much rhetorical sense for a company to offer gift wrapping at other moments in the ordering process. The moment of "checkout" provides the best timing for offering these options.

When making your own arguments, you should consider when the best time would be to launch your message, whether it's a flyer you post for a lost pet (as soon you notice the pet is missing) or a poster for a new movie (before the movie releases, but not too early that the buzz about the movie has time to quiet down). You should also be aware of other events taking place—such as holidays, celebrations, or memorials—and how they may affect the timing of your message.

Credit: VOA Video

Figure 2.22
The unfortunate shooting at Sandy Hook Elementary School provided a kairotic moment to discuss gun control.

http://www.youtube.com/watch?v=gAmr-A-F8K8

"*Kairos is really about ***when*** you communicate a message, so kairos is more concerned with web interactions such as those encountered during a user flow for an e-commerce checkout, a tutorial, subscription process, web app interaction (such as those on Rdio or Mint), search apps, or office apps. An example of what I mean is when a new user logs into Google Docs for the first time and they are presented with a pop-up box offering an optional tour. That first login is a kairotic moment where Google can educate its new users about how they'll benefit from using the application. Another example would be when a user is buying flowers on FTD.com and during the checkout process is presented the option of adding a gift card or a box of chocolates to their order before submitting their payment information.*"

—Stuart McCoy

MAKING CONNECTIONS

AS A CLASS

Kairos can be understood as an opportunity to speak. However, the Greeks also understood that *kairos* was accompanied by metanoia: regret. In other words, if you miss the opportunity, you may experience regret. However, this regret can teach you how to act in future situations so that you don't experience it again. As a class, share your experiences of regret at not having said something at the right time. Keep a list of the examples for future reference.

IN A GROUP

Examine a typical news website and the role that *kairos* might play in posting news stories. How does the site try to make use of *kairos*? Does the site try to present news at an opportune time, or simply as it happens? Make sure you consider all the facets of news it presents, from news stories to editorials to blogs.

ON YOUR OWN

Locate a famous speech by a politician, leader, or celebrity, and analyze the speech in terms of *kairos*. To complete this assignment, you will have to research the context and time at which the speech was given. How did the speaker make use of the most opportune moment? Do you think his or her timing could have been better? Draft a short report and share your results with the class.

RHETORICAL MAPPING

While the rhetorical tetrahedron provides a way to understand the major choices and appeals when writing, there are a few other elements that you should plan for. Before you begin to write, you should map out the rhetorical situation in which you find yourself, such as your reason for writing and the purpose of the document. Also, although it was discussed in Chapter 1, techniques for mapping the audience are also detailed below since it is such an important part of understanding your reason, purpose, and rhetorical strategies. This section will point out some of the elements you'll need to figure out before fully committing to a final draft of a design, whether that design is visual and based in new media, or simply a standard written assignment.

Exigency

Most writing starts with an *exigency*, a word that refers to the reason one writes. For example, a teacher assigns a writing task so you have to write for class. Perhaps you have to remember what to get from the store and need to write a list to make sure you don't forget anything. Exigency can also refer to some imperfection in the world that compels you to write, such as a vote by your congressman that you don't agree with, prompting you to write him a letter expressing your disapproval. Exigency simply refers to the reason or situation that requires you to write.

For instance, if your dog runs away, this situation prompts you to write a flyer to inform others that you've lost your dog (Figure 2.23). Such an exigency could possibly have many different writing strategies to solve the problem that demands writing as a solution. You'll have to carefully consider the entire situation and determine what audiences you're trying to reach, what outcomes you desire, and the best medium in which to convey your message.

In this example, the situation requires that you communicate to the public to solve the problem of finding your dog. Since the dog is probably still nearby in the neighborhood (or nearby neighborhoods), you might devise a strategy that delivers your message locally. You could possibly solve the problem by placing phone calls, but a flyer is probably more efficient. Of course, with new media, traditional flyers, phones, and other technologies work together (Figure 2.24).

Some other examples of exigencies for writing include:

- A nonprofit organization is losing funding from one of its major donors and must write a grant proposal to compensate for this loss.

- An online business is having trouble getting new customers and considers how a social media marketing campaign might increase traffic.

Credit: Bill Nicholls

Figure 2.23
An unfortunate exigency has prompted someone to make this flyer.

Credit: AT&T

Figure 2.24
This AT&T ad shows how writing technologies can work together to solve problems more quickly.

http://www.youtube.com/watch?v=cZwEIKBxgtU

- Two national companies have merged, and the new combined company requires a new brand mark that integrates both their identities.

- A band is about to release a new CD and needs a music video to accompany the release of the first single.

- A NASA engineer notices a faulty part on a new space vehicle and must communicate this to her superiors before the first, highly-anticipated test launch.

Each of these examples has a very different reason for writing and will require different kinds of writing to solve each problem. The exigency may seem obvious and not really worthy of thorough investigation. However, fully understanding how the writing situation developed can help you plan a rhetorical course of action and determine the best path for your message.

For instance, in the example with the NASA engineer, suppose that she has noticed faulty parts before and that each time she contacts her superiors, they brush her off and rarely heed her warnings. Knowledge that the launch is highly anticipated and that the project has been behind schedule might cause the engineer to aim her message at someone else besides her immediate superiors, such as the local or national press. This, she might think, would put more pressure on the project managers to stop the launch and repair the faulty parts. If she simply reports directly to her superiors, they may ignore her, possibly resulting in a destroyed space vehicle or worse. Of course, this decision might anger her superiors and also cost the engineer her job. Knowing the bigger picture behind the immediate reason—the larger ecology of exigency—can help you craft a more effective and efficient argument and get that argument heard (or seen).

As illustrated in the above examples, remember that exigency influences not just those documents written with alphabetic text but also those written with images, whether they include Web content, a new brand mark, or a music video. The release of a new movie often requires its marketing and promotion; this problem is often solved in part with commercials and movie posters.

MAKING CONNECTIONS

AS A CLASS

Gather and examine various political cartoons. Discuss the exigencies for each cartoon that you think compelled the cartoonist to create it.

IN A GROUP

Choose a website such as Facebook, YouTube, or Twitter. Research the background of the site, and find or conjecture on the exigency (or exigencies) that caused the founders to create the site. What problem did the site solve?

ON YOUR OWN

In 2011, the Miami Marlins, a professional baseball team, changed their team's visual identity, including the brand mark and team colors. Using this example (or your own), determine the exigency for this change? Why were a new brand mark and colors needed? Again, what problems did the design change solve?

Purposes and Outcomes

After you consider the exigency, you should identify the *purpose* and *outcome* you want to achieve. A flyer letting people know you've lost your dog informs them of your situation, but informing may not have been your purpose. Instead, you probably want to inform *and convince* the reader to take some action. Your purpose is to convince the reader to act by letting you know if he or she has seen your dog.

Part of thinking about your purpose for writing, then, is to consider what outcomes you want to achieve. Do you simply want your audience to be aware of some sort of information? Do you want your audience to have a better understanding of something they might already be aware of? Do you want the audience to perform some action after reading your document? These are all different outcomes that require different strategies and involve different purposes from the outset.

When assessing your purpose, examine the outcome that the document is meant to achieve and the practical ways that the document fulfills that outcome. If you create a flyer to inform people about a local issue, what elements must it contain so that a reader can make use of it? Is this document's purpose to contain all the information that the reader needs to know or only pique their interest so they can learn more? If the latter, then the document's purpose isn't just to inform, but to propose that they seek out more information on the topic. For the flyer to be successful, you should include a website URL or a phone number so that the reader can make use of the interest that your flyer generated and act.

Typically, a document will have at least one or more of the following purposes:

- **Inform**: Convey information to readers that they might be unaware of.

- **Define**: Convey the characteristics of something the audience needs to better understand.

- **Explain**: Convey how to go about a particular action or engage in a process, how a past action has unfolded, or how a future action will unfold.

- **Propose**: Convey a particular outcome that you want the audience to make, whether this is an action or simply a decision.

DOG MISSING

REWARD

DISAPPEARED FROM THE DUNEWOOD BAY BEACH,

KOKO IS A SHEPARD / COLLIE MIX, VERY FRIENDLY, BUT ALMOST DEAF SO MAY NOT RESPOND TO HIS NAME.

PLEASE CALL WITH ANY INFORMATION :
LAURA (646) 269 3714
ALEX (917) 747 2241

Figure 2.25
This flyer uses multiple photos, places important information in a different font color, describes where the dog was last seen, and includes contact information. The flyer also includes other important information, such as the dog's deafness and friendliness.

A well-written flyer advertising a lost dog would exhibit all of these different purposes. For example, it would inform the audience that a dog has been lost and define different aspects about the dog, such as its breed, color, size, name, and other important features. The flyer would also explain how the reader should proceed should they find the dog, such as giving them a phone number to contact. Finally, the flyer should propose an action to the audience, such as contacting the owner. Notice that not all of these purposes need to be presented as "written" text—you might "define" the pet by offering a picture that shows what it looks like (Figure 2.25).

Consider also that your purpose for writing may not be your audience's purpose for reading and reacting to a document. While *you* care about the dog you've lost, your audience may not. However, you might persuade them to act by offering a reward for their help, hoping that the audience will be moved to act based on financial compensation if not simply wanting to do a good deed. When creating an argument, be aware of the multiple purposes in a document, considering not only your own reasons for writing but also your audience's reasons for responding.

MAKING CONNECTIONS

AS A CLASS

Search for "lost pet" flyers in your neighborhood. Using a camera (or camera phone), snap a picture of these flyers. As a class, look through the flyers and analyze each one, noting their strengths and weaknesses and whether you think the flyer will achieve its purpose (not necessarily of returning the lost pet to its home but at least convincing someone to act upon the flyer's message).

IN A GROUP

Recall memorable television commercials you've seen or find ones on Internet video sites such as YouTube. Watch the commercials and consider the many purposes involved. For instance, what was the purpose of the company who sponsored the commercial? What outcome does the commercial try to achieve? What strategies does the commercial use (i.e., does it inform, define, explain, propose)? Finally, what purposes do you think the audience might have for acting upon the commercial?

ON YOUR OWN

Take one of the flyer designs from Prompt #1 above and revise it so that the flyer is more effective at achieving its purpose. Once you've created the new flyer, you might contact the owner of the original flyer and ask if they would like to adopt your new one.

Audience

As discussed above, you need to clarify your purpose when creating a document, and the outcomes you wish to happen. However, you must also consider your *audience* and their needs to ensure that they can fulfill their own purpose after reading your document.

Even if neighbors want to start looking for your lost pet, they may not be able to if you fail to include a photo or description of the dog—they wouldn't know which dog to look for. Also, if you simply include the breed of the dog, such as "border collie," the audience may not know the physical features of this breed and be equally lost and unable to help. If you don't include any contact information, then even if a reader found the dog, they wouldn't be able to let you know the good news, and they may be forced to take the dog to the local animal shelter instead. To avoid these undesirable outcomes, you need to anticipate these needs and clarify your intended audience when planning any text. To meet audience needs, map how they might interact with a document according to the guidelines below.

Map Multiple Audiences

When you write, you must typically account for multiple audiences who may view your documents. Each of these audiences may have a different reason for reading, and you need to consider how to address their reasons and needs.

Several strategies allow you to adapt your writing for these audiences. First, you might tailor your document toward a very narrow, specific audience. For example, if you were writing a software book about Hypertext Markup Language (HTML), you might focus it toward an audience of computer science students who would have extensive background with computers and coding, and you could leave out a lot of information that a novice would need to understand.

On the other end of the spectrum, you might write the same book very broadly, such as the "Dummies" series, that provides enough information for readers with any experience level to learn. The computer science majors would probably roll their eyes at a lot of the language and information in this book, but they could still use it (just not as efficiently). Focusing in on your audience is an important step when planning to write.

Also, you must consider the secondary and tertiary audiences that read your writing and account for their needs as well. For example, you are the primary audience for your course's syllabus. You use the syllabus to understand the course policies, learn which books to purchase, and see what assignments are required and when they're due. Your purpose when reading the document is to learn about the class.

However, your instructor probably also has secondary and tertiary audiences that she or he must consider. Many of the course policies are most likely dictated by university policy. Your instructor needs to make sure that these policies are present and will satisfy a reader from the university's compliance department. Sometimes specific course requirements are dictated by the state legislature, so the instructor must consider this possible audience.

You should also consider the access that multiple audiences have to your writing. If you were to place a document on the World Wide Web, are you intending that anyone be able to read and understand it, or only a certain group or demographic? Of course, you should realize that even if you only aim your writing toward a smaller group, almost anyone can gain access to it, so you should make sure that the contents are not sensitive.

Map Audience Expectations

Different audiences will expect different things from a document. As the syllabus example above demonstrates, students will expect certain information to be in a syllabus, while university officials will look for other information to be present.

As another example, consider a television program. The typical viewer only cares about the actual content of the show, and not usually the commercials. In fact, she or he may change the channel during the commercials and watch a different show (Figure 2.26). However, the sponsors that pay for commercials will want to make sure that their ads actually air during the breaks and may hire someone to watch all the commercials and make sure their ads appear. In other situations, both viewers and sponsors might expect and seek out good commercials during certain events, such as the Super Bowl.

Audiences also have different attitudes to what they view and read: positive, negative, and neutral. If you're watching a machinima (the process of making real-time animated films by utilizing the 3-D graphics technology of computer games) on YouTube, such as *Red vs. Blue*, you're probably familiar with the video game *Halo*, engaged in the material, and have a positive attitude when initially viewing fan-based clips. In this case, the creator of the video does not anticipate any hostility toward their message (Figure 2.27).

Figure 2.26
Many television viewers have a negative attitude toward most television commercials.

If you see a political advertisement from a political party you disagree with, however, you would probably approach this ad with a negative attitude. If you were the advertisement's intended audience, the creators of the ad would need to find rhetorical ways to overcome that negative attitude to convince you of their point of view.

Finally, if you have no particular attitude toward the author or content, perhaps a documentary about penguins, then the filmmaker would simply need to show you their point of view by presenting the benefits of their particular message. They don't have to overcome a negative attitude, just show you why the documentary is important and why you should pay attention.

Credit: Rooster Teeth Productions

Figure 2.27
Most of the audience members of Red vs. Blue machinima probably have a positive attitude toward the clips.

In each of these examples, your audience's expectations and attitudes will determine how you craft your message, design your document, and what rhetorical techniques you'll need to use.

Map Audience Use

Imagine opening up a road atlas and trying to find an alternative route around a serious accident on the highway. Typically, you would expect to find a map of the county or state that includes road names, distances, points of interest, and other features that would help you navigate via automobile.

What if, instead, you found maps that included the political information for each state, county, and city—which areas voted Democrat or Republican, or how different areas responded to political issues? Most likely, this particular map would be useless to you, and you would be stuck in traffic for several hours. In addition to the expectations audiences have, they also have different uses for documents. This political map might make sense when discussing politics, but not while traveling. Likewise, the road atlas wouldn't do much good to navigate a state park, which requires more detail and includes roads and trails not normally accessible by cars (Figure 2.28).

The environment in which audiences use a map may be much different as well. An atlas usually has very large pages that can contain enough detail to make reading easy for the driver (or passenger) in a moving vehicle (Figure 2.29). A hiker in the woods doesn't usually need this large of a map—in fact, a smaller, more compact map might be ideal. The hiker, however, might appreciate a map printed on waterproof paper in case it rains or she accidently drops it in a lake or stream. How you plan and design a map for use in a car would be very different from a map you would design for use in the woods of a state park.

Figure 2.6, the screenshot of Clemson University's home page you looked at previously, demonstrates sensitivity to multiple audiences, audience

Figure 2.28
A road atlas doesn't do much good once the road ends.

Figure 2.29
Using an atlas in a cramped car is much different than using it in other environments.

expectations, and audience use. If you look at the menu (you can also actively use the site at www.clemson.edu), you can see that it's divided by the multiple audiences that Clemson expects to use the site: prospective students, students, faculty/staff, parents/families, corporations, families, visitors.

Each of these audiences has different needs and expectations of the site and will use it differently. Prospective students need to learn about application procedures, tuition rates, information about the university, and academic programs. Current students will need to find the academic calendar, schedule of classes, community information, and Blackboard access. Faculty will expect links to their class rolls, human resource information, and other administrative content that affects them. As you go online and explore the other links, you'll see that each section of the menu specifically tailors its information for a particular audience, anticipating what they'll need and how they will use the site.

Beware of Unintended Audiences

Remember that these guidelines primarily help you target your *intended* audiences. As briefly discussed in Chapter 1 and as you'll read more fully throughout the rest of the book, digital technologies make the delivery to *only* your intended audience nearly impossible. When nearly any kind of document can be forwarded through e-mail, or posted on someone else's website, Facebook page, or Twitter profile, you never really know who your final audience will be (Figure 2.30). While you might think that such worries don't affect you (for you're probably not a celebrity, government official, or top secret agent), even the wrong phrasing in an e-mail can turn into a piece of evidence in a court of law.

For example, many of the internal memos sent between the football staff and administration of Penn State University eventually became public during the hearings for Jerry Sandusky, who was accused and found guilty of sexually

Credit: Lance Armstrong via Twitter

Figure 2.30
Lance Armstrong probably regrets tweeting this photo of him lying next to his Tour de France jerseys. Only a few months later he would admit to doping (bad kairos?), and Oprah Winfrey showed the image during her television interview with Armstrong.

abusing children. Once the documents were made public through legal proceedings, they then appeared online, on TV, and on many other outlets. While you might think that it was right that such documents came to light, you might feel different about documents you'd like to keep from ESPN, CNN, and other media organizations. Keep in mind, then, that any document can reappear in other contexts, and have possible negative effects. Be careful, very careful, with the kinds of documents you distribute online.

MAKING CONNECTIONS

AS A CLASS

Look at your own college or university's home page. How is the page designed to account for multiple audiences? Does it use similar menu choices as Clemson, or employ a different navigation system? Do you think the two universities have the same kinds of audiences? How might they differ?

IN A GROUP

Search for Coca-Cola advertisements (still and video). Find as many as you can from many different time periods. For each advertisement, speculate on what audience you think each ad was trying to reach. For example, do some ads cater to adults, while others focus on younger viewers, teenagers, or children? How do these ads adapt to audience expectations over time?

ON YOUR OWN

Search engine robots provide another (nonhuman) audience that find documents on the Web for search engines. Search Engine Optimization (SEO) is a practice that attempts to maximize the possibility that a search robot will find a particular site and index it so that it appears as high as possible in a search result. Research search robots, SEO, and some of the practices used by marketers to write for these invisible audiences. Prepare a research report with your findings and present it to your instructor.

Rhetorical Fallacies

Rhetorical fallacies, faults in rhetoric, often affect *logos*, the logical argument you're trying to make. These fallacies can affect the soundness of your evidence, and—if noticed—affect how your audience responds to your argument and you as an author. Fallacies in *logos* can also affect your *ethos*. For these reasons, rhetorical textbooks often advise against making these fallacies. However, logical fallacies can still significantly affect emotion, appealing to *pathos*.

Ad Hominem

This fallacy attempts to discredit the speaker's argument by attacking the speaker's character (Figure 2.31). For example: "The president's policies won't work because he's a socialist." Rather than debating the merits of the president's actual policies, the author attempts to attack the president's person, switching the debate from the substance of the policies to the president's perceived character (something which would also have to be proven rather than just claimed).

Credit: Zach Weiner

Figure 2.31
"Your face" is never a good reason to support an argument.

Begging the Question

In this fallacy, rather than proving a particular question and reaching a conclusion, an author assumes the conclusion and incorporates it into a claim. For example: "Irresponsible teenagers should not be allowed to drink alcohol before the age of 21." Rather than making an argument that teenagers are irresponsible, which would prove the claim that they should not be allowed to drink earlier than age 21, the author inserts that conclusion within the claim by using the word "irresponsible," assuming the conclusion and bypassing the question that really needs to be answered.

Circular Argument

A circular argument restates the claim as evidence of its proof, rather than developing logical reasons to support the claim (Figure 2.32). For example: "LeBron James is a good basketball player because he plays basketball well." In this case, the evidence just rephrases the initial claim and doesn't actually add any evidence to support it. Instead, the author might focus on James's statistics, work ethic, knowledge of the game, or other qualities that good basketball players typically have.

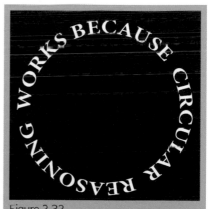

Figure 2.32
Circular reasoning doesn't really work—logically at least.

Either/Or

This fallacy reduces an argument to only two possible options when many are probably available (Figure 2.33). For example: "We can either stop all fishing or all the fish will become extinct." While some fish stocks are becoming significantly depleted, others are not, so a combination of different regulations could allow for some fishing to occur without destroying the populations of all fishes. Also, there are different kinds of fishing that affect populations differently. For example, many game fish are caught but immediately released back into the sea, which affects their populations much differently than food fish such as tuna. The choice is much more nuanced than just an either/or.

Credit: Benjamin Franklin

J O I N, or D I E.

Figure 2.33
Benjamin Franklin's famous cartoon actually presents an either/or fallacy.

Genetic Fallacy

When one assumes that a person's origins determine his or her character, one commits a genetic fallacy. For example: "Even though the presidential candidate was born in the United States, his parents were not, so he must not be American enough to run the country." Where the candidate's parents were born does not logically equate to how "American" the candidate is. This type of fallacy also pertains to the origins of objects and ideas. For example: "The new policy in favor of universal health care is stupid because a democrat came up with it." In this case, the speaker is creating his opinion of the idea based upon his opinion of the political party that advocates it, when the two are not innately connected. This fallacy can also pertain to the "genetics" of the speaker as well, and how he or she incorrectly interprets data based on its origin. For example: "My parents told me that dinosaurs never really existed, so I don't care what paleontologists say."

Hasty Generalization

This fallacy occurs when one reaches a conclusion without considering all the evidence, sometimes due to preexisting bias. For example: "All terrorists plotting against the United States are Muslim extremists." Such a statement could come from a kneejerk reaction based on the sole case of the World Trade Center attacks. However, many terrorists in the United States are not Muslim, such as Timothy McVey, who bombed the Alfred P. Murrah building in Oklahoma City, or Eric Rudolph, who committed a series of bombings, most notably at the Olympic Park during the 1996 Olympics in Atlanta, Georgia.

Moral Equivalence

This fallacy attempts to equate acts or atrocities that are not equal in their severity. For example: "I get paid so little, I feel like a modern-day slave." Unlike the employee, who actually receives a paycheck and has the choice to leave the job, slaves had neither pay nor choice, and so this is not an equivalent comparison. Moral equivalencies may also invoke prior acts to excuse new ones. For example: "Our administration has recently used torture to get information, but so have our enemies." Here, the fallacy is claiming that because their enemies commit torturous acts, it's okay for the administration to do so as well. Just because torture has been used in the past or by others does not mean it's all right to use it in the future.

Post hoc ergo propter hoc

This Latin phrase translates to "after this therefore because of this," which identifies a fallacy in cause and effect relationships between two actions or events. This fallacy makes the assumption that if Y happened after X, then X must have caused Y. For example: "After downloading and installing a program from the Internet, your computer crashes. You assume that the program must be faulty and caused the crash." Without more evidence, you can't assume that just because the computer crashed after you installed the new program that the program caused the crash. The computer may have had other problems and the timing is just coincidence.

Red Herring

A "red herring" occurs when a speaker attempts to divert the conversation by introducing a tangent line of thought to avoid discussing the main issues at stake. For example: "Oil consumption may be leading to climate change, but how will we run our cars and maintain our economy if we don't use oil?" In this example, the speaker is attempting to shift the debate from climate change itself to the economic issues of oil consumption. While these issues are interconnected, it is still important to discuss the workings and dynamics of the atmospheric conditions and not just cast them aside.

Slippery Slope

In this fallacy, an argument is made that if a particular action or event occurs, then an unwanted consequence will inevitably follow. For example: "If we let homosexuals marry, then what's to stop someone from polygamous marriage or marrying a horse?" Letting humans marry is not the same thing as letting humans and animals marry, and one does not logically lead to the other.

Straw Man

Just as a man built with straw is easy to destroy, a straw man fallacy indicates when a speaker attempts to reduce an opponent's argument so that it seems weak or flimsy, thereby making it easier to defeat rhetorically (Figure 2.34). For example: "Anyone who favors gun control hates freedom." One can advocate for gun control and still support freedom. However, by reducing the argument to such a simplistic motive, and by eliminating the nuanced debate that accompanies the arguments for gun control, the speaker diminishes the argument to a minimalistic phrase that's easy to side with.

Figure 2.34
Sometimes saying a statement is "just rhetoric" makes a straw man out of both the speaker and rhetoric. This statement reducing someone's argument to "just rhetoric" is itself rhetorical.

MAKING CONNECTIONS

AS A CLASS

View a political debate performance. While you watch, keep track of how many fallacies you notice. Once you're done watching, discuss the fallacies you think occurred, and whether you think the debaters intentionally committed these fallacies for rhetorical purposes, or if you think they simply used bad logic in constructing their arguments.

IN A GROUP

With a partner, visit YouTube, and try to find television commercials that demonstrate each of the fallacies listed above. Consider whether you think each fallacy was committed intentionally or accidentally. Present your findings to the class.

ON YOUR OWN

Through an image search, find cartoons, diagrams, or other visuals that represent each of the fallacies listed above. Create either a blog or digital scrapbook of these examples and share them with the class.

KEY TERMS	
audience	*outcome*
ethos	*pathos*
exigency	*purpose*
kairos	*rhetorical fallacies*
logos	*visual rhetoric*

3
READING VISUAL ARGUMENTS

As mentioned in the preface, this text's primary goal is to have you making your own images for your own rhetorical purposes. However, an understanding of how to "read" or view other people's images from rhetorical perspectives can help make you a better designer and producer of new media texts. In other words, while reading is not the same activity as writing, they influence each other and are interconnected, and being a better reader can make you a better writer, even if you're writing with images.

This chapter will look at a variety of different kinds of visual texts and provide tools for how to analyze them, pointing out the argumentative features in each example. While the chapter is not an exhaustive rehearsal of all the possible readings an image may have, it will help you think rhetorically about different kinds of visual arguments.

The following strategies for reading visual arguments closely follow some of the elements you'll use to construct new media texts, especially those discussed in Chapter 2 on rhetoric, Chapter 4 on media convergence, and Chapter 10 on design. Since Chapters 4 and 10 provide an extensive overview of analyzing and composing, this chapter will primarily focus on the rhetorical aspects examined in the last chapter, although it will touch on some basic design questions you should ask about any visual text.

 When reading a text, you can use the rhetorical tetrahedron as a starting place to ask questions about the text, mapping those questions (and answers) about the text onto the edges of writer, audience, message, design, medium, and genre, or onto the surfaces of the tetrahedron to think about *logos*, *pathos*, *ethos*, and *kairos*. In other words, use the tetrahedron as a rubric or guide when both reading and writing.

MAPPING RHETORICAL FEATURES

Writer and Purpose

The *writer* should be one of the first elements of the rhetorical tetrahedron you examine when analyzing a text since knowing a writer of a work can help determine the exigency of a text and its purpose. Behind every kind of writing is at least one writer who created it, and while a text can be read and understood without knowing the writer's identity, the originator of a text can help explain much about it. For example, much of ancient Egyptian art depicts stories of Egypt's pharaohs. While these rulers didn't write Egyptian art and hieroglyphics by their own hand, they did sanction their creation and probably had very important reasons for doing so (Figure 3.1).

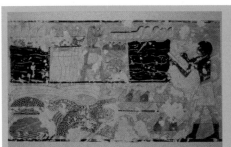

Figure 3.1
Egyptian pharaohs often required scribes to write for them. In this wall painting, a scribe is recording deliveries for the pharaoh.

Figure 3.2
Wall Carving of Ramesses II, located inside the Abu Sembel temple.

In the context of the Egyptian empire, a pharaoh needed to keep his or her kingdom united by ensuring that subjects remained loyal and enemies didn't attack. These concerns provide the exigency for the large amount of artwork on Egyptian buildings for the purpose of propaganda, a kind of political art designed to influence an audience to think a particular way (usually in support of the rulers). The Egyptian pharaohs needed their subjects to respect and fear them (lest some ambitious individual try to overthrow him or her and take over) and make any enemies think twice before attacking. Any art depicting the pharaohs should be full of praise and exaggerate their feats.

Figure 3.2 depicts a wall carving inside the Abu Sembel temple that shows the pharaoh Ramesses II fighting in the Battle of Kadesh. From this relief, the audience understands that Ramesses gained a great victory, forcing his enemy—the Hittites—to agree to a truce. However, documents found in the Hittite capital Boghazköy claim that the Hittites were the true victor. The writer of the document can determine a great deal about the exigency, purpose, and ultimate message of a particular text.

Such propaganda by the ancient Egyptians can teach a lot about text authorship in the modern age. While Ramesses might have commissioned the images on his temples, he did not do the actual carving. Those who did carve the stone surfaces worked collaboratively, sometimes over many years or generations. Of course, these craftsmen receive little credit for their writings.

Similarly, many of the images you see around you are not attributed to the "writer" who actually created it. Typically, a graphic, poster, billboard, film, and even book are not written by a single person but by a team of specialists. Graphic designers might determine how an image should look, but experts in computer drafting might actually create the final version in Photoshop. Often, a single individual doesn't decide on the final draft of a design, a committee does, by voting to make a final decision.

Finally, like Ramesses, a company may provide the motivation and basic narrative that needs to be told and leave it to others (either in-house or contracted technical writers or graphic designers) to create the finished piece. Typically, you may never know the writers of these images, such as company brand marks or advertisements, unless you were to conduct background research and find out. When you're trying to read a visual text and want to consider how the writer affects your analysis, you might have to dig a little deeper to find out the writer's identity (or, of course, identities).

When you attempt to identify the author of a text, you often have to make a decision about what level of authorship is important. This level of detail about the writer will help you better identify the writer's intentions for creating a text, but to research this information you'll have to isolate the level of authorship you feel is most important to your reading. For instance, is it more important to consider the sponsor of the work, or the individual(s) who physically created it? Your own motivations for looking at a work will help you answer these questions.

MAKING CONNECTIONS

AS A CLASS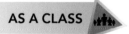

Analyze the writers of a news website. Discuss how you would define authorship at various levels, such as micro-levels of individual reporters, and macro-levels, such as the sponsor of the site as a whole. Remember to consider information that might be crowd-sourced, such as invitations to comment on a story. How would you consider the rhetorical dimensions of authorship in these cases? Do exigency and purpose fluctuate across the site?

IN A GROUP

Locate the credits from a video game that you enjoy playing or are familiar with. How does the video game represent its authors? What terms does it use? Are any of these terms similar to those used in other genres such as books, movies, or music? Which ones are different? How would you ascribe authorship to this video game as a whole? Present your findings and thoughts to the class for further discussion.

ON YOUR OWN

Identify a logo from a company whose products you frequently use or like (perhaps such as Apple, Nike, Coca-Cola, etc.). Research the origins of their brand mark and map the various kinds of writers that went into producing these marks. If possible, try to identify the individuals that created the brand marks, and if different, the artists who took that design and produced the first renderings.

Audience

Besides the writer, you can also use the rhetorical tetrahedron to analyze a text for the writer's intended audience. You usually never write for a totally general audience but instead imagine a specific, intended audience. In order to determine what this intended audience is for the writer of a particular work, you'll have to do just as much (if not more) research into the writer and the text. The following list provides some specific questions that can help you begin your research:

1. What was the original publication that published the text or image?

This question has two main parts. The first is the organization behind the publication of the text. For instance, a writer published by the magazine *The Economist* will reach a much different audience than if she were published in *People Magazine* (Figure 3.3). The first magazine covers politics and world affairs, while the second mainly explores celebrity life. You would probably need to determine the publication's history and goals and its targeted readership, as well as the kinds of advertisements it includes. You might ask some of these same questions about the advertisements as a way to investigate the text's audience.

Figure 3.3
The magazine for which an author writes will determine the audience they reach.

Such questions might relate to the audience's income, education, lifestyle, or other characteristics.

The second question concerns the medium in which the text was originally published. Does it appear in a print advertisement, a newspaper, a website, or on television? Different audiences use media differently and read different kinds of media, and someone who reads a newspaper might expect a different writing style than someone who reads a blog. By researching this information, you can gather clues toward the audience that the writer most likely intended to reach.

2. Does the writer provide any clues about his audience within the text itself?

Sometimes the writer will directly address a particular audience, making it clear whom you need to research. However, sometimes indirect clues can provide direction. For instance, the Federal Emergency Management Agency's advertisement in Figure 3.4 displays a flooded street and hardware store with a banner "Liquidation Sale." This ad clearly targets small business owners, which is also evident in the ad's text. However, because of the flooded street, this ad also targets those business owners near rivers and oceans, or those subject to hurricanes, and not necessarily those subject to other disasters such as earthquakes. If you research the ad's creation, you'll learn that the advertisement was created a few months before hurricane season starts in the United States.

Credit: FEMA

Figure 3.4
The Federal Emergency Management Agency would like to help keep small business owners from going underwater.
http://www.fema.gov/medialibrary/media_records/12398

3. What does the writing or image say about the intended audience?

Often, the writer will leave other textual (or visual) clues about her intended audience. For instance, if she provides significant background information about her topic, then she's probably addressing an audience who's unfamiliar with the subject. In addition, the kind of evidence she provides can offer clues. If she were quoting Bible scripture as a way to make her argument, then she might imagine her audience to be mostly Christian. If she included lots of statistics, she might be targeting someone who values quantitative data when assessing an argument, such as scientists, economists, or engineers. Finally, the emotional appeals she makes also hint at her audience. Does she try to persuade the audience with anger or sympathy? If so, what audiences might respond to such emotional appeals?

This outline provides a beginning for researching the intended audience of a writer. As you analyze a text and identify clues, you might have to research these clues further to get the information you need. Of course, this line of questioning only attempts to discover the "intended" audience. The actual audience will be much more fluid, especially in a new media environment where you can never know every person who reads or looks at a particular text. However, focusing on the intended audience can tell you about the text itself as well as the writer who created it.

MAKING CONNECTIONS

AS A CLASS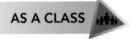

Collect various print magazines that also have a Web presence. Compare the difference between how the content is written for the print versions of the magazines versus their websites. Does the style of the writing differ? The length? Are the advertisements different, or the same? Note all the variances you discover and predict the intended audience for each version of the magazine. Are the audiences the same, or are they subtly different?

IN A GROUP

Locate a variety of print advertisements from a single company, preferably marketing the same product (such as a soft drink company). How do you think the ads are designed to appeal to different audiences? Are the words different? Do the ads use different celebrities or models? Does the use of color change? Try to anticipate the different audiences that each ad is meant to reach. Write your findings in a brief report, and share them with the class.

ON YOUR OWN

View various commercials for products that you buy. Does the commercial contain any clues to its intended audience, such as language, setting, actors, or other elements? Whom do you think this commercial is targeting? What makes you believe so? Do you feel that you, as a buyer of this product, are represented as one of those intended audience members, or do you think the commercial doesn't reach you even though you buy the product? If this is the case, how might the company alter the commercial with you in mind as the intended audience member? Record your thoughts and share them with the class.

Context and Subject

When looking at "message" on the rhetorical tetrahedron, some of the questions you might ask about the message are the *context* and *subject* that inform how an audience understands the message. Researching the context of an image can provide important information about a text, including what the message is actually about. As you saw with the example of Ramesses's propaganda, a text always exists within a historical moment and is created to meet certain needs of a particular time and place (even if this time is a potential, future time, such as letting your decedents know how great you were). Without knowing anything about that image's context, it's difficult to determine the subject of the work (the Battle of Kadesh), as well as other questions such as why the image was constructed, how, when, or by whom.

Analyzing the context can provide important clues to reading an image. You cannot know what an image is really "about" unless you know this larger historical context in which it appeared (or appears currently), and so the subject and context are always intertwined. Since images often offer less evidence about their context than alphabetic writing, you'll have to look for other clues to provide details.

You've already examined how knowledge of the writer and audience can provide information for reading an image. In addition to these elements, you can also research the larger historical context, which includes not only who created the image and whom it was created for, but also when the text was created, in what part of the world, the perceptions or attitudes of the audience at the time, as well as how that audience originally received the image.

Figure 3.5 shows an artwork titled *The Physical Impossibility of Death in the Mind of Someone Living* by Damien Hirst (Figure 3.6). The facts that you can easily learn from a simple Web search include data such as its materials (tiger shark, glass, steel, 5% formaldehyde solution), dimensions (213cm x 518cm), the

Credit: Agent001

Credit: Christian Görmer

Figure 3.5
The Physical Impossibility of Death in the Mind of Someone Living by Damien Hirst

Figure 3.6
Damien Hirst

date of its creation (1991), and the person who funded the artwork (Charles Saatchi).

From just this information, more questions arise, such Damien Hirst's background and how he got the tiger shark. Hirst was a British artist and became associated with the art movement Britart, or Young British Artists, a group that was known for creating art that had shock value, was composed of throwaway materials, and had an attitude that Kate Bush writes is "both oppositional and entrepreneurial." Knowing this, you can clearly see the shock value of the tiger shark, as well as the simple materials of glass and steel, which are not especially valuable in their own right.

The shark, as a dead carcass, can also be considered "throwaway." Hirst acquired the shark by paying Australian fishermen to specifically catch a large shark that was clearly big enough to devour a human. While the artwork was commissioned by Saatchi, the shark itself was commissioned by Hirst for £6000. Here, you can begin to see the purposes and motivations for the particular piece.

How did audiences respond to the artwork? As with many works of art, Hirst's piece elicited mixed responses. Upon the artwork's visit to the New York Metropolitan Museum of Art in 2007, Roberta Smith writes:

> Will the shark attract a new audience to the Met? Maybe. Is it worth the trip? Definitely. Mr. Hirst's detractors accuse him of being a Conceptual artist, with the implication (misguided even for most genuine Conceptual art) that you don't need to see the work in person. Mr. Hirst often aims to fry the mind (and misses more than he hits), but he does so by setting up direct, often visceral experiences, of which the shark remains the most outstanding.
>
> In keeping with the piece's title, the shark is simultaneously life and death incarnate in a way you don't quite grasp until you see it, suspended and silent, in its tank. It gives the innately demonic urge to live a demonic, deathlike form. (2007)

Credit: Albert Kok

Figure 3.7
A live tiger shark in the Bahamas.

Smith finds that despite the artwork being "conceptual" rather than aesthetic, it is definitely worth seeing, and the artwork will leave the viewer with a "visceral experience." Others, however, did not see the same value in the artwork and criticized it as contributing to the decline of British art, or simply refused to recognize a dead shark encased in a tank of formaldehyde as art at all.

However, despite concerns about the artwork's status as art, others question the attainment of the shark itself (Figure 3.7). Some critics (many from outside the art circle) chastised Hirst for killing a shark specifically for this project rather than using a shark that was already dead. Organizations such as People for the Ethical Treatment of Animals have condemned Hirst's work that involves killing animals, and artist Bill Gusky writes:

The shark in Damien Hirst's Conceptual piece The Physical Impossibility of Death in the Mind of Someone Living—*a spectacular fourteen-footer— was caught and killed in Australia specifically for this work.*

It doesn't get much more sickening than this.

Almost as if to match Mr. Hirst's and Charles Saatchi's moral character, the original shark has slipped into an advanced and irretrievable state of decay, rotting so terribly that its tiny sheltered world became dark and murky with the sickness of it. Those standing outside and looking in could only marvel at the stench from which they were protected by a thin wall of unimaginable wealth.

At first Saatchi performed a fairly standard taxidermy by skinning the shark and stretching the skin onto a fiberglass form. Doesn't this beg the question why not use a fake shark in the first place and save hapless, beautiful sea creatures from becoming the victims of the weak-minded egotistical fantasies of a British art punk?

But that solution apparently wasn't realistic enough for someone. After all, the dead shark had sure as hell better look real or else Hirst's precious multi-million-dollar concept goes sailing out the window, right?

So now they've killed another shark. This majestic and most unlucky victim is fully thirteen feet long. (2006)

Given the title of the work, Hirst's subject was much larger and more complex than just a dead shark: the psychological interaction that occurs when one sees a dead animal. While this interaction might have occurred subconsciously, for many viewers, the subject was simply the shark itself and the concept of "shock." When researching a particular image, then, the larger context in which it originally appeared can tell you a great deal about the work itself. Given that much of the shock around Hirst's artwork developed because he killed a shark to make it, you can deduce that his audience values living animals more than killing them to create new artwork. Of course, the context covered here is only a fraction of all the information that might be important to reading this particular image. Current events, the political leaders at the time, and other coincidences can also affect how one reads an image.

Context changes through time, and an image that was created and seen in one historical period can change in meaning and value when viewed in another. You probably recognize the swastika (Figure 3.8) as a symbol for Nazi Germany as it existed during the 1930s through World War II and associate the symbol with fascism, white supremacy, and the holocaust. Whenever most people see the symbol, they usually view it in this context and negatively view its use.

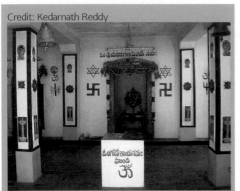

Credit: Kedarnath Reddy

Figure 3.8
You can see the Hindu version of the swastika on the walls of the Vinayaka Swamy Temple. The word "swastika" translates to "all is well."

However, the swastika has existed for more than 5000 years, originating from the Indus Valley region near modern day India. The symbol spread through the ancient world, eventually being used by many civilizations in the Western world, and it was also used by some Native American cultures.

Generally, the symbol had positive meanings of good luck and often served as a religious symbol as it still does today for Hindu, Buddhist, and Jain religions. Translated from Hindu, swastika means "all is well." As the swastika entered each culture, it took on new meanings and associations, and was used in a variety of ways. Of course, because of recent historical memory, the symbol has largely become taboo in much of the Western hemisphere. Researching an image more deeply will give you a richer understanding of how to approach a given text and why an author might include it in her design.

MAKING CONNECTIONS

AS A CLASS

List various symbols that commonly appear in visual culture, such as a four-leaf clover, an arrow, or a lightning bolt. Once you have several to work with, discuss how you think the symbol was originally created, what it meant, and of course, what the symbol means today. Then, break into groups and have each group research one of the symbols. Once finished, come back together as a class and share your results.

IN A GROUP

Choose a famous painting or photograph. Analyze the photograph according to some of the suggestions above, including who created it, why it was created, the historical context around its creation, and how audiences typically view the image now. Write your findings in a brief report and share them with the class.

ON YOUR OWN

One of the symbols used regularly in daily Twitter interactions is the # symbol, typically when identifying a conversation or topic in Twitter messages. Research the history of the # symbol and how it evolved into its current uses (for instance, while Twitter calls it a "hashtag," other contexts refer to it as the "pound" symbol. Why?). Compose a report detailing your findings and share them with the class.

MAPPING RHETORICAL APPEALS

Another way to analyze texts is based on the classical appeals included in the rhetorical tetrahedron: *logos, ethos, pathos,* and *kairos.* As discussed in the last chapter, the rhetorical tetrahedron can be modified to study these rhetorical appeals by placing them on the four sides of the tetrahedron. While you can use the rhetorical tetrahedron to construct an argument, you can also use it to read arguments that you find in a variety of texts. When you need to evaluate an image, use the rhetorical tetrahedron according to each of the appeals below as a mode of analysis when looking at any text.

Credit: TBWA/Yehoshua, Tel Aviv, Israel

Figure 3.9
This ad for the Toyota Prius attempts to use *logos* to compare and contrast the car with a sheep.

Logos

Logos, as you remember, is an appeal to the reader based on logical claims. When looking at an image from this point of view, you want to examine how a text attempts to convince the reader by making a reasoned argument.

Figure 3.9 depicts an ad that appears in Israel for the Toyota Prius, a hybrid car that runs on both electric batteries and gasoline. In this advertisement, the designers present an argument based on comparison and contrast between their car and a sheep, demonstrating that the car has fewer greenhouse emissions than the sheep (which naturally emits methane, a greenhouse gas). The ad attempts to make the logical point that the car is in some ways more natural than a natural animal and is therefore good for the environment. Deeper analysis would be required to determine if the comparison is accurate (can one really compare a car and a sheep in this way?), but on the surface, the ad uses *logos* to make its case.

Credit: youarethetechnology.com

Credit: Harvard University

Figure 3.10
This online ad for Vibram FiveFingers shoes makes use of the interactive nature of the Internet.

Figure 3.11
Daniel E. Lieberman practices what he preaches in this photo.

Figure 3.10 shows the online advertisement for Vibram FiveFingers, a shoe company that makes minimalist footwear that is popular among barefoot runners and other barefoot enthusiasts. This interactive "ad" makes its appeals based upon the science of running, the anatomy of the human body, and other claims based on *logos* in an attempt to persuade the viewer that minimal shoes provide a more "natural" way to run.

The ad also uses comparison and contrast between their shoes and more traditional footwear in order to establish why their shoes are healthier and cause fewer injuries. The company also refers to Daniel E. Lieberman (Figure 3.11), a researcher at Harvard, who performs clinical studies on runners with different footwear, and uses his data to further bolster the company's argument. When analyzing texts for *logos*, you should look for the source of such information and whether these sources are credible and not just based on misleading data.

Of course, as you'll see below, *logos* usually doesn't exist alone, and you could probably make the case that *ethos* and *pathos* also appear in these ads. However, on the surface at least, *logos* is one of the more prevalent appeals in these advertisements.

MAKING CONNECTIONS

AS A CLASS

Many companies include a section on their website that lists various press releases and media campaigns, including advertisements and commercials. As a class, choose a company with such a section and look at the various ads on this site, noticing which advertisements predominantly use *logos*. What kinds of claims does the company make? Do the ads use facts and statistics, comparison and contrast, definition, or other kinds of arguments? Whom do you think the company imagines its potential audience to be for these ads, and do you think the ads would be effective for these audiences.

IN A GROUP

Logos comes from the ancient Greek word for "word." Appeals to *logos* are based in thinking with the word, typically analytical thought. With a partner, look through a variety of company brand marks. Do you think any of these brand marks attempt to use the rhetorical appeal of *logos* to make a connection with the audience? Which elements suggest this? How might a company's brand mark connect with the meaning of *logos* based in its early meaning as "word"? Report your findings to the class.

ON YOUR OWN

Locate an advertisement for your favorite food. What kinds of appeals to *logos* does this advertisement make? What kinds of evidence does it provide? If the ad doesn't seem to appeal to *logos*, what logical claims would you include in the ad in order to persuade readers to eat the food? Share your ideas with the class.

Ethos

You can also analyze a text based on the writer's *ethos*: their credibility as an author. You'll want to know what qualifications the writer has to make the statements he or she does. What is the author's background and experience? Is the author presenting the argument for good reasons, or does he or she have a secret, ulterior motive? Basically, is this someone you can trust?

For example, the *ethos* of two writers already discussed, Ramesses and Vibram, differ quite radically. Since Vibram is a shoe company, you expect that it's trying to sell you something. In order to establish its arguments with some basis in independent data, the company cites an authority figure to increase their *ethos* rather than just stating claims without expert testimony.

To do so, they cite Lieberman, a professor of human evolutionary biology at Harvard University, someone who is well trained to look at the biomechanics of human running, make determinations about how humans evolved to run, and predict the impact that modern-day footwear might have on the human body. Also, as a scientist, and with no affiliation with any particular shoe company (he's not paid by Vibram), Lieberman makes his assessments mostly independently and for the advancement of knowledge, not for any kickbacks from a particular sponsor. In addition, his research is usually peer-reviewed by other scientists, so the knowledge he produces is verified as good work.

Ramesses, on the other hand, was the pharaoh of Egypt and could write whatever he wanted. His status as ruler doesn't necessarily make his statements more truthful but probably makes them more suspect. As you've already seen, both Ramesses's texts and those found at the Hittite capital Boghazköy claim victory at the Battle of Kadesh. Most historians believe that Ramesses was able to force a truce (he was losing badly for much of the battle), and so neither civilization truly won. Given that the very purpose of the carving inside the Abu Sembel temple is selfish, a piece of propaganda aimed at keeping Ramesses's empire together with him as ruler, you can definitely question that his motives for writing weren't as independent as Lieberman's, and that he's not entirely trustworthy as a writer (or, at least, as the sponsor of the carvings).

Figure 3.12
Based on this rusty sign, would you trust this body shop to repair your car?

Besides a writer's credentials, other structural and formal elements can affect how you read a writer's *ethos* within a text. Audiences often find fault with a writer who makes spelling or grammatical mistakes in their writing, and their *ethos* as a writer often diminishes for their readers. You can make the same assessment of visual works. Does the image seem well-designed, making good use of elements such as color, white space, typeface, and other design choices? Or is the image hastily composed, sloppy, and look amateurish? Would you say, "That text looks like it was created by a professional," or would you remark that "My five-year-old niece could compose something better than that"? Most images you see around you are professionally created, but simple mistakes can make the audience question the creator's *ethos* (Figure 3.12).

When analyzing a text for *ethos*, then, consider these facets of the writer's credibility. Is the writer credentialed to make the claims she or he does? If not, does she use supporting evidence that is credentialed, as Vibram does with Lieberman? Does the writer seem to respect his or her reader, or does he treat the reader condescendingly? Does the writer use any of the logical fallacies discussed in Chapter 2 that would make the audience question how well he or she understands the argument? Finally, does the writer craft a well-written or well-designed text, or does the text look unorganized and difficult to read? These questions will help you begin to make sense of the writer's *ethos* when reading a text.

MAKING CONNECTIONS

AS A CLASS

Visit a news website and view some of the articles and photographs. How does the site attempt to establish credibility for each article? Does it appeal to the writer's credentials? If so, what are they, and do you think they're relevant to the article? Does the website make good use of formal design and appear well-organized and error free? Do you feel you can trust the website and the writer's motivations for writing? What makes you think so?

IN A GROUP

Look through a variety of articles from Wikipedia. How does each article attempt to establish *ethos*? What kinds of sources do they site? Are these sources credible? Is the article free of major mechanical and grammatical errors? In addition to looking at the articles, research how Wikipedia works, and the role of moderators at the site. Finally, look through the same (or similar) entries in a print encyclopedia (or an online version of a print encyclopedia). How does this version create *ethos*? Does it establish *ethos* in the same way as Wikipedia, or does it use a different approach? Record your results and share them with the class.

ON YOUR OWN

In the last section (on *logos*), you found advertisements for your favorite food. Look back at these advertisements, and consider how they use *ethos* to supplement their argument. Do they use celebrities, famous chefs, or perhaps endorsements from nutrition or health organizations? What elements appear that suggest you can trust the claims they make? Do you believe in these claims? Why or why not? Record your ideas and share them with the class.

Pathos

In many cases, images that make an argument will use appeals to *pathos*, as you've already seen with examples of cigarette ads in Chapter 2. As discussed in the introduction, images appeal to the parts of the brain that respond emotionally to visual stimuli. While text can certainly produce emotional responses, images can do it more quickly and with greater force. Reading *pathos* in a visual text becomes an important skill in order to understand more systematically how the image is attempting to reach a viewer.

Figure 3.13 displays an advertisement that encourages riders to wear their helmets while on a bicycle, motorcycle, or other open-air vehicle. Here, the message relies mostly on the fear of receiving a significant brain injury, one that could require life-long care or possibly death. While the text also attempts to use logical arguments, citing statistics of how many people injure themselves each year from not wearing helmets, the ad's predominant appeal is toward *pathos*, creating an emotional response to make people reconsider their actions and protect their heads out on the roads. The appeal is sometimes called a "fear" appeal, because it plays on readers' fears of what might happen if they do not act on the message.

Another appeal to *pathos* plays on one's desires to be socially accepted and to attain social status and approval. These social appeals often portray a product that makes the customer part of an "in" crowd, or someone with special privilege. Figure 3.14 shows a commercial for AT&T's 4G network. Because the two main characters have this cell phone service, they are able to receive information before any of their friends or acquaintances, centering them as in-the-know. Their responses (always paired with how long they have already known a particular piece of information) have a tone of superiority and condescension, making the other characters (and the viewer) feel inferior for not having as fast a wireless service, and not knowing such "crucial" information sooner.

This ad also uses an appeal of humor, but not as well as Figure 3.15, a commercial for Old Spice deodorant. This ad depicts whimsical transitions from scene to scene, making the viewer laugh at its improbability. The success of such ads can be confirmed by their views on YouTube. On Old Spice's official YouTube page, this commercial has more than 39-million views. The power of humor not only helps the viewers recall a particular product

Credit: Ogilvy & Mather Vietnam

Credit: BBDO Atlanta

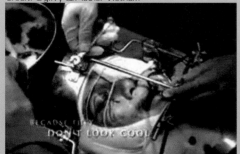

Figure 3.13
Note how this ad uses *pathos* to convince you to wear a helmet.

http://www.10ad.org/wear-a-helmet-and-protect-your-life/

Figure 3.14
This AT&T ad makes an appeal to social privilege.

http://www.youtube.com/watch?v=VZv_duAByDI

when making a purchase, but also to circulate that ad among their friends, increasing the total audience.

As you've probably noticed by now, most of these examples use a variety of emotional appeals, blending social, humor, fear, and other appeals to persuade an audience. The Old Spice commercial could also fall into the category of "sex appeal" or "adventure appeal"—appeals that a product will make one's life more adventurous and fun.

Many companies and organizations that offer outdoor products and services rely on this appeal. Companies like Columbia, The North Face, or Coleman often display ads that depict remote, inaccessible wilderness areas explored by an outdoor enthusiast. The North Face's slogan, "never stop exploring," solidifies this appeal. Nonprofit organizations such as the U.S. Forest Service also appeal to a sense of outdoor adventure and other positive activities many associate with being in natural environments (Figure 3.16).

Often, images can appeal to shared values, which usually include a sense of community, either in the regions where audiences live, a country as a whole (patriotism), or in a global context. Figures 3.17, 3.18, and 3.19 offer an example of each of these.

Figure 3.17 is a website for "Don't Mess with Texas®" aimed at keeping people from littering in the Lone Star State. While their ads offer many logical arguments about not littering, their main message is one based on local pride—and the warning of a veiled threat as in the popular saying "don't mess with Texas" (this campaign also uses the pun of "mess" to provide a bit of humor to the ads).

Credit: Wieden + Kennedy, Portland, OR

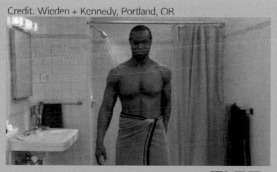

Credit: Ad Council/USDA-Forest Service

Figure 3.16
The Forest Service appeals to a sense of adventure.

http://www.discovertheforest.org/about

Figure 3.15
This Old Spice ad uses improbable transitions to appeal to the viewer.

http://www.youtube.com/
watch?v=owGykVbfgUE

Credit: Don't Mess with Texas*

Figure 3.17
If you litter, you mess with Texas. Don't do it.

Credit: Greenpeace/Lowe AG, Switzerland

Figure 3.19
This Greenpeace ad appeals to a sense of being a citizen of the world.

Credit: James Montgomery Flag

Figure 3.18
This advertisement clearly calls for the patriot in you to "wake up."

Figure 3.18 appeals to a national audience. This advertisement from World War I attempted to persuade Americans to join in the war effort. The female figure is depicted as "Miss America," asleep to the war being fought overseas.

Figure 3.19 goes beyond nation and appeals to the global citizen. This ad for Greenpeace shows not a school of fish but a school of litter flowing through the seas. This image might produce feelings of shame, pity, or sadness, or appeal to the need that humans be more responsible with their trash disposal. It is not aimed at any particular body of water but oceans in general, something that everyone shares in one way or another.

When analyzing an image for its emotional appeals, think specifically about the particular kinds of emotions it appeals to (fear, humor, love, anger) and which desires it taps into (social acceptance, adventure, sex). This strategy will help you then determine the kinds of audiences that the image is attempting to reach and can give you ideas about how to compose your own images toward your own audiences.

MAKING CONNECTIONS

AS A CLASS

Revisit the company's press release and media campaign site that you looked at in the *logos* section above. You've already analyzed the ads that use logical appeals. Now, identify which ads use *pathos*. Which emotions do they appeal to? What desires are they attempting to exploit? How do you think the creators view their audiences differently between those ads that use primarily logical appeals versus those aimed at emotional appeals? Do you find one more effective than the other? Why or why not?

IN A GROUP

Look back at the company brand marks you selected to research regarding their *logos*. Do any of these brand marks have an emotional component? If not, can you think of brand marks that do? Do they appeal to your desires for adventure, social status, or patriotism? Are the brand marks that create an emotional connection from newer companies, or long-established companies? Discuss why you think the brand marks create an emotional connection, and share the results with the class.

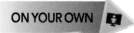

ON YOUR OWN

In the last two sections, you looked at advertisements for your favorite food, considering their appeals to *logos* and *ethos*. How do ads for this same food create appeals toward *pathos*? Do they create a sense of nostalgia? Do they present you with an appeal toward social acceptance? Adventure? Do they make you hungry, and would you consider hunger a type of emotion? Record your findings and share them with the class.

Kairos

You can also analyze an image for its timing—when it was placed within a particular moment. As discussed in Chapter 2, *kairos* identifies the best rhetorical moment to help make a particular argument. When analyzing a specific image, you might ask some of the following questions to help you determine why the author created the text at a particular moment or opportunity:

- What's in the text that relates to other local, national, or global events?

- Is there a pressing need to communicate that cannot wait until a later time?

- Is there a certain mood or atmosphere that the image attempts to tap into?

Figure 3.21 depicts an advertisement for relief after Hurricane Sandy struck the east coast of the United States. To achieve maximum effectiveness—or to seize the opportune moment—this ad should've appeared shortly after the hurricane struck. If the ad had appeared too late, then many people may have forgotten about this disaster, or another may have created other exigencies.

Credit: Ad Council

IN THE WAKE OF HURRICANE SANDY YOUR DOLLARS ARE HARD AT WORK

help where it's needed most.

Even a small donation can make a big difference
Sandy.AdCouncil.org

Figure 3.21
This advertisement from the Ad Council asks for donations and lets the audience know that their contributions are "hard at work" toward medicine, water, and construction.

Political campaign ads usually only appear during election seasons. Advertisements for presidential elections usually air according to how a political candidate is doing in a particular location. Or, if a scandalous story were to come out, the opposing politician might create an ad pertaining to this scandal to make sure everyone became aware of it. However, the politician must time the ad's release at the right moment. Releasing the ad too late might make it seem like old news and no longer relevant; opportune moments to communicate have limited time frames.

As a conversation enters into a community's consciousness, it matures until it reaches a peak. However, over time, the conversation dwindles and it no longer matters as much. For example, at the Conservative Political Action Conference (CPAC) of 2012, presidential candidate Rick Santorum made a remark about women serving on the front lines in military operations, saying that allowing them to do so could create a "compromising situation where people naturally may do things that may not be in the interest of the mission because of other types of emotions that are involved." Bob McDonnell, governor of Virginia, also spoke at CPAC after Santorum and used his speaking platform as an opportunity to rebut this idea (Figure 3.22). McDonnell seized the kairotic opportunity to speak about this issue while it was circulated by the media and in the public's mind.

You might also look at uprisings in Africa and the Middle East during the spring of 2011 as examples of seizing the kairotic moment. For the protesters, the most opportune moment to send Twitter messages about the situation was during the protests, to let media outlets know what was happening so that the outside world could support their efforts (Figure 3.23). To make such tweets well before the peak of the protests or well after any of the regimes were overthrown would not have had the intended impact or reaction. Writers must make use of *kairos* during this short window of time before it closes.

Figure 3.24 displays a modified "Apple" advertisement from a group called "Freedom From Porn" located in San Francisco, California. If you were to ask how *kairos* relates to this image, or why the writers might have posted the image when they did, you could search for events that occurred during the same time period.

Figure 3.22
Governor Bob McDonnell uses a kairotic moment to discuss the role of women in the military.
http://www.youtube.com/watch?v=Hx9bKObcoPo

Credit: Sherif9282

Figure 3.23
An Egyptian protestor in Cairo's Tahrir Square with a flyer that refers to social media's role in the 2011 Egyptian Revolution.

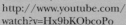

Figure 3.24
The group "Freedom From Porn" waited until the Apple Worldwide Developers Conference to spread their ads protesting Apple's policies on pornography.

Credit: BBDO New York

Figure 3.25
General Electric taps into the kairotic moment of environmental conversations.
http://www.youtube.com/watch?v=MCH-T8kMh7A

Since the group seems to be juxtaposing the iPad and pornography for some rhetorical purpose, you might also ask if any events that involved Apple products occurred in San Francisco during this time, such as an iPad or other Apple product release. Researching these questions, you would discover that Apple did not release any major product, but the Apple Worldwide Developers Conference, a meeting of Apple developers, did take place in San Francisco during this time. The creators of the ad clearly timed its delivery to correspond to this meeting and to make sure the developers attending the conference got the message.

Many companies are tapping into the zeitgeist of environmental consciousness that has been increasing since the 1970s. Now, many companies attempt to portray their products in at least a few commercials that highlight how their product reduces pollution, is recycled, or is otherwise environmentally friendly. Figure 3.25 shows a commercial from General Electric that attempts to tap into the current kairotic moment regarding such environmental discourse.

MAKING CONNECTIONS

AS A CLASS

Return to the company's press release and media campaign site that you looked at in the last few sections above. Look at the timing of each release, and research how each release corresponds to a particular opportune moment. You may have to research other events that require the exigency for the releases and speculate on how the authors used *kairos* for their rhetorical advantage.

IN A GROUP

Visit a news website. Analyze the opinion pieces, and determine how each meets a kairotic opportunity. Do you think any of these opinions appear too late or too early for a particular conversation? For example, discussions about women's rights to vote would probably be too late, since this debate occurred nearly 100 years ago. However, there may be authors who write about arguments that you feel have been settled long ago. What new exigency occurs to make the timing of these pieces appropriate? Write your results in a report and share them with the class.

ON YOUR OWN

In the last three sections, you looked at advertisements for your favorite food, considering their appeals to *logos, ethos,* and *pathos.* How do ads for this same food tap into *kairos*? Do they enter into a conversation that is already going on about particular dietary fads, health advice, or concerns about food safety? Do they relate to current events at the time of their release such as sporting events or holidays? Consider some of these factors, think of your own, and research how the writers might have used *kairos*. Compose your results in a report and share them with the class.

MAPPING THE ARGUMENT

Finally, you should also consider the argument itself that the writer is attempting to make, as well as how she or he makes that argument. While a visual argument isn't necessarily the same as a written argument, it does make use of some of the same strategies, such as argument by analogy, definition, comparison and contrast, as well as stating claims and reasons. While a visual text often doesn't have the space (or if a video, time) to develop an argument the way an essay does, you can still look for some of these features when analyzing an image.

Claims, Reasons, Evidence

In other classes, you may have been asked to compose an argument by making a *claim* and then supporting it with *reasons* and *evidence*. These argumentative elements may also be present in visual texts, although sometimes hidden from view. To investigate a visual text and uncover these elements, you can start by asking yourself the following questions:

1. What is the main claim of the image?

Of the main parts that compose an argument, a visual text will usually have some sort of claim. Although not in complete sentences, you can probably easily interpret the claim in Figure 3.26, an advertisement for Chik-Fil-A restaurants. The text above the image of the cows, which reads "Go De-Calf This Mornin," indicates by juxtaposition that the ad refers to "de-calf" as "without cow," and thus eating chicken. Here the text anchors the meaning of the image.

Figure 3.27 provides another example of how text can anchor the claim of the image. In this ad, the model, Patrick Ribbsaeter, appears chained, and the text reads "Wild animals don't belong in chains: keep elephants out of zoos." Here, the main claim appears in the second line, "keep elephants out

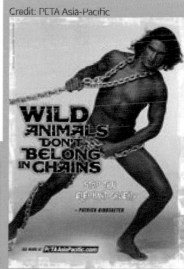

Credit: PETA Asia-Pacific

Credit: Chik-Fil-A

Figure 3.26
Despite very little text, this Chik-Fil-A ad still makes an argument.

Figure 3.27
This ad makes a very direct claim. What role does the visual play?

of zoos," with the first part, "wild animals don't belong in chains" as a reason for the claim.

However, some images may make claims while not using any text (or very little text) to provide a specific meaning. Figure 3.28 displays a clump of rainforest in the shape of a set of lungs. In the right lung, loggers are clear-cutting the forest, destroying the lower lobe. The text at the bottom, "before it's too late," doesn't provide a claim, but instead provides support for the claim, which may be something like "the rainforests are the lungs of the earth, and we need to protect them," which then may be coupled with "before it's too late." The use of visual metaphor is an effective and powerful way to quickly make a claim without resorting to the use of text. The downside, of course, is that your readers might misinterpret your metaphor without any text to guide them.

Credit: World Wildlife Fund

Figure 3.28
If you had to interpret this ad's argument, how would you phrase it?

2. Does the image provide any reasons to support its claim?

Figure 3.29 shows Paul McCartney, one of the members of the band, the Beatles, in an ad promoting vegetarianism. While the most prominent text "I am Paul McCartney, and I am a Vegetarian," is most likely the main claim and could be continued into "and you should be a vegetarian too," the main reason for this argument is provided in the anecdote in the upper right-hand corner of the image where McCartney tells of the time he caught a fish and realized "that his life was as important to him as mine is to me." In this example, the reason for becoming a vegetarian relates to the consciousness of animals. While this reason can be debated further, it provides some indication of why one might want to accept the main claim.

Many images, however, do not provide explicit reasons for a claim, and instead leave it to the

Credit: PETA

Figure 3.29
This ad provides a very explicit reason to back up its claim.

audience to fill in those reasons themselves. Figure 3.30 depicts a stork labeled as "resources" carrying ten children to their expectant families. This image provides an analogy for overpopulation and the strain it will have on Earth's finite resources. However, this image doesn't state that overpopulation is bad and why it is bad. Instead, the audience is left to fill in the unstated reasons or realize that the image is suggesting that overpopulation is bad, because it puts undue strain on resources and will send them (like the stork) crashing to the ground. Since the audience knows it needs resources to survive, the cartoon doesn't have to provide that reason. The audience provides it on its own.

The reasons may also be built into the claim. Figure 3.31 provides an image of a man with a fish's head. The main text of the image states, "Stop climate change before it changes you." Here, you might read the main claim as "Stop climate change" with the reason "if you don't, it will change you." The image of the "merman" suggests that climate change will change the

Credit: Clay Bennett

Credit: World Wildlife Fund

STOP CLIMATE CHANGE
BEFORE IT CHANGES YOU.

Figure 3.30
This cartoon only uses two words. How would you phrase its argument?

Figure 3.31
If you had to interpret this ad's argument, how would you phrase it?

planet in a way that will force humans to adapt, perhaps becoming more fish-like as sections of landmasses become submerged. The second part of the main text, as well as the image, provides reasons for the claim.

3. What kind of evidence does the image provide for these reasons?

Although reasons for a claim are often missing from visual texts, authors do include evidence on occasion. Figure 3.32 depicts an advertisement against human trafficking. Its main claim is "Human trafficking is more active than ever. YOU can help." The writer does not state the reasons why this is a problem. He or she probably assumes that the audience will think that "of course we shouldn't traffic in human beings."

While the author doesn't provide reasons for this problem, the author does provide evidence about the statistics of victims: "99% of victims

Credit: thea21campaign.org

99% OF VICTIMS
ARE NOT RESCUED

Human trafficking is more active than ever. YOU can help.

Figure 3.32
This ad uses a powerful statistic as evidence.

are not rescued." Should someone be taken and in this situation, chances are he or she will never be seen again, making this statistic very powerful. When creating your own visual, you might c members of the former pop band, the hoose to be selective about the evidence you provide since you have little space to do so. Choose claims/evidence that you think will most impact your readers and get their attention.

4. Does the image provide any counterarguments?

As discussed previously, most visual texts don't have the space to provide a

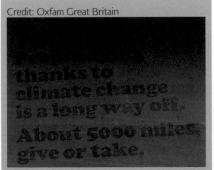

Credit: Oxfam Great Britain

Figure 3.33
This ad provides a counterargument but is all text. Do you find it effective?

full-fledged argument as you might typically think of when writing a paper. In this literate context, you are often taught that you should address counterarguments to your claim and then discuss how they aren't applicable or are otherwise wrong. Figure 3.33 uses its main title to provide one of the counterarguments to global warming before then explaining how this statement is incorrect. This example is completely text-based with no image and is the exception that proves the general rule that most visual texts do not include this level of counterargument. However, you should still be conscious of them when analyzing a text, for they do occasionally appear.

While some of these claims may be literally "spelled out" through text, many visual arguments are composed simply of images without text. Keep in mind that many of the arguments you're looking for may be implicit rather than explicit.

MAKING CONNECTIONS

AS A CLASS

Revisit some of the websites of the companies whose press releases you examined. Locate where the company makes claims about their products through written descriptions. Do the companies include reasons, evidence, or counterarguments for their claims? After you've examined the written copy, reexamine their ads, and analyze how they incorporate claims, reasons, evidence, and counterarguments within visual media. Do the ads use text to secure the meaning of any images, or do they use images alone?

IN A GROUP

Choose a company that has a product for which they create print and
television advertisements. After locating these ads and commercials,
compare how the authors modify their use of claims, reasons,
evidence, and counterarguments for each medium. For television
commercials, does spoken dialogue substitute for written text?
How much does the visual still play an important part? Record your
findings and share them with the class.

ON YOUR OWN

Return to the advertisements for your favorite food. If possible,
examine the company's website for this food, and compare the
information it contains with their advertisements (in as many media as
you can locate). How does the company's argument (or construction
of the argument) change from website to print ad to television
commercial (and to other media)? Write a report of your analysis and
share it with the class.

Symbols and Analogies

When you analyze an image, you
should also pay attention to how
that image uses familiar *symbols* or
analogies to make its argument. For
instance, the Apple logo uses an
apple, which has many
connotations, depending on its use.
Since Apple makes computers,
audiences learn to associate their

Credit: pop culture geek

Figure 3.34
This ad for *Desperate Housewives* appeals to the
"sinfulness" of the show.

logo not with the apple from the Biblical story of genesis
and how it relates to sin but from the classic story of the
apple that fell on Isaac Newton's head and how it relates to
knowledge.

Alternatively, the apple used in Figure 3.34, an
advertisement for the television series *Desperate Housewives*,
does use the apple in its relation to the Garden of Eden.
New York City sometimes uses the image of an apple to
promote some of its business and events since its nickname
is the "Big Apple" (Figure 3.35). Of course, the apple is
often associated with teachers, education, and knowledge.

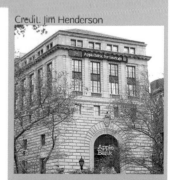

Credit: Jim Henderson

Figure 3.35
The apple used for this
business refers not to sin but
to a bank.

Some symbols may be obvious, such as using a bald eagle to
connect one's message with American patriotism. Others,

such as the apple above, can be common but require context to understand how they relate to the whole of the messages. Some images may use historical figures or celebrities as symbols. The visage of Abraham Lincoln may be used to symbolize honesty, while Marilyn Monroe may be used as a sex symbol. If you come across an image that you believe makes use of a symbol, research the meaning of that symbol as well as its uses in other contexts. This information will provide more depth for your analysis of a particular image and help you make connections between all of its parts.

Credit: World Wildlife Fune/ Ogilvy & Mather

Figure 3.36
This ad uses an analogy to combine two realms, golfing and tree removal, to argue how they're connected.

Images may also use visual analogies or metaphors, and you should notice when they occur. You've already examined the analogy of rainforest as "lungs" in Figure 3.28. The World Wildlife Fund has a series of similar ads, such as the one in Figure 3.36. Here, a golfer has just taken a shot, but instead of a golf club, he holds an ax. The ad is implicating the golfer in the destruction of forests to make space for the fairway he's standing on. While the golfer probably didn't directly cut down any trees himself, his patronage of the golf course pays for those who did. The analogy (and thus the claim) might be written out: "A golfer is like a lumberjack." To follow up on this claim, you would then have to do more research to determine how accurate it is. What is the impact of golf courses on deforestation? Depending on what you uncover, you can then determine if you feel this argument made by the analogy is fair or if it misrepresents the golfing industry. Unpacking the symbolism and analogies in an image is only the first step toward a deeper understanding of visual arguments.

MAKING CONNECTIONS

AS A CLASS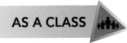

Search for standard symbols in images such as a light bulb for insight, invention, or creativity, or perhaps a heart for love and romance. How do these symbols affect the meaning of the images? How does the presence (or absence) of text contribute to that meaning? Would the meaning change if the symbol were changed to another symbol? Would the meaning substantially change if the symbol was missing altogether? Do you think the symbolic message the image attempts to make is effective?

IN A GROUP

Create your own argument using a visual analogy without using text. You can use some of the examples in this chapter as models. Share your work with the class.

ON YOUR OWN

Return to the advertisements for your favorite food. In the ads that you've examined so far, do any use traditional symbols to sell their products to the audience? If so, what do you think is the significance of the symbol? What does it contribute to the ad? Do the ads use metaphors comparing their food to something else? What is the relationship the ads are trying to establish with these symbols? Do you think it's rhetorically effective? Write a report of your analysis and share it with the class.

MAPPING DESIGN, MEDIUM, AND GENRE

As discussed in Chapter 1, the rhetorical tetrahedron provides a model that accounts for *design, medium,* and *genre* in addition to writer, audience, and message. This section considers these first three elements, which you should analyze through the rhetorical tetrahedron as you consider a new media text as a whole. Remember, just as all six of these rhetorical elements appear together in the rhetorical tetrahedron, they also exist and effect each other in real-world rhetorical situations. Although the following discussion isolates these elements, they're always affecting, and affected by, the other parts of the rhetorical tetrahedron.

Design

While design is taken up more extensively in Chapter 10, below are a few elements to consider when analyzing a text. Use this information to help you ask questions about visuals and investigate how they use different design characteristics. Cross-reference the information here with Chapter 10, however, for a more complete understanding of how images make use of design.

Color

The use of color can help contribute to an argument by selecting hues associated with particular themes or emotions. Typically, the colors red, orange, and yellow stimulate the appetite, and so these colors are often used in food advertising. Figure 3.37 depicts a photo of a typical McDonald's restaurant which uses red and yellow in this way." Of course, McDonald's was clever enough to compose their visual identity in red and yellow, so whenever one sees their logo or food packaging, the appetite has a greater chance of becoming excited.

Figure 3.37
This McDonald's building uses colors that appeal to your appetite.

Credit: Nick Moreau

However, these colors also signify caution, warning, and danger signs on technical documents and dangerous machinery, and of course, you commonly see red on STOP signs.

The color green has been used extensively when creating messages with an environmental theme, but it also represents money, and so may be found on a variety of advertisements promoting financial products. When analyzing a particular image, pay attention to the dominant colors that are present, and research the possible meanings of those colors. How do they influence the way you respond to an image?

Figure 3.38
This ad for Apple's iPod uses contrast to clearly show its product.

Credit: Cancer Patients Aid Association/Touchstone Advertising

SMOKING REDUCES WEIGHT
(one lung at a time)

CANCER PATIENTS AID ASSOCIATION

Figure 3.39
This ad uses typography to effectively "show" its argument.

Color can also be used to contrast different information, making different design elements stand out. Figure 3.38, an advertisement for Apple's iPod, uses only three colors to establish high contrast, so that the white iPod and headphones are clearly visible in the advertisement. Also, the font color is the same as that of the product in the ad, making it clear what the text refers to in the image.

Typeface

Like color, typeface can bolster an argument implicitly by creating a mood or atmosphere. For example, conservative, clean typefaces like Helvetica may suggest the idea of uniformity or convention. Typefaces such as Comic Sans may suggest a whimsical nature. Other typefaces, such as Broadway, literally invoke their namesake, such as the large marquis typeface that displays a Broadway production's title. A typeface such as Futura is intended to evoke the future.

Typefaces can provide personality or characteristics to text that say something beyond the words in which they're composed. In any image you're analyzing, determine which typefaces the advertisement uses and research the creation, intended use, and typical response to that typeface. In addition, other font characteristics can be used to contribute to an argument, such as Figure 3.39, which changes the font from bold to normal to thin in order to portray the idea of losing weight, an important part of the advertisement's message.

Layout

How a particular image is laid out will determine many other important elements, such as emphasis, balance, harmony, use of white space, and other design consideration. For any particular image, you might ask what elements does the writer emphasize over others? While you can probably tell which words an author wants to stand out based on font typography and font weight, you should also pay attention to which visual elements hold more importance than others.

Figure 3.40
The stars, which represent the 50 states, are united by proximity.

For example, proximity offers one way to arrange a design's layout. The United States flag, for instance, uses proximity to group the stars together in one location, visually and metaphorically suggesting that they're together and thus "united" (Figure 3.40).

Figure 3.41 uses isolation by placing a figure in an organ against empty black background, separating the joined figures from any other visual elements and making it the focal point of the public service announcement. This design also isolates the liver from the rest of the body,

Credit: Red Cross/JWT, Shanghai, China

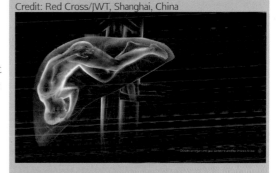

Figure 3.41
This image isolates the organ/man on a black background.

making the message clearer. How and where elements of an image are placed in relationship to each other can create rhetorical effect, drawing the readers' eyes to certain parts and helping to persuade them of a certain point, even if only by placing the reader in a particular mood or atmosphere regarding the message.

MAKING CONNECTIONS

AS A CLASS

Look at a variety of random advertisements and analyze their layout. How do these ads achieve emphasis within the layout? Do they use isolation? Proximity? Color? Contrast? Do you feel that each use of emphasis helps make their argument clear, or does it detract from it? How might you revise each image to make the argument stronger? How might changing the layout change the message of each image?

IN A GROUP

Select an image that makes an argument using juxtaposition of both text and image. Using a photo editor, create different versions of the image by erasing the current text and recreating it (using the same words) by changing the typography. How does changing the typography change the atmosphere (and the message) of the image as a whole? Share your different versions of the image with the class, and discuss how you think the meaning changes for each.

ON YOUR OWN

As discussed in this section, food companies often select colors that appeal to the audience's appetite. Look back at the food advertisements you've collected for the previous assignments in this chapter. Analyze the colors of the ads and note which ones use colors such as red, orange, or yellow. Do these colors appeal to you in these ads? Why or why not? What other colors are used? Do you find these colors attractive when considering a food product to eat, or do the colors make the food unappetizing? Write a brief report detailing the use of color in these ads and share the results with the class.

Genre and Medium

When analyzing an image, you should also examine the genre and medium in which it appears. These two rhetorical elements are very closely connected, and thus worth discussing together.

You're probably already familiar with genres and mediums as they occur in more traditional workplace documents. For instance, the genre of a letter is more formal than that of an e-mail. If you wanted to recommend a change to your boss or colleague, you might do so in the genre of a recommendation report rather than a laboratory report; these two documents obviously serve different functions for different audiences.

Visual documents also require carefully selected genres as well as the medium in which that genre takes its ultimate form. Such genres might include photographs, illustrations, maps, charts, graphs, paintings, commercials, websites, posters, or flyers. Any of these genres could appear in a variety of media, such as print/paper, audio, video, or an assortment of digital formats.

For example, you might ask if the image appears as a flyer, a poster, or a billboard. Is the billboard paper-based or on an LCD display? Is the image painted on the side of a bus, making it a moving image, or does it appear electronically as a commercial, a website, or a commercial within a website? How the image is delivered affects how the reader responds to it. A commercial placed on television can usually only be viewed once, unless the viewer has a digital video recorder and can rewind live television. Of course, the viewer might be equally inclined to fast-forward through the commercial. Online commercials, however, can typically be viewed repeatedly, and also shared among friends, especially when posted on YouTube. This form of medium greatly increases the distribution of the typical commercial genre.

Some companies use the standard genre of the advertisement in some very interesting and creative media. Figure 3.42 is a photograph of an advertisement for Bounty paper towels. Here, the traditional product shot and tag line of the product is combined with a huge coffee cup that has been spilled on the sidewalk. The overall message is delivered through the scale of the "mess" being made.

In Figure 3.43, a billboard for the television program *Law & Order*, the image integrates with

Credit: Bounty/Publicis New York

Figure 3.42
This ad for Bounty paper towels makes the viewer interact with it, even when trying to avoid or ignore it.

Credit: Colenso BBDO, Auckland

Figure 3.43
This ad for *Law and Order* makes use of the existing physical space for a unique effect.

Credit: Papa Johns/Zimmerman Advertising

Figure 3.44
This clever ad for Papa John's pizza changes what a "door flyer" can be.

the building itself, so the police detective holds the building's light as if it were a light in the interrogation room.

Credit: bigantinternational.com

Figure 3.45
This ad, arguing for the United States. to stop the wars in Iraq and Afghanistan, is designed specifically for this particular physical environment.

The door flyer in Figure 3.44 uses the peep-hole to help deliver its message, one that looks like a pizza delivery person at the door. This modifies the traditional flyer that hangs on a door knob and places it within a slightly different medium, one that sticks onto the door and integrates with its design.

Finally, the poster in Figure 3.45 is specifically designed to be wrapped around a round column so that the message ("what goes around comes around") is actually enacted by the poster itself. If this poster were laid flat, or wrapped around a square column, it would lose its effectiveness.

Whenever you analyze a visual text, ask yourself "Why did the designer create the text in this genre?" and "Why did she create the text in this medium?" Some of the answers to these questions might be obvious. For example, if the visual text appears outdoors, the medium might need to be waterproof to withstand the elements. The medium may need to be a static medium that is not electronic (of course, some electronics are waterproofed to be placed outside). Placing an advertisement on a bus might help to increase exposure as it moves about a city. While a YouTube video isn't located outside where people can see it, placing a video in an online medium might actually garner more attention because people can more easily share it. Decisions about genre and medium are rhetorical choices meant to reach particular audiences and persuade them. They are important considerations when analyzing a visual text.

MAKING CONNECTIONS

AS A CLASS

Review the websites of the companies whose press releases you examined. Analyze the different genres that their advertisements use. Are some of these ads print ads while others are video-based commercials? Search online for where these appear besides their website. Do some appear on buildings? On buses? On T-shirts? Do you recall ever seeing them outside of the classroom? How does the environment in which they appear affect the choice of medium on which they appear?

IN A GROUP

Walk through campus and take photographs of different visual texts.
Analyze and discuss the genre and medium used for each text, and
consider if you think the use is effective. Could the designer have chosen
better options? What creative ways can you come up with to deliver
the same message (using the examples above as models)? Share your
examples and results with the class.

ON YOUR OWN

Think of a restaurant or fast food chain that you frequent. How does
the company make use of different genres and designs to market and
provide information about their products? Make a list of as many genres
and media as you can (from menus to nutritional information and from
websites to food containers). How does each provide a specific purpose
or niche for making particular arguments about its product? How might
each be modified or improved? Share your list and ideas with the class.

KEY TERMS	
writer	*evidence*
context	*symbol*
subject	*analogy*
argument	*design*
claim	*genre*
reason	*medium*

OUTPUT: BLOG

While you might keep a blog for this class or write a blog on your own already, this output will focus on creating a focused, sustained blog and some suggestions for developing an audience and keeping them engaged. According to *Technorati*, a website that studies and tracks blogs, a new blog is created every half-second (that's 120 a minute). However, many of these blogs are quickly abandoned by their creators, and are considered "dead."

When you create your blog, use the rhetorical tetrahedron to consider its audience, message, and design. You already know your medium (the Internet, text, visuals) and your genre (a blog), but consider how the other elements of the rhetorical tetrahedron interact with these predetermined elements. In addition, the following suggestions will help you sustain a blog over a longer period of time and reach your target audience.

Write Good Content

You may have heard the phrase "content is king." No matter how slick or fancy your blog may look, users won't return to it if you don't include good content. Try to post information that will help your readers, or at least be interesting or entertaining. This, more than anything, will help you build and retain a long-lasting readership.

Read Other Blogs

Reading other blogs can be a great way to see what other bloggers are posting, how they compose posts, and how they interact with their readers. While you don't have to do everything other bloggers do, studying other blogs can help you write better content for your own site, even if the other blogs are on different topics. Just as you read other essays to help you write better essays, reading other blogs can help you better write your own blog.

Blog Regularly

Readers won't frequent your blog if you don't keep it fresh with new material. Try to blog regularly, preferably several times a week. If a reader returns to your page and doesn't find new content, they may move on to other sites that offer something current.

Create a Bank

In order to help you blog regularly, consider making a bank of prewritten blog posts. This bank allows you to quickly add a new post if you don't have time or can't think of anything to write for that day. However, make sure these posts are not tied to any current event. If you submit the post a year after the event happened, then the post obviously won't be timely. Add posts on current events when those events are still current, seizing the kairotic moment.

Chunk Your Text

When reading online, readers generally prefer short chunks of text rather than long, dense paragraphs. If you're composing a longer blog post, make sure to break it up into smaller, digestible paragraphs of only a few sentences.

Proofread

Part of building up and sustaining a readership involves *ethos*. As a writer, spelling and grammatical errors can quickly erode your *ethos*, so make sure that you proofread your text before you publish your posts. Errors in spelling can also affect SEO (for instance, if you misspell a keyword), so proofreading affects how both human and nonhuman audiences interact with your site.

Post Images and Multimedia

In addition to small, chunked text, images and videos help to break up writing as well as provide illustrations, examples, and more interactive ways to engage with your content. You can add images, videos, podcasts, or other media that help support your written text.

Disseminate New Posts

When you add a new post to your blog, disseminate the news via social media platforms such as Facebook or Twitter. If you visit the technology blog Mashable.com and visit its social media pages, you'll notice that Mashable's administrators and users post and tweet about the site's articles, thereby allowing its readership to know when new material is on the site.

Write for Nonhuman Audiences

In order for Web robots to better find and index your blog, use the search engine optimization practices noted in Chapter 6, especially those related to selecting titles for your blog posts and including keywords within the written content.

Interact with Other Bloggers

In addition to sending out blog updates through social media, you can also engage with other bloggers who might direct traffic to your site. Interacting with other bloggers is a great way to engage with the larger blogging community and establish yourself as an expert in your particular niche.

Choose a Niche

Speaking of niches, choose one that is not too broad but not too narrow. For instance, if you blog about sports, you might select a particular sport to blog about, or even a particular team. This would narrow down your focus and give you plenty to blog about (but not so much that it would be overwhelming). However, blogging about an individual player on a team might be too narrow a focus, since your readership would be much smaller and you would have less to blog about on a weekly basis.

Blog Comments

Most blogs allow you to activate a "comments" section where your readers can respond to your posts. You can usually turn this section "off" in the blog template so you wouldn't have to worry about keeping up with comments or worry about negative comments that could hurt your argument or offend other readers. However, allowing comments from readers can help to create a larger sense of belonging and participation among the users, and it might create a larger sense of community, helping to keep readers coming back for more. If you do allow comments, you need to be aware that some readers will post negative comments no matter what you write. This practice is referred to as "trolling," and arguing with such posters (called "trolls") can sometimes make things worse. If possible, you might set your comment section so that you have to moderate comments before they're posted. This allows you to see the comments before all your readers do, and so only those comments you approve will appear publicly.

Respond to User Comments

If you do allow users to comment on your blog, try to respond to each one. This helps you establish a good rapport with your audience, gives your readership a sense of belonging, and helps your *ethos* as a writer. However, try to make the responses meaningful. Don't simply include "thanks!" when responding to a compliment, but direct the reader to other resources related to that compliment, showing the reader that you have more to offer as an expert on your topic.

Tag Your Posts

For organizational purposes and to help readers find related posts on particular topics, tag your posts with descriptive keywords.

List Your Blog in Directories

Blog directories will help generate more exposure to your blog. You can visit the site below to find out more about directories, including a list of 23 blog directories where you can submit your blog information. There are many more blog directories, but this should get you started: http://www.searchenginejournal.com/20-essential-blog-directories-to-submit-your-blog-to/5998/.

4

MEDIA CONVERGENCE

As technology continues to evolve, scholars such as Henry Jenkins point to the increasing convergence of technologies (Figure 4.1). For instance, while phones, televisions, computers, GPS units, alarm clocks, and other devices used to be separate products, now you can find all of these on your smartphone. While you will probably never have a single "black box" that does everything, technology continues to develop toward this end (Figure 4.2).

However, while your devices converge, so do the logics that support their use and how you interact with them. How you look at a website is often not much different than how you watch television (for most websites contain television content),

Credit: Derzsi Elekes Andor

OSA ARCHIVUM

Figure 4.1
Henry Jenkins proposes the theory of media convergence.

Credit: Blake Patterson

Figure 4.2
There's still not a single "black box," yet.

and television channels often contain multiple references to online content. For instance, many television broadcasts, from news to sporting events, will display tweets from celebrity or ordinary Twitter users.

Toward this convergence of media, this chapter includes a variety of techniques and principles that can work across media production technologies toward a logic of media convergence. While you can use many of the principles here in literary contexts (and this text encourages you to make these connections), the chapter mainly focuses on visual media and how these media interact and converge. The chapter will emphasize how each principle might be used toward the output of a brand mark, a kind of image that often appears across media in print, television, Web, and other platforms. However, these principles are applicable to all the outputs discussed in this text.

As you read about the various ways that image logics converge across media, consider how these elements fit along the various edges of the rhetorical tetrahedron. For instance, how does a particular rhetorical technique affect audience? What kind and how many writers are required? How does a specific medium encourage particular design and genre choices, and vice versa; how do particular techniques encourage one medium over another? Keep these questions in mind as you read the chapter.

PRINCIPLES OF CONVERGENCE

Analogy

Analogies are one of the most basic structures of communication and are present in how humans understand the world through both alphabetic writing and writing with images. For example, when you use a map, you're using an analogy to make sense of the world (or a part of it). The map is not the territory itself but an analogous representation. That is, the outline of Florida on a map (A) is analogous to the actual coastline of Florida (B), setting up the formula A is to B (Figure 4.3).

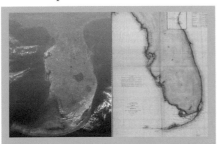

Figure 4.3
A map creates an analogical relationship with the land it represents.

On a larger scale, a model of the solar system provides another analogy for how the planets are arranged spatially at a given point in time. Because you are used to such analogies, you are not confused when someone points to a map and says, "you're here." You know she means the place the map represents, not the actual spot on the map.

Analogies may appear in a variety of sub-types, such as associations, comparisons, correspondences, metaphors, proverbs, idioms, and icons. A complex analogy like a map may be comprehensive and include several of these analogical types. The scale on a map may be used for comparisons in distances, while color coding may be used to create associations, such as using the colors red and blue when discussing Republican or Democratic representations of certain U.S. states (Figure 4.4). On topographical maps, the proximity of lines around a mountain indicate an association of elevation and gradient (the closer the lines, the steeper the slope). On a weather map, however, lines represent isobars and indicate wind speed (the closer the lines, the higher the wind speed).

Consider a series of commercials from Pacific Life (Figures 4.5-4.7). Here, a humpback whale is used as a symbol for the company. The humpback whale provides an analogy between the animal and the company through characteristics such as the whale's size, strength, and intelligence. Given that the humpback whale, as well as whales in general, is often viewed positively by U.S. audiences, Pacific Life hopes to create similar favorable associations by analogizing their company to the whale.

Credit: Spitfire19

Figure 4.4
Map depicting the electoral votes from states during the 2008 presidential election. In this example, the color red is associated with the Republican Party and blue for the Democratic Party.

In this first example (Figure 4.5), the analogy is somewhat direct: just as the whale steadily breathes, so must investors breathe in the marketplace; just as whales have been around for millions of years, Pacific Life has also been around for a long time (140 years).

In the second commercial (Figure 4.6), Pacific Life analogizes the relationship of a mother guiding her calf to the relationship of Pacific Life guiding the next generation of financial investors.

Finally, in the third commercial (Figure 4.7), Pacific Life uses the analogy of how the sound of humpback whales caused people to stop slaughtering whales and start conserving them. The company analogizes this pause in action with the need to stop and think about protecting one's own (investment) future.

Another kind of analogy used in narrative, both print and visual, is the proportional analogy. As a formula, proportional analogies might be written as A is to B as C is to D. In other words, the character (A) in her situation (B) is analogous to me (C) in my situation (D). Also called a structural portrait, this kind of analogy helps the audience identify with a character in a book or movie.

For instance, in a crime drama, you might identify with the victim because you have undergone a similar event. In science fiction or fantasy, you might identify with a character like Luke Skywalker, feeling stuck at home and wanting to escape and find adventure. The proportional analogy would be Luke (A) feels trapped and restless in Tatooine (B) just as you (C) feel trapped in your hometown (D).

This kind of analogy also appears in commercials. The insurance company Allstate runs a series of television ads featuring a man personifying the state of "mayhem" (Figure 4.8). The premise of each commercial is that you, the viewer, can identify with the character victimized by mayhem, foresee this character's situation as your own possible future, and purchase All State insurance in case "mayhem" ensues. The direct language of these commercials, especially the use of the second person "you," help to anchor this meaning so that you identify with the victims.

Credit: Pacific Life/Engine Company 1

Credit: Pacific Life/Engine Company 1

Figure 4.5
Pacific Life has been "breathing" for 140 years.
http://www.youtube.com/watch?v=i2-wtfR98Kg

Figure 4.6
Pacific Life continues to "guide" its customers.
http://www.youtube.com/watch?v=rR4WBVrfYCA&feature=youtu.be

Credit: Pacific Life/Engine Company 1

Whale populations
BEGAN TO RECOVER.

Credit: Allstate/Leo Burnett Chicago

Figure 4.7
Pacific Life "listens" and adapts when necessary.
http://www.youtube.com/watch?v=ELYjfrsNxpU

Figure 4.8
Allstate commercials often personify "mayhem" to create an analogy.
http://www.youtube.com/watch?v=6QIxySt3e-g

Notice also how the brand mark for Allstate helps to reinforce the company's identity (Figure 4.9). Like Pacific Life, Allstate's brand mark is iconic, representing an actual object rather than presenting a word (like Publix, a supermarket chain) or an abstract figure (such as Mercedes). Allstate's brand mark looks like a pair of hands, hands that will help protect and assist you

Credit: Allstate, Mercedes Benz, and Publix

Figure 4.9
Allstate, Mercedes, and Publix brand marks create identity in different ways.

should you encounter an accident. As you work through the following chapter, notice how you might use each element to construct your own brand mark.

MAKING CONNECTIONS

AS A CLASS

List as many brand marks as you can think of and analyze them as a group. What kind of analogy do they create between the brand mark's design and the company's identity? Is the brand mark iconic, representing an actual object? Or, does the brand mark use an abstract design? How does either design make the brand mark effective?

IN A GROUP

Perform an Internet search for "visual analogy." What kinds of examples does the search return? In your group, analyze what analogy the image is attempting to communicate and whether or not you feel it is effective. Share your examples and analysis with the class.

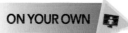
ON YOUR OWN

Research your college's or university's mascot or the mascot of your favorite sports team. What kind of analogy is being made between the mascot (cardinal, lion, gator, tiger, etc.) and the university or town of the team? Does this analogy fit, or does it seem forced?

Metaphor

Metaphor is a type of analogy that you use every day in many situations. If you've ever claimed that a test was a "slam dunk," you've used a metaphor to express how easy it was or how well you did (Figure 4.10). Metaphors help express ideas by using something familiar from one domain (such as a slam dunk in basketball) and applying it to another (test taking). Metaphors (which in Greek means "to carry over") help carry across meanings that might otherwise be difficult to grasp. Obviously, doing well on a test is not too difficult to communicate. You might simply note that it was easy, or use a number of other metaphors: you aced the test; you passed it with flying colors; it was no sweat; it was easy as pie.

However, some terms can be more complicated, and a metaphor helps express them to nonexperts. LIFO, an accounting acronym that stands for "last in, first out," refers to the accounting practice of inventorying goods according to the order in which they're purchased. With LIFO, the last good inventoried will be the first one sold, ahead of any other inventory that already exists in the store. One metaphor to help understand this might be a suitcase. The last item you put into a suitcase is usually the first one you take out when unpacking. This metaphor helps visualize the unfamiliar concept of LIFO with a familiar concept of packing and unpacking for a trip (Figure 4.11).

Metaphors also appear in the images that are seen every day. Rather than using words to represent concepts between domains, images are used. Consider the image in Figure 4.12. Here, a gas hose is depicted in the shape of a noose, juxtaposing the domains of gasoline consumption with that of capital punishment or suicide. The noose helps to carry across the idea that gasoline consumption (either through high gas prices or the reliance on foreign and domestic oil) provides a means of hanging oneself. The caption anchors the meaning, suggesting sarcastically that "things are just fine," and so you don't need to exercise your vote and find an alternative solution that won't kill you (see section on "anchorage" below).

Visual metaphors such as this one are heavily used in advertising, although they may be harder to pick out. During the 2010 Super Bowl, Snickers ran a commercial featuring Betty White and Abe Vigoda playing football (Figure

Credit: Keith Allison

Figure 4.10
This is a picture of a literal slam dunk, although the term can be used metaphorically as well.

Credit: mattbuck

Figure 4.11
When you pack and unpack a suitcase, the last item in is the first item out...usually.

Figure 4.12
This image suggests that society is hanging itself through its use of gasoline.

4.13). View the commercial, and consider the following questions:

Credit: Mars/BBDO North America

- What is the metaphor being used in this advertisement? That is, what is the "vehicle" that attempts to convey meaning to the audience?

- Although reinforced with the tagline "You're Not You When You're Hungry," how well do you think the metaphor conveys this meaning without that additional text? Are there other meanings that you interpreted before viewing the tagline?

Figure 4.13
If you're not you when you're hungry, are you like Betty White?
http://www.youtube.com/watch?v=UbMN7wvIw_s&feature=youtu.be

- If the audience doesn't know who Betty White or Abe Vigoda is, do you think the advertisement is still effective? Why or why not?

How you select a metaphor depends on audience and context. If you suspect that your audience has never played or seen a basketball game, then you might not want to use the "slam dunk" metaphor. Likewise, if the audience doesn't know what a humpback whale is or has a different set of values associated with the humpback whale (if they think humpback whales are lazy instead of majestic), then the metaphor won't have the intended effect. Just as word choice is important when writing text, image choice is important when converging media into multimodal compositions.

Metaphors also appear in the icons and brand marks you see around you every day. Figure 4.14 is the brand mark for the United States Postal Service. The brand mark consists of a bald eagle's head stylized in a particular way to make it unique and recognizable. However, this stylization has specific, visual effects:

Credit: USPS

Figure 4.14
Modern USPS brand mark

- the abstracted outline of the head makes it more universal.

- the slanted design shows movement, and makes the visual more dynamic.

- its angular shape suggests a sense of speed and direction.

What associations between the eagle and the postal service is the USPS trying to make? Because the USPS is a part of the federal government, it makes sense for it to incorporate the bald eagle, the national bird, into its brand mark design. Of course, the bald eagle has other characteristics, such as its ability to fly, speed, and numerous other qualities that you might associate with an eagle. By incorporating the eagle into its brand mark, audiences now associate these qualities with USPS. At least, this is what the USPS hopes an audience does. Moreover, this particular brand mark is a part of its older brand mark (see Figure 4.15), which helps to maintain continuity of its brand identity as the brand mark changes and becomes updated through the years.

Credit: USPS

Figure 4.15
Modern USPS brand mark

Certainly, composing metaphors will be one of the primary techniques that you will use to write through images. Having a good understanding of how others make metaphors through images will better help you select and compose metaphors that suit your purpose. At the end of this chapter, you'll be asked to compose your own brand mark. Part of writing this kind of genre involves selecting visual metaphors that bring out those aspects about yourself that you wish to communicate.

MAKING CONNECTIONS

AS A CLASS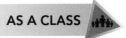

Visit YouTube and search for television commercials. Together, identify what metaphors, if any, the company is trying to make between its product or service and the secondary domain.

IN A GROUP

As shown by the examples above, animals are a common motif used to create a metaphor. With a partner, select an animal for each of the businesses below that you might use for creating a brand mark, and provide a rationale for your choice. Share your ideas with the class, and note which animals others selected.

a. advertising firm

e. skydiving

b. personal trainer

f. automobile dealership

c. lawn maintenance

g. private security firm

d. bicycle shop

h. defense attorney

Although you might not have chosen a major, select a specialized term in your field (or something that interests you), and develop a metaphor to help explain the term to someone who is unfamiliar with it (as in the LIFO example above). Exchange your metaphor with a classmate, and test whether your metaphor was effective. In addition, research the specialized term and consider how it might already provide a metaphor. (For instance, why do police call the location of a crime a "scene"?)

Enthymeme

Enthymemes derive from syllogisms, which are three-part deductive arguments. Syllogisms are used scientifically to arrive at conclusions but are also used rhetorically to present an argument. Syllogisms are composed of three parts: 1) a major premise, 2) a minor premise, and 3) a conclusion. One of the most common syllogisms states that Socrates is mortal because he is a man.

Major premise: All men are mortal.

This major premise sets up the situation or conditions under which a test case is applied, which appears in the minor premise.

Minor premise: Socrates is a man.

If Socrates is a man, and all men are mortal, then the conclusion is easily reached.

Conclusion: Socrates is mortal.

While you might consider mortality to be somewhat scientific, syllogisms might be expressed argumentatively. For example,

Major premise: Smoking marijuana is unhealthy.

Minor premise: Alexia smokes marijuana.

Conclusion: Alexia is unhealthy.

As you have probably already concluded, the outcome of a syllogistic argument depends upon the ingredients put into the syllogism. Rather than expressing a clear-cut fact, this syllogism makes an argument about what constitutes an unhealthy state of being. This argument relies upon a major premise that is also argumentative, i.e., whether or not smoking marijuana is unhealthy. One might argue that this syllogism is invalid because little evidence exits to support the major premise. Alternatively, even if sufficient evidence or common opinion supports the claim of the major premise, Alexia might be unhealthy because of other factors, or she might be completely healthy despite the accuracy of the major premise.

An enthymeme relies upon this syllogistic structure but omits one of the elements, either the major or minor premise, or the conclusion. This omission makes the syllogism into a kind of puzzle or riddle that requires the audience to fill in the missing part themselves. The enthymeme provides a kind of pleasure to the audience once they figure it out, the way that you experience pleasure when you get the punch line of the joke. In addition, because the audience fills in the missing part themselves, they're more likely to remember it. This is one reason advertisements rely heavily on enthymemes. Many of the Geico commercials, such as the one in Figure 4.16, rely upon enthymemes to make their argument.

Credit: Geico/The Martin Agency

Figure 4.16
Do woodchucks chuck wood? If so, then Geico can save you money on your car insurance, according to the enthymeme they construct.

http://www.youtube.com/
watch?v=4faBo4PdFpU&feature=youtu.be

In this commercial, the announcer states the major premise in the form of a question, asking "Can Geico really save you 15 percent or more on car insurance?" He then asks a rhetorical question, "Do woodchucks chuck wood?" The overall major premise would be, "Geico can save you 15 percent or more on car insurance if woodchucks chuck wood." The commercial then fills in the minor premise through a visual demonstration, showing that woodchucks do indeed chuck wood. The conclusion, "since woodchucks chuck wood, Geico can save one up to 15 percent on car insurance," is left for the viewer to figure out. This enthymatic structure has worked well for Geico, and they have adapted it for many other commercials.

MAKING CONNECTIONS

AS A CLASS

Find examples of syllogisms and enthymemes. Find examples that are both print-based and visual examples in photographs or videos.

IN A GROUP

Create your own syllogism based on something familiar. For example, a syllogism based on my dog might be as follows:

Major premise: Border Collies are smart dogs.

Minor premise: My dog is a Border Collie.

Conclusion: My dog is smart.

Once you have your syllogism, make an enthymeme from it. For the example above, you might simply state, "my dog, a border collie, is smart," omitting the major premise.

ON YOUR OWN

Using the syllogism created in the group exercise above, try to express the enthymeme as an image.

Metonymy

Metonymy is a technique that uses part-to-whole relationships to stand in for another idea, and can offer you ways to succinctly represent an idea through image. You may have encountered these terms from their literary context. Metonymy occurs when a speaker represents a larger idea or process by mentioning a smaller piece of that larger whole. For instance, the phrase "Washington passed the budget today" uses the location "Washington" to represent the larger organization of the federal government. "Washington" itself isn't the government, but you usually understand what someone means when they use the term this way.

Consider the request "lend me your ears." You probably don't interpret this literally to mean "Remove your ears from your body, and lend them to me." Instead, the speaker most likely means this metonymically to mean, "Give me your attention," and this task may even be specific to the ears: "Listen to me." The ears, however, stand in for the larger idea of giving one's attention rather than actually lending the ears themselves (Figure 4.17).

In a visual example, a cross sometimes serves as a metonymic function for Christ and Christianity. Similarly, the Star of David or the crescent does the same for Jewish and Muslim faiths. A

Credit: Andreas Praefcke

Figure 4.17
The phrase "lend me your ears" usually means to "listen."

country's flag may perform this function as well. When you see the U.S. flag, you typically think "America." In this way, any brand mark can become an image that serves a metonymic function. Over time, this metonymic function can lose its transparency so that the brand mark seems to *be* the thing which it stands for.

MAKING CONNECTIONS

AS A CLASS

Look at the United Way brand mark (Figure 4.18). Research a bit about the organization, and answer the following questions.

Credit: United Way

- Describe the different parts of the brand mark and how they work together.

- How do the elements serve metonymic functions? What are the larger wholes they represent?

- Find two examples of metonymy, one visual and one verbal, and share them with your class.

Figure 4.18
United Way brand mark.

IN A GROUP

Think of as many sayings as you can, such as "lend me year ears," that have a metonymic function. If it's not obvious, research how the saying came about. Report your findings to the class.

ON YOUR OWN

Read through news reports, or watch news reports on television, about large organizations such as governments or corporations. Pay attention to the language used in these reports, and note how many uses of metonymy occur. Do they use the organization as a whole to refer to the actions of unnamed individuals? Visually, do they present a brand mark to stand in for the organization? In the next class meeting, report your findings to the class.

Synecdoche

Synecdoche is similar to metonymy, and the two are easily confused. While metonymy stands in for some larger process or idea, synecdoche occurs when a part of a person or object stands in for the whole.

Instead of "lend me your ears," consider the request "lend me a hand." Like ears, you usually don't interpret this literally to mean "Remove your hand from your body, and lend it to me." Instead, the speaker most likely means this metonymically to mean, "Can you help me?" However, sometimes this task may be specific to the hands: "Can you lend me a hand to hold this nail while I hammer it?" While the hand stands in for the larger idea of helping rather than actually lending a hand itself, the hand is a part of the body that is being called forth, not simply a process like "listening" (Figure 4.19).

Synecdoche can provide a powerful narrative element if used properly and can simplify an image by playing to the audience's imagination by only showing a part of a larger picture. If you've ever seen the movie *Jaws*, you most likely remember the shark's dorsal fin cutting through the water (along with hearing the famous theme music).

Credit: Mary Popejoy

Figure 4.19
Christopher Lynch (U.S. Navy) literally lends a hand to build a school in Ethiopia.

Credit: Mary Evans/Universal Pictures/ Courtesy Everett Collection

Figure 4.20
This dorsal fin from the shark in *Jaws* performs a synecdochal function.

Spielberg, because the animatronic shark kept breaking down, resorted to showing either none of the shark, or just the dorsal fin (Figure 4.20). Now, you probably think that the movie would be ruined with constant appearances of a cheesy shark, especially compared with today's special effects. Most critics agree and argue that the absence of the shark makes it more terrifying because the audience has to use their imagination. This is a similar technique used by Ridley Scott in *Alien*, where the viewer only sees the full creature toward the end. The rest of the movie only shows the alien's tail as it moves about the ship.

Music, to the extent that it provides a theme for a particular character, can also provide a synecdoche. Whenever the *Jaws* theme plays, the audience knows the shark is present. In *Star Wars*, the composer John Williams wrote themes for different characters, so that the "Emperor's March" can stand in for Darth Vader himself.

Besides just a part for a whole, however, synecdoche has a few other modes. It can also:

- represent a part via a whole; this kind of metonymy occurs in such instances as using "car" to refer to any and all automobiles, including trucks, or using "meat" to refer to any animal flesh.
- refer to a larger class: although "Kleenex" is a brand name, many use it to refer to any kind of tissue.

- refer to an object made of a certain material by mentioning that material; you've done this if you've ever referred to your credit card as "plastic."

- refer to the contents by citing its container; rather than saying beer, you might refer to it by its container, such as a bottle or a keg.

While metaphor works because of the similarity between two things, metonymy and synecdoche work because of contiguity. That is, a shark fin IS a part of a shark and thus can easily stand in for the whole shark. Of course, a shark fin also can serve as a metaphorical function as well. If a shark fin were used in the brand mark of a law firm, the metaphor would suggest some of the clichéd dispersions made against lawyers. Or, if a shark fin where used for a sports team, it might promote the idea of aggressiveness and competitiveness (Figure 4.21). Just like any word or image, the meaning of images or words used in synecdoche and metonymy depend on the context in which they occur. You can create a particular meaning more effectively by using these elements within contexts that favor a particular interpretation. A shark fin would make more sense as a brand mark for a sports team than as a brand mark for an animal rescue organization.

Credit: Leech44

Figure 4.21
The San Jose Sharks create metaphorical meanings with its brand mark.

MAKING CONNECTIONS

AS A CLASS

Look at some of the brand marks for different companies and organizations. What different parts make up the brand marks? Do any of these parts fulfill any of the above categories for synecdoche? If so, explain their synecdochal function.

IN A GROUP

Choose an animal and create a brand mark for it based on a part of the whole. For instance, if you choose a tiger, you could use the paw (as in Clemson University's athletic brand mark), or you might choose its stripes (as the Cincinnati Bengals football team does). Think about how that particular part creates meaning for the brand mark. Next, repeat this exercise with a different part of the animal. How does the meaning change from one brand mark to another?

As mentioned above, sound can also serve to create synecdoche. Think of, or re-watch, a favorite movie or television show, preferably one that is suspenseful or dramatic. How does the film use music or sound effects to associate particular sounds with certain characters or moods? Share your findings with the class.

Ekphrasis

Ekphrasis—a Greek word that means to "speak out"—is an ancient concept that attempts to understand visuals through spoken (and written) language. Whenever you attempt to describe a picture, object, or other visual through language, you are engaging in ekphrasis. However, while denotation (discussed below) seeks to identify what an image is, ekphrasis usually attempts to describe an image for rhetorical effect.

One example of ekphrasis appears in Homer's *Iliad*. In Book 18, Hephaestus, the god of fire, creates new weapons for Achilles, who has decided to rejoin the battle of Troy (Figure 4.22).

Credit: Angelo Monticelli/Public Domain

Figure 4.22
This is an artist's fabrication of what Achilles's shield might have looked like.

He made a shield first, heavy and huge,
Every inch of it intricately designed.
He threw a triple rim around it, glittering
Like lightning, and he made the strap silver.

The shield itself was five layers thick, and he
Crafted its surface with all of his genius.
On it he made the earth, the sky, the sea,
The unwearied sun, and the moon near full,
And all the signs that garland the sky,
Pleiades, Hyades, mighty Orion,
and the Gear they also call the Wagon....
On it he made two cities, peopled
And beautiful. (369-370)

—Iliad

You might say that—rhetorically—the scene on this shield offers a contrast from the world of war at Troy with a scene that depicts peace. The cities are still "peopled and beautiful," for war has not killed and maimed them. The shield provides the reader with a "view" of what life was like, and what it could be like, if men stopped fighting wars. In this way, it makes an argument against war.

Another example of ekphrasis appears in the *Odyssey* after Odysseus finally returns home following the Trojan War. Penelope requires Odysseus to describe their bed, which he built by hand, before she'll believe that he is truly who he claims to be and not an imposter. In this scene, she asks him to produce an ekphrastic description of an object in order to convince her of his identity (Figure 4.23).

Credit: Johann Heinrich Wilhelm Tischbein

Figure 4.23
Penelope isn't convinced that Odysseus is who he says, and poses a test that requires him to describe their marriage bed.

Through his description, Odysseus proves his identity, convincing her that his claim is true. However, while the *Iliad* and *Odyssey* use poetry to describe a visual scene, ekphrasis can occur via other images, not just those in written and spoken language. A press photograph of a work of art, for instance, is an attempt toward rhetorical vividness, to explain the art through the medium of photography and bring that piece of art to the viewer within a larger story about the artwork.

"Strange man,
I am not making too much of myself,
or ignoring you. Nor is it the case
that I'm particularly offended.
I know well the sort of man you were
when you left Ithaca in your long-oared ship.
So come, Eurycleia, set up for him
outside the well-built bedroom that strong bed
he made himself. Put that sturdy bedstead
out there for him and throw some bedding on,
fleeces, cloaks, and shining coverlets."

Penelope said this to test her husband.

But Odysseus, angry at his true-hearted wife,
spoke out:

"Woman, those words you've just uttered
are very painful. Who's shifted my bed
to some other place? That would be difficult,
even for someone really skilled, unless
a god came down in person—for he could,
if he wished, set it elsewhere easily.
But among men there is no one living,
no matter how much energy he has,
who would find it easy to shift that bed.
For built into the well-constructed bedstead
is a great symbol which I made myself
with no one else. A long-leaved olive bush
was growing in the yard. It was in bloom
and flourishing—it looked like a pillar.
I built my bedroom round this olive bush,
till I had finished it with well-set stones.
I put a good roof over it, then added
closely fitted jointed doors. After that,
I cut back the foliage, by removing
branches from the long-leaved olive bush.
I trimmed the trunk off, upward from the root,

The photographer will most likely use other rhetorical techniques inherent to photography, such as framing, lighting, or perspective, to visually tell the story that the newspaper piece is attempting to illustrate. In many ways, ekphrasis is a multimodal attempt at discussing a visual.

Films can use ekphrasis to tell of an event not present in the movie itself. One example is the scene in *Jaws* where Quint and Hooper are discussing their scars, describing how and where they received the wounds. When asked about a particular scar, Quint begins to narrate his experience during the sinking of the USS Indianapolis (Figure 4.24).

cutting it skillfully and well with bronze,
so it followed a straight line. Once I'd made
the bedpost, I used an augur to bore out
the entire piece. That was how I started.
Then I carved out my bed, till I was done.
In it I set an inlay made of gold,
silver, and ivory, and then across it
I stretched a bright purple thong of ox-hide.
And that's the symbol I describe for you.
But, lady, I don't know if that bed of mine
is still in place or if some other man
has cut that olive tree down at its base
and set the bed up in a different spot."

Odysseus spoke, and sitting there, Penelope
went weak at the knees, and her heart grew soft.
For she recognized that it was true—that symbol
Odysseus had described to her. (456-457)

—Odyssey

In this moment of ekphrasis (called notional ekphrasis), Quint dramatically recounts the story to create a mental image of the experience, and the film uses it to create tension within the scene and propel the plot, foreshadowing what may happen to Quint, Hooper, and Brody if the ship they're on were to sink. In this way, ekphrasis operates differently than other forms of describing an image via words. In fact, this very paragraph, describing a scene in a movie, especially to make a rhetorical example to help you understand how ekphrasis works, is itself ekphrasis (as are many verbal descriptions of images throughout this text).

Credit: Universal Pictures

MOVIECLIPS.COM

Figure 4.24
Quint tells Hooper and Brody of the night the USS Indianapolis sunk.

http://www.youtube.com/
watch?v=u9S41Kplsbs

MAKING CONNECTIONS

AS A CLASS

Agree on a single image to examine. Individually, create your own ekphrastic description, writing no more than 250 words, or about one typewritten page. Then, back together as a class, share your descriptions and analyze the similarities and differences between them. Ask each other why you agreed on some descriptions, and why you might have chosen others.

IN A GROUP

Visit the website for a museum, such as the Museum of Modern Art, and browse its online catalogue. On the page for any given work of art, you should notice a verbal description explaining the piece. What sort of information does this description provide? What does it leave out? Develop your own ekphrastic description that complements what the museum provides, and explain why either might be preferable in different rhetorical contexts.

ON YOUR OWN

Within the arts section of a newspaper, find a story (preferably with a photograph) that attempts to discuss a visual work of art. Notice how the story uses ekphrasis in both the written piece and any visuals that accompany it. How does the visual create ekphrasis compared with the written piece? Can either the written or visual stand alone and convey a description to the reader? What does the combination of verbal/visual ekphrasis offer that either alone cannot?

Anchorage and Relay

Related to ekphrasis, anchorage and relay are two kinds of relationships between an image and text. If one of the primary ways that a reader tries to interpret an image is through language, through an ekphrastic action, then anchorage and relay are two modes of interpretation. However, they are also modes of production. That is, they may become rhetorical techniques to converge image and text.

Roland Barthes, a French theorist of linguistics, developed these terms and notes the primacy still given to the verbal even in an increasingly visual world: "Today, at the level of mass communications, it appears that the linguistic message is indeed present in every image: as title, caption, accompanying press article, film dialogue, comic strip balloon. Which shows that it is not very accurate to talk of a civilization of the image—we are still, and more than ever, a civilization of writing" (38).

If you heed the cliché "a picture is worth 1000 words," anchorage and relay aid to fix those 1000 words to only a few specific ones that you might want the reader to focus on. When juxtaposed with an image, a title or caption helps to situate what the picture is about, and this is a rhetorical strategy, whittling down all the possibilities of what the image means to only the one intended by the author. Results are not guaranteed, of course, but anchorage and relay can help maximize the intended message.

Consider the picture and caption in Figure 4.25. You probably already know this picture as the image of Barack Obama and some of his cabinet watching the raid on Osama Bin Laden's compound in May 2011. In fact, the caption that accompanies the image on one of CNN's pages tells as much: "U.S. President Barack Obama was able to monitor the raid that led to the death of Osama bin Laden 'in real time' from the White House, it has been disclosed." However, if you didn't have that caption to "anchor" the message of the photograph, what other meanings might you come up with?

Credit: Pete Souza

Figure 4.25
Depending on the caption, this image can be anchored in many ways.

You could list the people in the picture; describe the colors of their clothes; analyze their demeanor. Also, without the caption to explain what they're watching, you might conclude that they're focused on the final minutes of a close basketball game. Such a caption would also have larger consequences for how you might subsequently view the president himself. (For instance, why would they be using the situation room for this superfluous purpose?)

The caption, however, typically restrains the audience from reading "too much" from a photograph. It aids in narrowing the focus from 1000 words to only a few, and thus affects how the audience understands photographs. As Barthes writes, anchorage becomes "a kind of vice which holds the connoted meanings from proliferating" (39). But primarily, "the anchorage may be ideological and indeed this is its principle function; the text directs the reader through the significance of the image [...] it remote-controls him towards a meaning chosen in advance" (40).

The caption of this photo directs the reader toward Obama, toward his intense gaze at the monitor out of the picture frame (one that you know is there from the focus of all of the spectators in the room, but also from the caption letting the reader know the action of the photograph). The very action ascribed to Obama, that of "monitoring," provides an ideological reading positioning the president as someone engaged in the operation, supervising as commander-in-chief.

Figure 4.26
The caption on Fox News gives a different interpretation.

The same picture on the Fox News website has a different caption, which provides a different understanding of the picture: "Top-level officials get updated on the status of the mission to kill Osama bin Laden" (Figure 4.26). The caption no longer puts the focus on Obama but on all the officials in the room, so that Obama is no longer as important. Moreover, the caption doesn't indicate that these officials are watching the operation in "real time," only that they are receiving updates.

Figure 4.27
The text in the speech balloon helps the reader understand what's going on in the image as a whole.

While anchorage most commonly occurs with fixed images, relay operates alongside moving ones, such as film, or images in a sequence, such as a comic strip. While anchorage fixes the meaning of an image, relay develops meaning through the back and forth interplay between image and text to create a larger narrative than either provide individually.

For example, imagine a comic strip with just images. The text balloons help provide context for the images and move the story along (Figure 4.27). Without text, comics would be difficult to interpret. Alternatively, imagine a comic strip with no pictures, and only text balloons. Such a comic would be equally unfulfilling in its narrative structure.

Such would be the same for a film without sound. Dialogue and music often provide information and clues that move the images of the story along through a plot or some other narrative. "While rare in the fixed image, this relay-text becomes very important in film where dialogue functions not simply as elucidation but really does advance the action by setting out, in the

sequence of messages, meanings that are not to be found in the image itself"
(41). When serving as a relay rather than an anchor, text helps the image by
moving its meaning along from one image to the next, filling out the parts of
the world that the audience needs to know when encountering the next image
that doesn't show the whole picture.

MAKING CONNECTIONS

AS A CLASS

Decide on a single image. Individually, write captions for the image.
Once you've finished, come back together as a class and share your
captions with each other. How do the captions differ? How are they
similar? Try to agree upon a common caption that the whole class
thinks best describes the image.

IN A GROUP

Locate the same picture or photograph on at least three different
websites and note how the caption changes. How do these different
captions affect the meaning that you take away from the photograph?
What different ideological meanings do you think these captions
create? What key words in the captions do you think have the most
effect toward these different meanings? Write your own caption for
this image, and share it with the class.

ON YOUR OWN

Find a comic strip from the comic section in your local newspaper or
online. Without looking at the comics themselves, cover the speech
balloons with a strip of paper. Next, try to deduce the plot of the
comic from just the images, writing down your interpretations as
you proceed. After a few tries, remove the paper and see how your
narrative compares to the actual balloons. Share your comic with the
class, both in its original form and how you interpreted it.

Polysemy (the Puncept)

Signs, whether words or images, are polysemous: that is, they can have many
meanings. The word "screen" can refer to the computer monitor you might
be reading this on, but it could also mean the screen from a window, a screen
set in basketball, the action of screening your phone calls, or numerous other
definitions. These polysemous meanings provide the comedic device of the
"pun," such as in the joke: "The comedian used puns that stunk so bad that

his routine was pungent." Here, "pungent" plays on both the bad taste of his material as well as his use of puns (pun + gent). To the extent that a pun can create multiple associations, it can also be used for rhetorical effect. Many businesses incorporate puns into their names, such as "The Great Frame Up," a business that sells picture frames (punning on "frame" as "to frame someone for a crime"), or "Boo's Liquor" (punning on booze).

Figure 4.28
This image creates a visual pun on "semi conductor."

Credit: Maxo

Figure 429
How does this image of a "facebook" help you think more about Facebook?

Images can also provide puns. For instance, look the image in Figure 4.28 of a "semiconductor." Typically, you might think of a semiconductor as an element in computer circuitry. In this visual pun, however, a man is conducting semi-trucks, making him a "semi conductor." Like the effect produced by many puns, your first response might be to groan. However, the associations created by overlapping the two meanings can provide new insights to each of these ideas.

As a practice, Gregory L. Ulmer has developed the term "puncept" to describe a kind of concept-making based on the pun. By using a pun like an analogy—relating two things that may seem dissimilar—an argument or new understanding can be made that can make your audience think.

In this way, puns can provide an important tool to understanding larger concepts. According to a Chinese saying, if you want to understand *li* (justice), you should study *li* (the plum). This statement establishes a connection between the concept justice and the plum, asking the student to study the elements of the plum tree that might help him or her understand the nature of justice. In a North American context, one might say that justice is like a tall, straight, strong redwood. In Chinese, they can explore this relationship within a single word. As an image-based puncept, we might ask how the image of a "facebook" in figure 4.30 helps us think about our relationship with the social media platform Facebook.

The puncept is possible because, as Roland Barthes writes, "all images are polysemous (38-39)." Often, the reader has to guess what you're trying to communicate. Anchorage and relay are attempts to limit an image's polysemous nature so that the reader can be more certain of the text's meaning. However, sometimes the pun within an image should not be "fixed" but open to interpretation so that the audience becomes more engaged.

MAKING CONNECTIONS

AS A CLASS

Search through advertisements for the use of polysemy or puns. Do the advertisements make use of verbal puns, visual puns, or both? What kind of information or argument do you think the advertisement is trying to communicate by using a pun?

IN A GROUP

Take any object and try to create a visual pun with it (like the "semi conductor" example above). Use whatever photo editing software you have available to make the image.

ON YOUR OWN

Attempt to create a nonlinear relationship as in the "li" example above. Choose a thing (noun) that can also be a verb, and make the image. What new insights do you glean from creating this kind of association? Share your example with your class.

Juxtaposition

Images (and text) are usually always present with other images. Look at a typical website, from CNN and ESPN, to Ebay or Facebook, and images always exist near other images. These images are juxtaposed, placed together in a single space. Often, the presence of any particular image next to another may be accidental. Different images on a news site may have little to do with one another, other than both being related to the day's current events. The images juxtaposed on your Facebook page go together because they come from your friends (or ad banners based on your interests), but otherwise there isn't much thought in placing images together in such ways. Juxtaposition, however, can be used in a purposeful, rhetorical way to create meaning and communicate ideas to an audience. While you inhabit a visual world full of juxtaposed images, here you'll look at juxtaposing as a rhetorical move to make an argument.

In the section on metaphor, you looked at the Snickers commercial featuring Betty White and Abe Vigoda. While White and Vigoda become metaphors for how one plays football while hungry (i.e., the tagline, "You're not you when you're hungry"), this commercial also uses juxtaposition to make its point. In the opening shots, Betty White struggles to make a play. These scenes are juxtaposed with later footage of the player after he has eaten a Snickers, once he "becomes himself again." Here, juxtaposition operates as a way to compare and contrast the character's two states before and after eating the candy bar. This kind of juxtaposition of sequences over a longer period of time is called montage, which this chapter will discuss later.

You can juxtapose elements in a single space, such as a still image, or through time, through video. While the Snickers commercial uses video, juxtaposing different images one after another, a still image can include contrasting elements within a single frame to create associations and connections between what it juxtaposes.

Figure 4.30 shows the movie poster for *Terminator 3*. Clearly, this poster juxtaposes the two main characters of the film, the terminator unit played by Arnold Schwarzenegger, and his adversary, another terminator unit played by Kristanna Loken. The poster uses the images of each character—the stylization of each one's face, blending from human into machine—and juxtaposes these two elements to set up the internal distinctions that make up each character. In this example there are at least two levels of juxtaposition, and although a still cannot make multiple juxtapositions through sequence as video does, it can be used to layer many elements into a single image.

Credit: Warner Brothers

Figure 4.30
Poster for *Terminator 3* juxtaposing the two main characters.

Juxtaposition can be used for much more than just selling movie tickets and offers a powerful technique for creating your own visual arguments. Figure 4.32 depicts two very different kinds of transportation: a play toy tricycle and a tank. The first of these you probably

Credit: Corona/Cramer-Krasselt

Figure 4.31
This Corona commercial juxtaposes different scenes to create a mood.
http://www.youtube.com/
watch?v=ETPxQu1TQcA

Credit: Chris Gee

Figure 4.32
What does the juxtaposition of this toy tricycle and tank say to you?

used as a very young child, while most of the audience have probably never driven a tank. What meaning is created by combining these two items? From a stylistic perspective, you could argue that the large tank imposes itself upon the smaller tricycle and threatens to crush it (or fire upon it).

You might also consider how the two vehicles serve as analogies for those who use it. A young child most likely uses the tricycle, while a young adult probably operates the tank. Each object, the tricycle and the tank, might represent aspects of a single individual at different stages of their lives, prompting questions such as how someone who innocently used a tricycle can now wage war in an armor-plated vehicle? Other aspects, such as color, lend to this analysis. The tricycle is bright, multicolored, which might signal the curiosity and optimism of childhood, while the "olive drab" color of the tank is just that—drab—suggesting a loss of optimistic spirit. When placed together, these objects offer a trajectory of their user's life. A single image juxtaposing two simple objects can offer many new modes of thought than each object presented alone.

In the Corona beer advertisement in Figure 4.31, juxtaposition provides the main rhetorical device to support its argument. The opening shot depicts a man sitting in a lounge chair on the beach, his back to the audience, holding a Corona. If you research other Corona ads, you'll see that most start with this style of shot. From camera left, a flight attendant rolls a beverage cart through the sand and approaches the lounger. After she asks him, "Are we doing okay here?" the next shot juxtaposes the same man sitting on an airplane, without anything from the beach except his Corona. When the woman across the aisle also takes a Corona, the airplane scene is again juxtaposed with the beach, with the woman now sitting beside the man. The link between these juxtaposed shots is the beer bottle, which gives the experience of being on the beach to anyone who drinks Corona. The juxtaposition, using the bottle as this visual link, establishes a comparison and contrast between what a Corona drinker experiences versus that of someone not drinking the beer. While a visual juxtaposition occurs, an emotional or experiential juxtaposition occurs as well.

Many brand marks juxtapose images with text, but the total image of a brand mark can also have several images juxtaposed within it besides text. For instance, the brand mark for the United Way, which you looked at earlier, juxtaposes an open hand, a rainbow, and the figure of a person to create its overall brand mark. Each element relates to each other and creates the total message that the United Way is attempting to capture visually. As you continue to think about how to create your own brand mark for this chapter's assignment, consider how you might juxtapose multiple elements together to create a unique and rhetorical message.

MAKING CONNECTIONS

AS A CLASS

You and each of your peers should select a different image of an object. Display your image with one of your peer's on the classroom's overhead projector (if available). As a class, discuss the associations created between these objects, and how these associations might produce arguments or support for arguments. Repeat this exercise with the images from each of your peers.

IN A GROUP

Select two images, and using a photo editor, juxtapose them. Analyze the image and consider what new meanings emerge between the two objects. What relationships can you think of between them that you might not have noticed before? Share your new image and findings with the class.

ON YOUR OWN

Find an icon or brand mark that juxtaposes two images, such as the brand mark used by United Way. Without any research into the brand mark, what associations does juxtaposing the elements in the brand mark create? What message do you think the company or organization was attempting to communicate? When you've finished, research the company's intent when designing the brand mark, and compare what you've found with your original ideas about the brand mark's design.

Denotation

 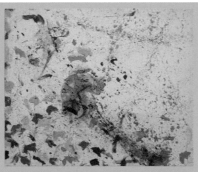

Look at the image in Figure 4.33. If you had to describe the picture with words, how would you do it? Take a minute to write down as many words as you can think of.

Which words did you use? How did you describe the image? Did you write a definition? Did

Figure 4.33
How would you describe this image?

Figure 4.34
What words would you use to describe this painting?

you describe features such as colors and shapes? Did you define it by naming a category it fits into?

How about the image in Figure 4.34? A bit trickier? What words would you use to describe this image?

This image is more difficult to describe and requires different terms in order to say "what it is." For instance, it doesn't seem to have recognizable relationships between parts that follow linguistic grammar. There is no clear subject (noun) doing something (verb) to an object. So besides naming its colors, what else could you say about it?

Naming an image in this way defines its "essence," its literate definition...or in semiotic terms, its denotative message. The denotative meaning usually refers to the abstract meaning of a signifier, that is, what something "is" apart from what it "means."

Denotation is the "literal" meaning of a sign (or image). The denotation of a linguistic sign is the literal meaning, or dictionary definition. Similarly, the denotation of an image is what you and anyone else would literally see when you view the image. If you wanted to make a denotative description of an image, you would describe the image in the most objective and unbiased way you could.

Usually when you see a symbolic object as familiar as the American flag (Figure 4.35), you don't think of "red, white, and blue" as simply colors. When you "read" a symbolic object like the American flag, you not only see the colors and the shapes of the stars and stripes, but you also see the symbolic meanings those colors and shapes represent.

Figure 4.35
What are the denotative meanings of the United States flag?

The denotative meaning does not include any of the flag's symbolic meanings. Denotation is a literal description of the visual elements in the image:

A photo of the American flag on a flagpole. The flag has dark stars on a blue background in the upper-left corner, and white and red horizontal stripes. The flag appears to fold like it is waving in the wind. It appears against a blue sky and is backlit by the sun...

You might tend to think of denotation, such as the definitions of words, as being fixed and unchanging. If this were true, and denotative meanings were permanent and stable, then the meanings of words would not change over time, and furthermore, different languages would use the same words to describe things. The fact that dictionary meanings change over time and different languages use different words to describe the same things shows that "naming" at the denotative level becomes "slippery," as discussed above with "polysemous" words and images.

Some signs are more polysemic than others, but all signs are polysemic to some degree. If you compared several different people's denotative descriptions of the abstract painting, you would probably see that some parts of the descriptions were similar, while other parts were very different. The abstract painting is more polysemic than the rose photo, but even the rose photo is polysemic. Look at three possible descriptions of the first image.

You might have simply described the first image as

- "a rose" or
- "a red rose."

Or you may have written something more descriptive, such as:

- A photo of a red rose, a flower in the Rosaceae family, with a green stem and three green leaves on a wood table, situated diagonally across the picture from the upper-right corner to the lower-left. The photograph was taken from a slightly overhead view, and the red rose bud is the focal point, in focus and set slightly off center according to the rule of thirds, while the leaves and stem behind it are not in focus...

Even though all three are denotative descriptions of the same image, they are all different ways of interpreting the reality of the image. The words one uses to "name" the photo don't "stick" to the image but are "slippery" because other people can use different words to describe the same image. People's descriptions of the rose photo may be slightly different, but they are still more likely to be similar than descriptions of the more polysemic abstract painting.

The way you describe an image at the denotative level is affected by your specific situation and your point of view. The third description of the rose photo requires some knowledge that not everyone would have, such as an understanding of basic photographic composition, such as the rule of thirds (discussed in Chapter 10).

As seen in the earlier examples, the denotative message of an image can be interpreted in many different ways, and the exercise can be almost exhausting for some images. When thinking about the denotative message for the images you use, try to approach the question of image selection from the point of view of the audience: What image will most make them understand your intended message? Should the denotative message be "simple," such as a rose, or must it be something more complex, such as an abstract painting? Try to use an image most appropriate for the rhetorical situation.

Toward the final output of this chapter, a simple Google search for "brand mark" will reveal brand marks that are very literal, using just a word for the brand mark, to ones that are more abstract. Analyze these various kinds of brand marks to help decide which would be best for yours.

MAKING CONNECTIONS

AS A CLASS

Find a random image online. Individually or in a word processor, take five minutes and write down as many denotative meanings as you can. After five minutes, share your denotative meanings as a class, noticing the similarities and differences between them.

IN A GROUP

Visit YouTube and find a "literal version" of a music video. These videos attempt to provide the denotative message of the video as the lyrics of the song to explain what occurs visually. These literal versions change the lyrics and the actual song itself to give a denotative description of the video. Analyze the literal version of the video you find, or the one in Figure 4.36. What does the denotation mainly focus on? What kind of meta-analysis occurs through the lyrics? What do the lyrics miss?

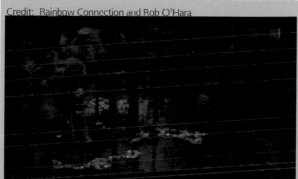

Credit: Rainbow Connection and Rob O'Hara

Figure 4.36
Literal version of "Rainbow Connection."
http://www.youtube.com/watch?v=Ywvwp0aQz-o&feature=youtu.be

ON YOUR OWN

Find an original version of a music video and attempt to write your own literal version of lyrics. What visual elements do you find yourself including? Which do you seem to exclude? Why? Share your literal version with the class.

Connotation

Look again at the rose image (Figure 4.33). The section on denotation discussed that the denotative message is the literal message apart from symbolic meanings or association. Connotation, however, pertains to those messages of an image that include the symbolic levels.

What connotative, symbolic messages might an image of a rose invoke? Romance? Love? Valentine's Day? You can probably come up with many. Connotation provides the image with a set of cultural conventions that help the reader navigate and make sense of it and in some ways provide the audience with its meaning. You didn't always associate a rose with romance but learned that this flower and behavior have been connected in the past, so that the rose becomes symbolic. The rose comes to signify ideas beyond its denotative meaning.

Barthes points out that the stylistic techniques and elements used when taking a photograph—such as "framing, distance, lighting, focus, speed" (44)—are all elements of connotation. Typically, an audience is unaware of these techniques (and probably can't tell which settings a photographer used), but these are still design choices selected to create specific effects. Such effects may also be "recorded" into the denotative meaning (such as the "rule of thirds" discussed above) but are meant to evoke connotative meanings.

Credit: Corona/Cramer-Krasselt

Figure 4.37
Corona attempts to show a mood that's "miles away."

For example, using a black-and-white setting might convey a feeling of nostalgia or timelessness, while framing a subject at a long distance against an expansive backdrop might create a feeling of smallness compared with the vast space. Since any photograph or video relies on such choices (even if made without much thought), there is no clean separation between denotation and connotation; even if a photographer attempted to capture an image of an apple, that apple is not simply a thing by itself but related to the larger context in which the photo was taken.

As an example, consider Jonathan C. Hall's description of a Corona beer advertisement:

"Miles Away From Ordinary"

In these days of wane for traditional media advertising, Corona's "Miles Away From Ordinary" ad campaign seems almost quaint. While most marketers are looking to guerrilla and viral techniques to spend less and circumvent the kind of instinctive consumer ad resistance I expressed above, Corona simply blanketed the mass media—from 30-second spots on primetime TV to graphic wraps on the trucks of their distributors to those banner-flying planes that buzz up and down the Jersey Shore in summer—with the visual and aural sensations of a subdued tropical beach, a picture always completed by that iconic Corona bottle and obligatory lime wedge.

Whether in Web, TV, print and outdoor media, Corona ads consistently offer a flight of the senses to an idyllic, tropical place "miles away" from our ordinary worries and woes. Beach scenes and ocean sounds are powerful triggers of the so-called "relaxation response"—some psychotherapists use these exact tools to help patients cope with anxiety. The Corona drinkers in these scenes silence their cell phones and engage in other stress-neutralizing activities. A trope in the ads is the use of the Corona bottle in fanciful optical experiments: a bikini-clad woman appears to swing on a hammock between two Corona bottles (pictured) [Figure 4.37]; a beer-drinking beach-goer re-positions his Corona bottle to block his view of less attractive neighbors; a crescent moon over tropical waters appears in the mouth of a Corona bottle as if it were a lime wedge. These images emerge from the kind of idle mental play that only occurs to a vacationing mind.

All of these media ladle onto us, day after day, the promises and meanings of the Corona brand: namely, that drinking Corona is tantamount to a temporary escape, a vacation, from the punishing, daily fray of our ordinary modern lives. But how could Corona beer itself, that sad drink, ever deliver on such a promise? How could I have enjoyed the stuff?

Alcohol content is certainly part of it. But I suspect the phenomenon also has something to do with what Baylor College of Medicine researchers found with Coke drinkers: that brand knowledge can have "a dramatic influence on expressed behavioral preferences and on the measured brain responses" to beverages. In other words, all those ad dollars spent by Coca-Cola over the years haven't been just to persuade us to buy Coke; they've also been part of the content of the product experience.

Connotation helps to deliver this "experience." Barthes discusses a similar example with the pasta company Panzani, and he explains that what it offers is "Italianicity" in the same way that the Corona ad offers the experience of vacation. As Hall points out, the features of the Corona ad that led to this reading include various images and sounds of ocean and beach life, including palm trees, hammocks, beach balls, deck chairs, and similar elements. At the level of denotation, these items are just a list, a series of parts. However, the overall mood they evoke exceeds the sum of those parts and creates an atmosphere (Figure 4.37).

Credit: Laurent Rich

Figure 4.38
Budweiser has crowned itself the "king of beers."

Of course, that mood, that experience, might be different for each person. Such ads, however, assume that their audience has a certain shared set of ideas so that connotation might be achieved. Corona hopes that most Americans associate the beach with vacation (as well as some of its international audience), and thus drinking their beverage will induce that atmosphere. Someone who hates the beach or is afraid of the ocean, however, might have a negative reaction to such images, although they might still understand what the advertisement is trying to evoke.

Brand marks use connotation as well. In terms of denotation, Corona's brand mark, a crown, makes sense given that Corona means "crown" in Spanish (Corona is made in Mexico). But beyond this initial denotative meaning, a crown has other connotations, such as royalty, superiority, and other meanings. What the crown begins to connote, then, is a message of "the best," which most advertisements use as an argument. Note that Budweiser also uses a crown as part of its brand mark and anchors the image with the tagline, "the king of beers." Rather than create the experience of "miles away from ordinary," Budweiser offers another kind of experience (Figure 4.38).

MAKING CONNECTIONS

AS A CLASS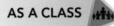

Look at campaign advertisements from recent national elections on YouTube and image searches. Discuss what experience you think the videos and images are trying to convey. How do you think they achieve this? What feelings, associations, or symbolism is connoted?

IN A GROUP

Locate a brand mark from a familiar company, such as McDonald's "Golden Arches" or Target's "target." Research what the brand mark means, why it was designed or selected, and other details that affect its connoted message. What message do you think the company was trying to convey by using a particular brand mark? Do you think the brand mark is successful at this message, or could it be improved?

ON YOUR OWN

Locate a print ad for your favorite food. What kind of "experience" do you think the ad is trying to convey? What elements in the advertisement add to that message? Record your thoughts and share them with the class.

Visual Narrative

Typically, a narrative is simply a method for telling a story. While you're probably familiar with narrative as it appears in books, narrative can also use images to tell a story. The most common genre of visual narrative that you're probably familiar with is a film or television program. In fact, films and television shows often begin with a written script before a single image is captured, and so image and written text go hand-in-hand when making these kinds of visual narratives.

Visual narratives usually make use of relay to move the story along. The images often aren't enough to support the narrative on their own, so dialogue, voice-over, subtitles, or other kinds of verbal language are used to help the audience understand the story. Other genres, such as comic books, create visual narratives in the same way, using speech bubbles rather than audible dialogue.

However, stories do not have to only serve entertainment purposes; they can also function rhetorically. For instance, photojournalists use images to tell the stories of the events they cover, and you'll compose your own photo essay later in this textbook. In photo essays, photos provide a tool for telling a larger story and usually integrate some sort of verbal counterpart into the essay, either through audio narration or written text. Such narratives are usually used to make a rhetorical point, a call to get the reader to act in some way.

For instance, Figure 4.39 depicts a commercial by Chipotle that tells the story of a farmer who turned to factory methods of farming. He realizes that he made a mistake and returns to his former practices. Although Willie Nelson's cover of Coldplay's "The Scientist" relays this message thematically, the visuals provide the main narration of the story and attempt to persuade the audience that Chipotle only buys agricultural products that sustain the environment and animal well-being.

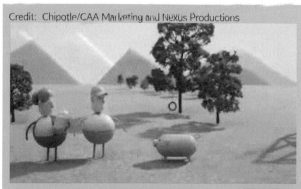

Credit: Chipotle/CAA Marketing and Nexus Productions

Figure 4.39
This music video attempts to tell a story to make an argument.
http://www.youtube.com/watch?v=aMfSGt6rHos

Some of the historical documentaries by Ken Burns deftly integrate video, audio, and still images to create a narrative of a historic period, usually to make some point about what life was like during the time. However, still images alone can also contain narrative content that helps them make a rhetorical point.

Credit: AP/Nick Ut

Figure 4.40
Image of Phan Thi Kim Phuc taken by Huynh Cong Ut.

Consider the image of Phan Thi Kim Phuc taken by Huynh Cong Ut during the Vietnam War (Figure 4.40). From the various elements in the photo, such as the naked girl and other children running, the nonchalant soldiers following them, and the plumes of napalm in the background, you can construct a narrative. Obviously, any reading without historical context is open-ended and imprecise, but you can generally assume that some sort of military action is taking place, and the children are fleeing from danger. You might also assume that since the men aren't aiming their weapons at the children, they are providing some sort of escort. Overall, though, the narrative in this image can be used to argue against the horrors of war.

MAKING CONNECTIONS

AS A CLASS

Search for "famous photographs" and discuss how each photo creates or provides a narrative. You might individually record your own version of a narrative based on a particular photograph, and compare how you see the photograph's narrative with how others see it. Note not only where the differences in narration appear but where similar events/themes might also overlap.

IN A GROUP

Create a visual narrative that tells the story of one of your school's recent athletic seasons. You may complete this assignment in a variety of ways, via an image collage that contains multiple images from each important moment or as a video narrated with audio dialogue. Share your narrative with the class.

ON YOUR OWN

Choose a commercial online and analyze its narrative structure. Does the commercial tell a story? If so, does it mainly use visuals, written text, narration, or a combination? Which of the three, if any, dominate? How does the narrative in the commercial tie into the larger narrative of the company or organization as a whole? Share you analysis and conclusions with the class.

Adaptation

If you've ever seen a Disney movie, you've mostly likely seen a visual adaptation of a written work. The narrative in the movie *Aladdin* comes from the Middle-Eastern folktale "Aladdin's Wonderful Lamp," while the movie *The Little Mermaid* is adapted from a tale by Hans Christian Andersen (Figure 4.41). Many visual works that you see—from historical epics like *Troy* to modern best-sellers like *Harry Potter*—originate in print and are adapted into other media from television and film to video games.

Credit: Hans Christian Andersen

Figure 4.41
Disney wasn't the first to draw a little mermaid.

Of course, an adaptation isn't an exact copy of the original but rather an adapted version of one medium into another. In a broader sense, adaptation is a process in which an individual or group changes to better live in their environment. Similarly, a novel "as is" wouldn't work well within a movie and would need major changes within the new medium.

This principle can be applied to written texts as well. For instance, you would typically adapt your writing style when sending a professor an e-mail versus sending your friend an e-mail. You would also write a text message or Twitter update differently than you would an answer on a test. While the content for each might be the same, you would adapt the style for each audience and medium.

Credit: Sesame Workshop and Columbia Pictures

Figure 4.42
These two Draculas were adapted for very different audiences.

When you consider adaptation, think more broadly than the kind of film adaptation you're used to, and instead think of how a particular message might be adapted for a particular genre and for a particular audience. An adaptation of Bram Stoker's *Dracula* would be much different for a children's cartoon compared with an adult-rated movie (Figure 4.42).

Brand marks also can (and should) adapt over time. The John Deere brand mark has undergone many changes since its creation in 1876 (Figure 4.43). These changes occurred to match contemporary aesthetics but also because John Deere understood its audience. Because many of its customers already knew the brand by 1962, it could eliminate unnecessary text (such as "Moline, ILL.") and simply display the deer silhouette and company name. Over time, the deer changed from a specific deer to a more stylized, abstract deer. Note the description next to the 2000 brand mark and how the company created a brand mark design for the new millennium.

Credit: John Deere

Figure 4.43
A history of John Deere brand marks.

MAKING CONNECTIONS

AS A CLASS

Select a story that has been adapted into a film. Read the story, and then watch the film in class. As you watch, keep notes on how the book differs from the film. What did the director change? What did he or she leave out or add? Discuss your observations with the class, and develop reasons why you think the director made the choices they did.

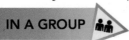

IN A GROUP

Choose a short poem. Using video clips from the Internet, create a visual adaptation of the poem, integrating images with the poem's words. How does the meaning of the poem change once you create it as a visual?

ON YOUR OWN

Research a film that you've seen lately or one you remember seeing as a child. Was this film adapted from other sources? If so, what other adaptations have been made from the original? Create a diagram mapping the various relationships between the original and all of the adaptations produced from it. If the film you researched wasn't adapted, choose another or look up *The Little Mermaid* and complete this exercise using this film as a starting point. Share your diagram and results with the class.

Montage

"Even *Rocky* had a montage."

If you've ever seen *Team America: World Police* by South Park creators Matt Stone and Trey Parker, you might remember these lyrics. They offer commentary about the film-making process of montage, a technique used to reduce a longer period of narrative time down to a few minutes so that a movie doesn't have to last many months to tell a whole story. As an example, watch the *Team America* montage clip in Figure 4.44.

This montage occurs at a point in the film where the movie's main character, Gary Johnston, needs to regain physical fitness and skill after becoming depressed and despondent from an earlier failure. As the lyrics explain, a montage shows "a passage of time" with "a lot of things happening at once" within only a few minutes (or even seconds), for "to show it all would take too long." Using this logic, the montage depicts Johnston target shooting, running on a treadmill, practicing martial arts, shaving, flying in a simulator, strength training, reading, as well as

Credit: ©Paramount/Courtesy Everett Collection

Figure 4.44
Team America shows how to make a montage.
http://www.youtube.com/
watch?v=oJc0PxeikfA&feature=youtu.be

as a few clips of other characters to maintain context for why he's preparing. Obviously, even though Johnston's training only takes "one day," all of these actions would be too long to show in a full-length film.

A photo montage is made of several images stitched together into a single visual. Rather than compressing time in the mode of a film montage, an image montage juxtaposes images that might not fit within the same space of a single camera shot. Photo montages might be used for scientific purposes, such as the photo montage of the surface of planet Mars in Figure 4.45, or to create visual metaphors, such as the grasshopper/rabbit in Figure 4.46. Such montages can be used for rhetorical purposes and create visual arguments, as in Figure 4.47, a photo montage by Peter Kennard, which combines photos of the Earth, a screaming mouth, and a gasoline hose to suggest a response that the Earth might have from filling it with fossil fuel emissions.

However, some photo montages can be unethical. Figure 4.48 presents a hoax created by combining two real photographs: one of Navy SEALs training outside San Francisco and another of a breaching white shark in Africa. Like other photo montages, this one collapses geographic space but does so to create a false sense of reality.

Credit: NASA

Figure 4.45
Photo montage of the surface of Mars.

Credit: Nevit Dilmen

Figure 4.46
Photo montage of a grasshopper and rabbit.

Credit: Peter Kennard

Figure 4.47
What argument is Peter Kennard trying to make with his photo montage?

Credit: Unknown/Charles Maxwell/Lance Cheung

Figure 4.48
This photo montage, a hoax, fooled many.

While you might create images such as these for fun to practice photo editing skills (as in the grasshopper/rabbit example above), or to make an argument, the creator of this montage (who still remains unknown) tried to pass the photo off as real and even claimed that it was the 2001 National Geographic Photo of the Year. Depending on how you intend to use a photo, you must be careful about the ethical (or even legal) consequences of photo composition and manipulation.

MAKING CONNECTIONS

AS A CLASS

Watch the montage scene from *Rocky IV* (Figure 4.49), where Rocky prepares in the Russian countryside to fight his main opponent, Drago. As you watch, write down the answers to the following questions: What are all the activities that you notice in the montage? How long do you think it would take all of these activities in real time? How does the montage order and link the scenes together to create a narrative arc? How does this particular montage use comparison and contrast to create a narrative? As a class, discuss your answers.

Credit: MGM/United Artists

Figure 4.49
The *Rocky* movies make frequent use of montage scenes.
http://www.youtube.com/watch?v=rV7rjT_dGbY&feature=youtu.be

IN A GROUP

Find one montage each from a television show or movie. Compare the two montage sequences. What features do they have in common? How do they differ? What are the formal features? How many seconds does the director dedicate to each part of the montage? How many parts are there? What else do you notice? Share your montages and findings with the class.

ON YOUR OWN

Using a video camera—either a camcorder or a video camera on your phone—take brief video clips from each part of your day, and try to create a montage depicting the whole day in two minutes or less. Share your montage with the class and revise your montage based on their feedback.

Remediation

One of the most common practices of new media is remediating materials from existing works into new ones. Often, this occurs in music, where an artist may sample an older music track and incorporate it into a new work. Figure 4.50 features a video of the song "Changes" by Tupac Shakur. This song borrows from the song "The Way It Is" by Bruce Hornsby.

Credit: Death Row Records

Figure 4.50
Tupac Shakur's "Changes" remixes Bruce Hornsby's "The Way It Is."

Shakur uses Hornsby's work rhetorically, summoning for the viewer an older song they may have heard that has similar themes of prejudice and hardships and then applying them to his own context. The combination helps orientate the viewer to the proper mood of the song.

As Jay David Bolter and Richard Grusin explain, remediation is the most common characteristic of new media, appearing in nearly all the media that you consume. For instance, a typical news website such as CNN.com not only contains hypertext (HTML) but also photographs, video, podcasts, and other media. You might take this construction of hypermedia for granted now, but the current Web experience only came about due to the interaction of all these media together.

While the Web developed to most closely align with the logic of television, you can now see television adopting components of websites, such as on-screen information for e-mail or Twitter accounts. CNN.com re-uses video also shown on CNN the cable channel, and the cable channel will also display blog posts, e-mail responses to questions, as well as videos posted on its website. Whenever you compose any new media text, you are probably also committing an act of remediation.

Credit: Franklin Templeton

Credit: Joseph-Siffred Duplessis

Figure 4.51
Brand mark for Franklin Templeton Investments.

Figure 4.52
One-hundred dollar bill featuring the portrait of Benjamin Franklin.

Figure 4.53
Portrait of Benjamin Franklin

Although you might typically think of remediation as a more recent method for composing works, especially works using new media, remixing is actually a very old practice. When a new kind of media emerges, usually the first content presented in the new medium is a work from older media. After the invention of alphabetic writing, people didn't immediately invent new works specific to writing, such as the novel, but recorded oral works already circulating within their culture. When cinema was invented, some of the first films were book adaptations.

Brand marks can also remediate other images. Figure 4.51 depicts the brand mark for the financial company Franklin Templeton Investments, which remediates the image of Benjamin Franklin found on the one-hundred dollar bill (Figure 4.52), which further remediates a portrait of Benjamin Franklin by Joseph-Siffred Duplessis (Figure 4.53). Franklin Templeton Investments hopes that the potential customer will connect the positive characteristics often associated with Benjamin Franklin with the company. While you might have to consider copyright issues, remediating a common image within a brand mark can convey a particular argument about your brand by using the *ethos* and symbolism associated with the image.

MAKING CONNECTIONS

AS A CLASS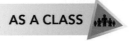

Open a well-known website of a television channel, such as ESPN.com. Discuss how the website remediates its television content or other media. Then, discuss how its television coverage remediates its website.

IN A GROUP

Find a trailer for a movie that fits within a particular genre, such as horror, romance, thriller, or comedy. Using a video editor, remix the trailer and add appropriate music to make it seem like the film is actually from another genre. For example, you might take the trailer or clips from the movie *Jaws* and remix it into a trailer for a love story. Share your video with the class.

ON YOUR OWN

Find a song on your iPod or in your music collection that makes use of remix or sampling. Research the origins of the sampled recording. Why do you think the artist of the newer song sampled the original? Does the older song add anything to the story or point the song is trying to make? Share your findings with the class.

Celebrity

While it may sound odd, celebrity is becoming a mode of argument in itself. Mostly, the rhetorical force of celebrity comes from its use of *ethos*, channeling the reputation of the celebrity to help sell a product. This technique is common, and it would probably be difficult for you to watch any commercial break or open any magazine and not see celebrities used in a rhetorical way.

Credit: Davidoff/SELECTNY

Figure 4.54
This Davidoff fragrance ad appeals to your sense of "adventure."

In addition to the celebrity's *ethos*, advertisers can use the logic of juxtaposition by placing a celebrity and the product in proximity. In advertisements, simply placing the two together is enough to make a link to the viewer, and just like analogy, traits carry over between the two.

In Figure 4.54, the company Davidoff advertises its fragrance, "Adventure," by juxtaposing it with Ewan McGregor. Davidoff is relying on your knowledge of McGregor in his many action movie roles such as the second *Star Wars* trilogy (where he played Obi-Wan Kenobi) or various other characters. The ad provides very little information otherwise and expects the viewers to fill in their own gaps, associating the adventurous nature of McGregor's characters with the experience of wearing the cologne.

Another aspect of celebrity logic is circulation, putting one's image in the public sphere and hoping that the image might become viral. In response to a question regarding rumors about her love life, Mariah Carey once responded that, "My image is having more fun than I am." An image can take on a life of its own that is independent of what it references, and even if you're not famous, your image can still circulate broadly if it appeals to a wide audience.

However, one must obviously take into account the negative consequences of posting images of oneself online. As Figure 4.55 reminds you, once you post an image online, it's impossible to guarantee that someone else hasn't already saved it and that it won't appear elsewhere on the Web. Once an image starts circulating, which occurs whenever you upload an image, it's impossible to get it back.

Credit: Ad Council

Figure 4.55
You should always "think before you post" online.
http://www.youtube.com/
watch?v=KhbxOxftr-U

Brand marks themselves have taken on a celebrity nature. When you see the Golden Arches for McDonald's, you probably know what it means and what it represents. Corporations typically don't have any individual that can fulfill this celebrity status (although some, such as Apple, had Steve Jobs), so the brand mark and brand fill this role. Some celebrities create their own brand to represent themselves. Tiger Woods uses a simple "T W" (Figure 4.56), while the artist Prince has used a more elaborate image (Figure 4.57).

Credit: William Selby

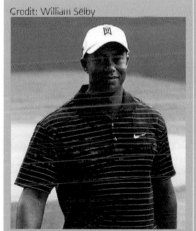

Figure 4.56
Tiger Woods with his personal brand mark displayed on his hat.

Credit: El Pantera

Figure 4.57
"Love Symbol #2" used by Prince.

MAKING CONNECTIONS

AS A CLASS

Look through some celebrity gossip blogs such as TMZ, Perez Hilton, or the entertainment sections of other news sites. Discuss how these sites might be using celebrities for a rhetorical purpose. Can you think of other venues that use celebrities to make arguments?

IN A GROUP

Find an advertisement using a celebrity. Discuss how the advertisement uses the celebrity rhetorically. Is there an analogy the ad attempts to make between the product and celebrity? Is this analogy implicit or explicit? Share your findings with the class.

ON YOUR OWN

Choose a product with which you identify, and create an advertisement in which you endorse the product. Juxtapose images of yourself and the product together in some way and create a small blurb on the page explaining how/why you use it. Share your advertisement with the class.

KEY TERMS

media convergence	*puncept*
analogy	*juxtaposition*
metaphor	*denotation*
enthymeme	*connotation*
metonymy	*visual narrative*
synecdoche	*adaptation*
ekphrasis	*montage*
anchorage	*remediation*
relay	*celebrity*
polysemy	

OUTPUT: BRAND MARK

This chapter has offered some ideas for how to incorporate different rhetorical strategies into a brand mark, from juxtaposition to remediation. This section will take a more direct, step-by-step approach for how to construct a brand mark.

Brand marks provide a way for companies or organizations to connect with their audience through a simple, visual composition. A brand mark also provides a means of identifying who made a certain product or service or who is responsible for a certain event (just think of the sponsorship brand marks on the back of a race T-shirt from a running competition, or the brand marks covering a racecar in NASCAR). Over time, audiences often form strong relationships with the brands that they use, and the brand mark often provides the "face" or identity of that relationship.

As the quote by Mariah Carey indicates, we are all becoming an image in one way or another. We post more and more pictures of ourselves, and our identities are becoming more and more visual as people can search for us online to see what we look like.

For this assignment, you should construct a brand mark for a client in your community. If your class isn't working with a client, you can create a brand mark for yourself as an alternative. This brand mark will provide you with a way to brand yourself in the future, should you need it, and also help you develop skills to create brand marks for other organizations.

The guidelines below describe the kinds of brand marks you might consider making as well as questions to answer as you design the brand mark. These are general principles, however, and not hard rules. Remember that writing a brand mark—like an alphabetic text—is not always a linear process and will require drafts and revisions. You can make your brand mark through photo editing software or by hand-drawing it. Use whatever resources you have available.

Also remember to consult the rhetorical tetrahedron as you consider your brand mark. For instance, you know the writer; what is the message of the brand mark? What audience would you like to reach? How will you design it? While you know the genre (a brand mark), onto which media do you expect to place the brand mark (paper, Web, clothing)? Make sure you keep all these elements in mind as you compose.

Types of Brand Marks

Below are several types of brand marks that you might consider when crafting your own. You may use any of them, although your instructor may want you to focus on a particular style for this assignment.

Wordmark

A wordmark is perhaps the basic form of a brand mark, and simply represents the organization's name through stylized font. Common examples are Coca-Cola, Google, or Netflix (Figure 4.58).

Credit: Netflix

Figure 4.58
Wordmark brand mark for Netflix.

Letterform

A letterform provides a shortcut to the name of the company. Rather than using the whole name as in a wordmark, the letterform presents only the letters necessary to make a connection with the brand. Examples include IBM, CNN, or Honda (Figure 4.59).

Credit: Honda

Figure 4.59
Letterform brand mark for Honda.

Emblem

An emblem contains a pictorial element combined with a wordmark or letterform. The brand mark for BMW is an emblem (Figure 4.60), while the brand mark for Mercedes is not. Other examples include the brand mark for the National Football League, or the brand mark for the hardware store Lowe's.

Credit: BMW

Figure 4.60
Emblem brand mark for BMW

Pictorial Brand Mark

A pictorial brand mark uses only an image but one that's clearly identifiable as an object. The brand mark for Apple—an apple—is pictorial (Figure 4.61). Mascots for sports teams are also often pictorial, although sometimes they're presented as an emblem, incorporating the name of their team into the design.

Credit: JoeInQueens

Figure 4.61
Pictorial brand mark for Apple

Symbolic Brand Mark

Symbolic brand marks convey an abstract idea, one that usually connects to the company in a symbolic way but doesn't necessarily say anything about

Credit: Craig Sunter

Figure 4.62
Symbolic brand mark for Nike

what the company does. The Nike "swoosh" represents a wing and the ideas of flight, speed, and victory (Figure 4.62). However, the "swoosh" doesn't provide a pictorial representation of the company's name (as does the Apple brand mark), nor does it look like any of their products, such as shoes and apparel. Other examples include the brand marks for Pepsi or the "donkey" and "elephant" for the Democratic and Republican parties (respectively).

Questions for Designing a Brand Mark

Answering the following questions will help your thought process about the brand mark and help you to focus in on particular aspects, both practical and aesthetic.

Why are you creating a brand mark?

In this case, you're creating a brand mark as part of a class assignment but also for an external client who depends on sending the right visual identity. Ask your client what the company intends to gain by creating a brand mark. Even if you already know the purposes of creating a brand mark, it's good to hear this explanation, which may lead to ideas on how to create it. If you were going to create a brand mark for yourself, you might want a brand mark to create a visual identity apart from your photograph, one that expresses certain parts of your identity, experiences, or skills that your own image may not necessarily show.

Who is your brand mark intended for?

Ask the client who will see the brand mark. Current users or customers? New ones? Current staff and employees? Just as you should understand your audience before writing with words, you should also understand the audience who sees the brand mark and anticipate the expectations that a particular audience might have. If this is a personal brand mark, do you intend to use this as a job marketing tool for potential employers or simply to post on your social media pages as a form of self-expression for your friends to see? Either audience would probably expect different designs.

What is the purpose of the brand mark?

Does the client expect to grow its brand, reach new customers, or create stronger ties with the clientele it currently serves? If you're creating a personal brand mark, what do you intend the brand mark to help you with? Make new contacts? Represent yourself visually to potential employees? This brand mark becomes a part of your visual identity and how others remember you, and this "how" and "why" are important questions to figure out.

What are the organization's attributes?

In addition to the questions above, this question provides the biggest research phase of brand mark design. Find out about your client's organization specifically and its field in general. Research its products or services, whom it serves, and what it does. Within this research, you'll find rich ideas that capture the essence of its specific organization that can then be captured visually in a brand mark. If you're creating your own brand mark, this step is equally important. Write down your interests, skills, background, and other elements, which may lead to your own visual identity (or at least part of your identity).

Is your brand mark simple?

The best rule for designing a brand mark is to keep it simple. This simplicity will provide flexibility on where you place the brand mark and how well an audience will understand and remember the brand mark. The rest of the guidelines reinforce this principle.

Where are you going to place the brand mark?

Where you plan to place the brand mark will limit the design of the brand mark. A brand mark that's very complicated might be difficult to read on a variety of surfaces, such as a T-shirt, since the fibers may reduce resolution and blur the different elements of the design. The best answer to this question, then, is that the brand mark will be placed everywhere. Try to create a brand mark that will look good on nearly every surface, from a piece of paper to a brick wall. To do this, keep your brand mark as simple as possible. The brand mark for Apple computers, for instance, looks visible and clear on a variety of surfaces.

Is it easy to understand and remember?

You want your audience to remember your brand mark after they see it. Again, simplicity helps here. The Apple brand mark is not only a simple shape but also a familiar one, since you've probably seen an apple. It is also iconic, using the representation of an apple for a company of the same name. If you use a shape that's too abstract that an audience can't "name" it as a circle, square, eagle, or bicycle, then your audience will probably have a hard time remembering the brand mark.

Can your brand mark withstand the test of time?

You don't want to create a brand mark today that looks outdated in five or ten years. You can update it, as the John Deere example in Figure 4.43 shows, but it's easier just to create a brand mark with a timeless look. For instance, the CBS brand mark has existed since the 1950s—and although it has been cleaned up a bit over the decades—looks relatively the same as the brand mark used today (Figure 4.63). View the video in Figure 4.64 for a brief history of the CBS brand mark.

Credit: CBS

Figure 4.63
CBS "eye" brand mark.

The brand mark is simple, which allows CBS to place it on a variety of media as the video depicts (even a necktie). The video also mentions that the sources of inspiration for the brand mark come from Shaker artwork. To create your own brand mark, you might research older symbols and artwork as a way to invent the basic shape of your design.

Credit: CBS

Figure 4.64
History of the CBS brand mark.

http://www.youtube.com/
watch?v=wB63odkphhg

Does your brand mark display well on a variety of backgrounds?

Although related to where you will place your brand mark, the question here pertains mostly to color considerations. For example, if you originally construct a brand mark that is all black, it would look good on most light-colored backgrounds. However, will the brand mark also look good in white? If you make a brand mark of several colors, will the brand mark still work as a single color for situations in which multiple colors aren't possible? If your brand mark makes use of both black and white, you could place the brand mark on a red background—but if you place it on a white sheet of paper, the white elements will disappear. If your brand mark is simple, such as the Apple brand mark or CBS eye, then you can create the brand mark in any color for a variety of backgrounds.

Is your brand mark attractive?

Your brand mark should look like other kinds of brand marks but also stand out as an original creation. Your brand mark should be eye-catching, giving the viewer a positive experience of looking at it. Also, an attractive brand mark helps your *ethos* as a designer, for the better your design looks, the more reason an audience has to be impressed with your communication skills. One way to see how your brand mark "fits" within a conversation of brand marks is to place it on a page with other established brand marks. For instance, in a photo editor, you might copy and paste various brand marks, and in that collage, include yours. Does your brand mark look like it "belongs" with the other brand marks while still appearing different enough that it stands out? This should be your last step in the creation of the brand mark. If it doesn't look right, start the revision process and return to the drawing board.

5

SCOUTING MEDIA ENVIRONMENTS AND ECOLOGIES

Chapter 3 considered how the circumstances of a visual text affect the way an audience receives and responds to that text. Writing doesn't occur in a vacuum but reacts to and exists within a particular situation. Ramesses had particular problems he was trying to solve by creating the wall carving in the Abu Simbel temple and particular audiences that he hoped to reach. Just as you've considered these contextual elements when analyzing a visual text, you should now consider them before composing your own texts.

Credit: Steve Owsley/Public Domain

Figure 5.1
Ian Bryce scouts the flight deck of the USS John C Stennis for filming *Transformers 2*.

Credit: Jack Johnson/Brushfire Music Group

When creating a movie, a director or assistant director will usually scout locations where filming might take place before shooting begins. The director not only looks for the places themselves for scenery but also the overall logistics that a location can offer, such as proximity to lodging, food, casting extras, and other elements (Figure 5.1). Likewise, when writing for visual modes, you must often consider the entire environment in which the visual will appear.

Using the film practice of scouting as a metaphor, this chapter asks you to

Figure 5.2
Jack Johnson discusses selecting an environment for his music videos and concerts.

consider the "scene" of writing as a larger environment. For example, the video in Figure 5.2 shows an interview with the musician Jack Johnson and some of the environmental details he considered when deciding the location for shooting one of his music videos. When a media composition is placed at a location with other media, these media create relationships that may be advantageous, neutral, or damaging to your argument. This chapter will help you begin to consider these variables and use them to maximize your rhetorical effectiveness.

Although "environment" isn't one of the sides of the rhetorical tetrahedron, you can still use the rhetorical tetrahedron when you consider the environment in which you situate your writing. For example, how does the message of the text change once you place it within a particular environment? What is the audience doing in the environment where they encounter your text? How does the environment affect your design choices? Does the environment affect the kind of medium you make your text out of? Is a particular genre more effective in one environment over another? As you read through the rest of the chapter, funnel questions about environment through the rhetorical tetrahedron to create a more complex understanding of the larger rhetorical environment.

ENVIRONMENT

In their work *Natural Discourse*, Sidney I. Dobrin and Christian R. Weisser explain the interconnections between writing and environment and how the two are always closely connected. For example, some of the letters in the Latin alphabet most likely derived from natural objects. The letter A, which was originally called an "aleph" in the Phoenician alphabet, means "ox" and derived from a drawing of an ox's head (Figure 5.3). Humans' first attempts at creating images were probably attempts to recreate the forms of animals, such as those of the Chauvet Cave in southern France, which may be up to 30,000 years old.

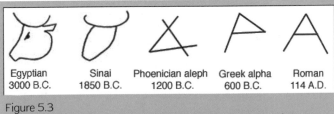

| Egyptian 3000 B.C. | Sinai 1850 B.C. | Phoenician aleph 1200 B.C. | Greek alpha 600 B.C. | Roman 114 A.D. |

Figure 5.3
A possible origin and transformation of the letter "A" over time.

You might also consider that all writing technologies inevitably come from the environment, whether this includes clay for tablets, animals for skins, trees for paper and pencils, blood and other substances for ink, graphite for pencil lead, or oil for the plastics in your computers and cameras. In this sense, you cannot write without incorporating the environment into your compositions (Figure 5.4).

Credit: Chris Wightman

However, thinking about the environment and writing includes thinking about "environment" in a more generic sense. The term does not (only) mean the environment of the Earth through conversations about pollution, recycling, or climate change. While this narrow sense of environment is important as it pertains to writing (as discussed later), you should also think about environment as a more general term.

Figure 5.4
Older writing technologies were much more "natural" than those used today.

For instance, how does your immediate environment influence how you write? Some writers prefer to write indoors, while F. Scott Fitzgerald occasionally wrote outside in his garden. Some prefer total silence, while others write better with background or white noise. Still, others write while listening to their iPod. You, no doubt, have your own preferences for a particular environment when writing.

The overall environment can influence how your audience responds to a text, as well as if they even notice it at all. As you've already examined, the advertisement for paper towels in Figure 3.42 uses a mock-up of a spilled coffee cup in order to draw attention to the ad and make its argument, which is that this paper towel can handle big spills.

However, consider the environment in which the advertisement takes place: it appears outside, on a sidewalk, in what looks like a metropolitan area. Most likely, then, pedestrians who use the sidewalk will have to walk around it, making the ad more noticeable since it might be in their path (but possibly more annoying as well). These same pedestrians might also be used to seeing coffee cups littered on the streets, and thus the presence of a giant coffee cup defamiliarizes their setting and makes them take particular notice.

Credit: Anthony M.

ROMA

La città saluta

BENEDETTO XVI

Papa
e
Vescovo di Roma

Because the ad is exposed to the elements, the material out of which it's made must be water-resistant, and if intended for long-term use, also UV-resistant. Or, the ad could be designed to be brought inside the store upon closing or during periods of inclement weather. Also consider the environments in which this ad could not appear. Because of its size, it probably wouldn't be

Figure 5.5
This city proclamation saluting Pope Benedict XVI didn't hold up to the elements very well.

practical to place this particular ad in a small indoor space. This ad also wouldn't work very well on a flat, vertical space the way a poster would. This detail may seem obvious, but you should consider the pragmatics for how your design will function within a specific environment, including the constraints and ways that it cannot be used (Figure 5.5).

Credit: Oldtimer/Demner, Merlicek and Bergmann

Figure 5.6
This advertisement wouldn't work the same way if it was just a typical billboard.

Figure 5.6 shows another example of how a visual can be integrated into the existing environment. This ad, affixed to the side of a mountain, makes use of the preexisting tunnel to draw attention to the image as a whole. In addition, even though this ad doesn't move, it is in some ways "interactive" as the viewers drive through it. Since the image advertises an all-you-can-eat rest stop, the mouth, one of the main focal points through its connection with the tunnel, is important conceptually as it "swallows" the viewer "down the hatch" to the nourishment just ahead. If this image was portrayed on just another roadside billboard, without the presence of the mountain and tunnel, the ad wouldn't be as effective or make much sense. The overall environment in which the image appears creates a symbiotic system of meaning-making for the audience.

Credit: David Evers

Figure 5.7
These billboards in Egypt attempt to capture the attention of a fast-moving audience.

Of course, a designer of a billboard advertisement also has to consider the environment in which that billboard exists. The billboard has to be high enough above trees or other landscape features so that motorists can see it, but not so high that it escapes their view. The images also must be big enough to be clear from far distances, and the font size of any text also has to be readable. Motorists don't have the option of walking up to the billboard to get a closer look. In fact, they usually can't go back to it at all without considerable inconvenience once they drive by. Because of this environment, designers of such images need to capture drivers' attention quickly and, in turn, quickly deliver that information before their audience passes by (Figure 5.7).

You probably won't be designing your own billboards (though you certainly could), but you should think about how the environment in which your image appears influences how you design it. One of the first steps in planning a design is to scout the locations where you plan to place the image, and part of determining where to place it includes finding the locations where your targeted audience will most likely see it. Below are some questions that can help you consider all the facets of the environment in which your image will appear.

MAKING CONNECTIONS

AS A CLASS

Share your own experiences of unique ways visuals have been integrated into their environments. Did you find the visual effective? Why or why not? If possible, find an example online, and compile a class wiki of these examples for future reference.

IN A GROUP

Walk through campus and notice where different kinds of signage and visuals appear. Do they make use of the surrounding environment in order to convey their message? Do you think they could be better placed to improve their appeal to their audience? Does their placement leave out certain audiences who may not be able to clearly see the images or text? If you have a camera, snap a few photos of these signs, and share your examples with the class.

ON YOUR OWN

Consider the environments in which you typically write best. Where are they located? What sounds are present? Are there few or many people? Do you write best with food around? Think through these variables, compile a short report, and share them with the class.

WHO IS YOUR INTENDED AUDIENCE?

As mentioned in the introduction to this chapter, consulting the rhetorical tetrahedron can help you consider questions when screening environments. Targeting your intended audience is not only the first step when deciding how to craft the argument of your message but also for deciding in which environment you should deliver it (delivery is covered in more detail in Chapter 12).

For instance, if you lost your dog in the neighborhood, then your target audience for a "Lost Dog" flyer would probably be your neighbors or people passing through the area. For a billboard, the audience includes motorists who cannot avoid driving past the billboard (unless they take a previous exit). If you own a restaurant and need to design a menu, then your audience consists of your potential customers.

The audience for a restaurant varies between restaurants. Those who frequent a high-class, expensive restaurant will expect a different kind of menu experience than those who visit a less expensive restaurant, even if this audience is the same person who happens to eat at both. For example, a more expensive restaurant might have its menu encased in a leather folio (Figure 5.8), while a less expensive establishment will simply have it laminated.

Credit: Enoteca Vino Bar

Figure 5.8
Usually, a leather binding signals that the menu belongs in a high-class establishment.

Credit: Sharky's on the Pier

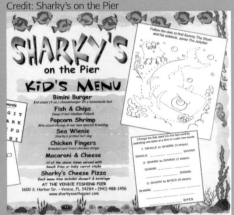

Figure 5.9
A disposable kid's menu with puzzles and activities.

Credit: Ildar Sagdejev

Figure 5.10
You don't look "down" at the menu at McDonald's.

Figure 5.11
The menu outside a fast food restaurant must be visible from a car and withstand the elements.

If you consider the users, you might see why. Most patrons do not take young children to more expensive restaurants, and so there's little chance that the more expensively designed menus will suffer any damage. With less expensive restaurants, there's a good chance that something sticky will wind up on the menu, and so cheap, laminated, or disposable menus save money. Some restaurants even skip the lamination process and include menus that can be written or colored on by children and are then disposed of by design (Figure 5.9).

In many cases, the menu itself reflects the environment in which it exists, sharing such elements as typefaces, graphics, and color schemes. This attention to visual identity is apparent in fast food restaurants, which create menus full of company brand marks and colors.

However, consider the design of a fast food menu and the audience it caters to. In fact, consider both kinds of fast food menus, neither of which the customer even gets to hold in their hands. Inside, the menu typically appears on the wall behind the registers. In this location on the wall, the customer can make a decision without needing to look down at a document while talking with the cashier. The customer doesn't need to grab a menu when getting in line and won't slow down foot traffic, increasing the number of people the restaurant can serve (Figure 5.10).

Outside, the drive-through menu must address an audience sitting in their vehicles and must be at a height viewable by cars, trucks, and SUVs. The menu must also be visible from a certain distance (as must the inside menu), for the audience cannot realistically get any closer to the menu than the distance from their car seat (Figure 5.11). Toward this particular audience, in this particular environment, drive-through menus often use large pictures so that the motorist can easily see what kinds of foods the restaurant offers. Calculating this basic information about your intended audience can tell you a lot about where to place your texts as well as how to design them based on audience expectations and how an audience will use a document.

MAKING CONNECTIONS

AS A CLASS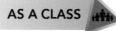

Share your favorite restaurants and consider how these establishments design their menus (if the menus are available online, you might look at each as you discuss them). How do these menus differ? What kinds of audiences do you think each menu is attempting to target? Do you find that you fit within that target audience? Why or why not? Would you revise any of the menus to better fit within the environment of their respective restaurant? How so?

IN A GROUP

Revisit the visuals you identified in the earlier assignment above. What kinds of audiences do you think were targeted for each visual? Do you think the visual reaches that intended audience (in other words, is it well-designed specifically for that audience)? How does the surrounding environment help or hinder the audience's reception of that visual?

ON YOUR OWN

Consider the writing within the environment of a car. What kinds of writing are present and for what purposes? How does the manufacturer take into account the interior space when constructing messages? Does each text have the same intended audience, or does each differ between driver, passenger, mechanic, or other audiences? How does the writing differ between the front seat and back seat? Inside or outside the vehicle? Record your thoughts and share them with the class.

WHERE IS THE BEST LOCATION TO REACH YOUR INTENDED AUDIENCE?

For the examples above, the answers to this question are pretty clear: the neighborhood where the dog was lost, alongside the highway or major road, and within a restaurant. However, other locations might not be so obvious or may have multiple options.

Figure 5.12
Although they all have maps on the insides, atlases need to compete on the outside.

If you intended to create a road atlas for the same driver above, you might consider two locations: the place where the motorist purchases the atlas and the car in which the motorist uses the atlas. For the first, the cover of the atlas might be designed in such a way to double as advertising, making it clear to the potential buyer the benefits and features that the atlas includes (Figure 5.12).

This message is a persuasive one by letting the reader know how he will benefit. You also should consider the other atlases that exist in this same environment, for the audience will have other atlas options, so your atlas should stand out. This same design principle would most likely hold true for online environments, such as Amazon.com, where the audience could still see the features that persuade the audience to "buy me."

Knowing your target audience and deciding on a location often go hand-in-hand. Consider this story from Dan Merica (CNN) that demonstrates how the organization American Atheists places billboards (Figure 5.13) in strategic environments to target specific communities with their message.

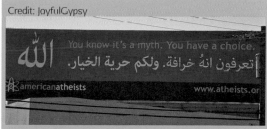
Credit: JoyfulGypsy

Figure 5.13
The group American Athiests has a difficult time placing their billboards without controversy.

Atheist Group Targets Muslims and Jews with 'Myth' Billboards in Arabic and Hebrew

The billboard wars between atheists and believers have raged for years now, especially around New York City, and a national atheist group is poised to take the battle a step further with billboards in Muslim and Jewish enclaves bearing messages in Arabic and Hebrew.

American Atheists, a national organization, will unveil the billboards Monday on Broadway in heavily Muslim Paterson, New Jersey and in a heavily Jewish Brooklyn neighborhood, immediately after the Williamsburg Bridge.

"You know it's a myth ... and you have a choice," the billboards say. The Patterson version is in English and Arabic, and the Brooklyn one in English and Hebrew. To the right of the text on the Arabic sign is the word for God, Allah. To the right of the text on the Hebrew sign is the word for God, Yahweh.

Dave Silverman, the president of American Atheists, said the signs are intended to reach atheists in the Muslim and Jewish enclaves who may feel isolated because they are surrounded by believers.

"Those communities are designed to keep atheists in the ranks," he says. "If there are atheists in those communities, we are reaching out to them. We are letting them know that we see them, we acknowledge them and they don't have to live that way if they don't want to."

Silverman says the signs advertise the American Atheists' upcoming convention and an atheist rally, called the Reason Rally, in Washington next month.

Atheists have long pointed to surveys that suggest atheists and agnostics make up between 3% and 4% of the U.S. population. That number increases when

Americans unaffiliated with any religion are included. The Pew Center's U.S. Religious Landscape Survey found that 16% are unaffiliated, though only a fraction of those are avowed atheists and agnostics.

Silverman acknowledges that the pair of new billboards will likely cause a stir.

"People are going to be upset," he says. "That is not our concern."

"We are not trying to inflame anything," he continued. "We are trying to advertise our existence to atheists in those communities. The objective is not to inflame but rather to advertise the atheist movement in the Muslim and Jewish community."

The billboards will be up for one month and cost American Atheists, based in New Jersey, less than $15,000 each, according to Silverman.

Mohamed Elfilali, executive director of the Islamic Center of Passaic County, laughed when he learned the Arabic billboard would go up in the same town as his office. He says he's surprised that someone is spending money on such a sign.

"It is not the first and won't be the last time people have said things about God or religion," Elfilali says. "I respect people's opinion about God; obviously they are entitled to it. I don't think God is a myth, but that doesn't exclude people to have a different opinion."

But Elfilali bemoaned the billboards as another example of a hyper-polarized world.

"Sadly, there is a need to polarize society as opposed to build bridges," he says. "That is the century that we live in. It is very polarized, very politicized."

Rabbi Serge Lippe of the Brooklyn Heights Synagogue had a similar response.

"The great thing about America is we are marketplace for ideas," he says. "People put up awful, inappropriate billboards expressing their ideas and that is embraced."

But Lippe acknowledged that there are a lot of agnostic and atheist Jews. A recent Gallup survey found 53% of Jews identified as nonreligious. Among American Jews, 17% identified as very religious and 30% identified as moderately religious.

"When you have two Jews in the room, you have three opinions," joked Lippe.

American Atheists have used the word "myth" to describe religion and God on billboards before. Last November, the organization went up with a billboard immediately before the New Jersey entrance to the Lincoln tunnel that showed the three wise men heading to Bethlehem and stated "You KNOW it's a Myth. This Season, Celebrate Reason."

At the time, the American Atheists said the billboard was to encourage Atheists to come out of the closet with their beliefs and to dispel the myth that Christianity owns the solstice season.

The Christmas billboard led to a "counter punch" by the Catholic League, a New York-based Catholic advocacy group. The Catholic League put up a competing billboard that said, "You Know It's Real: This Season Celebrate Jesus."

Silverman says his group's billboard campaigns will continue long into the future.

"There will be more billboards," Silverman says. "We are not going to be limiting to Muslims and Jews, we are going to be putting up multiple billboards in multiple communities in order to get atheists to come out of the closet."

In this example, American Atheists plan to place billboards in environments where they know their target audience congregates, "in heavily Muslim Paterson, New Jersey and in a heavily Jewish Brooklyn neighborhood." They also plan to place the billboards on a busy street (Broadway) and in a location after the Williamsburg Bridge that motorists probably notice when getting back onto land. American Atheists also cater each message to each audience, making both signs bilingual with English and either Arabic or Hebrew languages. Because the organization has thoroughly scouted its audience and knows their general habits, it was able to make a rhetorical decision about the environment in which it hoped to place its message.

However, other groups have interests in what gets posted within a specific environment as well, and these other actors may pose constraints to delivering a message to a targeted audience.

A week later, CNN reported that the building on which the American Atheists planned to place its billboard is owned by a Jewish landlord who refused to let it install its billboards. While the billboard was "moved out of the residential area and put up in a pricier spot off a major highway at no additional cost," thus gaining more visibility because of increased traffic, Silverman noted that "his group was specifically targeting that Brooklyn neighborhood" because of his group's targeted audience: "We wanted to get into the residential neighborhood because so many Hasidic are closeted atheists." This highway is a much different environment with a different audience than a neighborhood. Sullivan was very aware of such placement as a rhetorical choice, but was denied the opportunity by someone with a competing interest. Just as living organisms compete within a natural environment, writers compete within a rhetorical one.

MAKING CONNECTIONS

AS A CLASS

Think of a single business or organization, and brainstorm all of the places you've seen its ads. In what kinds of environments do you find these ads? Cities? Rural areas? Electronic spaces? Vehicles? Think broadly about what might constitute an "ad." With this in mind, can you think of any more examples? Keep a list as you think of ideas.

IN A GROUP

Research the rules for where you can post information on your campus. This may be found at your university or college's website, or the information may be available from student political groups on campus. Which spaces are listed as designated areas for posting information? Do you notice posters adhering to these rules, or do you find visuals posted in other locations as well? Of the permitted and nonpermitted spaces, which do you think are more effective environments for reaching target audiences? Record your results and share them with the class.

ON YOUR OWN

Choose a company with which you're familiar and whose ads you frequently see. Research how the company modifies their ads for different locations, such as different regions of the United States, or for different countries abroad. How do companies take into account these different environments, either by where they place the ad or how they portray different kinds of environments within the image of the ad? Record your findings and share them with the class.

WHAT IS YOUR INTENDED AUDIENCE DOING IN THIS ENVIRONMENT?

When considering the environment in which you place a visual text, you also have to consider the usability of that text, which also means considering how the audience is using the environment as a whole when they use or encounter your text.

Returning to billboards, the audience is typically driving a vehicle, commuting on the roads adjacent to the billboards. However, different environmental and user variables can alter the audience's encounter with a billboard. If the traffic is light and moving fairly quickly, the user has more attention to focus on billboards and scenery rather than the immediate cars in front of them. However, because of their reduced attention to traffic, they may also be doing other things in the car, such as talking on the phone or thinking about tasks they have to accomplish. If the stretch of road is typically congested with stop-and-go traffic, one might think that they driver hardly has a chance to shift her focus from the flow of cars to any external stimuli. However, slow traffic might give the driver more time to read the billboards along the route.

During long drives, motorists typically get hungry, need a rest stop, or need to refill their fuel tanks, sometimes on stretches of highway where these services may be spread across long distances. Billboards for these kinds of needs will probably be actively looked for by motorists more than billboards for other services that don't address their immediate needs or environmental situation. Of course, especially during long trips, motorists may become bored and engage with billboards as something to do during the drive, presenting opportunities to offer them other kinds of information besides those of their immediate circumstances.

Staying in the car, you can also consider the usability of the atlas discussed earlier. While in the vehicle, the motorist needs to be able to quickly and easily use the atlas within the cramped environment of the car or truck. To make the atlas easier to use for the reader, the pages need to be large enough to view quickly but not so large that the atlas can't easily be opened and held within the driver's or passenger's lap (Figure 5.14).

In addition, the content of the atlas should be large enough for the driver to quickly find their location on the map, and the content should include other information relevant to a highway environment, such as major roads, exits, rest stops, or points of interests. If you pick up and explore an atlas, you'll notice that many of its maps make detailed use of color contrasts to separate different elements such as highways, state roads, national parks, mile markers, and other features (Figure 5.15).

Audience use is also very important when thinking about how to design the

Figure 5.14
An atlas is a collection of particular kinds of maps to be used in particular kinds of environments, especially a car.

Figure 5.15
Atlases use many colors to help the reader easily find different kinds of roads and locations.

environment of a website. At first, you might not think of the Internet as comprising an environment, but the very metaphors you often use—such as cyberspace or the World Wide Web—conceptualize the Internet as a virtual environment that can be "navigated" and "surfed." Moreover, although you still can't upload yourself into such an environment as in the *Matrix*, you do use the Internet in the context of other kinds of environments, whether they're desks, libraries, office spaces, or any variety of real-world places via mobile devices (Figure 5.16).

As you looked at in Chapter 2, the website for Clemson University (Figure 2.6) has in mind particular audiences who will use the site: prospective students, current students, faculty/staff, parents/families, corporations, visitors, and alumni. Clemson's website tailors each of these specific sections and makes the Web-based environment easy for these audiences to use and navigate. However, what does Clemson expect their users to be doing on the website within their immediate, real-world environment? Most likely, they probably expect users to be sitting at a computer terminal in a variety of environments depending on if they're students (which could range from their dorm room to an outside plaza) or alumni (their work or home computers). In most of these cases, the outside physical location probably plays a small role in how the user chooses to navigate the site.

Some websites are a bit more difficult to use in the places where they'd be most helpful. If you were using an online bird guide to identify a bird in your backyard, you could probably look it up on the computer while viewing it from your house. However, this online guide would be more difficult and clumsy to use when out in the field. You might, of course, use a mobile device to view the site as long as the cell signal is clear, but in this particular environment, a traditional paper-based field guide might be best. It won't lose signal, it probably has a larger viewing area for quick identification, and—if it gets wet—it won't short circuit and shut down.

Other Internet-based content, however, requires access to the user's specific environment in order to work correctly at all. Consider augmented reality (AR), which makes use of GPS and mobile Apps to provide a real-time augmented view of a physical location. One of the most familiar examples of AR is Google's Sky Map (Figure 5.17).

Credit: Oregon Department of Transportation

Figure 5.16
Texting and the environment of a car and highway do not go

Figure 5.17
Google's Sky Map "augments" reality by "writing" on the sky, showing you the locations of planets and constellations.

While in this app, a user can hold her smartphone to the sky and see the constellations in space. While at first glance you might not consider this "writing," many of the augmentations are produced by users, entering not just constellations but also historical facts about ancient buildings, reviews of restaurants, free Internet hotspots, and even virtual graffiti. Just hold up a mobile device to an augmented location, and this information appears on the screen.

This technology has the potential to create new forms of visual rhetoric, many of which will be difficult to predict. However, it's clear that any form of argument that might occur within AR apps will require careful attention to the environment. But for all modes of producing visuals in both physical and cyber spaces, knowing where and how your audience will use a text is an important part of screening the location and environment for which your text should be designed.

Looking at this question through the rhetorical tetrahedron, these examples all show that the "medium" and "genre" in which you create a text depends on the environment. How the audience uses a text, and where they use a text, will help you determine if the information should be presented as a map, manual, website, or other genre and whether the medium should be paper, electronic, or something more substantial than either.

MAKING CONNECTIONS

AS A CLASS

Bring in a variety of instruction manuals. These manuals can be for a lawn mower, MP3 player, computer, hair curlers, or any variety of products. First, consider where these instruction manuals are probably read by the average user. What else, besides trying to read the instructions, might they also be doing within the environment? Then, discuss how well these instruction manuals attempt to accommodate the environment in which they'll most likely be used. Did the designers do a good job in predicting this use, or might they have designed the instructions differently? How would you redesign the instructions based on the probable user's environment and purpose?

IN A GROUP

Research how to augment reality via AR apps and websites. What kinds of reality are being augmented by these programs? In what ways? Do you find augmented reality to be useful or superfluous? Record your results and share them with the class. If you or your partner has a smartphone that can make use of one of these AR apps, try viewing an example of augmented reality and perhaps construct one yourself.

ON YOUR OWN

Think of the most popular Web-based media you use on a weekly basis. Facebook? Pandora? Twitter? Pinterest? Create a list of the environments in which you use these services. Do you only use them at your desk, or do you use them in other locations, either via a laptop or smartphone? What else are you doing while using these media? Share your list and results with the class, and compare how the class as a whole integrates media and environment.

HOW CAN YOU BEST INTEGRATE A TEXT INTO THIS ENVIRONMENT?

To determine how to best place a text within an environment, it's important to consider the particular audience, the best environment to reach them, and the particular activities they may perform while encountering this text. In addition, you must also consider the constraints of the environment when making this decision, including not only physical constraints but also legal restrictions.

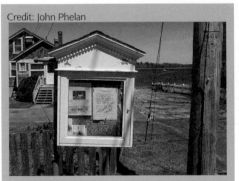

Credit: John Phelan

Figure 5.18
Some spaces are intended for community posting.

Some spaces, such as community bulletin boards, are clearly demarcated for most anyone to use (Figure 5.18). In addition, these spaces are expected to contain information, so your users may logically congregate to these areas in order to find what they're looking for. However, one cannot simply erect a billboard on the side of the road but must lease an existing billboard or a plot of land on which to build a new one. Ads such as that for Bounty paper towels in Figure 3.42 often require special permitting to place it on the street. If you're working for a client, the company may take care of these legal aspects for you.

However, legal requirements affect what you can post and where you can post it, as is evident in the example of the American Atheist billboard above.

Good integration requires an awareness of the larger media ecology in which your text will exist. While you might typically think of ecology in scientific terms, here "ecology" refers to the combination of images, videos, sounds, and other media within a space and their interaction with each other. According to media theorist Neil Postman, the field of media ecology considers the following aspects:

What is Media Ecology?

Media ecology looks into the matter of how media of communication affect human perception, understanding, feeling, and value and how our interaction with media facilitates or impedes our chances of survival.

The word ecology implies the study of environments: their structure, content, and impact on people.

An environment is, after all, a complex message system which imposes on human beings certain ways of thinking, feeling, and behaving.

- It structures what we can see and say and, therefore, do.
- It assigns roles to us and insists on our playing them.
- It specifies what we are permitted to do and what we are not.

Sometimes, as in the case of a courtroom, or classroom, or business office, the specifications are explicit and formal.

In the case of media environments (e.g., books, radio, film, television, etc.), the specifications are more often implicit and informal, half concealed by our assumption that what we are dealing with is not an environment but merely a machine.

Media ecology tries to make these specifications explicit.

It tries to find out what roles media force us to play, how media structure what we are seeing, and why media make us feel and act as we do.

Media ecology is the study of media as environments.

Copyright 1980 Pitman Publishing Corp. Reprinted by permission.

A media ecology (and really, any writing environment) has many varied parts that interact with a larger network, just as natural ecologies do. This ecology concerns not only the physical attributes of a text and all the objects within a space but also the intellectual and emotional responses that people have with those objects (and each other). Just as a natural environment is affected by animals that respond in different ways to various stimuli, humans affect the media ecology by how they react to the media environment.

Part of this effect comes from simply writing texts and adding them to this media ecology: you do not simply place your texts within environments, but your texts help construct environments. Furthermore, just as natural ecologies have "rules" that govern most of their interactions (such as the instinct of prey to flee from a predator or else be eaten), media environments have rules as well. Sometimes, as Postman points out, these rules are explicit, such as where you can or cannot place a text. But other rules, such as those of design, help a writer to determine the best way to create a text so that it best reaches the target audience.

Of particular note is Postman's insight that an interaction with media "facilitates or impedes our chances of survival (161)." It might be argued that seeing a particular visual message can save one's life. "STOP" signs certainly try to save lives. As another example, the cigarette ads looked at in Chapter 2 might convince someone to stop smoking and literally save their life (or, at least prolong it). Alternatively, ads convincing someone to start smoking can have the opposite effect, and media would—in a sense—take life.

Such messages compete for your attention, influencing your chances of survival in a very literal sense. The flyer for a lost dog, which you started to think about in Chapter 2, also has life and death implications. For the designer of a text, the effectiveness of a design can have ramifications for whether she maintains employment or is fired, affecting if she will be able to afford food, rent, and other necessities. From a variety of perspectives, media not only communicate ideas but also have physical effects on the actors in an environment and upon the environment itself. Just consider the sign in Figure 5.19, which affects both actors and environment.

This competition among the authors of texts becomes a competition by proxy, where the designs stand in place of the author within the media environment. The author does not directly survive or perish (although this can happen as a result), but her text instead faces a test of survival. In order to integrate your text within a media environment, you should pay attention to how the other texts within the environment will interact with it and where to best place a text so that it gets noticed. However, you should also ensure that your text's

Figure 5.19
By not complying with this sign, audiences can hurt the environment and their wallets.

Figure 5.20
Placing an ad in the wrong place can have unintended effects.

Figure 5.21
Another example of the pitfalls of ad placement.

meaning doesn't become diluted or transformed by images that appear around it.

Figure 5.20 demonstrates some of the pitfalls of not considering the larger media ecology into which you place another text. If you're the cigarette company, you probably don't want your ad next to another billboard telling your audience about the fight against cancer, as this can focus the viewer's attention on the negative aspects of smoking rather than "the best tobacco money can buy." If the top billboard, however, had been more specific, such as an anti-smoking/cancer message, then this juxtaposition would be perfect for the designer of

Figure 5.22
Bad ad placement can also happen online.

the nonsmoking ad. Just as the new warning images on cigarette packs create association by juxtaposition—making the repercussions of smoking clear—an anti-smoking billboard placed next to a cigarette ad would have the same effect and perhaps deter someone from smoking.

Figure 5.21 makes the same sort of indirect argument, since many people associate fast food with the rise in child and adult obesity. Whether this sort of juxtaposition was planned, and thus rhetorical, you can't be sure. But if predetermined, this placement provides a very clever rhetorical use of the media environment.

Figure 5.22 presents one problem with media juxtaposition in online environments. In this case, a story about coffee's possible role in triggering heart attacks appears alongside an advertisement for Folgers coffee. This inclusion is most likely an accident, but appears insensitive given the content of the story. This example also highlights the role that human psychology plays within a media ecology. Combining the story and ad is not inherently bad but becomes so because of social norms and the values held by society. Ecology, as discussed by Postman, is much larger than just the physical objects within it.

However, you can also use the media environment to your advantage, especially in finding "niches" where other forms of media don't yet occupy. Figure 5.23 presents an example of this. Here, the grab rails on a public transport vehicle have been made to look like watches. Not only do you notice the advertisement as you hold on to the strap, but you can also see how the watch looks on your wrist, "trying it out" before you buy. This business found a location within the environment in which no media existed and used the empty space to their advantage.

Figure 5.24, an advertisement for the San Francisco Zoo, used existing light posts for the "necks" of a giraffe, which hopefully catches the attention of people in the area, making them want to visit the zoo to see a real giraffe.

Figure 5.25 presents another clever example of using an existing environment in which to integrate an ad. Along the wall of an airport or subway system, the camera company Nikon placed a photograph of paparazzi taking photographs of an unknown celebrity with the company's cameras. The perspective is such that the viewer walking by experiences the point of view of this unseen subject. The existing environmental feature that really "makes" the experience is the red carpet that runs through the long corridor, simulating the clichéd red carpet that celebrities walk on at major Hollywood events. Without featuring any moving images or parts, this advertisement becomes dynamic, interactive, and more engaging than if simply placed along a highway.

Credit: BBDO West

You can also consider smaller-scale environments, such as those within the layout of a print document. Figure 5.26

Credit: IWC SchaffHausen

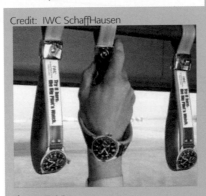

Figure 5.23
This niche advertisement makes use of safety straps on buses.

Figure 5.24
San Francisco Zoo ad using existing light poles.

Credit: TheCoolHunter

Figure 5.26
Although printed in a magazine, this Ikea ad is still interactive and makes use of a familiar environment.

Figure 5.25
Nikon ad using the existing environment.

shows an advertisement for the store IKEA, which sells a variety of furniture and other home furnishings. This design simulates the environment of a bedroom closet, designing the top page so that it "slides" as if it were an actual closet door. Although the ad doesn't appear in a three-dimensional physical environment, it plays with the media environment of print to create a clever gimmick that mimics a known, familiar household space. When you consider the media environment in which you write within, you must consider all of the pieces of the media ecology and how they interact with each other.

MAKING CONNECTIONS

AS A CLASS

Think about advertisements that seem inappropriately placed (like those in Figures 5.11-5.13) and take on additional meanings not intended by the author. How many can you think of? If you're having trouble, search for these ads online, and discuss how the surrounding media ecology influences how they might be inappropriately understood. As you find examples, keep a list and post them to a class wiki.

IN A GROUP

Brainstorm how you might place an ad for a product in a clever way, such as the example in Figure 5.23. What niches in the media ecology do you notice are unoccupied that could be filled with some sort of visual text? For example, some companies advertise on toilet paper located in public restrooms. Make sure that your ideas mesh well with the surrounding media environment and that you account for how the audience will use the environment. Share your ideas with the class.

ON YOUR OWN

Consider the spaces that you frequent that consist of a rich media ecology. One popular example might be Times Square in New York City, but most cities usually have their own version of a media-saturated area of town. Revisit this space and create a list of all the kinds of visuals you see. How are these visuals in competition with each other? How might they help each other? Do you notice spaces that are not being used but could be? Write up a brief report and share the results with your class.

ELECTRONIC ENVIRONMENTS

As you've already seen in Figures 5.17 and 5.22, online, virtual environments must also be considered within a larger media ecology. Online texts such as Web pages, videos, and streaming audio and television interrelate and affect how each is experienced on a page. These texts have their own internal environments and internal consistency that can be used rhetorically to better help your reader navigate a space and understand your argument. However, these electronic environments also affect the external environment as well, and the two are never really separated.

Online environments allow for a range of possibilities when reaching an audience. websites, blogs, social media, and video sites such as YouTube are all environments where you may reach your target audience through different kinds of media. Such sites easily allow for media convergence, juxtaposing image, text, sound, and video to create a multimedia environment that is more dynamic than print (even though print itself can include multimedia—such as this textbook, assuming you're reading the print version). These media can all display a similar message for different user preferences, or include multimedia that complement each other, offering something unique to the overall argument.

News sites such as CNN or ESPN do this fairly effectively. Not only do they include print stories, but they also integrate clips from their television shows so that you can often choose to read or watch a story, depending on your preference. Often, the text and video differ in the kind of content they provide (facts versus opinion or expert analysis) so that the two kinds of media converge and supplement each other, increasing the effectiveness of the piece. Such sites obviously also include images to illustrate the stories, hyperlinks to related stories, and occasionally include podcasts for listening.

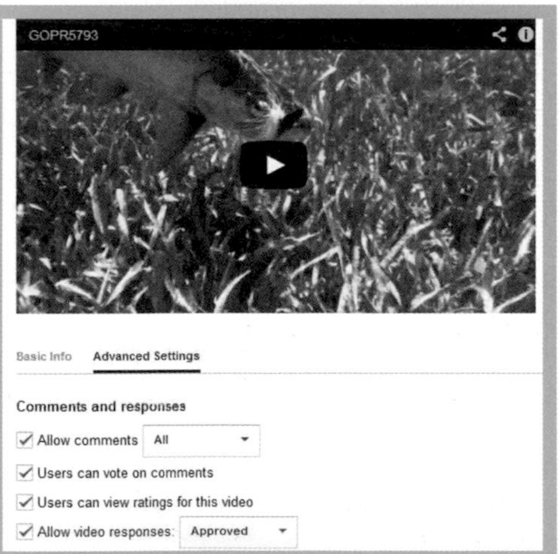

Figure 5.27
YouTube and other social media sites usually let you control the comments section.

As you've seen in Figure 5.20, the juxtaposition of different messages does not always produce the best environment for your argument. Just as billboards juxtaposed in a physical space can influence each other's meaning, online juxtaposition can also have unintended readings or consequences, such as that in Figure 5.22. The author might not have much control over what ads are placed on their site, which may sometimes lead to unfortunate pairings of texts and images (unless you have the power to make contracts for your own advertisers, which often isn't the case on free sites such as YouTube).

As discussed in Chapter 3, one option you can typically control on such sites is the comment feature. The decision to allow comments is a personal and rhetorical one (Figure 5.27). Do you want others to be able to interact and respond to what you write online, or do you wish to more carefully control the message? You may want, for instance, to create the perception that your YouTube channel or blog is friendly, inviting, and open to the opinions of others. This creates goodwill between you and a reader and affects how your *ethos* as a writer is perceived.

Facebook's major comment area, called a "Wall," allows those with access to one's account (a user's "friends") to post messages, photos, and various comments. For most users, these interactive, communicative features make social media worth using. However, for companies using Facebook to advertise their brand, the environment of the Wall can pose particular problems (Figure 5.28).

One of these affected industries is the pharmaceutical sector. Originally, Facebook allowed these companies to opt out of including the Wall on their Facebook accounts so that visitors could not post comments. Pharmaceutical companies were afraid that users might comment negatively about their drugs and obviously wanted to avoid bad publicity. However, Facebook put a stop to this privileged behavior, as described in the story below from National Public Media (you can also listen to the podcast): http://www.npr.org/blogs/health/2011/08/22/139859210/why-drug-companies-are-shy-about-sharing-on-facebook)

Why Drug Companies Are Shy About Sharing On Facebook

People love how Facebook lets them comment on and share other people's posts. But the idea of sharing on social media has got drug companies scared. When Facebook told drug makers that they had to start allowing comments on their Facebook pages, some of those pages started disappearing.

"Take On Depression" suddenly disappeared. "ADHD Moms" vanished, too. So did "Epilepsy Advocate." In the past, drug companies had been reluctant to create Facebook pages without a guarantee that they'd be closed to public comments—a unique accommodation on Facebook's part. But that accommodation ended last week.

Diabetes blogger Amy Tenderich thinks it's high time the drug companies quit walling themselves off. She's the founder of Diabetes Mine, an independent site. She says: "The notion that they would be able to put up these Facebook pages and then close them off to comments is ridiculous."

On her site, people with diabetes comment a lot. They share information on what drugs they're taking, give each other advice on dosages, and tell people which drugs are working for them, and which are causing side effects. For Tenderich and others, the whole point of social media like Facebook and Twitter is to comment on other people's posts.

But drug companies have to play by different rules. The Food and Drug Administration requires that each drug manufacturer mentions a prescription drug, they also have to list its risks and side effects. That's called fair balance.

"You see some of those magazine ads that are three and four pages long and you wonder why they are?," asks Tony Jewell, who supervises drug maker AstraZeneca's social media efforts. "It's because we're communicating the full risks, benefits and appropriate use of the medicine. That's a little bit harder to do in a social media channel like Facebook and Twitter."

One big reason companies cite for killing Facebook pages is that they wouldn't be able to adequately police comments with inaccurate information about prescription drugs.

"So they might say, 'Lipitor's great at whitening your teeth,' which it's not approved to do," says Jonathan Richman. That's his example of a potentially dicey comment. He's a group director for the Possible Worldwide ad agency in Cincinnati, and he closely follows the drug industry's social media efforts on his Dose of Digital blog. "The question becomes, what's Pfizer's liability? What action could the FDA take, based on somebody else posting that?"

So far, the FDA hasn't come down on a single drug company for allowing public comments. The only action the agency has taken against use of social media was last year, when it warned Novartis that a Facebook "share" widget for the leukemia drug Tasigna violated fair balance.

But the FDA also hasn't told the companies how to use social media and still follow the "fair balance" rule. In November 2009, the agency held public hearings on how pharma companies should use social media. But the FDA has yet to issue official guidance.

Jewell says that because of that, his employer and other companies are erring on the side of caution.

Tenderich says patients would benefit from a rich interaction with drug makers. She sees more and more drug company employees interacting on her site, giving advice on behalf of their employers. That's a huge benefit for patients, she says.

The pharmaceutical companies could benefit, too, she says, by learning what problems patients are having with drugs, and how to make them better.

"They could get so much fantastic, free, very high-value feedback," she says.

Pharmaceutical companies have a very complicated media environment to navigate, one that can't be easily controlled and requires thinking about how new inhabitants to the environment (visitors to their Facebook page) might interact with the content. As described in the article, the short, chunked style of online writing environments is not conducive to the long legally required list of side effects the companies must post each time one of their drugs is mentioned, either within their own posts or in the comments of users. They must also correct each user who makes false claims about what a drug could do. These concerns don't even cover those who may be unhappy with how a drug performed. Such possibilities that require constant monitoring and correcting don't occur within printed text, which isn't as malleable as hypertext. When you create a document online, be aware of your target audience and how they might use it and how such use could potentially undercut your own message.

Finally, not all your target users will be human. Much of your audience may attempt to find your site through a search engine such as Google. In order to index your site in its directory, search engines send out bits of code called "robots" or "spiders" to crawl the Web and create an ecology of websites and keywords. The robots organize these sites according to meta data (or, data about your site) such as listed keywords or the text it finds on your pages. In many of your writing classes, you've probably heard teachers say that you shouldn't use the same word again and again within your writing, that it sounds stylistically unsophisticated. For search engine robots, this repetitive style can be good, for the recurrence of a single keyword signals to the robot that this site must be about that keyword. Within online environments, especially ones you intend to be searched, you must balance between these two audiences—humans and robots—so that you write stylistically soundly for both.

MAKING CONNECTIONS

AS A CLASS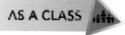

In a previous prompt, you looked at ways that ads were inappropriately placed in physical environments. As a class, reconsider this prompt in the context of electronic environments. Visit various Web pages to find these ads or search for examples that have already been documented (as in Figure 5.22). Discuss why the juxtaposition of certain ads is inappropriate and how you might prevent such juxtaposition in your own texts. As you find examples, keep a list, and post them to a class wiki.

Consider the reasons why a company (besides a pharmaceutical company) may or may not want a social media page that allows comments. What are the reasons for including comments? Why wouldn't a particular company want comments? How can comments help or hurt the company's image and its message? Provide examples of both, and share your results with the class.

Recall a website that uses a variety of media genres, such as print, images, video, podcasts, or even video games. Do you find this integration of various media within a single electronic environment to be effective, or distracting? Why or why not? Is any media genre missing that should be included? How would you redesign the environment to better fit its purpose and target audience? Share your ideas with the class.

NATURAL ENVIRONMENTS

In the beginning of this chapter, you looked at how natural environments and writing intertwine before moving onto larger understandings of "environment." While this chapter has mostly focused on "media" environments and ecologies, it would be unethical not to also mention the way that writing in new media also affects natural environments and ecologies.

Returning to the "natural" sense of these terms "environment" and "ecology," it's probably clear now that such environments can influence how you write.

Credit: Frank Donat

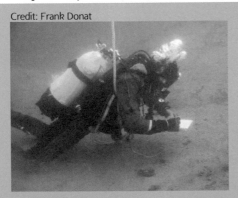

Credit: Ebyabe

Figure 5.28
Different environments can require different writing technologies.

Figure 5.29
This sign helps to designate this beach as a state park.

Writing on a boat would be much different from writing in an office, and each environment would demand different writing technologies (Figure 5.28).

What and how you write can also influence these environments. The designation of a specific area of land as a "state park" is a legal, written definition that doesn't exist outside of writing (Figure 5.29). This official designation determines what can and cannot occur in such a location. For example, one might not be permitted to hunt within a state park, yet be allowed to hunt within contiguous wood located just beyond the park's boundary. These woods are really the same and are only separated by writing (and perhaps a fence). Sidney Dobrin and Christian Weisser explain how language and writing affects how tourists and locals relate to the environments of Hawaii:

Natural Discourse: Toward Ecocomposition

Half a world away on the "Big Island" of Hawaii, words demarcate where natural sites exist. Each year, thousands of tourists flock to Hawaii Volcanoes National Park to get a glimpse at a "real" volcano. Most of them stop at the small town just outside the park, aptly named "Volcano," to purchase T-shirts, coffee mugs, and postcards emblazoned with images of Mauna Loa or Kilauea [Figure 5.30]. Little attention is paid to the fact that it is all volcano, that the Hawaiian Islands themselves are volcanic peaks formed over the course of millions of years. In fact, this mapping and classifying of environments extends even below the depths of the world's oceans, encompassing sites as yet inaccessible to human beings. Fifteen miles south of Hawaii, more than three thousand feet below sea level, lies the volcanic seamount Lo'ihi. Despite the fact that it will not reach sea level for tens of thousands of years, tour guides, residents, and even some scientists have begun referring to Lo'ihi as the next Hawaiian island, thereby mapping and inscribing a long political, cultural, and social history upon this island that is yet to be [Figure 5.31].

Credit: R.W. Decker

Figure 5.30
Although tourists consider Mauna Loa a "real volcano," the whole island is actually a volcano.

Credit: Kmusser

Figure 5.31
Lo'ihi is still underwater, but Hawaiians have already named it.

Credit: Matthias Feilhauer

Figure 5.32
Much e-waste from the United States ends up in other countries.

Credit: Curtis Palmer

Figure 5.33
E-waste is becoming a significant problem as humans discard obsolete technology.

In this example, writing names the physical objects and locations in Hawaii, but writing also expresses how people relate to those objects and locations, as in the example of "volcano" given above.

Besides places, writing also affects how humans relate to living beings. Some animals are labeled as food but others consider them as pets, and those animals that are typically consumed are further identified with other labels such as meat, poultry, and fish. Some species of plants are usually labeled as good, such as grass, and some as bad, such as weeds. These distinctions, however, are completely arbitrary and constructed through writing. In this way, writing not only establishes relationships with the environment, but also affects the very environments in which an audience reads such relationships. If such relationships were written differently, turkeys might be kept as pets (and some are), or weeds might be considered more desirable than grass.

Writing also affects environments through the writing technologies themselves. Many writing instruments are electronic and made from plastic, metals, and toxic materials. When you throw these technologies away, they become electronic waste, or e-waste (Figures 5.32 and 5.33). Such refuse typically contains many poisonous or harmful substances. If disposed of improperly, these substances can cause serious environmental problems.

While you may never have to dispose of any of this equipment yourself, you should consider the materials your texts and writing technologies are constructed out of and how they may impact the environment if abandoned or forgotten. While it may be obvious that you should retrieve flyers you may have posted once an event is past, or that you should print on recycled paper, you might also consider the kinds of inks or paints used on a billboard or other kinds of visual installations. Learning this information requires more research on your part, but choosing safe materials will also help you earn goodwill and have a more positive impact on the environment.

MAKING CONNECTIONS

AS A CLASS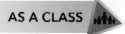

Often, state parks and recreation areas post signs that read "Take Only Photographs, Leave Only Footprints." As a class, discuss the purpose and rationale behind this message. Then, discuss how the very act of taking a photograph—which this sign takes to be benign— might alter the environment in unintended ways. Also consider how environments are sometimes altered or constructed in order to make photography more accessible.

IN A GROUP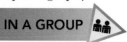

Research how an electronic writing technology is made, such as a computer, tablet, smartphone, or camera. What materials go into this technology? Which are poisonous to humans and the environment? How does the company recommend you dispose of the technology after its use? How, in actuality, do most users dispose of the product, and what effects does it have on landfills? Compose a report with your findings and share them with the class.

ON YOUR OWN

As in the volcano example above, think of your own hometown and how language and environment interact. Was there a physical feature or some local wildlife that influenced how the town constructed its idea of nature? As a starting point, you might use your university as a model. Many college campuses have an animal-based mascot that affects how they think about their own campus (for example, the University of Florida—whose mascot is an alligator—refers to their football stadium as "the swamp"). This mascot might further affect how the university interacts with the larger environment, perhaps by including locations on campus for wild alligators to live or donating to causes that help the local environment. Do similar naming conventions appear where you grew up or at your university? Write a report with your findings, and share them with the class.

KEY TERMS	
media environment	*location*
media ecology	*electronic environment*
scouting	*natural environment*
intended audience	*e-waste*

OUTPUT: ADVERTISEMENT

In this output, you'll create an advertisement. What you advertise is up to you and your instructor, but the possibilities are numerous. You can choose a pre-existing product and create your own advertising approach that the company may not have considered. For instance, you might create your own Gatorade advertisement with you as the subject selling the product. You might want to create an advertisement for something you need to sell. If you're moving out of your apartment at the end of the semester, you might want to sell your furniture rather than moving or tossing it in the landfill. Or, if you perform a service, such as yard maintenance, child sitting, or Web design, you could focus this assignment on advertising that service.

As you plan your advertisement, remember to view your assignment through the rhetorical tetrahedron to make sure you consider the basic and important elements, from audience to genre, and from *logos* to *kairos*.

Target your audience

As discussed above, determine which specific audiences you're attempting to target. Try to narrow down this audience as much as possible so that you can create an advertisement that will be as effective as possible.

Research your audience

Once you've identified your audience, research as much information about them as you can. For instance, consider questions such as: Who are they? What kinds of interests do they have (hopefully interests that correspond to your message)? Where do you expect to find your audience (i.e., where should you place your advertisement)? How will they use your advertisement or advertised product/service?

Identify your niche

What can you say within your advertisement that is unique and will make the viewer stop, read, and respond? If the advertisement is for a concert, does the talent draw the most attention? The location? Perhaps a combination of a certain artist playing at a certain arena? If you were posting an advertisement to sublease your apartment, what makes your apartment stand out from the others? Location? Price? Amenities? What benefit does it provide above other competing advertisements? Knowing your audience and what they care about can help you identify your niche as well. Determine what unique, but relevant, reason sets your service or item apart and make it the main focus of your design.

Plan an effective message about the subject of the advertisement

First, you should make sure "what" the ad is about is clearly apparent, either from text or an image. However, you should also make sure you clearly display information about the niche that your advertisement fills. You may also include the necessary details that allow the reader to use the advertisement. Again, if you're advertising a concert, make sure to include where, when, and perhaps how much the tickets will cost (and where to purchase them).

Think about the larger situation

Consider how the user will encounter this advertisement and the larger environment in which you post it. Will the advertisement be located among a variety of other ads? If so, you'll want to create a design that stands out from the others and captures the reader's attention. Will the reader see the ad while walking? Driving? At home on the computer? These questions about the larger context and ecology will help you avoid pitfalls and also position your ad in a more rhetorically advantageous environment.

Consider what images you might use

Images can help the reader to easily identify what your text is about, or create a unique design that sets the ad apart from others. Think about which images will convey your message about the ad's niche and also what your target audience might expect to see. If you were advertising a car, the audience would most likely expect a photo of the car (if not several). The audience for a concert advertisement might expect cover art from one of the band's albums. When deciding which images to include, determine how to balance these audience expectations with making sure you communicate how your subject matter is unique. Of course, you should also determine what right you have to use certain images. If you didn't take or make the images yourself, are they within the public domain, or might you have to pay a copyright royalty to use them?

Consider the amount of text you'll need

Think of the more memorable advertisements you've seen. How many words did they include? Most likely, the actual word count for these ads was very low, and images dominated the space. While advertisements in the 1930s-1950s typically included several hundred words (Figure 5.34), today's ads use a fraction of this amount. Consider using as few words as possible while still conveying all the relevant information that the audience needs to understand how the advertised subject matter applies to them and how it offers something unique. You may also need to include text to help your audience understand how to use the ad (as discussed with the concert ad example above). However, you should place text so that it is clearly identifiable and separated from other textual elements (see Chapter 10 for more suggestions on layout).

Automatic Telephone

Long Distance Service

To Our Visitors:
    Your independent telephone in Peoria, Bloomington, Joliet, Aurora, Elgin, Clinton (Ia.) and intermediate points is now in instantaneous communication with 40,000 Automatic telephones in Chicago.

    If you are an independent telephone user in Illinois or surrounding states, you may now call your home town from Chicago via Automatic long distance service. Just place your finger on the dial in the opening marked "long distance," give a complete turn, release the dial, and you are instantly connected with long distance service.

    For complete information and rates on Long Distance service call on the dial. Remove the telephone from the hook before operating dial.

Illinois Tunnel Co.
162 W. Monroe St.   Chicago, Ill.
Contract Department 33-111

Figure 5.34
By today's standards, this ad has too many words.

User-test the advertisement

When you have completed the ad, find others who can look at it and determine if it conveys the information you're trying to communicate. Also, have users look at the ad within the final environment you expect to place it in and get their feedback. This user testing can be informal, or you might create a questionnaire that asks specific questions about the user's experience. Such feedback should go beyond simple proofreading and ask questions about the choices you made as a designer if the ad doesn't seem to work quite right.

Edit your advertisement

Based on the feedback you get from user testing, re-think the advertisement through the rhetorical tetrahedron. Why didn't a particular phrase or word work? What didn't a design catch the reader's attention? Would a different medium work better in a particular environment? What message is the overall advertisement, in a particular environment, saying to an audience? Once you've hashed out these questions, revise and user-test again.

6

SCREENING AUDIENCES AND ACTORS

The ultimate goal of any rhetorical communication is to get your audience to act (or not act) in a particular way. However, especially with new media texts, audiences can also be actors who interact with your texts in ways that go beyond simply responding to the text itself, and you should account for the possible ways that this interaction occurs. In addition, your audience may not even be human. They may include search engine robots that scour the Web on behalf of search engines such as Google or Bing. This chapter will offer guidance on how to research and analyze your multiple audiences and how to design different media to maximize their activity with new media.

 Most of the decisions you make when writing will revolve around your understanding of what your audience wants, expects, likes, dislikes, and will find persuasive. Determining these preferences requires a careful analysis of your audience, and you must screen them before writing. Thinking about how the audience acts with the other parts of the rhetorical tetrahedron is a good way to do this.

CASTING A TEXT

To screen actors for a film is—in some ways—to literally screen them by placing them on film and seeing how they appear on the screen (Figure 6.1). How do they look? How do they move? How do they relate to other actors on a flat, two-dimensional medium? Just as you should user-test your designs before posting them, directors want to see how actors will test before casting them.

Credit: ©Universal/Courtesy Everett Collection

Figure 6.1
This was a successful screen test for Henry Thomas for the movie E.T.
http://www.youtube.com/watch?v=t0Cinb1j5-s

Just think how different some well-known movies might be with a different cast. For example, in the film *Terminator*, director James Cameron originally considered Lance Henriksen for the lead role (Figure 6.2). However, after Arnold Schwarzenegger read for the part of Kyle Reese, Cameron decided to "revise" his choices, placing Schwarzenegger in the title role (Figure 6.3). Henriksen was cast as a minor character and still appeared in the film, but the movie would have been much different without Schwarzenegger as the over-built, intimidating presence, not to mention his signature line, "I'll be back."

Credit: Orion Films

Figure 6.2
Can you imagine Lance Henrikson as the *Terminator*?

Credit: ©Orion Pictures Corp./ Courtesy Everett Collection

Figure 6.3
Of course, Arnold Schwarzenegger got the part.

If you're a fan of the *Indiana Jones* movies, you might think that Harrison Ford was the perfect choice to play Indiana; however, he wasn't the first choice. George Lucas originally considered Tom Selleck to play the part (Figure 6.4). Selleck auditioned for the role but had already signed a contract to play Thomas Magnum in the television series *Magnum P.I.* when Lucas offered him the role. CBS, who created *Magnum P.I.*, wouldn't release Selleck from his contract, and because of this contractual conflict, Lucas and Stephen Spielberg selected Ford for the part (Figure 6.5). You may find that contractual or legal conflicts force you to choose elements in a design that aren't your first choice, such as copyright issues around already existing media. However, if you think creatively about what your audience really needs, you can usually overcome such constraints.

With audience in mind, you should screen the elements of your own design to test how they interact within a specific composition before making that work public. In many ways, you can consider the text that you create as an agent in the world that acts on your behalf, whether it's the advertisement you created in Chapter 5 or the video resume you'll compose at the

Figure 6.4
Tom Selleck in Hawaii to shoot *Magnum P.I.*

Credit: ©Universal Television/Courtesy Everett Collection

Credit: © Paramount/Courtesy Everett Collection

Figure 6.5
Now in his 70s, Ford still has what it takes to play Indiana Jones.

end of this chapter. And like any actor, you have to screen your text and make sure it fits the part. Martin Wikner offers the following advice on what to look for while *screening* actors and *casting* a movie:

There's a lot that have to work to make an actor or actress suitable for your production. It might be great to cast a shy person, depending on the role, or an excellent performance may have been performed by an unpleasant person. What you're after depends on the role, the movie, and yourself. If you have filmed the audition, here are some things to think about while watching it:

- **Chemistry.** Does the chemistry between you and the actor or actress work out well? Often this means that you can communicate well and that the person seems nice, but there might very well be a reason for you to prefer someone nasty. However, think about it this person will cause issues with other members of the crew.

- **Looks.** Simply, do the person's looks and movement suit the role? If not, perhaps it's still possible to make the person look right with make-up or training.

- **Performance.** Is the person good at acting? Perhaps it was a solid performance, but not what you asked for. A performance that came natural may really make your preparations with the actor or actress a lot easier, but could also mean that if you change some trait for the character, he or she cannot make the change, being a one trick pony.

- **Voice.** Does it sound right? This is easy to forget with everything else going on, but the voice and accent must fit the character and sound believable.

It is a good idea to get a second opinion from someone else about the performances, while watching. But the most important thing is to think through what you value the most and what you could make without. You're really lucky if you get someone that is both a good actor or actress in all ways possible and is nice to be with.

Casting as Writing

This analogy can be useful in how to "cast" your own production, even if it doesn't consist of live humans. Instead, your "actors" become the different elements that you include within the design—from images, to typefaces, to medium, to environment—all of which have to fit and work together for a text to be effective and act on your behalf toward your target audience.

For example, you might think of chemistry in terms of harmony (see Chapter 10), how all the elements relate to each other and create an overall balanced aesthetic. You might select visual elements based on whether they "look" right for the role. For instance, you might use a certain typography because it looks right for a title or header, or you may choose an image because its colors fit the color scheme of the design. If the image doesn't look quite right, you can use a photo editor (instead of makeup) to augment it.

You might think of an actor's performance as reflecting the versatility of a particular visual element. A particular element might look like it fits naturally and conveys a certain message in one setting, but if that design changes or is converted from one kind of genre (flyer) to another (video), will the element have the same effect?

In terms of writing, an author's "voice" often becomes synonymous with an author's "style." You can also look for this kind of voice-as-style in visual texts. If you analyze a design as a whole, does it have an overall style, a voice, which transcends the individual parts? Do the textual elements have a particular voice or tone that matches the message you want to send?

Finally, getting a second opinion—either through peer review or by having someone you trust analyze your writing—is important when deciding on how to screen individual elements for your overall project. Some elements might not work the way you see it, or some may be unnecessary and actually detract from the goal and purpose of your design. Since, hopefully, lots of eyes will fall upon your text, you want to make sure you solicit feedback from lots of eyes before making your design public.

MAKING CONNECTIONS

AS A CLASS

Look at a variety of ads (in several media, including print and digital) that feature celebrities. Why do you think companies chose particular actors, recording artists, or sports figures over others? Their popularity? Looks? Voice? Would you have cast someone else in these advertisements? Why? Discuss your opinions as a group and note how each of you interpret the qualities of the actors and needs of the audience differently.

IN A GROUP

Choose two or three movies that you love to watch in which the main character is iconic (such as Arnold Schwarzenegger as *The Terminator*). Now, for each movie, recast the main character of the film with other actors. How would the movie change? How do you think audiences would react to the main character? Share your casting ideas with the class and discuss how they would react to such a change.

ON YOUR OWN

Think of a fictional work that you've read lately. If you had to cast the various characters for a movie, whom would you consider? Why? How would you consider the traits mentioned here such as chemistry, looks, performance, and voice? Would you use well-known actors, or do you have people in your own life (who are not celebrities) that you would cast instead? Create a casting list with your rationale, and share it with the class.

FUTURE AUDIENCES

Usually, you think about a *future audience* when writing (unless the audience happens to be looking over your shoulder). You also write for an imagined audience, an audience that you try to predict will be like your actual audience. While these two audiences ultimately differ in many ways, some audiences are more futuristic and imaginary than others. The following examples provide some insights toward screening audiences you will probably never meet and toward thinking about how your designs will need to operate long into the future to affect those audiences.

According to a report by the U.S. National Academy of Sciences, current stores of nuclear waste could take as long as 3 million years to decay to normal levels. Because of this danger, the world's nuclear waste must be safely stored in a way that shields humans from the radiation that continues to emit from spent fuel rods and other forms of used nuclear materials. However, even when safely stored, humans must be warned of the potential dangers at these storage sites, for the waste stored in them can pose potential hazards to life for tens of thousands (if not hundreds of thousands) of years.

Figure 6.6
Original radiation warning sign outside the Chernobyl accident site.

Credit: International Atomic Energy Agency

Figure 6.7
New radiation warning sign.

Since humans have existed for much less time than it takes nuclear waste to decay, who knows what languages, cultures, or even physical features will exist at that time? Governments and scientists have to design technical documentation that can warn future audiences about the impending threats, warning them not to enter waste facilities. This task is quite difficult. As an analogy, consider how you would tackle trying to read the inscriptions on the Egyptian pyramids if you were the first to find them. While you might have unleashed the curse of King Tutankhamen, future archaeologists might unleash something much worse.

Such future warnings are already being designed and created, but this rhetorical situation raises certain questions about future audiences that may be unanswerable. For instance, no one knows the languages that future audiences will use, nor does anyone even know if future humans will still "see" using eyes.

The long-standing international sign for radiation appears in Figure 6.6. While this warning sign is an elegant symbol, it doesn't offer much other context. In an attempt to update it, the International Atomic Energy Agency (IAEA) revised the warning to that in Figure 6.7. As the IAEA describes it:

With radiating waves, a skull and crossbones and a running person, a new ionizing radiation warning symbol is being introduced to supplement the traditional international symbol for radiation, the three cornered trefoil.

The new symbol is being launched today by the IAEA and the International Organization for Standardization (ISO) to help reduce needless deaths and serious injuries from accidental exposure to large radioactive sources. It will serve as a supplementary warning to the trefoil, which has no intuitive meaning and little recognition beyond those educated in its significance. The new symbol is aimed at alerting anyone, anywhere to the potential dangers of being close to a large source of ionizing radiation, the result of a five-year project conducted in 11 countries around the world. The symbol was tested with different population groups - mixed ages, varying educational backgrounds, male and female—to ensure that its message of "danger—stay away" was crystal clear and understood by all.

The new symbol, developed by human factor experts, graphic artists, and radiation protection experts, was tested by the Gallup Institute on a total of 1650 individuals in Brazil, Mexico, Morocco, Kenya, Saudi Arabia, China, India, Thailand, Poland, Ukraine and the United States.

The symbol is intended for IAEA Category 1, 2 and 3 sources defined as dangerous sources capable of death or serious injury, including food irradiators, teletherapy machines for cancer treatment and industrial radiography units. The symbol is to be placed on the device housing the source, as a warning not to dismantle the device or to get any closer. It will not be visible under normal use, only if someone attempts to disassemble the device. The symbol will not be located on building access doors, transportation packages or containers.

From the description of the design process, you can see how thoroughly the IAEA attempted to account for audience when creating the new warning label. Their target audience is literally anyone and everyone, and their research reflects this, testing the label in many countries and with many different demographics, such as "mixed ages, varying educational backgrounds, male and female" to make sure a diverse audience can understand the message.

However, despite such extensive user-testing, the IAEA can only test a current, existing audience, not the audience that may read the warning label in 500 or 10,000 years. For instance, as the IAEA notes, only some people can read the current symbol of the trefoil "which has no intuitive meaning and little recognition beyond those educated in its significance." Others may think that it looks like a fan, a propeller, or any variety of circular objects. Incorporating the trefoil into the new design includes some of the original problems with this symbol. John Brownlee, writing for *Wired Magazine*, discusses the problem of the new warning:

Building a Better Radiation Warning Symbol

The old radiation symbol was certainly a timeless masterpiece of paranoid Cold War aesthetics, but it only makes sense if you already know what it means. If confronted with the relic of such a symbol on the side of a barrel of toxic ooze that has been dug-up a hundred thousand years from now, how would the super-intelligent space monkeys of the future know it was a danger to them? The radiation warning symbol would tell them nothing: our simian descendants would crack open that container with an industrial sized can opener and start smearing the fluorescent toxic waste through their hair like styling gel.

To prevent this, the International Atomic Energy Agency is launching a new symbol, which they hope more clearly spells out the threat to those who don't already know what a radiation symbol means. But what is that threat? According to the new symbol, it's when a blowing fan causes a gigantic skull to chase a man into the side of an equilateral triangle, which then probably knocks him cold.

Credit: Ben Crum

Figure 6.8
You shouldn't monkey around with radiation.

There's a lot of weirdo problems with this symbol, the biggest one being that it still uses the original radiation symbol without any sense of context. You want to warn people a hundred thousand years in the future that there's dangerous radioactive elements about? All you need is two panels stenciled on the side of every barrel of nuclear sludge [see Figure 6.8]. In panel one, a monkey wearing a space suit and with a throbbing, exposed brain levers open a barrel of sludge. From the sun in the background of the panel, you can tell it's early morning. And in panel two, the monkey is just a skeleton standing in a sloughed-off puddle of his own melted skin at midnight, silently screaming before the open background. An arrow leads readers in the intended direction of the comic. Who's going to mistake that warning sign?

Copyright 2007 by *Wired.com.* Printed by permission.

Brownlee illustrates the problem with writing in visuals: more so than words, images are usually much more open to interpretation. While someone might understand that the "man" is attempting to run from the outcome of death that radiation causes, this conclusion is based on several assumptions and causal relations. Perhaps these future space monkeys will think that the man whom the skull belonged to died when some other man ran away from him, leaving him without help.

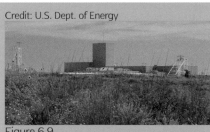

Credit: U.S. Dept. of Energy

Figure 6.9
The Waste Isolation Pilot Plant in Carlsbad, New Mexico.

In addition to the new symbol, some locations such as the Waste Isolation Pilot Plant (WIPP) in Carlsbad, New Mexico have begun to use the "Rosetta Stone" approach (Figure 6.9). The Rosetta Stone helped archaeologists decipher hieroglyphs because it included three languages: Egyptian hieroglyphs, Demotic script (another Egyptian script), and ancient Greek (Figure 6.10). Since archaeologists already knew ancient Greek, they were able to compare the known script to the unknown, and crack the hieroglyphic code.

Similar to the Rosetta Stone, the WIPP will include 25-foot tall granite markers located around the WIPP facility, engraved with a message in seven languages: English, Spanish, French, Russian, Chinese, Arabic, and Navajo (Figure 6.11). Even if one or several of these languages become extinct or radically altered, hopefully future audiences will be able to make sense of the text should they still use any of the other seven languages or their variations. In addition to these monument-sized markers, the WIPP facility will also include 9-inch clay markers buried throughout the site, information rooms at the surface and underground, as well as radar reflectors and magnets so that future detection technologies should be able to tell that something strange is located at the site (Figure 6.12).

Credit: Hans Hillewaert

Figure 6.10
The Rosetta Stone was inscribed in three languages.

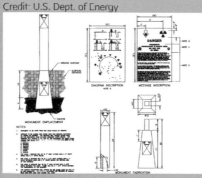

Credit: U.S. Dept. of Energy

Figure 6.11
The plans for these larger markers include inscribing them in seven languages.

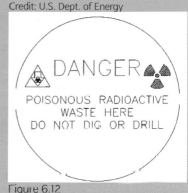

Credit: U.S. Dept. of Energy

Figure 6.12
These 9-inch clay markers will be buried throughout the site.

KLM, Inc., a management consulting company, frames the radioactivity communication problem in terms of branding:

> *If there ever was a brand challenge, this could be it. How can we communicate the mortal, and almost unending, danger of radioactive waste across all present and future cultures and civilizations and possibly, even to non-human alien beings from outer space?*
>
> *The essence of good branding is creating an identity, with a specific meaning, that endures through time. Thus the challenge of univocally communicating or branding radioactive waste into the future is a unique case study in both the nature and the limits of branding.*
>
> —KLM

To tackle this problem, WIPP uses a variety of branding strategies, including different kinds of markers, several languages, and other techniques to get the audience's attention and ensure the message is understood. Looking at more traditional attempts at branding, you probably notice some similarities with this example. Companies often create many different kinds of advertisements, in diverse languages, using focus groups and test screenings to make sure that the ad resonates with each kind of audience. Even though the WIPP location isn't trying to sell a product, many of their problems and tactics relate to those used by marketing companies. Of course, any brand message can fail, and only time (a lot of time) will tell if the WIPP site and IAEA are successful in their strategy.

MAKING CONNECTIONS

AS A CLASS

Locate other signs or symbols that attempt to warn audiences about imminent dangers. How might you interpret these images differently than their official message? What audiences do you think these images are designed for? Which audiences do they exclude? How are the messages distributed within the environment? Does this distribution strategy make sense?

IN A GROUP

Revisit the nuclear waste example above. Research more into this issue and what particular audiences the IAEA or WIPP considered. Can you think of any potential audience members that they neglected? Can you think of alternative ways to reach these audiences? Share your research findings and audience considerations with the class.

ON YOUR OWN

Using the information in this example, as well as the research you conducted in Prompt #2 above, design your own warning symbol for the nuclear waste site and a strategy for branding the WIPP location. How would it differ from the current WIPP strategy and IAEA symbol already in use? How would it accommodate audiences better than the current strategy? Share your new branding strategy with the class.

EXTRATERRESTRIAL AUDIENCES

The nuclear waste example above could apply to potential alien visitors as well. How would you warn these E.T.s to stay away from radioactive dump sites so that they don't accidentally unleash an intergalactic disaster? Moreover, if future cultures can't recognize the current symbols or languages, how would a being from another planet? While this hypothetical audience might seem far-fetched, many attempts have been made to create messages for this audience. While you might never have to construct a design targeted at aliens, thinking about such a practice can help you consider Earthly audiences in a more sophisticated way.

In 1972, the National Aeronautic and Space Administration (NASA) planned to launch the Pioneer 10 spacecraft (and, a year later, the Pioneer 11), which would be the first human-built object to leave the solar system.

During a visit to the Jet Propulsion Laboratory (JPL), which helped design and construct the Pioneer 10, journalist Eric Burgess suggested that in the event an alien species should intercept the spacecraft, the Pioneer should carry some sort of message to let the aliens know where the spacecraft came from as well as information about the human race.

Burgess approached Carl Sagan, who had previously discussed ways humans might communicate with extraterrestrials, and NASA agreed to let Sagan design a message to be attached onto the Pioneer 10 (Sagan's wife at the time, Linda Salzman Sagan, created the artwork for the design).

Sagan chose to create a visual message in the form of a metal plaque (Figures 6.13 and 6.14). Given the limited space, he could only convey so much information, and selected details that he thought his audience might want to know. First, he included basic scientific facts he figured any intelligent, space-going life form would know, such as the most abundant element in the universe, hydrogen, as well as including details about its hyperfine transition, which refers to the electron spin (top-left corner).

Figure 6.13
Carl Sagan, pictured here, helped to create the Pioneer 10 plaque.

If you look at this inclusion from the perspective of *ethos*, then Sagan is suggesting that humans are intelligent enough to understand some basic physics about the cosmos. This electron spin provides a relatively specific unit of length and time, allowing the message to convey a sense of distance and time other than arbitrary units of feet, meters, kilometers, seconds, minutes, or hours.

The large, line-based schematic on the left indicates the position of the sun in relation to the center of the Milky Way galaxy, as well as fourteen other pulsar stars, and uses the unit in the hydrogen diagram to signify distance/time of

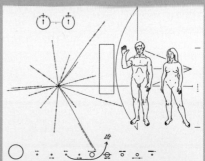

Figure 6.14
Pioneer 10 plaque designed by Carl Sagan and Frank Drake with the artwork by Linda Salzmann Sagan.

each from the center of the galaxy. Portraying this many pulsars provides a way to ensure the aliens can triangulate the origin of the spacecraft, even if some pulsars are missing, much as the multiple languages used at the WIPP location allow for cross-referencing of different languages like on the Rosetta stone.

The longest line that extends to the right represents the sun. Note how this line reaches toward the proximity of the human diagrams, helping to establish a line of trajectory to the creators of the spacecraft. To help ensure that aliens can find Pioneer 10's point of origin, Sagan also included a diagram of the solar system, noting the trajectory of the spacecraft from the third planet from the sun, Earth.

Of course, now that Pluto is no longer a "planet," one should hope that any aliens don't count from the outside of the solar system, otherwise they might deduce that the spacecraft was launched from Venus. Aliens, like many human cultures, might read from right to left instead of left to right, or they may try to read the plaque upside down. In addition, when the plaque first appeared publicly, *Scientific American* pointed out that the arrow-based symbol derives from arrows used for hunting and warfare. If an extraterrestrial audience never invented such tools, they would be unclear that the arrow represents direction and movement. Then again, all of this assumes that they categorize "planet" the same way humans do, or that they even reason with "categories" at all.

Finally, a diagram of human beings appears on the right side of the plaque. This diagram offers a nude perspective with most of the anatomical features of both a male and female. While many humans had negative reactions to depicting these figures in the nude, this choice probably makes sense to beings who might not use clothing (as seems to be the case with most Hollywood portrayals of aliens), and might be confusing if included in the design.

Sagan also designed the male to provide the typical gesture of a wave. Of course, Sagan had no idea how an alien race might interpret this gesture; they might find that it offers a sign of aggression. However, Sagan also wanted

Figure 6.15
The Pioneer 10 plaque was mounted so that it faced into the space probe.

to show that humans have limbs that can be articulated, as well as an opposable thumb. By contrasting the male's pose with the female's lack of pose, it's hoped that the aliens will deduce that the arms can bend, and that humans don't simply have one straight arm and one in a fixed, raised position. Behind the diagram of the humans is a line drawing of the Pioneer 10 spacecraft itself, drawn to scale to provide a way for aliens to determine the approximate size of Earthlings.

Although the last chapter covered environment, you might also think about the constraints between balancing environment with audience. As you can see in Figure 6.15, NASA decided to place the plaque facing toward the spacecraft. Given the amount of small space debris Pioneer 10 might encounter, this orientation helps protect the message from being destroyed. In addition, the material of the plaque was made of gold-anodized aluminum to minimize corrosion (since gold is inert and does not rust). Hopefully, the aliens that intercept the spacecraft will eventually remove the plaque and notice the image (even if they notice with senses other than sight). However, they might also miss it, or assume the piece of metal is blank on both sides.

MAKING CONNECTIONS

AS A CLASS

Discuss the Pioneer 10 plaque. In addition to some of the observations already made, what other information does it exclude about humans that might be useful? What other assumptions might an alien make that would be incorrect and cause potential communication problems should humans and aliens meet? How might the plaque be redesigned or displayed differently on the spacecraft itself?

IN A GROUP

Research later plaques that were designed for spacecraft launched after Pioneer 10, such as the Voyager, which contained a golden "record." How and why did NASA change the design? What modern ways of extraterrestrial communication are being used, if any? How have these designs and media changed? Which seem the most probable of being decoded by an alien race? Record your ideas and share them with the class.

ON YOUR OWN

Assume that you're an alien from another planet who just landed on Earth. As you explore, you find a dime on the surface of the planet. Since you have no pre-existing knowledge of the planet's cultures or languages, and thus can't decode the writing, what kind of information can you deduce from the other features of the dime? Create a list of possible meanings or assumptions about humans and share them with the class.

TRANSNATIONAL AUDIENCES

While you will probably never have to write for audiences that will exist 10,000 years from now, nor extra-terrestrials, you do have to consider the various ways in which audiences that do not share your language or culture might view your visual texts. Figure 6.16 demonstrates a simple failure to communicate with a *transnational audience*. This image provides visual instructions on how to remove fallen rocks from a railroad track for South American miners who could not read alphabetic text.

Credit: William Horton, *Technical Communication.* Copyright 1993 by Society for Technical Communication (STC).

Figure 6.16
While English speakers read this graphic from left to right, other cultures may read it from right to left.

At first glance, the image provides a pretty clear set of instructions: in frame one, the miner finds a rock; in frame two, the miner picks up the rock; in frame three, the miner carts the rock away. For the miners, the image also provides a pretty clear set of instructions: in frame one, cart a rock to the tracks; in frame two, set the rock on the tracks; in frame three, leave the rock on the tracks. As you've probably concluded, the South African miners read the image from right to left (as many cultures read), and thus for them the instructions meant the opposite of what they were intended to convey by the image's creator. A simple user test or conversation with some of the miners might have avoided this error, but the designer failed to properly screen his or her audience.

However, it's easy to screen for a single, local transnational audience. When you're McDonald's, and serve 68 million customers a day with restaurants in 119 countries, user testing and accounting for these various audiences can be more difficult. To make their nutritional information more globalized so that anyone could understand protein from carbohydrates, McDonald's attempted to create universal icons to represent each of these categories. The fast-food giant wanted to avoid any icons that might be ambiguous in meaning, especially meanings that might offend other cultures. To avoid these pitfalls, McDonald's teamed up with the marketing firm ENLASO to head the research. As Maxwell Hoffmann explains:

McDonald's and ENLASO focused on five main nutrient visuals (calories, fat, carbohydrates, protein, salt) that would be used globally on packaging, and also designed and evaluated half a dozen supplemental nutrient visuals that might be needed in some locales. The team had to deal with four main challenges:

1. What visuals can communicate the desired nutrients?

2. Does the visual work in 109 countries without evoking negative or socially/politically inappropriate connotations?

3. Will the visual print or display well in all media, including packaging?

4. Does anyone else already own rights to the image that might prevent it from being used in this context (22)?

For example, Figure 6.17 is one of the early icons that ENLASO tested. Take a moment and analyze the icon. What do you see? While McDonald's intended the image to represent grain or wheat, ENLASO ultimately classified it as an icon at high risk of being misinterpreted based on their market research. What did many respondents think it looked like?

Credit: Dell

Figure 6.17
This early nutritional icon referred to "fiber" was widely interpreted as being an "alien."

Figure 6.18
If you look at Dell's Alienware brand mark, you can see why many saw Figure 6.18 as an alien.

Figure 6.19
This early nutritional icon for "fiber" was widely interpreted as being a "bird."

Figure 6.20
This early nutritional icon for "fiber" was widely interpreted as being a "marijuana plant."

Figure 6.21
While you might think of a "bone" as referring to calcium, not all audiences understood it this way.

A "scary alien" of course, such as that in Figure 6.18, the brand mark used for Dell's Alienware line of computers. Other ambiguous icons were also rejected. Many thought Figure 6.19 looked like either a slippery slope or the neck and head of a bird, perhaps signifying a bird sanctuary, while some users thought Figure 6.20 resembled a marijuana plant.

Other icons also confused transnational audiences. Besides calories, protein, fat, carbohydrates, and salt, McDonald's attempted to create icons for other nutritional information such as calcium. Figure 6.21 depicts an original design of a bone, which makes sense when connected to calcium. However, some users thought of dog bones or dog food when looking at the icon, which also has potentially insulting meanings in some Muslim cultures. As discussed in chapter 4, all of these meanings are various connotations of the image, cultural meanings that extend beyond the denotative meanings in the icons. Even if a design looks innocent at first, it might be perceived by audiences from other nations and cultures as unclear, or even worse, insulting. Do your best to research the cultures you're writing for, and when possible, get feedback from members of those cultures to avoid any negative reactions.

MAKING CONNECTIONS

AS A CLASS

Look at various traffic signs used in other countries. How well do these signs match with U.S. traffic signs? How do they differ? How might you read these signs differently than their intended meaning? Could accidents result from these misreadings?

IN A GROUP

Create an icon for "candy" with transnational audiences in mind, similar to McDonald's attempts in the example above. After you've created the icon, research how different cultures think of candy: some might consider candy to mean all kinds of sweets, while others have specific ideas of what a "candy" is. Also consider other objects that your icon might resemble for these audiences. Once you've gathered this information, revise the icon to better reflect your research, and share both icons with the class.

ON YOUR OWN

Suppose you work for a design firm and you're hired to create a company brand mark for a fish and aquarium shop that is opening stores in both the United States and China. How would you screen your audience? What kinds of information would you gather to discern the differences between the two nations? Would you also have to consider cultural variance within each country as well? What kinds of design choices might you have to make so that each audience recognizes that the brand mark is for "pet" fish and not "food" fish. After you create the brand mark, how would you ensure that the audience responds to it in a desirable way? Compile a research plan of what you think you would need to consider and share this plan with the class.

AUDIENCE AS ACTORS: RHETORICAL VELOCITY

So far, this chapter has mainly considered how audiences use the texts that writers produce. In this sense, they become actors but usually as end-users. However, audiences can also become actors that serve your rhetorical purposes. Jim Ridolfo and Dànielle Nicole DeVoss have theorized such a practice they call "*rhetorical velocity*," through which a rhetor anticipates how her audience will make use of a particular text or document to further her own purposes.

For instance, Ridolfo and DeVoss offer the example of an author disseminating a press release. Rather than this press release being simply read, the author anticipates that the audience will remix and remediate it into other texts, such as online or print news articles, blogs, or video content, whether live or recorded. In this way, the original audience doesn't just consume media but reshapes and delivers this media to other audiences, who then may remix it again. The press release reaches a maximum velocity where as many people see it as possible, thanks to the actions of these audience-actors.

Credit: Comedy Central/Viacom Entertainment Group

AUG. 10, 2006

Figure 6.22
Stephen Colbert's Green Screen Challenge prompted audience participation that also produced content for the show.

You might say that comedian Stephen Colbert practices rhetorical velocity on his television show *The Colbert Report.* Occasionally, Colbert will offer a "Green Screen Challenge," in which he films himself doing something in front of a green screen (used for special effects), and then distributes the video footage on his website (Figure 6.22). He challenges his audience to take that video footage and edit and remix it to create something new. His audience, who become authors, uploads the new video to his site and he plays them on the air, providing content for his show.

The band the Decemberists mimic this idea by asking fans to create their own music videos of the band playing their song "O Valencia!" in front of a green screen. This request was noted

Credit: Comedy Central/Viacom Entertainment Group

Figure 6.23
Colbert would re-use his Green Screen Challenge to create a "feud" with the band the Decemberists.

by Colbert, who, in jest, accused the Decemberists of stealing his idea and challenged them to a guitar duel, further using the original green screen idea to create new material for the show (Figure 6.23). The "Green Screen Challenge" creates a more nuanced relationship between author and audience that turns the audience into actors and the author into the audience.

Viral videos also exhibit some characteristics of rhetorical velocity. In 2011, Volkswagen released a Super Bowl advertisement in which a child dressed as Darth Vader attempts to use the Force to move objects (Figure 6.24). This video quickly spread across the Internet, and as *Advertising Age* states, "With 600 placements, the video is on pace to become one of the most-watched viral ads of all time."

Credit: Volkswagen/Deutsch, Inc.

Figure 6.24
This Volkswagen commercial was widely shared.
http://www.youtube.com/watch?v=R55e-uHQna0

The next year, Volkswagen created a trailer for their actual Super Bowl advertisement, generating buzz for a commercial as movie companies do for their films. While such advertisements do not necessarily invite users to manipulate and repost their works of media, the companies who produce them are hoping that audiences will actively share the videos through YouTube, Facebook, and Twitter, spreading the commercials to a much wider audience.

Finally, Internet memes can also integrate users and make them into actors. Some companies have begun

Figure 6.25
Will it blend? This question has made it a popular meme.
http://www.youtube.com/watch?v=lAl28d6tbko

Credit: Stephen Cannon

Figure 6.26
Virgin Media used a pre-existing meme to sell its product.

to create their own memes that circulate online. For instance, the company Blendtec, which makes blenders, created a meme called "Will it Blend?" in which they attempt to blend a variety of objects (Figure 6.25). Other companies, such as Virgin Media, incorporate existing memes created by others as a way to tap into the recognition of the meme.

As Matthew Branson writes:

Virgin Media opted to use an existing meme for their marketing and advertising campaigns. Recently, "Success Kid," has been spotted on their advertisements and website (Figure 6.26). This adorable, fist-pumping boy is a variant of a meme born on Flickr in 2007.

Pros: Using "Success Kid", Virgin Media can tap into a new audience without alienating any of their other customers. If their users don't know about "Success Kid," they will simply see a cute mascot. If they do know about the meme, they could associate him with the brand and generate potentially risk-free traffic. Such a campaign requires significant research about your customers.

Cons: Without actively engaging in the meme's community and encouraging the growth of it, it could shorten the meme's lifespan and the source of free traffic. Eventually, the meme could lose popularity and leave Virgin Media looking for a new one.

Also, if the buzz behind the meme is not being properly tracked, things could take a turn for the worse if the meme were to change. Without seeing Virgin Media's results, it's impossible to tell whether or not this strategy will bring the company long-term success. It is still an interesting take on leveraging memes for marketing and paves the way for future campaigns.

In this case, the creator and subject of the photograph become actors in the design of an advertisement of which they are also a potential audience. But such strategies can backfire as well. Sometimes, an audience may take your content and then remix and redistribute it in a way that reflects negatively on you or your client/company. As Branson also explains:

FreeCreditReport.com's foray into the world of Internet memes came to an abrupt halt. In 2007, after being targeted by two major lawsuits, the company attempted to rebuild its brand by releasing online videos and commercials depicting people with poor credit being helped by its services.

Internet communities soon caught wind of the company's history, however, and began creating their own parody videos poking fun at the company's services (even the FTC joined in). These spread virally across the Internet, further damaging the brand. Since then, the company has had to refocus its efforts on other campaigns.

The moral of the story is that Internet memes can work both ways—for you or against you. It's very important to properly research any marketing campaign before starting it to minimize your chances of being labeled something you may not be able to hide from.

While any audience has the potential to take an active role in reshaping your intended message, new media make it easier to both manipulate and disseminate a pre-existing text. As Ridolfo and DeVoss point out, you should consider how an audience will become actors and engage with your texts toward both positive and negative results. Such considerations are rhetorical in nature, and require your attention before you deliver a text to the public sphere.

MAKING CONNECTIONS

AS A CLASS

Visit www.knowyourmeme.com, and analyze the various memes on the site. Why do you think these memes gather audience attention and participation? What features do they all share? How does each meme invite participation beyond simply viewing the clip?

IN A GROUP

Create your own idea for an Internet meme that you think would be widely emulated and shared online. What features from Prompt #1 would you include? How would you encourage audiences to extend your meme by copying its idea? If you have video editing software, enact your idea by creating the meme and posting it online. Share it with the class and get their feedback.

ON YOUR OWN

Consider your favorite Internet memes and viral videos. What do they have in common? Why do you consider them worth watching? Why do you think others watch them? Have you shared any of these mcmes or videos online with friends? Why or why not? Record your thoughts about these questions and share them with the rest of the class.

NONHUMAN AUDIENCES

You may think that your online audience consists of humans. Who else would be visiting your website or online documents? Those aliens mentioned earlier? Perhaps. More likely, though, your website is read by robots. Web traffic is driven by nonhuman audiences such as search engines and *web robots*.

These robots scour the Web looking for connections or associations between key words that search engine users enter, what kinds of search engine results they click on, and how such key words appear on other sites. Essentially, these robots try to make Web searches more useful so that when you search for something like "Internet memes" you get relevant content. However, these robots are using the Web more than humans do. As Peter Murray explains in his 2012 article:

51 Percent of Total Online Traffic Is Non-Human

It probably is no surprise to most that much of online traffic isn't human. Hacker software, spam, or innocuous data collection from search engines all get their slice of the bandwidth pie. But what might surprise you is exactly how much bandwidth is consumed by humans versus non-humans. It's pretty much an even split.

Actually, a slight lead goes to the non-human, web-surfing robots.

According to a report by Internet security company Incapsula, 51 percent of total online traffic is non-human. There's more bad news. Of the 51 percent, 20 percent of the traffic is accounted for by search engines, the other 31 percent are the bad bots.

Here's the breakdown:

- 49 percent human traffic, 51 percent non-human traffic

Non-human traffic:

- 5 percent hacking tools
- 5 percent "scrapers," software that posts the contents of your website to other websites, steals e-mail addresses for spamming, or reverse engineers your website's pricing and business models
- 2 percent comment spammers
- 19 percent other sorts of spies that are competitive analyzers, sifting your website for key word and SEO (search engine optimization) data to help give them a competitive edge in climbing the search engine ladder

■ 20 percent search engines and other benevolent bot traffic

The report was based on data compiled from 1,000 of Incapsula customer websites.

We always knew it was us against the machines. But until now the arms race had generally referred to virus versus anti-virus, malware versus anti-malware. Symantec wasn't warning us about the perils of non-human traffic. For web-based business owners though, that extra traffic can turn into lost business. Tagman recently reported that a delay of just one second in webpage load time decreases page views by 11 percent, customer satisfaction by 16 percent, and conversions—the number of people who buy something divided by the number of visits—by 6.7 percent. Incapsula says it's easy enough to get around the hacker, scraper, and spam software, but that most website owners aren't equipped to spot the infiltrators.

We already knew that robots did some amazing things, now we learn that they're doing things we're not even aware of—at least not the extent. They're not alive, yet they're surfing the web more than we are. So who will win in the end, human or machine? Better monitoring tools—for free—would help. You can't get rid of the critters if you don't know they're there in the first place.

This article portrays Web robots as living "critters" even though they are just bits of code. While these robots are not technically "alive," they do act. As an audience, these robots read what you include on a page, both that which a human audience typically sees as well as the HTML code underneath. As an actor, these audiences don't just "read" your sites but have agency, affecting and influencing the Web as much as any author who writes a blog post.

In relation to rhetorical velocity, you can make use of nonhuman audiences. You can use search engine robots, writing so that they index pages according to key words and help other audiences find your texts. For example, if you wanted to get search engine robots to index a site about apartments in your town, you would include key words in the HTML code such as "apartments," "rental units," "rental houses," or other terms that you think a human audience would enter.

While thinking about robots, you also have to screen your human audiences and how you think they'll search for your product or service. In addition, especially for this particular search, you should think about location. Since your apartments are probably in a fixed geographical area, you should include geographical key words within the site as well, such as the city in which the apartments are located, as well as the state (since many states have identical city names).

Such key words appear in several places. One of these locations is the <META> information within the header of a website (Figure 6.27). This information is specifically targeted at Web robots, and the human audience never sees it unless they right-click on a site and select "view source."

```
<meta name="robots" content="noodp, noydir" /><meta name="description" content="
Facebook is a social utility that connects people with friends and others who work,
study and live around them. People use Facebook to keep up with friends, upload an
unlimited number of photos, post links and videos, and learn more about the people they
meet." />
```

Figure 6.27
Nonhuman audiences, such as search engines, use metadata to index websites.

One of the other primary locations is within the page content itself, which is seen by both robots and humans. However, writing for each of these audiences requires a balance. Typically, the more times you include a key word such as "apartments" within a paragraph, the more a robot will think that the key word "apartment" is relevant to your page.

However, as you've probably learned from other writing classes, using the same word too many times in a sentence or paragraph does not meet most humans' stylistic preferences. While you might use synonyms to overcome this stylistic blunder, these synonyms can detract from how the web robot will view your page. Addressing both of these audiences is tricky, but you need to consider them simultaneously, for if the Web robot doesn't think your site is relevant to a particular key word, then you'll never reach your final human audience.

But in addition to simply posing as audiences, Web robots sometimes become actors that respond to writing. Andy Isaacson, writing for *The Atlantic*, discusses this phenomenon:

Are You Following a Bot?

One day last February, a Twitter user in California named Billy received a tweet from @JamesMTitus, identified in his profile as a "24 year old dude" from Christchurch, New Zealand, who had the avatar of a tabby cat. "If you could bring one character to life from your favorite book, who would it be?" @JamesMTitus asked. Billy tweeted back, "Jesus," to which @JamesMTitus replied: "honestly? no fracking way. ahahahhaa." Their exchange continued, and Billy began following @JamesMTitus. It probably never occurred to him that the Kiwi dude with an apparent love of cats was, in fact, a robot.

JamesMTitus was manufactured by cyber-security specialists in New Zealand participating in a two-week social-engineering experiment organized by the Web Ecology Project. Based in Boston, the group had conducted demographic analyses of Chatroulette and studies of Twitter networks during the recent

Middle East protests. It was now interested in a question of particular concern to social-media experts and marketers: Is it possible not only to infiltrate social networks, but also to influence them on a large scale?

The group invited three teams to program "social bots"—fake identities—that could mimic human conversation on Twitter, and then picked 500 real users on the social network, the core of whom shared a fondness for cats. The Kiwis armed JamesMTitus with a database of generic responses ("Oh, that's very interesting, tell me more about that") and designed it to systematically test parts of the network for what tweets generated the most responses, and then to talk to the most responsive people.

Can one person controlling an identity, or a group of identities, really shape social architecture? Actually, yes. The Web Ecology Project's analysis of 2009's post-election protests in Iran revealed that only a handful of people accounted for most of the Twitter activity there. The attempt to steer large social groups toward a particular behavior or cause has long been the province of lobbyists, whose "astro-turfing" seeks to camouflage their campaigns as genuine grassroots efforts, and company employees who pose on Internet message boards as unbiased consumers to tout their products. But social bots introduce a new scale: they run off a server at practically no cost, and can reach thousands of people. The details that people reveal about their lives, in freely searchable tweets and blogs, offer bots a trove of personal information to work with. "The data coming off social networks allows for more-targeted social 'hacks' than ever before," says Tim Hwang, the director emeritus of the Web Ecology Project. And these hacks use "not just your interests, but your behavior."

A week after Hwang's experiment ended, Anonymous, a notorious hacker group, penetrated the e-mail accounts of the cyber-security firm HBGary Federal and revealed a solicitation of bids by the United States Air Force in June 2010 for "Persona Management Software"—a program that would enable the government to create multiple fake identities that trawl social-networking sites to collect data on real people and then use that data to gain credibility and to circulate propaganda.

"We hadn't heard of anyone else doing this, but we assumed that it's got to be happening in a big way," says Hwang. His group has published the code for its experimental bots online, "to allow people to be aware of the problem and design countermeasures."

The Web Ecology Project has started a spin-off group, called Pacific Social, to plan future experiments in social networking, like creating "connection-building" bots that bring together pro-democracy activists in a particular country, or ones that promote healthy habits. "There's a lot of potential for a lot of evil here," admits Hwang. "But there's also a lot of potential for a lot of good."

Web robots can shape both social architecture and the cyber-infrastructure of the Internet. As you can tell from this article, much of the material that these robots read involves a user's personal information. These robots then use this information for or against the user. While you probably won't build your own bot, you can learn how to write toward this audience and manipulate them to your rhetorical advantage.

The practice of writing for these robots is called *search engine optimization* (SEO), briefly discussed in Chapter 1. Many complex practices of SEO exist and are constantly being invented, and no one knows the precise algorithms that search engine companies such as Google or Bing use to identify which sites get ranked higher than others. Although the audience is robotic and code-driven, writing for robots is a constantly shifting rhetorical situation, for search engine companies may change their algorithms at any time. If you don't think a computer-based algorithm can be both a significant audience and actor, consider the many online-dating sites that help match potential partners, or the TED talk by Kevin Slavin in Figure 6.28. Toward a practice of basic SEO, the guidelines below offer some information and techniques to help you write for your robot audiences.

Figure 6.28
Kevin Slavin explains how algorithms shape the world.
http://www.youtube.com/
watch?v=TDaFwnOiKVE

Understanding User Stats and Page Design

A search engine is a business. A search engine's product is search results. Google's goal, put simply, is to give you the website that gives you exactly what you're looking for in the top spot in the results. Google does not want spam in the results, nor does it want a harmful page in the results (such as one that might steal a user's identity or put a virus on their computer).

Search engine companies have spent millions of dollars trying to write programs that can understand the syntax of the key word terms that the user inputs. They want to know the user's goal—what the user is trying to achieve. If one puts "Nike" into Google, the search engine wants to know if you are looking for information, the Nike corporate website, product reviews, or websites that sell Nike products. The search engine categorizes many terms based on what it thinks the user is looking for and yields different types of results based on this estimation.

Search engines are in a constant state of evolution, tweaking their algorithms so that their top results are increasingly the correct result. You might say, then, that Google is performing a constant rhetorical adjustment. But how do they know if the correct result is displayed? They track and keep user statistics.

If searchers click on your link in the search engine results, go to your page, but decide it wasn't what they were looking for and bounce off the page (by hitting the back button), Google will count this against your page for that search term. Google has no way of knowing why the user bounced off: it could be because the page is not about the *key word* term, or that the user was looking for a page where she could buy something when your page is more informational, or because the page has really bad design. But when people bounce off, it counts against you. If lots of people bounce off (and the bounce rate is a higher percentage than those that stay at your site), your page will fall in the search rankings. Therefore, it's very important to establish that your Web page is about the subject, is well designed, and is designed for Web reading. Page design matters, for it creates a sense of *ethos* that makes users trust the site and stay once they find it.

Key Word Research

Researching a key word is perhaps the most important step in SEO, and the one that is probably the most neglected. If you do not properly research the search volume for your subject (how many times a key word is searched for over a certain period), you are bound to head off in the wrong direction. Before you begin optimizing, you need to determine which key word terms you are optimizing for. Here are some key points to consider:

- Never "guess" at what the popular key word phrase will be, or its search volume; often, users "dumb-down" the syntax they enter into search engines and use key word phrases that they would not use in their normal writing or speech. For instance, for someone searching for apartments in Gainesville, FL, where the University of Florida is located, the key word combination "gainesville apartments" gets more than four times as much search volume as "gainesville florida apartments," and twice as much as "apartments in gainesville" (even though you would probably use the term "apartments in Gainesville" in your everyday speech).

- You could probably come up with a list of more than 500 terms that people might use when searching for an apartment, but there is a short list of terms that will account for the majority of the search volume. These terms will be harder to compete for, but if you can come up high in the results, you will receive far more viewership. This is known as Long Tail SEO practice: there are hundreds of terms which, when aggregated, account for a large amount of traffic even though those key word terms individually get very low search volume.

- Since, at this point, you're probably not committed to an entire SEO campaign—which is highly competitive as hundreds of other pages on your subject are also vying for viewers' attention—you may be best served focusing on the long tail terms. This means that you will need to greatly vary your text within the actual visible content on the page to include as many of these terms as possible.

- In order to gain the most traffic, your link should appear "above the fold" in the first page of the search results for the term (the fold refers to the bottom of the monitor, so that users don't have to scroll down to see your link). Very few search users click to the second or third page of their search results; most don't even scroll down and click on the ninth or tenth result; it does you almost no good to come up fifteenth.

- A page that is optimized for the term "apartments in Gainesville" may not necessarily rank well for the term "Gainesville apartments." You'll have to optimize the page separately for each of the terms you are focusing on.

- As always, you will need to determine the target audience: laymen will use different key word terms than an expert—but there may be significantly less search volume for these technical terms.

Selecting Key Words

Once you have researched how people search—and what they typically search for—you can build your key word list.

- Begin by listing all of the related terms to your main key words. If you're writing an article on apartments, write down all of the words that relate to apartments. For example:

  apartments, apartment, housing, rental, home, dorm, flat, townhouse, loft, room, room for rent, one bedroom, pet friendly, apartment complex, for rent, rental, landlord, real estate, dorm, roommate, sublease, sublet

  If you're writing about a specific location, make a list of areas, states, counties, or cities that pertain to that area. Terms that are categories get the highest search volume; users generally start their search wide and narrow it down from there.

- There are lots of free tools that allow you to research search volume, such as Google Keyword Tool (https://adwords.google.com/select/KeywordToolExternal) or goRank (http://www.gorank.com/analyze.php). These sites will help you identify how dense key words appear on your page, as well as the key words that users input to search for a particular site. Find out the search volume for each of the terms and decide which terms you want to focus on in your first round of

SEO. For best results, you might focus on optimizing for the top ten terms first. If you're unsuccessful, go back and focus on the next most popular.

Links

Both incoming and outgoing *links* affect your page. Incoming links (links on other pages that point to your page) have a very big impact. Google seems to think of incoming links in a similar way to "votes" or "likes." The text of the actual link (known as anchor text) is critically important, as is the subject of the original page and how it ranks for a term.

Link building is one of the most important (and difficult to manage) factors in SEO. If you can find a page that is about your subject, which is listed in the Google search results and ranks well for the term, and you can get that page to link to your page, you will sometimes jump up in the search engine results. If and when you request a link, however, make sure you supply the owner of the other page with the exact text you want the link to read, using the key words that you determined from your earlier research.

Title Tags

If you "right click" on a Web page, and "view source," you can see the code that makes up the Web page. Near the top of this code, you'll find a variety of <meta> tags, including the *<title> tag* (Figure 6.29).

This information appears in the very top of the browser and is also looked at by Web robots. The <title> tag is one of the most important on-page SEO factors. Typically, you can include 70 characters within this tag—give or take—for the bigger search engines like Google. Search engines usually ignore characters beyond this amount. To reach this nonhuman audience, you should place important key words at the beginning of the tag.

Include both specific and categorical terms in this tag, and think wisely about how you include these terms since their placement affects both the ranking on search engines by Web robots and actual click through by human audiences. Remember that in most cases, the <title> tag is one of the biggest factors affecting your Web page's ranking, and for your human reader it's also the bold, blue underlined text in the search engine results pages. This tag not only optimizes the page for a robot audience, but must also encourage an actual click by the human hand. In other words, a good <title> tag has to not only be written for a good ranking, but also for humans.

As has been expressed above, this is the real problem of SEO—you are writing for two completely different audiences, which have very different needs. If you are writing about a company, you need your category term and the company name. All words used in the <title> tag must be used in the content of the page as well. For example: when optimizing for a company like Coca-Cola, you should include the top volume search term for your subject (such as soft drink, soda pop, etc.) and the company's name (Coca-Cola). You should also

```
<TITLE>Sean Morey, Sean W. Morey, Rhetoric and Composition, New Media, Electracy</TITLE>
```

Figure 6.29
The <TITLE> tag tells a search engine robot what a Web page is about.

include a message to the user, who will read the <title> tag and think that the page is helpful and therefore click on it. For instance: "soft drink | Enjoy the taste of Coca-Cola Classic, Diet Coke, and Coke Zero | The Coca-Cola Company."

File Names

Just as you name your word documents, you typically also name your individual Web pages. While the most common "home" page for a website is "index.html," your other pages may be named with descriptors such as "contact.html" or "aboutus.html." How you name these pages affects how these pages become indexed by Web robots, and you should use names that are relevant to both robot and human audiences. For example, a *file name* such as 0939201.html is pretty much meaningless to both humans and robots, while a file name titled "videoresume.html" conveys more information to both audiences.

Header Tags

Often, you will organize your Web pages with headers, just as you organize other kinds of documents such as letters, memos, reports, and various technical writing genres. On Web pages, you code these headers using *header tags*, which are often written as <h1>, <h2>, <h3>, etc.

These header tags should be used like subtitles within the content of the page, and should be followed by paragraphs of visible text that use the same key words as in the headers.

For instance, in the earlier example of a website about apartments, the title might be "How to Find the Best Gainesville Apartments." The headers might then be: "Cheap Apartments in Gainesville"; "Finding a Roommate in Gainesville"; and "How to Apply for Gainesville Apartments." Each of these header tags use key words that also appear in the title, and these key words should be repeated in the paragraph that follows each header. Don't repeat header tags (use only one <h1>, <h2>, <h3>, etc.), and the <h1> tag usually carries the most weight with Web robots. Header tags should be stylized so that they look like headers for the human reader: use a larger, bold font.

Include Key Words in the Main Text

When composing the text that the human user will read, you can insert key words into specific sentences in order to best write for Web robots.

- Use the top key word term (the one you chose for use in your title) in the first sentence of the first paragraph.

- Use that same key word term several times throughout the rest of the text (but no more than 1.5-2% of the text should be one single key word phrase). SEO experts often discuss finding the sweet spot in terms of key word density, so don't overdo it. Typically, you want between 2% and 7% of your text to be made up of all of the key word terms you researched earlier.

- Use variations of the key word term within the text: Gainesville apartments, apartments in Gainesville, Gainesville housing rentals. Not only does this replicate your key words for a robot audience, but it also creates stylistic variability for the human audience.

- Proximity matters. If you include the sentence "Gainesville apartments for rent are cheaper than you might think," Google will see the proximity of "cheap" to "Gainesville apartments"; the closer the words are together, the more likely you are to rank well for any given terms.

- Include key words at the beginning of a sentence.

- Bolding, italicizing, or underlining a key word may increase results.

- Write for a general human audience. Google and other search engines seem to like simple sentence structure.

Tag Multimedia with Key Words

Images, video, and other kinds of multimedia often include an <alt> or <image title> tag within their code. You should include the key word terms in these tags for any multimedia that you embed in the page content. These tags not only help Web robots index the page, but they also help screen-reader software identify the content of the multimedia for blind users who must rely on textual descriptions to understand what the visual content is about.

Make it Original

For each separate page on your website, make sure that each one includes original content. Google does not favorably rank websites that have two or three pages with the same information. If you're including a new page on the site, make sure it's unique.

Revise

Just like any kind of writing, you should revise how you code your page for SEO as you develop new incoming links, new content, and gain new information about how people search for your site. If you don't rank high for your targeted search terms, keep changing your approach. Remember, however, that it takes time for Web robots to reach your site and return, so several weeks may pass before you notice results.

MAKING CONNECTIONS

AS A CLASS

Look at the "page source" of a variety of websites. Compare how these sites use (or don't use) the SEO techniques mentioned above. Do they make good use of the <title> tag? Do they include key words in the page's main text? Do they include key words in the <alt> tags for images? Analyze the Web pages for these features and assess how well each page writes for search engine robots.

IN A GROUP

Besides search engine robots, many other kinds of bots scour the Internet. Create a list of as many different kinds of Web robots as you can find. Include what these robots do and whether they're considered helpful or harmful. Compose your list as a chart and share your findings with the class.

ON YOUR OWN

Select a website not discussed in the "as a class" prompt above. Engaging in the same analysis, write an SEO report on the site, noting what the site does well to write for nonhuman audiences, as well as what they do poorly. Offer suggestions on how they might improve this aspect of their site. After you've composed the report, share your findings with the class.

KEY TERMS

screening	rhetorical velocity	link
casting	Web robots	title tag
future audience	search engine optimization	file name
transnational audience	key word	header tag

OUTPUT: VIDEO RÉSUMÉ

For this output, you'll create a video résumé, a visual version of your résumé that allows you to make different kinds of persuasive appeals that you can't in a printed résumé.

If you've watched the television show *How I Met Your Mother*, or if you are familiar with the show's character Barney Stinson (played by Neil Patrick Harris), then you might have seen his "Awesome Video Résumé" (Figure 6.30):

Although a humorous example, Stinson's video is able to convey many qualities that one cannot communicate in a typical print-based résumé, such as making an emotional connection with the viewer. Moreover, he can demonstrate some of the qualities he proclaims, such as attention to detail through the details of the shots.

This example shows how attention-grabbing a video résumé can be, which is especially needed when trying to stand out in a stack of other applicants. While video résumés don't completely replace traditional résumés, they do offer a valuable supplement and can be vital when applying to jobs that require demonstration of new media skills. A video résumé can demonstrate your portfolio of work in a condensed, visual, and efficient way.

Credit: 20th Century Fox Television

BARNEY STINSON'S VIDEO RESUME
¡Click here to view

Sponsored by

GOLIATH NATIONAL BANK

Figure 6.30
Barney Stinson has a very imaginative video résumé.
http://www.barneysvideoresume.com/

Since you can compose a video résumé in many ways, the following guidelines offer some basic strategies and techniques rather than a strict how-to guide. Also, a simple YouTube search for "video résumé" will produce many examples on which you might model your own.

Like the actors mentioned above, a résumé "acts" on your behalf, letting the potential employer see certain aspects of you. Carefully consider what kind of "character" you want them to see as you craft the video.

Also, remember to read the rhetorical situation through the rhetorical tetrahedron. What kind of audience does a video résumé address? What is its message? How should you design it? How can you effectively use *logos, ethos, pathos,* and *kairos*? Keep these questions in mind as you read through the following guidelines.

Start with a Traditional Résumé

Although you're creating a video résumé, just like any video production, a written script will greatly help. This is where your traditional résumé comes in. If you don't have one already, create a list of the following:

- education history
- work experience
- activities you performed for each job
- skills (such as computer skills, foreign language fluency)
- awards
- other qualifications (such as certificates or licenses)

This list will help you develop your overall narrative for the video even though you might not use every item on the list.

Determine Your Audience

Like any document, determine your audience. Are you targeting a specific company? A specific industry? Once you know who you're applying to work for, research the company and determine how your experience and skills match up with what it's looking for. You can also study its website materials to determine smaller details, such as how to dress on camera (are they formal or casual?). After sketching the audience and determining what details from your résumé they're most likely to find appealing, you can start developing a more complete script.

Tell the Story of Your Résumé

You should incorporate some of the résumé items into your video résumé based on this audience, but unlike your résumé, which is essentially just a list of accomplishments, your video résumé should be an argument. In the video, you should have a pitch, a claim for why they should hire you, with your accomplishments and skills as reasons and evidence for that claim. Do not simply recite your traditional résumé, but tell a story about the items on your résumé. However, just like your traditional résumé (and like Barney), start with your name, ideally both spoken by you, and superimposed in text—this way they both hear it *and* see it.

Incorporate Aesthetic Elements

Since you're not simply reading your résumé but performing it, incorporate graphics, music, and other elements to create an overall atmosphere. While you don't need fighter jets soaring through the sky to create a metaphor for how awesome you are, you can use other images that might convey positive associations. Just make sure they're tasteful, and not tacky. If you're unsure, ask a friend.

Make Your Résumé Relevant

As mentioned above, a video résumé should not be used for just any kind of job. For example, you probably wouldn't submit a video résumé for a technical editing job. Instead, save the video résumé for jobs where showing off your personality would be beneficial (such as sales jobs), or for jobs where you need to show off visual production skills, such as a graphic designer or video editor.

Be Bold and Creative

While you don't need to be as creative as Barney—who uses Hollywood effects, stunts, and other unrealistic techniques—you can still think of creative ways to tell your story. For example, consider the video résumé by Matthew Epstein (Figure 6.31):

Credit: Matthew Epstein

Although Epstein didn't land the job with Google, he did get hired by another company doing his dream job. And although Epstein is bold in his approach, he nicely integrates his skillset and knowledge of the company into his dialogue, showing how he would perfectly fit with the Google team. While you don't

Figure 6.31
Matthew Epstein eventually landed his dream job with this video résumé.
http://www.youtube.com/watch?v=HRHFEDyHIsc

necessarily need to create this level of performance, you can still create an interesting narrative for how you tell a company about what you do, and what you can do for it. In addition, by marketing himself, Epstein is showing his marketing skills and not just talking about them.

Stay Professional

Although you want to develop a creative idea, make sure that you still demonstrate professionalism, that you would be an invaluable employee who would work hard and infuse talent into their company. For example, unlike

Epstein, you probably shouldn't appear in your video résumé without pants. And unless you're making a specific point by wearing a Batman costume, you should probably stick to more traditional clothing. Of course, the research you do about the company can tell you if they have a culture of three-piece suits or deck shoes and khakis. So unless it conflicts with a particular effect or rhetorical move, keep your speech, clothing, and general appearance as professional as is appropriate.

Keep it Brief

Keep your video short (unless it's particularly engaging, such as Epstein's), usually around a minute but no more than two. Most viewers of online videos don't like to watch more than one to three minutes at a time, and as you've probably noticed, most résumés are only a page long.

Rehearse

Don't assume you'll be able to complete your video résumé in one take. Performing in front of a camera can be a strange experience, even when there is no one else in the room watching. Practice your story and script in front of the camera, and watch these early attempts to improve your enunciation, posture, gestures, and other body movements. Also, practice adding stress to important words and delivering the script naturally, not as if you're reading from a page.

Prepare the Recording Environment

Make sure that the environment where you're shooting the video résumé is ideal. Check the lighting in the room, listen for ambient sound or outside noises that the microphone might pick up, and try to alter the surroundings until you eliminate these unwanted elements.

Deliver Well

After you've watched your rehearsal videos, refine your delivery. Try to act casual, and remember not to look or sound like you're simply reading the script. However, you can place your script below the camera to use as a guide but not to read from. If you're recording from a webcam, you can potentially leave your script on-screen. When you close the video, repeat your name, thank the audience for watching, and leave them with a smile.

Review

Like the other video assignments in this book, you should have other eyes look at the video and give you feedback. Consider their suggestions, and add them to your revision list. Technically, check the video's sound and image quality and listen for unwanted noises. Finally, note the segments you might cut out and what parts you need to reshoot because of poor delivery or other accidents.

Edit and Revise

Once you've reviewed the video and reshot any necessary video, use the techniques in Chapter 4 to edit the video into a final cut, incorporating any images, title sequences, or other effects you want to include.

Distribute

Although you can distribute your video résumé widely, you might want to be more selective in where you post a professional résumé. For instance, should you place it on YouTube, it may remain there forever, and old video résumés will show only past experience when you may have had several other jobs since. Instead, some job-finding websites such as CareerBuilder have options to upload a video résumé, or you could host it on a separate server and send employers the direct URL. YouTube can always be a backup option, but it might not be the best one. Also, like Epstein's résumé, include a link to your traditional résumé either embedded in the video, or in hypertext directly below it. This way, they can find out more about you should they be interested.

7

PREPRODUCTION (RESEARCH)

As with any writing project, composing in new media requires significant *research* to ensure that your document has the best chance of reaching your desired audience with your intended message. While you've probably conducted research when writing papers in previous composition classes, other kinds of research are often necessary when composing a text in new media.

Since you reviewed many research topics in Chapter 3 (such as purpose, audience, and context), this chapter will explain the research practices you'll need to consider in the pre-production phase of your writing that are more specific to visual-based productions. This research includes investigating the history of a particular visual element you might want to include in a design, finding images through search engines, or researching the copyright owners of a piece of media you want to integrate into a visual project. This chapter will cover some basics for you to consider before fully launching into design and production.

 When conducting research, make sure you go back to the rhetorical tetrahedron. As already discussed, you'll need to research your audience, but you'll also need to research when design, genre, and medium will best suit your particular project. For instance, if you're designing a fish identification card for fishing, you might research which kinds of paper are best for waterproof printing. Keep the tetrahedron at the forefront of the pre-production process.

FILM RESEARCH

As an example of the kinds of research you might have to conduct, consider how much research goes into a feature film. One has to screen the locations for where a movie will be shot, as discussed in Chapter 5. One also has to screen the actors that will be cast in the film, as discussed in Chapter 6. However, before each of these selections can occur, the location scout, casting director, and other key personnel must have researched what they're looking for before performing each of these tasks. That is, the location scout must research the kinds of places in which the film takes place so that the landscape best matches what the screenwriter and director have in mind. Likewise, the casting director should research the traits of the characters for which she'll cast so that she knows what physical features to look for in the actors who audition for roles.

Once cast, the actors themselves have much research to do before they ever visit the set, have their makeup and hair done, or stand in front of a camera. For instance, if their role is based on a historical character, the actor will most likely want to research the biography of the person, learn about their traits, habits, patterns, friends, family, pets, and any other information that's available. If the character is a living person, the actor may want to talk to the person.

Some actors go to extreme lengths when researching their roles. For the film *Cadillac Records* (2008), Beyoncé Knowles entered a rehab facility with recovering heroin addicts to research her role playing Etta James, an American blues and R&B singer (Figure 7.1).

Credit: ©Sony BMG Feature Films/
Courtesy Everett Collection

Figure 7.1
Beyoncé entered rehab to learn more about her role as Etta James.

Because Knowles had never experimented with drugs, she found the role challenging as James was addicted to heroin at the age of 21. In order to learn more about the struggles and characteristics of heroin addicts, Knowles felt she needed to conduct research in person to faithfully portray James. Such research isn't easy but necessary. As Knowles relates, "I never tried drugs in my life so I didn't know about it all…It was hard to go to the rehab. I learned a lot about life and myself."

Some actors go to even more extreme lengths to research and prepare for their roles. Jim Carrey used the technique of method acting when preparing for the role of Andy Kaufman in *Man on the Moon* (1999). During this production, Carrey (Figure 7.2) attempted to "live" as Kaufman, making everyone refer to him as Kaufman and not Carrey, and even surrounding himself with the same possessions that Kaufman owned.

Credit: ©Universal/Courtesy Everett Collection

Figure 7.2
Jim Carrey as Andy Kaufman.

Credit: ©Walt Disney Pictures/Courtesy Everett Collection

Figure 7.3
Johnny Depp as the Mad Hatter.

Johnny Depp, who has delivered some of the more bizarre and memorable performances in recent cinema, often thoroughly researches his roles and uses this research to create his own take on traditional, and not-so-traditional, characters. In describing Depp's preparation to play the Mad Hatter (Figure 7.3) in Tim Burton's *Alice in Wonderland*—part of which involves literally painting the character—Rachel Abramowltz writes:

Johnny Depp Explains How He Picked his Poison with the Mad Hatter

When he takes on a role, Johnny Depp often paints a watercolor portrait of the still-forming character to help find his face and personality. After putting the finishing touches on his painting for "Alice in Wonderland," Depp looked down at the Mad Hatter staring back at him from the canvas and giggled.

"I was thinking," the actor said, "'Oh my God, this one will get me fired!'"

Depp's extreme vision for the character…creates yet another vivid screen persona for the Hollywood chameleon who has played Sweeney Todd, Willie Wonka, Edward Scissorhands and a certain scoundrel named Jack Sparrow. The 46-year-old actor said his Hatter's springy mass of tangerine hair became a particularly important detail because of one of the suspected origins of the term "Mad as a hatter."

In the 18th and 19th centuries, mercury was used in the manufacture of felt, and when used in hats it could be absorbed through the skin and affect the mind through maladies such as Korsakoff's syndrome. Hatters and mill workers often fell victim to mercury poisoning which, in Carroll's time, had an orange tint—hence Depp's interest in adding brush strokes of that particular watercolor to his portrait.

"I think [the Mad Hatter] was poisoned—very, very poisoned," Depp said. "And I think it just took affect in all his nerves. It was coming out through his hair and through his fingernails, through his eyes."

Depp's research also took him down some unexpected literary rabbit holes with the writings of Carroll.

"There's a great line in the book where the Hatter says, 'I'm investigating things that begin with the letter 'M,'" Depp said. "So I started kind of doing a little researching, reading a bunch. And you start thinking about the letter 'M' and Hatters and the term 'Mad as a hatter' and 'mercury.'"

Depp was also intrigued by one of the Mad Hatter's nonsense questions during a dizzying tea party: "Why is a raven like a writing desk?" "I think he is referencing Edgar Allan Poe," Depp said, referring to the haunted author of "The Raven," which was published in 1845, two decades before Carroll's surreal tale reached the public. Depp let the two ideas germinate in his head and it informed his own Hatter concoction.

Burton, whose background in art and animation is well known, also draws his characters, and when he and his star compared their handiwork they grinned like the Cheshire Cat. "They were," Depp says, "very close."

As you can see, Depp's research is multifaceted, looking into the historical, literary, psychological, and physical aspects of his character-to-be. Depp looks into the historical instances of "mad hatter disease" brought about by mercury poisoning, a chemical used in the production of hats during the time Lewis Carroll wrote *Alice in Wonderland*. Such information influences how Depp paints his character's picture—such as the red hair and nails—and thus affects the choices of others involved in the production, such as hair and makeup artists.

Credit: Oskar Gustav Rejlander/

Figure 7.4
Mad Hatter disease was a problem in Carroll's time.

Depp now has psychological (and physiological) motivation for why the Mad Hatter should be mad and can inhabit his character more convincingly. Finally, Depp researched the work on which the movie is based rather than just relying on the script. Carroll's text offers him insights into the Mad Hatter that the screenwriter might not have included, and these bits of information help Depp deliver a performance that is both faithful and unique.

This research is not only multilayered and multifaceted, but also collaborative. As already discussed, others besides the actors are researching on their own, such as the casting directors who perform their own research on the Mad Hatter. And as Depp's final statement illustrates—that his and director Tim Burton's paintings of the Mad Hatter were "very close" (Figure 7.6)—this collaborative research eventually synthesizes into a shared vision of what the final project should look like.

Credit: Tom Friedel

Figure 7.5
Mercury poisoning is still an issue today, just not through the hatting industry.

Image courtesy of The Art Of Tim Burton. www. timburton.com

Figure 7.6
Tim Burton's painting of the Mad Hatter.

This synthesis is not unlike writing a research paper, where all of the different sources used to make an argument should be arranged and integrated so that they support the one voice of the author, rather than reading like disparate, unconnected statements. A large production requires all the actors and agents to research their own parts, distribute the work across the cast and crew, and leaving it up to the director to make sure all the research distills into a coherent vision.

If the different elements in your own compositions become actors that you have to screen before casting, then you will need to sufficiently research each of their roles before including them in your text (and unfortunately, such elements can't research themselves). However, part of casting actors involves looking at their prior work—what other roles they've performed—to help determine their suitability for a new role. Many images, techniques, genres, and other visual elements have their own history of roles that can help you determine how well they might fit.

Finally, *how much* research and *what kind* of research needs to be done depends on the type of film. Since *Alice in Wonderland* is based on a literary work, the cast and crew should read the work, research its creation, and perhaps research the author. They should also research the context in which the book was written, as Depp did, noting the historical moment and connections that influence the book and thus the film.

If the film is about the Civil War, then the producer, director, and actors have historical information to research, such as aspects of living and fighting in the Civil War, weapons of the time, meanings of colloquial vocabulary, or perhaps riding a horse.

Credit: George Pantalos

Figure 7.7
To research and prepare to play NASA astronauts, Tom Hanks and Kevin Bacon flew aboard a KC-135 "vomit comet." This aircraft can simulate zero gravity for up to 24 seconds.

If the movie takes place in outer space, then the production crew should research the environment of space, how features such as zero gravity or lack of atmosphere affect the way that physical actions might occur, as well as the psychological effects of living in space. This kind of environmental research must be done in addition to the other creative aspects that affect plot line and character development. Research becomes the most important part of making a successful film, and this occurs before the director ever shouts "action."

MAKING CONNECTIONS

AS A CLASS

Develop an idea for a movie. Once you have the basic concept, divide into groups and decide which group will represent a specific area of production, such as actors, set designers, makeup artists, location scouts, or casting directors. Within these smaller groups, create a list of research goals necessary to understand the job that needs to be done (acting, designing sets, creating makeup effects, etc.), and create a list of specific topics and sources you might use to find important information related to such research. After each group finishes, come together as a class and discuss what kinds of research need to be done in order to complete the film. After discussing everyone's lists and ideas, discuss how the research can be conducted more efficiently to produce a coherent whole. Can such research be done independently, or is it more helpful if the groups collaborate during the entire research process? What insights did you glean from researching for this kind of visual text?

IN A GROUP

Find examples of other actors who go to extreme lengths when researching their roles. What kinds of research do they perform? How do they research? How do they feel such research affects their performance? Do you think such research is necessary, or overkill? Why? Present your findings to the class, and if possible, show a clip of the role for which the actor prepared.

ON YOUR OWN

Think of you favorite film. What kinds of research do you think the cast and crew needed to do in order to create the film? Did they have to perform historical research? Environmental research? Literary research? Scientific research? Did they have to research similar movies that came before and thus influenced the new production (as when a movie is re-made)? Create a list of research you think was necessary, and share it with the class.

RESEARCHING ELEMENTS

When considering elements to incorporate into your own projects, research each of the categories below to determine how the element fits and how it will affect the overall message you're attempting to convey. You should pay attention to the reasons why you make certain choices in your texts, and researching the elements you use is a major step in understanding why you might compose a text in a certain way.

Subject

If you're incorporating another visual into your own design, you should know what it's about—its subject. Without this knowledge, you might include an image that has meanings contrary to your purpose, which may cause problems. While it's unlikely that you would include a swastika in your design—since you're already familiar with some of its history and understand the negative reactions such an image would produce—other visuals have their own histories that can affect how an audience understands and interprets the work in which you include them.

Credit: Eddie Adams/Associated Press

Figure 7.8
Adams's photo alone doesn't tell the whole story.

For example, Figure 7.8 depicts a photograph taken by Eddie Adams depicting General Nguyen Ngoc Loan, South Vietnam's national police chief, executing a Viet Cong captain, Nguyen Van Lem. This image would become one of the most iconic photos of the Vietnam War. However, the subject of the image is often misinterpreted by many who see it.

The photograph depicts Loan just as he is about to pull the trigger of his gun, executing Lem. The image—and the video of the act, which was also shown on U.S. nightly news programs—helped to change U.S. sentiment against the war and spur the antiwar movement.

Opponents of the war claimed the image depicted the brutality of the U.S. allies in Vietnam. From their perspective, Loan played the villain, killing the victimized, unarmed Lem who was captive and helpless. However, this interpretation does not tell the whole story, and research into the larger subject and context needs to be examined.

Prior to the photograph's creation, the Vietcong launched a military campaign—the Tet Offensive—which included death squads that targeted South Vietnamese National Police officers and their relatives. Lem, who led one of the death squads, was captured near the site of a mass grave containing thirty-four bodies and their relatives, six of whom were Loan's godchildren. South Vietnamese sources confirmed Lem's role in the killings, and Loan summarily executed him for his crimes, using his personal sidearm. While this knowledge perhaps doesn't excuse Loan's actions, it does put them in a greater perspective.

When originally running the story and photograph, the *New York Times* also included a photo of an infant killed by the Vietcong juxtaposed next to Adams's photograph of Loan. However, Adams's image alone became remixed into other media forms and circulated without this balance, causing a more skewed perspective and damage to Loan's reputation.

Adams later lamented that his audience did not interpret Loan's actions as heroic, the way that he viewed them: "The general killed the Viet Cong; I killed the general with my camera. Still photographs are the most powerful weapon in the world. People believe them; but photographs do lie, even without manipulation. They are only half-truths…What the photograph didn't say was, 'What would you do if you were the general at that time and place on that hot day, and you caught the so-called bad guy after he blew away one, two or three American people?"

An ethical use of images, or even an ethical interpretation of images, asks you to research what's really going on before jumping to conclusions or before leading your audiences to particular assumptions. Of course, leading the audience toward a particular outcome is the purpose of rhetoric. However, conducting thorough research before selecting various elements for your own work can help you argue in a more ethical and honest way.

Purpose

When using another's image in your own project, it's helpful to know the author's original purpose in creating it. As already discussed, Ramesses's main purposes for creating images included propaganda. If you were to include photographs of his carvings within your own text, others might think you're trying to distribute propaganda yourself. Then again, they might just think you're using a dead pharaoh's wall carvings. However, such knowledge of Ramesses's work as propaganda might influence how others see your work as a whole.

What does including past propaganda say about the overall message you're creating? This inclusion might have negative repercussions, but they may also have positive effects if your work somehow reflects or criticizes the nature of propaganda. While another writer's purpose might not reflect your own, it can help you think about the message you're creating, provide insight, and help you think more critically about how you remix such images within your works.

Audience

Another image property to research is the original audience. Was the image meant for a pharaoh's slaves? Did a press photographer take the image to disseminate it to the general public? Or, did a famous celebrity take photos for personal reasons—intending no other audience than immediate family—that then became leaked or stolen? Or, did the celebrity hope that "private" images became public as a way to get him or herself into the news?

Like purpose, the original audience of a particular image may not align with your target audience, but knowing who this image was intended for can help you understand the new image ecology you might be creating. Learning such details about audience can also help you place the image within its original historical context, and perhaps help you discover other details that inform how you might use the image in your design.

Influence

Many images are influenced by previous images, and, in turn, influence subsequent images. The famous image of Barack Obama by artist Shepard Fairey (Figure 7.9) was influenced by a photograph taken by Mannie Garcia, an Associated Press photographer (Figure 7.10). Subsequent to Fairey's image, many others have incorporated his technique to produce their own portraits, including a website that allows you to create your own "Obama" version of an image. Fairey was taken to court for using this photo without permission, although Fairey claimed that his new, artistic interpretation constituted fair use. However, this argument doesn't help Fairey's *ethos* when he denies others the right to use his own artwork depicting Obama.

Credit: Shepard Fairey

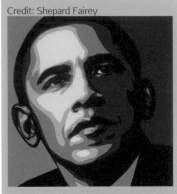

Figure 7.9
Shepard Fairey was influenced by
Mannie Garcia's photograph.

Credit: AP/Mannie Garcia

Figure 7.10
Mannie Garcia snapped the photo on which
Fairey based his work.

In his short documentary *Everything Is a Remix*, Kirby Ferguson notes that many of Hollywood's movies depend on previously made movies and other materials:

> *"Perhaps it's because movies are so massively expensive to make; perhaps it's because graphic novels, TV shows, video games, books, and the like are such rich sources of material; or perhaps it's because audiences just prefer the familiar: whatever the reason, most box office hits rely heavily on existing material."*

Figure 7.11
Kirby Ferguson explains that
"everything" is a remix.
http://www.youtube.com/watch?v=Z-HuenDPZw0

Credit: Hiroyuki Obara

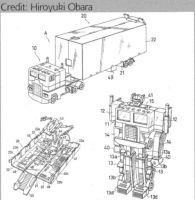

Figure 7.12
Transformers were toys before cartoons
or movies.

The movie *Pirates of the Caribbean* was based on Disney World's theme park, which further spawned three sequels. While you might generally think that toys based on television shows or movies come after their release, the movie

Transformers (Figure 7.12), which now has multiple sequels, originally came from a cartoon created to help sell toys already on shelves at the time.

Some of the biggest box office hits are influenced by other films. As Ferguson points out, George Lucas relied heavily on other films when creating *Star Wars*. Such influences included: Joseph Campbell's analysis of myth and the classic hero's story; *Flash Gordon*; Japanese director Akira Kurosawa; war films; westerns; and other science fiction films. As Ferguson concludes:

> *"George Lucas collected materials, he combined them, he transformed them. Without the films that preceded it, there could be no* Star *Wars. Creation requires influence. Everything we make is a remix of existing creations."*

Lucas's originality comes not from the individual pieces of his film but how he assembles them into a unique whole. While your own work will necessarily be influenced by other works, the overall design you create should have a uniqueness of its own.

From a research perspective, knowing how works were influenced and how they influenced other works can help you to understand more about how a particular visual was created and help you better create your own. For instance, the above knowledge about *Star Wars* helps you understand where different elements in the movie come from as well as their history and lineage. This research can provide ideas for source materials for your own works. If you were making a movie and wanted to incorporate a sword-fighting scene, you might turn to Kurosawa or Lucas's works and use samurai or Jedi duels as templates. If you were telling a story about zombies, you would research other zombie-related materials. If you were creating a political poster, like Fairey, you might look at past political posters, research their influences, and research the subsequent posters they influenced as well.

Credit: The Everett Collection

Figure 7.13
If you were researching Zombie films, you should probably check out George Romero's *Night of the Living Dead*, one of the earliest zombie films.

Details

While it's important to understand the main subject of an image—as the discussion of Adams's photograph illustrates—sometimes the details are just as important. When you analyze any type of visual, you should pay attention

Credit: City of Chicago's Clerk's Office

Chicago's Heroes

Figure 7.14
The details in Pulgar's design were upsetting to some.

to the details included within the whole and ask questions about why the writer included specific elements, where those elements come from, and what connotations they bring. Failing to research the particulars can create unforeseen problems if you incorporate such details without adequate investigation.

In 2011, the city of Chicago held its annual contest in which high school students had the opportunity to design the city parking decal, a decal affixed to all automobile windshields of Chicago residents. The winning decal (Figure 7.14), designed by Chicago teen, Herbie Pulgar, depicts a heart-enclosed skyline of Chicago along with various hands throwing up hats as symbols for "Chicago's Heroes": the police, firefighters, and emergency medical personnel that help keep the city safe. While the overall subject seems clear—celebrating local heroes—other elements may be interpreted in other ways. And they were, causing the city to reject using the decal even though Pulgar won the contest. As David Schaper explains the controversy:

Gang Signs And A Sticker: Chicago Pulls Teen's Design

"When you first look at the design, it's a beautiful design. It's recognizing Chicago's heroes," says former Chicago Police Superintendent Jody Weis.

But look a little more closely, and Weis sees something troubling.

"You've got the hands . . . configured in such a way that are very similar to a particular gang's hand sign. So that's one part," Weis says. "If you look a little bit back—imagine yourself 10 feet away from this—you've got a couple of hands in a position that could be viewed as horns. That's another symbol of this particular gang."

The gang in question is the Maniac Latin Disciples, and Weis, now president of the Chicago Crime Commission, says even the large heart that forms the artwork's centerpiece is a main symbol of that gang.

"When you add the heart symbol, you add the hand signs, you add the hand placements—you can see where there might be a perception that this could be in some way reflecting on a particular gang."

Weis and others also point out that Pulgar's Facebook page—since taken down—had several gang-related photographs and comments.

But Pulgar, a freshman at a high school for children with emotional and learning disabilities, insists he is not in any gang and did not try to sneak gang symbols into his vehicle sticker design.

"Our design doesn't have nothing to do with no gangs. Nothing," Pulgar tearfully told Chicago's WGN-TV. "It don't have nothing to do with no gangs, no violence, no nothing."

But in a city where gang violence terrorizes some neighborhoods, Chicago City Clerk Susana Mendoza says Pulgar's sticker design had to go, regardless of the boy's intent.

"I can't ask any Chicagoan to put on a city sticker that is mired in controversy related to gangs," Mendoza says. "So whether that was the intent or not, it doesn't matter. Because the perception is out there that there could be a correlation—and that's unacceptable."

Regardless of intent, perception of the final piece matters, and city officials had to choose the second-place design for the parking decals. While not necessarily derived from pre-made images, the hand signs are still visuals that signify certain meanings. Had Pulgar known this, he might have drawn the hands differently to avoid any connection to Chicago gangs. Although you might not expect students in a high-school competition to undergo the kind of research covered in this chapter, the unfortunate outcome presented here shows the importance of thoroughly researching the details of a particular image before placing them into your project.

Genre

Beyond the content that makes up a visual design, the genre in which a visual appears also has its own history. When considering an image, video, flyer, blog, poster, or other genre, you should research to determine why you might choose one genre over another.

Each kind of genre conveys information in different ways. A movie poster typically displays the title of the movie more prominently than other information, such as the production crew. However, viewers can glance at the poster as a whole, and scan it as they like.

A video, however, typically only allows the viewer to see it within a linear, controlled fashion. The viewer could fast-forward, pause, or rewind, but the video would typically make less sense.

A proposal for a new car design, however, may be purposefully designed to be read differently by different audiences. A CEO or manager might only read the executive summary, while those in finance will read the budget, and engineers the technical aspects. Knowing how a genre is meant to be used is important when deciding on the genre through which to distribute your message.

You might also consider subgenres. For example, the genre of film consists of many kinds of subgenres, such as drama, comedy, romantic comedy, horror, fantasy, and others. Each of these has further subgenres, with their own specific influences. Horror films can include such subtypes as slasher or zombie horror. You can probably think of others as well. Knowing the conventions and formulas for each of these subgenres can help you better understand how these films work, and help you better understand how to use them within your own works.

Typography

Like genres, typographies have their own histories as well. It's easy to forget that font types that come preloaded into word processor programs had to be designed and invented by a human being. Many of these font types were commissioned by an individual or group who wanted typography with a certain aesthetic, a particular look and feel.

The font type Helvetica (Figure 7.15), for instance, was designed by Swiss typeface designers Max Miedinger and Eduard Hoffmann in 1957. During this time period, designers were moving toward a cleaner, modernist look that was very simple and utilitarian. Because Helvetica displayed the characteristics that many designers were looking for, it became the designated font for hundreds of companies and organizations.

Credit: Pbarnola

Figure 7.15
Helvetica remains a popular typeface

However, during the Vietnam War, younger designers felt that Helvetica came to symbolize the very companies they felt were perpetuating the war and they started to create more unique fonts that moved away from Helvetica's simple forms. Reaction to Helvetica today is mixed: some designers feel it is so simple, easy, and timeless that it provides an important font that should still be used. Other designers, however, feel that Helvetica is overused, constricting, and lazy. Researching your typefaces before you include them in a design can help you understand how audiences might react to different typefaces.

Color

As discussed in Chapter 10, color choice requires extensive research since colors can mean different things to different groups and individuals. While the United States and many Western nations use the color red to symbolize danger, such as on a stop sign, some Asian countries consider red to symbolize good luck or happiness. In Ireland, however, green is the color for good luck.

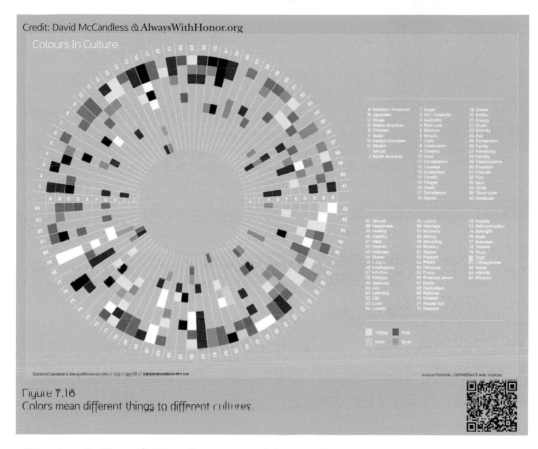

Figure 7.16
Colors mean different things to different cultures.

The chart in Figure 7.16 analyzes some of the moods associated with different colors in ten cultural contexts. Love, #53, is represented by red in Western/American, Japanese, and Eastern European cultures, green in Hindu, yellow in Native American, and blue in African cultures. The color for a "truce" is white in most cultures—which you may recognize in the expression "waving the white flag"—except in Muslim and African cultures, in which the color silver represents this idea. Such differences don't preclude you from using any particular color, but you should be attuned to your audience's perceptions and associations about colors when making your selections. Research how your various audiences might respond to colors when considering your design choices.

Composition Techniques

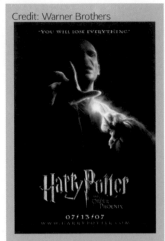

Credit: Warner Brothers

Figure 7.17
Even modern movies still
use low-key lighting to seem
"sinister."

When looking at a design, you might consider specific *composition techniques* that were used to create a particular effect. For example, low-key lighting (as seen in Figure 7.17), a method of lighting in which most of the frame is dark, was used in films in the early 1900s to depict "sinister" scenes. This technique is still used in many horror and suspense films, and it's easy to take for granted that scenes depicting dark subject matter should be lit darkly. However, the technique had to be invented, and part of this invention occurred when films began to shoot indoors or at night using artificial light.

The technique of montage, discussed in Chapter 4, also has a rich history as well as specific theories related to its use. If you notice a particular technique within a visual, consider researching more about it, learning who invented it, the kinds of effects it is meant to have on an audience, or where it appears in other works. Such knowledge will help you think more professionally about how you use these techniques yourself.

MAKING CONNECTIONS

AS A CLASS

Look at famous photographs without looking at their captions. Discuss what you think the subject of the photos is. What details make you think so? After you've shared some ideas, research the history of the photo. How does this information change your opinion of the photo's subject? Do you think that your own interpretation is still valid?

IN A GROUP

Choose a movie that you all enjoy. Identify the genre of the movie, as well as the director, time period, and other important elements. Next, identify previous movies that might have influenced it (based on your knowledge of the genre's conventions and other films within the same genre), the kinds of movies that influence the director, and any other information you feel is pertinent. Finally, what kinds of future films do you think this movie would influence? Write a short report on your results and share them with the class.

Online, search for a list of photographic or cinematic techniques and choose one that interests you. Research this technique, including its invention, the first photos or films in which it appeared and the photographer or director who is most associated with it. Compose a report based on your research and share your findings with the class.

RESEARCHING THE "CRYING INDIAN"

On Earth Day in 1971, the nonprofit organization Keep America Beautiful (KAB) distributed one of the most iconic images of the early environmental movement. Dubbed "The Crying Indian" (Figure 7.18), this public service advertisement against littering features the actor Iron Eyes Cody who is shedding a single tear at the environmental degradation that he sees around him. However, there's much more behind this famous image than meets the (Iron) eye, and researching this image turns up a variety of interesting facts.

Credit: Keep America Beautiful/Ad Council

GET INVOLVED NOW. POLLUTION HURTS ALL OF US.

Figure 7.18
Iron Eyes Cody and his "tear" became iconic.

While you might take the concepts and practices of environmentalism for granted, this wasn't always the case. Researching more about the image's larger context, you would discover some of the roots of the environmental movement. Gaylord Nelson, a former U.S. Senator from Wisconsin (Figure 7.19), proposed an "environmental teach-in" to educate students across universities about the effects of pollution, especially related to the massive 1969 oil spill in Santa Barbara, California (Figure 7.20). The day of these teach-ins would later come to be called "Earth Day," and the concept would quickly spread around the world. The exigency and purpose for the "Crying Indian" ad comes

Figure 7.19
Gaylord Nelson helped to found the first Earth Day.

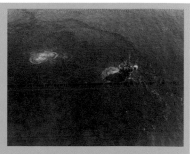
Figure 7.20
An oil spill near Santa Barbara, California was a primary exigency for the first Earth Day.

from this early movement, and making good use of *kairos*, was initiated during the second Earth Day.

Figure 7.21
Keep America Beautiful's commercial featuring "The Crying Indian."
http://www.youtube.com/watch?v=j7OHG7tHrNM

The advertisement in Figure 7.18 was not the only image to be released as part of KAB's campaign. As the organization discussed subjects related to ecology, they also created an ecology of media to put forth their message. One example appears in Figure 7.21, a television commercial that shows the pollution at which the Indian cries.

The commercial depicts stereotypical scenes of a Native American dressed in "traditional" costume, paddling down a stream in a canoe. As he paddles, he encounters debris floating on the surface and exits the river in a polluted harbor filled with exhaust-producing ships and factories. As he pulls his canoe upon land, he finds more litter strewn across the shore. Cody's character eventually reaches a highway packed with cars, and one of the motorists tosses litter out of the window, which splatters at his feet. The only narration, toward the end, states, "Some people have a deep abiding respect for the natural beauty that was once this country. And some people don't. People start pollution. People can stop it." The last two lines include the theme of the campaign, ascribing human agency—and therefore a human solution—to the problem.

Figure 7.22
Iron Eyes Cody meets with President Jimmy Carter in 1978.

However, what does the first line suggest, especially when juxtaposed with the figure of the Native American? One of the stereotypes that persists about traditional Native American cultures is that they are more connected with the Earth than peoples from colonist or immigrant backgrounds. Because of this stereotype, the character played by Cody has a particular *ethos* that helps these ads make a claim against pollution, since the audience would not expect the main character to have ever littered in his life. Knowing this, it becomes clear that casting a Native American to deliver this message is rhetorically savvy.

Shepard Krech III, however, finds some fault with these ads. In his book *The Ecological Indian*, Krech offers a critique of the "Crying Indian" campaign, writing that Keep America Beautiful played on common stereotypes about Native Americans and "cleverly manipulated ideas deeply ingrained in the national consciousness (229)." The ads worked, however, and Krech noted "Even though an invention of Madison Avenue, the Crying Indian is an effective image and advocate because its assumptions are not new" (229) (Figure 7.22).

The campaign plays well because of the stereotypes. However, what does research about the actor—Iron Eyes Cody—reveal? Iron Eyes Cody claimed throughout his life that he was descended from Cherokee-Creek ancestors. Furthermore, he married a wife of American Indian heritage, adopted several American Indian children, and supported causes that helped support American Indian communities.

However, in 1996 it was revealed that Cody was in fact of Italian descent (his original name was Espera Oscar de Corti), and both his parents—Antonio de Corti and Francesca Salpietra—were immigrants from Sicily. While this information could undercut Cody's *ethos* as an authentic American Indian, and therefore cast doubt on his ability to play American Indian characters, does it affect this particular campaign?

Since the information about Cody's Sicilian heritage wasn't released until close to his death in 1999, you might conclude that Cody's true ancestry makes little difference in this case. Just as KAB's audience in the 1970s bought into the stereotype of the Native American's environmental sensibilities, they most likely perceived Cody to be a "real" Indian and therefore somehow more directly affected by the average American's pollution. While such research about an image can reveal information that affects how an audience reads the image today, you must also consider what was known at the time the image circulated and how such knowledge (or lack of knowledge) affected the original audience's reception of the advertisement.

MAKING CONNECTIONS

AS A CLASS

Look at other public service advertising campaigns by Keep America Beautiful. How do these campaigns resemble the "Crying Indian" campaign? How do they differ? Does the information you now know about the "Crying Indian" images change your perspective of subsequent campaigns? What kinds of research would you conduct to find out more about them?

IN A GROUP

Find other public service announcements that use celebrities or well-known public figures. How much of the figure's background do they include in the advertisement? Does this background contribute to the overall argument? Research more about each figure and determine if there's any information that would undercut the spokesperson's effectiveness. Do you think that such background information is important to know about, or is it irrelevant? Why or why not? Share your examples and findings with the class.

ON YOUR OWN

Besides the information given above, conduct more research about the "Crying Indian" public service announcements. You might research more into the Keep America Beautiful organization, find out the photographer or equipment used to shoot the scene, or even the location in which the advertisements were shot. What does this new information add to what you already know about the campaign? Write a report with your findings and share them with the class.

COPYRIGHT

When looking for visuals to place in your own works, you have to be aware of *copyright* laws and how they affect you. Most works are copyrighted, a legal protection that designates that the creator has the exclusive right to his or her intellectual property and can determine if it can be used by others, where, how often, and for how much compensation.

Figure 7.23
Copyright symbol. This symbol designates that a work is copyrighted. However, a work can still be copyrighted without displaying this symbol.

Intellectual property is simply any original created work, such as music, a novel, a film, a poster, a photograph, computer program, or even one of your own college essays. If a work is protected by an existing copyright, you cannot use it without permission from the creator unless your project falls into a special category, such as fair use.

Generally, most of your class projects fall under fair use if they're noncommercial and for educational purposes. However, future projects beyond the classroom may not fall under this category. Below are some basic guidelines to follow when selecting works. However, what follows is not legal advice, and you'll have to conduct further research (or hire an intellectual property attorney) to make sure you can appropriate another's intellectual works.

Fair Use

Typically, work you complete for class will fall under *fair use*, a section in copyright law that allows you to avoid seeking permission to use another's copyrighted work. Fair use, however, is a legal defense that can only be tested in court and must hold up to legal scrutiny if a particular copyright holder feels that your use of their material isn't "fair." Here are four guidelines to research to determine if your overall project and use of copyright materials constitute the fair use doctrine. The better you meet all four criteria, the more likely you have used the work in good faith.

1. The purpose and character of the use, including whether such use is of commercial nature or is for nonprofit educational purposes.

2. The nature of the copyrighted work.

3. The amount and substantialness of the portion used in relation to the copyrighted work.

4. The effect of the use upon the potential market for, or value of, the copyrighted work.

The purpose and character of the work must be transformative in some way and not simply derivative. For instance, the law mentions the following specific uses: "criticism, comment, news reporting, teaching (including multiple copies for classroom use), scholarship, or research." While not every educational use falls under fair use, many do, including most of the projects you'll be working on.

The nature of the work often refers to what it expresses—fact or fiction. Generally, you can disseminate and incorporate facts into your works—such as journalistic reporting—much more readily than creative works.

The amount of the work you use is also important to consider. Generally, you should use as little of a copyrighted work as possible. If you were using a clip from a film, it should generally be 10% of the total film, or 2-3 minutes, whichever is less. If you were using a song, no more than 30 seconds should be used. The less of the original work you use, the more likely you'll be protected by fair use. However, even if the amount you use is very small, if it constitutes the "heart" of the work, fair use might not protect you.

Finally, courts will consider the effect that your work has on the market value of the work for the copyright holder. The less people that will see your work, and the shorter the time period it will be available for viewing, the more likely that it will not unduly affect the potential financial interests of the owner.

Public Domain

You can avoid dealing with fair use and copyright issues if you select works from the *public domain*. Usually, copyright only lasts for a limited period of time. If a work's copyright expires, then the work is in the public domain (Figure 7.24) and can be used without restrictions. Currently, any work produced before 1923 is now in the public domain unless its author, or estate representing that author, has extended it.

Figure 7.25
Creative Commons brand symbol. Users who publish their works under Creative Commons can designate that they want all, some, or none of their rights protected.

Figure 7.24
Public Domain Symbol. This symbol designates that a work is under the Public Domain and free to use without seeking permission.

Also, since they're paid for with public funds, most works produced by U.S. government agencies fall within the public domain. Some authors create work specifically for the public domain that may be reused and reproduced freely. Others utilize the copyright system of Creative Commons (see Figure 7.25), which permits use in certain contexts and conditions, such as whether the work will be used for commercial or noncommercial purposes, if it will undergo modifications, if it is properly attributed, or as long as the new work may be shared as well.

MAKING CONNECTIONS

AS A CLASS

Many ideas for Walt Disney films come from stories in the public domain. For example, *Cinderella* was adapted from a story written by seventeenth-century French author Charles Perrault. However, Disney guards the copyright of their own works very closely, even though their original ideas came from others. As a class, look up other stories that Disney has based movies on and identify the original writings. Then, discuss Disney's tough protection of its copyrights. Do you think they're fair, or should Disney allow others to re-use and remix their own works more freely just as they have done with others' works? What are the arguments for both sides?

IN A GROUP

The intent of copyright laws clearly states that "ideas" cannot be copyrighted, only their expression. Select an idea or concept that appears often in popular culture, such as zombies, vampires, aliens, etc. Then, find as many expressions of this idea as you can, either in movies, books, television, advertising, or other forms. How does each of these media create a new expression that can be copyrighted? Do any particular expressions seem to closely resemble others, perhaps creating a copyright infringement? Discuss how you see the difference between expressions in each case, create a report of your analysis, and share it with the class.

ON YOUR OWN

Music presents one of the most difficult copyrights to obtain, often requiring several types of permissions. Research the general process for acquiring the right to reproduce copyrighted music. Who owns the copyright? Who owns distribution rights? What kinds of licenses are required? Compose a report of your findings and share them with the class.

FINDING IMAGES AND VIDEOS

When looking for images and videos for your projects, you will probably start with a Google Image search or a search for videos on YouTube. For these searches, the selection of good key words is important. Start broadly, and then refine as needed. If you were looking for an image of a burning building, you might simply put in "burning building," or "building fire." If that search turned up results that don't meet your requirements for the project, you might refine "building" into other key words such as skyscraper, house, church, meeting hall, or other building types. You might also use other descriptors such as the color of the building you want, its age, architectural style, camera angle, and other adjectives.

Figure 7.26
Wikimedia Commons brand mark.
Wikimedia Commons has a wide variety of images, many which fall under public domain.

In addition to image searches supported by search engines, you can also look at image-specific databases. Some of these include the image search engine Picsearch (picsearch.com), Corbis Images (corbisimages.com), Getty Images (gettyimages.com), and AP Images (apimages.com). Of course, make sure you consider copyright laws when using databases such as Corbis, which offer stock photography for a fee. The website Wikimedia Commons offers images that are either in the public domain or fall under Creative Commons (Figure 7.26).

You can also look for images in the public domain through federal agencies such as NASA, as well as library websites that often scan and catalogue older, historical photos. The website Archive.org also has a range of media in the public domain, including still images, texts, videos, audio, and even software. While you will most likely find many more sites, these should get you started.

MAKING CONNECTIONS

AS A CLASS

Each student should bring in a random photo that they've taken. Exchange the photo with someone else in the class. Next, search the Web for a photo that looks as close to your classmate's photo as possible. Obviously it won't be an exact match, but try to come close. As you search, record the different search terms you enter. Which search terms worked or came closest? Which didn't? Record the different search strategies and discuss them as a class.

IN A GROUP

Create a list of as many image databases as you can find. Note which ones require payment for use, which ones offer their photos for free, and which require permissions. Once you've completed your list, share it with the class and merge it with the lists other groups produce.

ON YOUR OWN

Select another photo that you've taken not used in Prompt #1. If you were going to assign key words to this image so that it was easier to find through search engines, which key words would you choose? Shapes? Colors? Objects? Emotions? Create a list of all the possible key words you might use, and rank them in order of importance. How did you decide upon these key words? How did you decide upon their ranking? Which search terms are denotative, and which are connotative? Share your list and rationale with the class, and compare your system with those developed by your classmates.

KEY TERMS

research	*fair use*
composition techniques	*public domain*
copyright	

OUTPUT: IREPORT/PUBLIC SERVICE ANNOUNCEMENT

For this assignment, research a historic image or video. Research as many details as you can, such as the creator, subject, purpose, audience, influence, historical context, details, genre, and other aspects. Rather than a written report, however, compose a report via a Prezi presentation.

Prezi is a free, online-based presentation software that allows you to display information less linearly than PowerPoint. Prezi allows you to pan and zoom across a single canvas, so that you can look at multiple images simultaneously or zoom in on particular details. Prezi also allows the easy integration of images and video. Follow these basic instructions toward completing this project, although your instructor might have more details for you to consider.

Credit: prezi.com

Figure 7.27
Prezi offers a more dynamic way to present than other software programs.

1. Select an image; this image will hopefully be one you find motivating, appealing, or somehow interesting. You would do best to find an image that's fairly well-known and has much information available for you to study. You might also think about the disciplines in which to look for an image: artistic, journalistic, scientific, nature-based, or biographical.

2. Create a Prezi account. Visit Prezi.com to start your account. Prezi accounts are free to set up, and if you use an ".edu" email address, you can upgrade to the mid-level "Enjoy" license for free.

3. Start using Prezi. It doesn't take long to learn how to use Prezi and the website offers a thorough tutorial—both written and in video—to get you started.

4. Compose your Prezi. Insert the information you've gathered about the image to start constructing your presentation. Prezi offers a

few pre-designed arrangements for organizing your material, but you might also sketch your layout on paper before integrating your materials online.

5. Use images and video. Presentations are usually better received when you include visuals for the audience to see rather than just lines of texts for them to read. From your research, what images can you include? What videos? Perhaps you've found experts discussing the image on YouTube that you can include?

6. Present your Prezi to the class. When you present, do not read the text off of the screen, but instead try to paraphrase with different words to explain the different elements of your image.

8

STORY DEVELOPMENT (ARGUMENT)

While you've probably learned how to craft arguments in other writing classes, creating an argument in visual media can be a bit different. However, even though you'll be working with images, video, sound, and writing technologies other than a traditional word processor, these media can still be used to craft arguments that you might usually associate with traditional essays. Such arguments don't need to be explicit but can be designed in a way so that their arguments are implicit within a narrative and not overtly stated (Figure 8.1).

Often, these arguments are couched within a story that makes an argument as a plot unfolds and characters develop. Sometimes visuals become arguments without the intent of the creator, such as Eddie Adams's photograph of General Loan. When you argue with image, video, or sound, you're often developing a story as a rhetorical strategy to make your point. In this chapter, you'll analyze both kinds of arguments—explicit and implicit—as they occur in visual media, and discuss the strategies for crafting an argument within a visual discourse.

Credit: Carsten Tolkmit

Figure 8.1
Words aren't the only way to make arguments.

When developing an argument, the rhetorical tetrahedron that highlights *logos*, *ethos*, *pathos*, and *kairos* will be very useful. This version of the tetrahedron will help you consider these four rhetorical appeals and remind you to incorporate them into your arguments. However, factors such as message, audience, design, medium, and genre also affect your argument. For instance, an audience might respond more positively to one design or medium over another, and so these choices should also influence how you construct and deliver your argument.

EXPLICIT ARGUMENTS

Before turning to narrative arguments that are more prominent in visual media, you should revisit the basic structure of traditional, *explicit arguments* that you may be more accustomed to writing. While written arguments can be implicit—not directly stating what the reader should think—college classes usually ask you to write explicit arguments that state a claim and provide support for why the reader should adopt your point of view.

As discussed in Chapter 3, most arguments break down into three basic parts: a claim, reasons, and evidence. The first part of any argument is to make a claim. For instance, you might claim that vegetarianism is a better diet than one that includes animal meat. However, a claim is not enough by itself—you must also provide reasons why the audience should believe your claim. In order to accomplish this, you might state reasons such as: "a plant-based diet prevents more diseases"; "plants are packed with more nutrients"; or "a plant-based diet reduces animal suffering and cruelty."

Figure 8.2
"Eat More Kale" is a claim but has no explicit reasons or evidence.

However, just as a claim needs reasons to support it, these reasons need supporting evidence (Figure 8.2). You might then cite scientific studies that show reduced cancer rates in vegetarians, state findings that green, leafy vegetables have more protein by weight than meat, or demonstrate how plant-based foods are less acidic than meat and thus reduce inflammation and increase general health. Such evidence makes it more likely that your audience will accept your overall argument, depending on the credibility (*ethos*) of whom you cite.

In this example, *logos*, *pathos*, and *ethos* play a big part in your argument. If you're citing scientific studies, you're mainly appealing to *logos* (the scientific logic of the study) and *ethos* (the credibility of the scientists conducting the studies). Of course, you can also appeal to *pathos*, perhaps appealing to the emotions the audience might have toward the animals that suffer so that humans can consume them. As always, you have to know your audience and which appeals might work best. One audience member might balk at emotional appeals but appreciate a more scientific approach.

Toward an argument about new media itself, in an opinion piece for CNN, history and public affairs professor, Julian Zelizer, discusses the role of media in presidential elections. In the piece below, Zelizer argues that television has come to dominate how Americans choose a political candidate (figure 8.3). Read over his argument and pay attention to the reasons and kinds of evidence he provides.

How Political Ads Can Elect a President

Last week, American Crossroads, Karl Rove's nonprofit operation that was highly effective in 2010, launched a blistering ad charging that President Barack Obama has failed to help American families.

A woman described as the mother of two grown children without jobs says to the camera, "I supported President Obama because he spoke so beautifully. He promised change. But things changed for the worse."

Obama also found himself in the middle of a controversy when Cory Booker, the popular Democratic mayor of Newark, New Jersey, criticized a spot that had attacked Mitt Romney's work at Bain Capital. It had been paid for by the Obama campaign.

Credit: Pete Souza

Figure 8.3
Barack Obama effectively uses television to reach his many audiences.

Television spots are the medium through which the modern campaign is fought. The success or failure of the candidates at producing effective advertisements could have a huge influence on the outcome in November.

Each side of the campaign will spend inordinate amounts of money to pay for 30-second advertisements – which will also be spread through the Internet – that seek to define the message of the campaign of 2012 and the terms of the fight.

"Television is no gimmick," said Roger Ailes, Richard Nixon's campaign consultant, in 1968, "and nobody will ever be elected to major office again without presenting themselves well on it."

Ailes was right. Since 1952, when television had become a regular part of many American homes, the campaign spot has become a defining feature of modern politics.

According to The Living Room Candidate, an outstanding site that allows viewers to see many of these commercials, military hero Dwight Eisenhower

(Figure 8.4) launched a presidential campaign spot based on the advice of advertising executive, Rosser Reeves, who thought this was the best way to reach the electorate.

Figure 8.4
Dwight D. Eisenhower won his election through the use of television commercials.

Democrat Adlai Stevenson was disgusted by the use of commercials. "The idea that you can merchandise candidates for high office like breakfast cereal," he famously quipped, "is the ultimate indignity to the democratic process." Eisenhower won.

Like it or not, spots have dominated campaigns. Although there have been tremendous variations in the kinds of spots Americans have seen, there have been several consistent types that politicians have used that we are likely to see in the coming months.

The first is the character assassination spot. These are the ads in which candidates exploit a perceived weakness of their opponent, highlight this weakness and use it through the spot to shape how voters perceive them. The most infamous of all was the Daisy ad in 1964: Lyndon Johnson's campaign broadcast a spot featuring a little girl picking petals off a flower until viewers saw a mushroom cloud in her eye.

The point was to take fears that Barry Goldwater was a reckless hawk on military matters and craft them into a shocking image that could scare people into believing he would launch a nuclear war.

Another famous example came in 2004, when George Bush's campaign broadcast an ad featuring Massachusetts Sen. John Kerry wind sailing, moving in different directions. After going over a series of issues on which Kerry had switched his position, the narrator says, "John Kerry: whichever way the wind blows."

The ad played off perceptions that Kerry lacked core principles and sold this as the essence of his character. A more vicious ad in that campaign came from an independent group that featured veterans questioning Kerry's war record during Vietnam. The ad gave rise to the term "swift-boating" in modern campaigns.

Another type is the issue-based spot, which highlights a particular area of controversy that does not play well for the opposition or which triggers a debate about a subject that will raise problems for opponents.

One of the first ads by Eisenhower, called "High Prices," featured him answering questions to average citizens (who were filmed separately though it looked like they were addressing him), many of which revolved around the cost of living and inflation (Figure 8.5).

President Richard Nixon broadcast a powerful ad in 1972 that featured plastic soldiers being wiped off the table as a way to raise fears about defense budget cuts taking place under the Democratic Congress and which would accelerate if Sen. George McGovern was in the White House.

In 1988, campaign guru Lee Atwater filmed the "Willie Horton" ad, which revolved around a felon furlough program in Massachusetts when Michael Dukakis was governor, to talk about law and order.

There are also the guilt by association spots through which candidates try to tie an opponent to an unpopular figure or events through the power of image. In 2008, Barack Obama ran an ad that showed Republican John McCain embracing the unpopular George W. Bush repeatedly. In one of Richard Nixon's ads in 1968, the camera showed images of Vice President Hubert Humphrey juxtaposed with the chaotic Democratic Convention in 1968 where anti-war protesters clashed with the city police in Chicago's Grant Park. No words were needed.

Credit: Rosser Reeves for Ted Bates and Co.

Figure 8.5
Dwight D. Eisenhower argues that voting for his opponent will result in "high prices."
http://www.livingroomcandidate.org/commercials/1952/high-prices

The final spot is a very different kind, the candidate-boast spot. It is usually simple and direct, literally an advertisement for the person who is running. Jimmy Carter broadcast a very effective example in 1976, when he talked about his personal story in Georgia and used his own upbringing as the most important characteristic of the campaign. "1976. Across our land," the narrator says, "a new beginning is under way, led by a man whose roots are founded in the American tradition."

Ronald Reagan's campaign featured "Morning in America" in 1984 which highlighted the revival of the economy, and emphasized that the nation would be strong (Figure 8.6). "Under the leadership of President Reagan, our country is prouder and stronger and better." In 1996, Bill Clinton's campaign spoke about his being a bridge to the future.

This year both campaigns will likely draw on all of these kinds of spots to sell their message. They will be the subject of debate and play an important role in shaping the perceptions that voters have of each candidate.

Credit: Ronald Reagan Presidential Library

PRESIDENT REAGAN

PAID FOR BY REAGAN-BUSH '84

Figure 8.6
Ronald Reagan told a positive story about his presidency.
http://www.youtube.com/watch?v=EU-IBF8nwSY

Obama and Romney will need to be careful that the spots they broadcast, or which independent groups broadcast for them, don't backfire on them rather than their opponents, and they will need to make sure to convey enough positive messages along with the negative. But the candidate that pulls off the best ad campaign will vastly improve his odds of winning the White House in November.

Zelizer's claim is relatively easy to locate in this article: The best use of television by Obama or Romney will determine the outcome of the presidential election. What reasons does Zelizer provide for this claim? In several places, he states that television spots have become the primary medium through which candidates express their views and wage their campaign and that a huge amount of money is spent on these spots. As part of his rhetorical strategy, Zelizer incorporates the expert opinion of Richard Nixon's former campaign consultant, Roger Ailes.

With the reasons for his claim established, Zelizer goes on to offer a variety of evidence to support these reasons, primarily focusing on iconic and memorable examples of how the use of television helped or hurt various campaigns. Throughout, he balances *logos* and *ethos,* providing logical evidence to support his claim from the words of credible sources that have experience in politics. In order to avoid angering a reader through a particular bias (a negative aspect of *pathos*), Zelizer further balances his argument with sources from Democratic and Republican parties, as well as providing anecdotes about both past Democratic and Republican presidential candidates. These examples offer precedence for the modern day television campaign spots and how their use has steadily grown until they have become a necessity.

While some texts are more difficult to read than others, most literate writing can easily be analyzed in this way to identify the claim, reasons, and evidence that make up an explicit argument, and you should make use of this analysis when reading and composing any kind of text. However, as discussed later in this chapter, developing an argument within a visual medium requires different strategies.

MAKING CONNECTIONS

AS A CLASS

Find recordings of debates on YouTube or another video search engine. Watch the debates, and write down each arguer's claim, reasons, and evidence. After the debate concludes, share your findings as a class and discuss each speaker's strengths, weaknesses, which elements were missing, or other things you noticed.

IN A GROUP

Locate a) a written opinion piece, b) an opinion delivered through video, and c) an opinion delivered through radio (via recorded podcast). Analyze how each argument is constructed differently for each medium. Do all clearly state the claim and make the argument explicit? Do some use different kinds of evidence? How is each similar? Compile your findings into a report and share them with the class.

ON YOUR OWN

Locate a paper from another class in which you composed an explicit argument with a claim, reasons, and evidence. Create a script or storyboard for how you would turn this paper into a video that presented the same explicit argument. Would you simply read the text to a video camera, or add visuals to replace textual descriptions? Share your storyboard with the class and discuss what changes you made and why. If you have time, consider making the actual video.

IMPLICIT ARGUMENTS

Unlike explicit arguments, which directly state a claim, *implicit arguments* use more indirect means of persuasion to place an idea into the viewer's mind. For example, the photograph in Figure 8.7 depicts a naked infant breastfeeding.

This infant's skin is covered with tattoos of many well-known corporations and entertainment companies. This image doesn't make an explicit claim but attempts to plant some message into the viewer's mind, making an implied argument. You might deduce that the creator of the image wants the viewer to consider how such companies affect a person, even from birth, or how corporations dominate a person's life and owns him or her as much as he or she owns their products. Whatever idea you come away with, the fact that you come away with an idea at all proves the image's implied argument was successful. Even without a claim, reasons, and evidence, such implied messages make the audience think and come to conclusions itself, which can be an even more powerful form of persuasion, since the audience develops the answer on their own.

Credit: Tabula Rosa, 2004. Borjana Ventzislavova, Miroslav Nicic & Mladen Penev/Adbusters

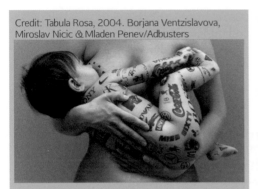

Figure 8.7
The organization Adbusters is trying to make an argument with this image.

Credit: Chang W. Lee/*The New York Times*

Figure 8.8
To make a visual argument, New York Mayor Michael Bloomberg presented the different sizes of soda cups juxtaposed by sugar cubes showing how much sugar is in each size soda.

In May 2012, New York City mayor Michael Bloomberg pushed for a city ordinance that banned food service establishments—such as restaurants or street vendors—from selling sugary soft drinks larger than 16 ounces (Figure 8.8).

His motivation was to decrease obesity—which he claimed was causing more than 5,000 deaths a year in the city—by limiting the amount of soda a person could order at any one time. When a skeptic of his proposal pointed out that a customer could simply by two 16-ounce drinks, thus bypassing the supposed intent of the law to limit soda consumption, Bloomberg commented that the proposed ban was:

> *"purely education. It forces you to see the difference, in the case of the two different sized cups... The public does act when they get the information. And all we're doing here is saying, 'If you want to order 32 ounces of soda, in a restaurant that we supervise, this restaurant must give you two 16-ounce glasses.'"*

While Bloomberg's justification of the soda ban is explicit, his ultimate goal is to make an implicit argument when someone orders a drink (or two). Bloomberg's two different sized cups create a visual argument, showing the customer the difference between one or two cups, an argument that he justifies with scientific studies (*logos*) about consumer behavior, but which isn't provided to customers at the time they order their drink(s):

> "*[the proposed ban] forces you to see the difference in the case of the two different size cups and you can decide. We're not taking away anybody's rights at all to do anything. All we're doing is forcing you to recognize that you're drinking an enormous amount of sugar.*"

Bloomberg doesn't want to convince his audience with a direct, explicit argument about soda but simply to make an implied, visual argument about how much sugar they might be drinking and to get his audience to further consider how that sugar might be affecting their bodies. Bloomberg simply aims to plant an idea. But this example shows that although implied arguments aren't direct, they can be forceful, and even forced upon a viewer.

When you compose your own visual arguments that use implicit means of persuasion, you might use various kinds of appeals such as *logos*, *pathos*, and *ethos*, and you might include some sort of evidence or reasons for what your visual is suggesting. In other words, you can use some of the tactics found in explicit arguments, but you're not tied to using all or any of them. Sometimes placing *logos* in a visual helps, but it's not necessary. You simply need to get your audience to consider your point of view. Of course, the better you do that, the more persuasive you will be in convincing them that your point of view is the best one.

MAKING CONNECTIONS

AS A CLASS

Bring in various political cartoons from newspapers or the Web. Look through all the cartoons and determine which ones might be considered explicit or implicit arguments. If explicit, map out the claim, reasons, and evidence. If implicit, what idea is the cartoonist trying to evoke? What visual elements suggest this? What rhetorical appeals are made to the viewer?

IN A GROUP

Compose a list of video games that you all have played or are familiar with. For each game on the list, try to determine if the game is trying to make an implicit argument about something. Note any implicit messages for each video game on your list and share your results with the class.

Through YouTube or another video search engine, try to find Michael Bloomberg's press conference where he announces his plan to ban sugary soft drinks. In this press conference, determine if Bloomberg makes an explicit or implicit argument about this ban. If explicit, map the various components of his argument, including claims, reasons, and evidence. If implicit, how does he try to convey this idea to his audience? Compare the argument he makes in the press conference with what he later tells reporters, such as in the statements above. Is he actually making multiple kinds of arguments between selling the idea of the ban to the public and the argument that New Yorkers need to reduce their sugar intake? Write a report of your findings and share them with the class.

IMPLICIT ARGUMENTS ACROSS MEDIA

Below are some examples of how implicit arguments show up in specific media and techniques that you might consider for your own projects. Study how these examples use different methods and rhetorical strategies for reaching their audiences and how those methods depend upon the overall rhetorical situation, including the constraints of the medium, the environment in which the medium is placed, as well as other factors you've looked at so far.

ARGUMENTS IN PHOTOGRAPHS

While photographs can serve a variety of purposes, such as to illustrate a point, provide an example, or simply as fluff to add a visual to a written document, photographs can also argue in their own right. However, since a photograph can't usually offer claims, reasons, and evidence, the argument they make is usually implicit for the reader to figure out.

Sometimes, spontaneous photographs can contain implicit arguments without the photographer's intentions, such as how Eddie Adams's photograph of General Loan was used by antiwar groups as implying an argument about the atrocities of war. However, often photographs that serve as implicit arguments are consciously created by the photographer to make a point.

For example, you can consider many of the images you've already examined, such as the photographs in the new smoking warnings, as attempts to persuade audiences of particular ideas without a fully explicit argument. The photograph in Figure 8.9 juxtaposes five different colors of crayons all labeled as "Flesh." This photograph suggests that although skin colors appear in many different shades, flesh is still flesh, all people are humans.

Photographs that already exist can be further remixed to create implicit arguments. Figure 8.10 juxtaposes two photographs, one of former presidents George H. W. Bush and George W. Bush fishing, and another of New Orleans, Louisiana during the flooding from Hurricane Katrina. You might guess that the creator of this remix is attempting to convey that while the people in New Orleans were struggling to find food, shelter, and survive the aftermath of the storm, President Bush was engaged in more trivial pursuits, ignoring the suffering of Louisiana citizens.

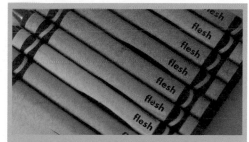

Figure 8.9
This image makes an argument about what colors count as "flesh."

Elements can also be added to photographs, as in Figure 8.11. Here, derogatory words are written in the shape of a hand strangling a crying child. While the image provides a claim, "Your words have power, use them wisely," the photograph and added elements can provide the argument with more power. Remove the explicit words, and you still have a powerful implicit argument. While text can help anchor the meaning and argument that a writer is trying to make with an image, sometimes a lack of textual anchoring can be more powerful, allowing the audience to interpret the argument in their own words.

Figure 8.10
This photomontage creates an argument through juxtaposition.

Credit: Juvenile Protection Association/ EuroRSCG Chicago

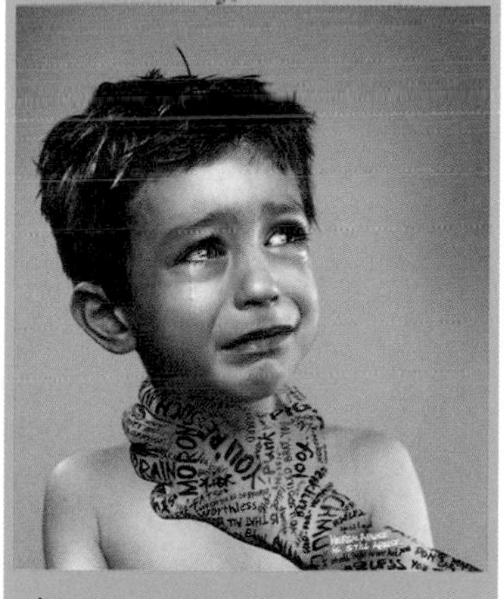

When developing your own arguments through photographs, consider the above techniques. You can randomly snap photographs and see what kinds of arguments you can make once you review the images, or you can pose objects or individuals in certain ways to make a rhetorical point. You can also crop, juxtapose, or otherwise manipulate photographs to develop an argument that might not be apparent in an unadjusted photograph. Finally, think carefully about how much textual anchorage you want to include in an image. A few words can guide your reader, but too many may undercut the power of your photograph.

Figure 8.11
This ad argues that, just like sticks and stones, words can also hurt.

MAKING CONNECTIONS

AS A CLASS

Look at various headshots that accompany syndicated newspaper columns. How are the photographs composed? What is the demeanor or pose of the author? Does this photograph make an implicit argument about the author and the column? If so, what is this argument? How does the author's photograph change how you read the column? How would this reading change if the author appeared differently in the headshot?

IN A GROUP

With a camera, create your own photographic argument. Consider what kind of story you can tell within a single snapshot, and what kind of implicit argument you'd like to make. In addition to the photograph, write a short description of what you tried to accomplish with the picture, noting your rhetorical choices, and share it with the class.

ON YOUR OWN

Like the example in Figure 8.10, mashup two different photographs to make an implicit argument. Share your photograph with the class and see if they can deduce your intended argument. Afterwards, explain your intended purpose to your classmates and explain how you created the image.

ARGUMENTS IN ADVERTISEMENTS

You probably consider images such as Figure 8.11 to be advertisements rather than simply photographs, and, of course, an advertisement's sole purpose is to make an argument for why you should buy a product.

As discussed earlier, visual advertisements rarely present a complete, explicit argument. Not only do ads often lack the space to present a full claim, reason, or evidence, but doing so would probably bore the reader and not be catchy enough to be memorable. Instead, arguments in advertisements often present themselves as a solution to some sort of problem.

Figure 8.12 is a gas station advertisement for Coca-Cola products. The ad simply states the solution: Mix and Match. What was the problem? The problem was choosing which of the Coke products to buy. The ad helps customers by offering them a way out of this dilemma.

Figure 8.13, an advertisement for Legos, shows an image that mimics Augmented Reality screens by demonstrating an alternative of the street scene if it were composed of their product (also consider how this advertisement makes use of its environment). The problem that the product attempts to solve for the viewer is one of "imagination," which they presume the audience may lack. The implied argument is that using their toy will help users improve their ability to imagine. The advertisement, however, doesn't provide reasons why users should improve their powers of imagination, nor evidence to support those reasons. Even though the advertisement makes the general claim or idea clear through the text "IMAGINE," it doesn't explicitly back up its claim or explain why Lego made it.

The implied argument, however, suggests that the viewer has a problem in the first place, which may or may not be the case. Figure 8.14 shows an advertisement for FedEx shipping. In this image, FedEx is making the implied argument that if you ship with the company, then your fragile merchandise will arrive safely at its destination, as safely as simply passing it from one set of hands to another. Through FedEx's careful service, the company solves the problem of packages that get broken in the mail. However, if you ship something that's not fragile, you might not have this particular problem, and so the unstated premise doesn't apply. FedEx, of course, would like you to believe you have this problem, and by

Credit: http://blackbulbcreations.blogspot.ca/

Figure 8.13
Like many of the images you have looked at in Chapter 5, this Lego ad makes clever use of its environment to support its claim.

Figure 8.12
This Coca-Cola ad offers a solution to your problem

Credit: Fedex/DDB Brasil

Figure 8.14
This FedEx ad makes a claim without printing a word of explanation.

Figure 8.15
The NHTSA and Child Car Safety want you to make sure you're using the right car seat for your child.

keeping the premise hidden makes it less likely for the audience to realize this.

Enthymemes often drive the argumentative structure of such advertisements. As discussed in Chapter 4, enthymemes offer a syllogism that suppresses either the major or minor premises or the conclusion. In doing so, they allow the viewer to figure out the logical structure of the argument as if it were a puzzle. The enthymeme leads to an implicit argument, since one of these premises or conclusions is suppressed. Articulating all the unstated parts of an ad can be difficult, showing just how unconsciously an audience often processes such images.

Figure 8.15 shows a public service announcement for the National Highway Traffic Safety Administration and Child Car Safety. This billboard asks a simple question "Is your child in the right car seat?" Rather than merely a yes or no, this question begs an analysis of what constitutes the "right" car seat, especially since the billboard shows four different options. The more complicated syllogism on which the question is based might go something like:

> Major premise: If your child is in the right car seat, he or she will be safe.

Which might have a minor premise and conclusion toward which the question prompts:

> Minor premise: My child is not in the right car seat.

> Conclusion: My child is not safe.

Alternatively:

> Minor premise: My child is in the right car seat.

> Conclusion: My child is safe.

These organizations would like you to react emotionally to this question, analyze your situation, and make sure that your child is safely secured with the right seat. By filling in the rest of the syllogism yourself, you remember the message better.

Within this implied argument is a narrative that the audience fills with whatever sport or activity they partake in. When creating your own advertisement, consider how you can develop a story that engages your reader and in which they can take some role. If you're advertising a product, develop a story in which the viewer can see herself using it in her daily life. If you're advertising a public service, create a story in which the audience can see themselves affected by or participating in the message.

Many public service announcements about cancer try to connect with the viewer by noting that many people will either get cancer or have a loved one affected by the disease. Such a statement helps to situate the viewer as a protagonist in the narrative against cancer. Even though you're not developing a full-fledged film narrative, such stories can be vital to your implied argument for why your audience should or should not act in a particular way.

MAKING CONNECTIONS

AS A CLASS

Analyze various advertisements and determine what problem they're trying to solve for their audience. What kinds of arguments do the companies make in trying to persuade the audience to accept their solution? Does the ad attempt to convince the audience that they have the problem in the first place? How? Are these arguments explicit or implicit?

IN A GROUP

Suppose that a group of scientists has just invented the first working teleporter and want you to help market the device. Create your own advertisement for this invention. Consider what kinds of arguments you will make and how you will make them. Will you use an explicit, straightforward argument? Will you present a narrative story? What problem does this device solve for potential customers? Is this audience monolithic, or does it have many problems? When finished, share your ad with the class.

ON YOUR OWN

At some point, you have probably identified with a product, the spokesperson for a product, or a story told about a product. Think of the brands that most appeal to you and create a list of products you identify with, whether or not you actually need or even buy the product. Think through some of the ways discussed in this section in which advertisements appeal to viewers and determine if any have influenced you. Write a report with your list and results and share it with the class.

ARGUMENTS IN MUSIC

While arguments appear in images, they also speak through the music you listen to, either through the songs on your iPods or the background music in film scores. Music that accompanies film or television can dramatically impact how an audience receives that media. The meaning of an image can change if combined with dramatic, suspenseful, sad, upbeat, or inspirational music, which triggers an emotional response and filters how an audience responds to other stimuli.

For instance, try thinking of how you would react to a horror scene of a zombie attack if a sensory-heightening suspenseful music was replaced by something romantic, or perhaps a heavy metal song from the 80s. The scene would change from scary to comical, and you might expect the zombies to start rockin' out, head-banging until their undead heads fell off. Such use of music develops an emotional response, which in turn develops the kind of argument the creator is trying to make about the scene's content (Figure 8.16).

Credit: Short Yellow

Credit: ©Buena Vista Pictures/Courtesy Everett Collection

Figure 8.16
When depicted with the music of Psy, Zombies aren't so scary (just stylish).
http://www.youtube.com/watch?v=B4hv0-FPDxc

Figure 817
The Lion King opens with what's commonly interpreted as African sounds and rhythms.
http://www.youtube.com/watch?v=JQ89RTVJB4c

In this way, music also provides a cue that helps to develop the story of a visual narrative. The famous music of *Jaws* lets the audience know that the shark is near, and provides an ominous atmosphere for its presence. John Williams, who composed themes for hundreds of movies that you've probably seen, developed individual themes for most of the main characters in the *Star Wars* franchise. "The Imperial March" indicates that the story is now depicting scenes with Darth Vader, while "Yoda's Theme" is, of course, about Yoda.

Rather than develop specific themes, music can help situate a location or character by cueing familiar kinds of music. *The Lion King* uses melodies and rhythms commonly associated with African-based music, helping to "authenticate" the story (Figure 8.17), while *Aladdin* uses music most listeners might connect with Middle Eastern sounds and instruments (whether or not such music is actually authentic to those regions).

The songs you listen to on MP3 players make arguments as well. Many songs can be somewhat explicit with their arguments. Michael Jackson's song "Heal the World" makes a direct claim to its audience, pleading for his listeners to heal the world to "make it a better place, for you and for me and the entire human race" because there are "people dying." Many of his other songs, such as "Man in the Mirror," "Billy Jean," or "Bad" also make direct claims and arguments about starting change in the world with one's self, denying paternity of a child, or claiming that he is "bad."

Many other songs make some kind of argument about love, either desiring, affirming, lamenting, or mourning for the emotion. Yet other songs make implicit arguments, often by telling some sort of story about a character or event and letting the reader create associations with modern life. U2's song

Credit: Island Records

Credit: Columbia

Figure 8.18
U2 argues against the violence in Northern Ireland through their song "Sunday, Bloody Sunday."
http://www.youtube.com/watch?v=Q59HvK2HM2c

Figure 8.19
Bruce Springsteen's "Born in the U.S.A." implicitly argues against how returning soldiers have been treated.
http://www.youtube.com/watch?v=EPhWR4d3FJQ

"Sunday, Blood Sunday" is about the Bloody Sunday incident that occurred in Derry, Northern Ireland, where the British Army killed twenty-six unarmed civil rights protesters. In the lyrics, U2 offers a series of rhetorical questions, asking for "how long?" must such atrocities go on, making an implicit argument against war and violence (Figure 8.18).

Back in America, while you might think that Bruce Springsteen's "Born in the U.S.A." is a patriotic song praising the country, it is actually a critique of the way that he feels the nation mistreats soldiers (Figure 8.19). Neither of these songs make an explicit claim but blend music and lyrics to make implicit, political points. Each of these songs tell a story of either a historical event or a fictional individual to help connect with viewers and affect them at the level of *pathos*.

Many songs made into music videos create even further arguments through the interplay of image and sound. Figure 8.20 shows the music video for the song "Words I Never Said" by Lupe Fiasco. The song comments on the current state of the world, and laments "words never said" by the author, supposedly referring to a missed opportunity to speak up when witnessing injustice.

Credit: Fox Studios

Figure 8.20
Lupe Fiasco's song "Words I Never Said" (featuring Skylar Grey) makes an implicit argument through its lyrics (and the images in the music video).
http://www.youtube.com/watch?v=2211sf5JZD0

The video parallels this theme but also shows a dystopian police state where citizens are gagged and/or jailed for speaking against the government. Part of the overall implicit argument suggests that unless citizens speak up, use freedom of speech and protest when needed, they will regret the "words we never said" and may ultimately lose that freedom. The lyrics anchor the meaning of the video just as text can anchor an image, but the video also offers a new perspective on the meaning of the song.

When you develop arguments in visual media that can use sound, you should consider how music can either become the secondary means of persuasion, reinforcing what the viewer sees, or the primary means, appealing to the audience via sound with images simply supporting the music. Consider how to develop an audio-visual argument with the previous examples in mind, using sound to signal emotional cues, incorporating songs that have an implied argument that reinforces your own, or by blending image and sound so that together they create an argument that is greater than the sum of their individual parts. Of course, if using copyrighted material, you should first ask for permission from the artist.

MAKING CONNECTIONS

AS A CLASS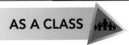

Find movie scenes that you vividly remember—but don't include dialogue—on a video search engine such as YouTube. As you play each clip, put the video player on mute and play different music in the background. Next, repeat with different music. Does the change in background music alter how you interpret the scene? How so? Discuss your reactions as a class.

IN A GROUP

Find and download a music video online. Insert the video into a video editor, and change the background music. How does the meaning of the images change with the new song? How does the meaning of the song change? How does the argument change? Alternatively, create your own video for a song forming a parallel argument. For either option, share your final version with the class and discuss your rationale for how you made it and what argument you hoped to convey.

ON YOUR OWN

Choose an album of songs and analyze their lyrics. What implicit arguments do you notice in each song? Does the album as a whole attempt to construct an argument? Does the title of the album suggest this argument? Do any important lyrics appear in multiple songs? Draft a report of your findings and share them with the class.

ARGUMENTS IN MOVIES

Movies provide a powerful medium for making arguments and use different degrees of explicit and implicit arguments depending on the movie's conventions, purpose, and audience. Documentary films usually offer a more direct claim and examination of an issue than your typical Hollywood blockbuster. The documentary *The Corporation*, for example, examines the modern-day corporation—which has legal status as a person—and asks what kind of person it would be according to psychological criteria (Figure 8.21).

The film argues that a corporation fits all of the characteristics of a psychopath. While this particular argument is explicit, providing reasons and evidence, the film makes other kinds of implicit arguments along the way, suggesting that perhaps one shouldn't want such psychopathic institutions to be so powerful.

But even the big blockbusters can offer arguments. Consider director James

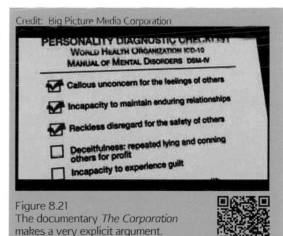

Credit: Big Picture Media Corporation

Figure 8.21
The documentary *The Corporation* makes a very explicit argument.
http://www.youtube.com/
watch?v=s5hEiANG4Uk&feature=relmfu

Cameron's film *Avatar*, the highest-grossing movie of all time (Figure 8.22). This film is a science-fiction action adventure with cutting-edge special effects, driven by classic narrative themes rather than an explicit exposition found in many documentaries.

Credit: ©20th Century Fox. All rights reserved. Courtesy Everett Collection.

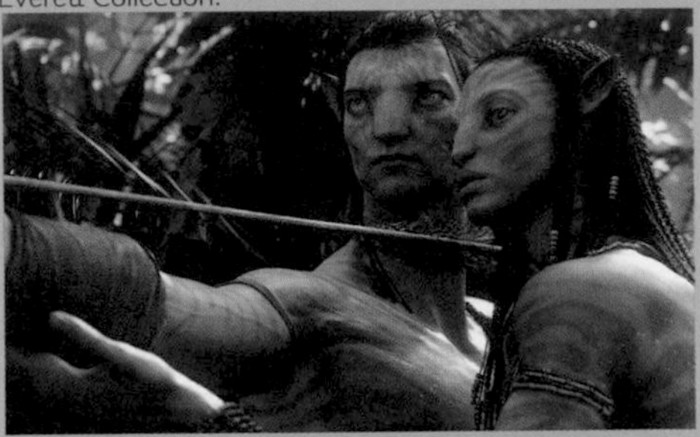

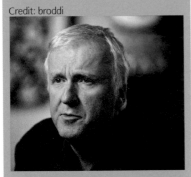

Figure 8.22
Avatar uses a story to create a complex set of implicit arguments.

Credit: broddi

Figure 8.23
James Cameron acknowledges that he hopes *Avatar* "opens" people's eyes.

Avatar borrows from the myth of the American Frontier (pushing the settled boundary of a civilization in search of wealth and opportunity), American Westerns (within this frontier, conflicts between Americans and the "Indian" other, in this case the Na'vi), and what Kirby Ferguson calls "sorry about colonialism" (films that show the destructiveness and injustice when one culture attempts to subjugate another). These themes, while traditional in many films, function as an argument in themselves, creating a particular set of expectations for the audience and constructing a particular atmosphere based on a common experience of these themes.

In addition, the film also has themes of deep ecology, forcing the audience to consider how it treats its own planet. As Cameron (Figure 8.23) has stated, he wanted to create an all-out adventure movie but also one "that maybe in the enjoying of it makes you think a little bit about the way you interact with nature and your fellow man." In that "making one think," you as a rhetorician should recognize an implicit argument about one's relationship to the world.

Cameron adds that "the Na'vi represent something that is our higher selves, or our aspirational selves, what we would like to think we are" while most of the humans in the film "represent what we know to be the parts of ourselves that are trashing our world and maybe condemning ourselves to a grim future." *Avatar*, then, makes arguments that pertain to what Cameron sees as the current situation regarding how humans treat the environment.

In addition, the United States was also engaged in two wars at the time of the film's release, and Cameron noted that his film touches on the role of warfare in culture as well. Consider the following article by Ben Hoyle of *The Times*:

Movie's Blue-skinned Aliens Aim to Open Our Eyes to War on Terror

YEARS have passed and superstar reputations burnt in the wait for a hit film about the War on Terror. Nobody imagined that that film might turn out to be *Avatar*.

James Cameron's 3-D science fiction extravaganza, conservatively estimated to have cost at least £240 million, had its world premiere in London last night.

As the director's first feature film since *Titanic, Avatar* is the most stratospherically hyped film of the year, as well as the most technologically ambitious and probably the most expensive film ever made.

However, it also contains heavy implicit criticism of America's conduct in the War on Terror.

As the director of *Aliens, The Terminator* and *Terminator 2*, as well as *Titanic*, the highest-grossing film of all time, Cameron has a formidable box-office track record.

However, a string of films about the wars in Iraq and Afghanistan have flopped at the box office in the past two years, including the Reese Witherspoon vehicle *Rendition* and *Lions for Lambs*, which starred Tom Cruise, Robert Redford and Meryl Streep.

Cameron said yesterday the theme was not the main point of *Avatar*, but added that Americans had a "moral responsibility" to understand the impact that their country's recent military campaigns had.

"We went down a path that cost several hundreds of thousands of Iraqi lives. I don't think the American people even know why it was done. So it's all about opening your eyes."

The film pitches the viewer 145 years into the future where a paraplegic US Marine called Jake Sully is flown to the hostile planet of Pandora to join a colony seeking to mine a rare mineral that can solve Earth's 22nd-century energy crisis.

The planet is home to the Na'vi, a species of 10ft-tall, blue-skinned hunters who enjoy a close bond with their bountiful natural environment and resist the humans' incursions.

Sully "remotely inhabits" a genetically engineered avatar created from a fusion of his DNA and Na'vi DNA and sets out to win the natives' trust. In the background is the looming threat of the heavily armed human colony who want the minerals under the Na'vi's land. This is where the politics comes in.

The hero is with the Na'vi when the humans attack their homes. The fusillade of gas, incendiary bombs and guided missiles that wreck their ancient habitat is described as "shock and awe", the term popularized by the US military assault on Baghdad that opened the Iraq war in 2003.

The humans' military commander declares: "Our survival relies on pre-emptive action. We will fight terror, with terror." One of the more sympathetic characters preparing to resist the human invasion bemoans the need for "martyrdom".

One theory for the box-office success of the *Star Wars* films in the 1970s and 1980s was that, in their depiction of a plucky guerrilla insurgency against a vastly better equipped superpower, they enabled a generation of Americans to refight the Vietnam war on the side of the underdogs. The same idea holds true for Avatar. The War on Terror references are more complex than simply equating the US with the villains in the film.

After the Na'vi homes collapse in flames the landscape is coated in ash and floating embers in scenes reminiscent of Ground Zero after the September 11 attacks.

Cameron, who was born in Canada, said he had been "surprised at how much it did look like September 11. I didn't think that was necessarily a bad thing".

Referring to the "shock and awe" sequence, he said: "We know what it feels like to launch the missiles. We don't know what it feels like for them to land on our home soil, not in America. I think there's a moral responsibility to understand that.

"That's not what the movie's about—that's only a minor part of it. For me it feels consistent only in a very generalized theme of us looking at ourselves as human beings in a technical society with all its skills, part of which is the ability to do mechanized warfare, part of which is the ability to do warfare at a distance, at a remove, which seems to make it morally easier to deal with, but its not."

Hoyle argues that *Avatar* is precisely engaged in the "war on terror," and many visual elements (such as the Na'vi tower) help to make this argument, offering a visual analogy. In this article, Cameron states that part of his goal with *Avatar* was to "open" people's eyes. As with the other media you've looked at, he does not argue explicitly, but implicitly, making his viewers think about the subject in an emotionally charged and invested way. Cameron attempts to make his audience identify with the characters in the story and side with the protagonist, Jake Sully, who comes to sympathize with the native Na'vi and ultimately fights with them against his own race of humans. As you develop your arguments, then, you might consider developing stories that create a world that parallels the situation about which you'd like to make an argument, using entertainment as a vehicle for persuasion as well as distraction.

MAKING CONNECTIONS

AS A CLASS

Analyze movie posters and discuss what kind of argument each poster is trying to make. How does the composition of the poster add to this argument? How do elements such as typography affect the argument? Does this poster attempt to offer some solution to a problem?

IN A GROUP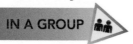

Find a movie trailer for a film of a particular genre, such as horror, western, suspense, fantasy, etc. Using the scenes from the trailer or additional footage from the film, create a new trailer that depicts the film as another genre, such as a comedy or romance (Figure 8.24). For instance, turn the trailer for Jaws into a romantic comedy. What kind of argument did the original trailer make, and what kind of new argument have you made in converting the trailer? Share your trailer with the class.

Credit: New Line Cinema

Figure 8.24
This trailer remixes scenes from the comedy *Dumb and Dumber* to make it seem like a dramatic thriller.
http://www.youtube.com/watch?v=zLDx-BPgxxA

ON YOUR OWN

Create a list of your top five favorite movies. Review these movies,
and determine what kinds of arguments they're attempting to make
as well as how they make these arguments. Share your list and results
with the class.

KEY TERMS
explicit argument
implicit argument

OUTPUT: PODCAST

For this assignment, create an explicit or implicit argument, and distribute it through a podcast. If explicit, make sure you incorporate a claim, reasons for that claim, and evidence. If your argument is implicit, consider how to win over your audience, such as by using anecdotes, presenting a fictional story, or by emotionally appealing to your listener.

A wide range of free audio programs can provide the basic software needed to make a podcast. Ideally, you will have access to a decent microphone, but some basic desktop computer microphones or webcam mics can be effective. While creating a podcast may seem simple beyond the initial technological setup, the following tips offer further suggestions to ensure your podcast sounds its best.

As discussed in the introduction, make sure you revisit the rhetorical tetrahedron through your drafting and revising process.

Planning: Write a script or overall outline of what you plan to argue. This script will help keep you on track while recording and make sure that your argument or story is the most logical or engaging. This script can also help you structure your claim, reasons, and evidence. Also, consider listening to podcasts created by others, such as the radio news organization National Public Radio. These podcasts can give you ideas about how to structure your own.

Testing, testing: Before recording your whole podcast, test your microphones and recording software a few times. Play back some of these test recordings and notice if the audio has too much static, too much background noise, too much hiss, too little volume, or if certain sounds like "p's" or "s's" stand out. If so, you might place a windscreen or "pop shield" in front of the mic to cut down on these sounds, or place a piece of paper between you and the microphone, testing this setup further to see if the sound improves. You can make some adjustments with an audio editor in post-production, but it's best to record the sound as cleanly as possible before moving to post-production.

Identity: While this principle is more important for a sustained, serial podcast, consider creating some sort of "identity" for your podcast. What does your podcast offer that others don't? What's your podcast's particular niche? You might also consider creating some sort of theme or catch phrase that's unique to your podcast.

Structure and organization: While you will hopefully organize and structure your podcast in the planning phase, make sure that it has a coherent beginning, middle, and end, either as an explicit or implicit argument. Within this three-part structure, introduce what you're going to talk about, discuss it, and then re-state what you just discussed or its conclusion. Since your audience can't easily go back and "read" what you said through audio, such structure helps them remember.

Don't Read: Although you should have a script or outline, try not to read the document when recording. You might read small sections of it, but try to sound spontaneous and free-flowing. Reading from a script tends to dull the material, sound unnatural, and decrease emotion in the voice.

Length: Although variable, try to determine the appropriate length for your podcast. If too short, you won't be able to present a whole argument to the listener. However, if you create a podcast that is too long, the audience may stop listening, either from boredom or time constraints. Try to find a middle range, usually at least five minutes, but no more than fifteen minutes.

Content: Since content is key, make sure you present something worth listening to. Why should an audience download your podcast? What does it have to offer? What will they learn? Will they be entertained? As always, you can't deliver your argument if your audience tunes out.

Review and revise: Just as you should ask your peers to review and comment on your written works, ask a classmate to listen to your podcast. Ask them where the content sounded dull, where they became confused, and if the audio quality detracted from the message. After you note this feedback, go back and revise or re-record any material that the reviewer found problematic.

Delivery: While you can electronically deliver your podcast in many ways, iTunes makes it simple to disseminate your podcast and allow anyone on the service to download it. Although you still have to host the podcast file on your own Web space, iTunes allows many more people to find it by including it in its database. You can read more about submitting podcasts to iTunes here: http://www.apple.com/itunes/podcasts/specs.html.

9

SCRIPTS (WRITING)

While many of the projects in this book will involve final outputs in new media, you'll still need to compose a lot of alphabetic writing during the planning, researching, and revising processes. This writing comes in a variety of forms, such as outlines, scripts, camera directions, and collaboration materials to help you communicate with other students you might partner with.

This chapter covers the kinds of writing that is necessary to produce the various new media artifacts presented in this text, writing that may range from a traditional research report to help you produce other documents, a script for a video, a list of shooting locations, or something as simple as a timeline to keep you on track so that you can successfully produce the final visual output (Figure 9.1). Writing in words has always been an important tool for writing in images, and this chapter will cover the ways that traditional writing can transfer to final outputs, which may not even contain words.

 As you read about the different kinds of writing that go into making visual texts, consider the elements of the rhetorical tetrahedron. As you draft different documents that you intend to turn into new media texts, keep in mind aspects such as design, medium, and genre, rhetorical choices that may change during the writing

Figure 9.1
Although this is one kind of "script," you'll write many other kinds when creating visual texts.

267

process, and which will certainly change as you move from alphabetic writing into new media. As you write on paper (or on a word processor), keep in mind the parts of the rhetorical tetrahedron and that your final product will look different once you change medium.

KINDS OF "SCRIPTS"

The word "script" derives from the Latin word *scribere*, which means "to write." In this generalized sense, any writing you produce is already a script, and there are many kinds of scripts you'll have to produce besides the actual "script" or screenplay. The following sections introduce the most common kinds of writing you'll encounter as well as a few tips on how to compose them.

Screenplays

When you think of writing for film or video, the script or screenplay probably first comes to mind. The screenplay provides the plan for the movie, the detailed outline for how to produce the visual and audio elements of the film. When a writer composes a screenplay, she is obviously writing words, but words meant to be transformed into images. These words need to be clear and easily adaptable to a visual camera shot or an action by an actor. When writing a script, one writes the visual elements, what the audience will see. Although you probably won't produce a screenplay for a full-length movie in your class, understanding the function and terminology of screenplays, and how to write them, can help you produce better new media texts, whether it's a photo essay or a short YouTube clip.

Credit: Academy of Motion Picture Arts and Sciences

The misconceptions of being a screenwriter

Figure 9.2
There are some misconceptions about being a screenwriter.
http://www.oscars.org/video/watch/
screenwriters_misconception.html

The screenwriter also composes what the audience hears, such as the dialogue or sound effects (the film's musical soundtrack is usually composed by a professional musician). However, as discussed in Figure 9.2, a film's dialogue—which many will probably assume is the most important writing within the screenplay—can be the least important part.

As Lawrence Kasdan notes in the video, "The biggest misconception about screenwriting is that the screenwriter writes the dialogue and someone comes up with the other stuff." So what is this "other stuff"? Dick Clement states that a screenplay includes the "architecture" or structure of the story. This structure typically follows some sort of narrative arc, with a beginning, middle, and end. Figure 9.3 shows Freytag's Pyramid, a diagram that helps explain the basic structure of narratives.

Aristotle, in describing ancient Greek drama, identified three main parts to a well-written play: a beginning, middle, and end. Gustav Freytag, a German playwright and novelist, designed a five-part pyramid with which he explains typical dramatic structure. Freytag's pyramid derives from a five-act play in which the following parts appear: exposition, rising action, climax, falling action, and dénouement. While Freytag based his pyramid on plays, this analytical device can also be used to understand other kinds of narratives, including fiction, film, and television.

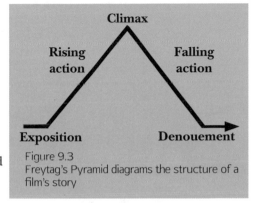

Figure 9.3
Freytag's Pyramid diagrams the structure of a film's story

The beginning of a story offers critical information, introductions to the main characters, and familiarity with the setting. In addition, the beginning presents the audience with a "hook": some situation that captures their attention and interest. You can think of a hook as the exigency of the film—what is the problem faced by the characters? What question is the director trying to explore? In other words, why is this story being told, and why is the audience compelled to watch it?

Typically, when considering that a typical screenplay is about 120 pages (with one page equivalent to one minute of screentime), this hook should occur within the first ten pages of the script (or first ten minutes of a movie). Of course, many of the videos produced on a daily basis aren't two hours long, and so you should consider getting to the hook sooner. If the video is informative rather than narrative (for example, an instructional video rather than a story), then this beginning should introduce the reader to those providing the information, what organizations they're affiliated with, and the hook can be thought of as the reason why the audience might be watching the video. If the video is a review of the latest smartphone, then this should be stated early to let the audience know what and why they're watching.

The middle section of a story is the longest and provides the rising action of the narrative. In this section, the main character attempts to solve a problem but the solution is complicated by other characters or situations. These characters have their own problems (subplots) that can get in the way of the main character's motivation or sometimes correspond with it. Often, alliances are formed between characters with similar interests.

In the movie *Jaws*, Brody (Roy Scheider) and Hooper (Richard Dreyfuss) work together since each has an interest in finding the shark. Brody wants to kill it to make the beaches safer, while Hooper wants to find it for scientific reasons. While their motivations are different, they come together toward a similar purpose. Brody and the town's mayor, however, struggle against each other. Brody wants to close the beaches because of the danger posed by the shark, while the mayor wants to keep the beaches open for tourists who bring money into the town's economy. These two characters help or complicate Brody's problem (the shark).

Credit: ©Warner Brothers/Courtesy Everett Collection

Figure 9.4
The Hangover introduces many complications for the protagonists to overcome.

You can also see this typical structure played out in the movie *The Hangover* (Figure 9.4). The hook, the problem that the characters confront, comes when Phil (Bradley Cooper), Stu (Ed Helms), and Alan (Zach Galifianakis) can't remember where they left their friend, Doug (Justin Bartha), who is soon to be married. Besides their hangover-induced amnesia, other problems complicate the search for their fiend, such as awakening to find their hotel room in shambles as well as a baby and a live tiger.

They further discover that they've stolen a police car (for which they're arrested), Stu was married to a stripper, they have stolen $80,000 from a flamboyant gangster, and that the tiger belonged to former boxer Mike Tyson. The main plot of the movie develops as the characters figure out how all of these complications occurred and trace them through the previous night to find Doug. Although the movie is a bit exaggerated in terms of its probability, it provides a useful example of how to include obstacles and subplots within the story that still drive the main plot.

Following the rising action, the story ends with a climax, the highest point of the rising action. The climax marks a point of transition for the protagonist. In *Return of the Jedi*, Luke Skywalker confronts Darth Vader, either to save him from the dark side, destroy him, or die himself. This final act provides the key moment when the plot will turn toward its fulfillment.

However, the climax itself is not the ending of the story. After this final buildup, a falling action occurs, where the actual conclusion is revealed. Often, the ending is still contingent, still in doubt and could go in either direction. The hero could win, or lose. Phil, Stu, and Alan might find Doug in time for his wedding, or they might not.

The actual conclusion, also called the dénouement, presents the outcome of the climax, and allows all of the unresolved situations in the film to become solved or untied (Figure 9.5). The dénouement may come quickly before the final scene of the film (such as Brody's killing of the shark right before he and Hooper swim back to shore), or a more lengthy conclusion as in *The Hangover*, where the final wedding scene depicts Stu breaking up with his controlling girlfriend, and the friends finding a camera with images of their forgotten exploits. Although the plot resolves when they find Doug and get him to the wedding, the falling action continues for several minutes before the final scene occurs.

Credit: Martino Altomonte

Figure 9.5
Dénouement literally means to "unknot," and describes the resolution to the story. In this painting, Alexander the Great cuts the Gordian Knot, creating a dénouement or final solution to his problem of untying it.

In addition to dialogue and the basic structure, Brian Helgeland explains that screenwriters have to write all of the smaller details as well, including the exterior shots, such as bridge explosions, car chases, fight sequences, and other action. In John August's words,

> *"Dialogue is a hugely important part of movies, but it's really one of the smaller parts of movies. The screenwriter's the person who figures out what's gonna happen, and when it's gonna happen, and how it's gonna happen...the screenwriter creates a plan for making the whole movie."*
>
> —John August

While a screenwriter won't create all the writing that goes into a film on her own, she does create the blueprint from which much of the other writing develops. As discussed in Chapter 7, most of the research that goes into movies derives from what the cast and crew read in the script.

In addition to the general structure of a script, you should also be familiar with how different parts of a script are labeled. The following includes some of the more common elements of a screenplay. These elements provide instructions to the audience for how they should read the script and are usually written in ALL CAPs to make it clear when they occur.

CHARACTER: When presented as dialogue to be spoken, a character's name or description is always written in ALL CAPs and centered on the page. If written in a description, the name appears in ALL CAPs for the first instance and can be written normally afterwards.

CONTINUOUS: This instruction indicates that a shift in scene location has occurred, but the time is contemporary with the action of the previous scene. This frequently occurs when two characters are talking on the phone, and the audience see shots of both characters.

CUT TO: One of the most popular transitions, this instruction indicates a simple cut in action from one scene to another.

CROSSFADE: A type of transition that fades from one scene to another with a black frame in-between the two scenes.

Credit: Grm_wnr

DISSOLVE TO: Another transition in which one scene fades as another appears, without any black frames in between (Figure 9.6).

FADE TO: Synonymous with "DISSOLVE TO" above.

JUMP CUT TO: Jump cuts are usually of the same subject, from similar camera angles, during a relatively short period of time. Often witnessed during interview sequences, the director may cut out unimportant parts of an interview, cutting directly to the next important thing the interviewee says, displaying a discontinuous, jarring look (Figure 9.7).

Figure 9.6
This transition dissolves one image into another.
http://commons.
wikimedia.org/wiki/
File:A2o_dissolve.ogg

Credit: UGC (France)

Figure 9.7
This scene from *Breathless* makes heavy use of jump cuts.
http://www.youtube.com/
watch?v=OwLH6-bDhuE&list=PLOToExF
aWoNJnJE6y3V3St32gtnmz9Cr8

Credit: ©Columbia/Courtesy Everett Collection

Figure 9.8
This aerial shot from *The Shawshank Redemption* also establishes the new location of the prison.
http://www.
youtube.com/watch?v=wyDifF2_
Csk&list=PLOToExFaWoNJnJE6y3V3St32gtnmz9Cr8

EXT: This instruction lets the reader know that the shot is exterior, that the action is happening outside of a building.

INT: This instruction tells the reader that the scene occurs within the interior of a building or structure.

AERIAL SHOT: This instruction indicates an overhead, or aerial, shot.

CLOSE ON: A typical shot that zooms in tightly on a particular feature, such as a face or other important detail that the director wants the audience to notice.

ESTABLISHING SHOT: Usually a shot taken from a long distance that helps orientate the viewer to the larger context of place. For instance, one might take a long exterior shot showing Shawshank Prison as a whole before cutting to an interior scene showing the prison yard, thus establishing that the scene takes place in the prison (Figure 9.8).

FREEZE FRAME: The motion stops temporarily, fixing the action into a still photograph.

INTO VIEW: This instruction describes a technique in which a character or object moves into the camera's view, or frame, while the camera is still or pans out.

MATCH CUT TO: A match cut is a kind of transition in which a "match" is made between objects in two different scenes. The two objects may be a similar shape, color, movement, or like characteristic. This transition not only provides a clever way to shift scenes but also links the two objects together,

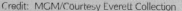
Credit: MGM/Courtesy Everett Collection

Credit: ©Amblin Entertainment/Courtesy Everett Collection

Figure 9.9
This match cut from *2001: A Space Odyssey* is perhaps one of the most famous.
http://www.youtube.com/watch?v=mI3s5fA7Zhk&list=PLOToExFaWoNJnJE6y3V3St32gtnmz9Cr8

Figure 9.10
This reverse angle from *Jurassic Park* reveals Tim to the viewer, but not the velociraptor.
http://www.youtube.com/watch?v=dnRxQ3dcaQk

creating a visual metaphor, suggesting one is in some way like or related to the other (Figure 9.9).

O.S or O.C: This acronym refers to "off screen" or "off camera" and provides a note to the director or actor that the sound or dialogue should occur outside of the camera's frame.

POV: Short for "point of view," this instruction indicates that the camera angle should come from the perspective of the character, as if the viewer is seeing through his or her eyes.

PUSH IN: For this camera direction, the camera should move toward (or push into) an actor, object, or the focus of the scene.

REVERSE ANGLE: A reverse angle shot provides the 180-degree view from a previous shot. It is often used when the director wants the audience to be able to see something that might be hidden from one of the on-screen characters. For instance, if someone is hiding behind a table from a movie monster, the reverse angle allows the audience to see the character but not the monster (Figure 9.10).

SPLIT SCREEN SHOT: This shot displays two scenes or locations at once. For example, rather than using a CONTINUOUS CUT TO for two people talking on the phone, you might show them simultaneously with a split screen shot.

STOCK SHOT: Any shot that you use that has already been recorded, such as clips from other films or from historical documents.

SUPER: This direction refers to "superimpose," when one image is superimposed over another. This technique is often used for titles and credits.

TIME CUT: A time cut chops up a long event into sections to display the most important part of each. This lets the director know to make transitions that show continuity and to eliminate the whole sequence of the action. For example, if you were making a movie about a marathon runner and wanted to include an actual marathon, you wouldn't show the whole race. Instead, you would show only certain important parts, such as the start, pivotal moments where the character struggles, and the finish. You might use TIME CUT to signal a cut in the time of the event while letting the director know that the marathon is still going on.

ZOOM: A camera instruction in which the camera lens is adjusted so that it zooms in on a particular subject.

SLUG LINE: The slug line precedes each scene, telling the director where, when, and sometimes what characters are in the scene. For instance, the slug line "EXT. DUVAL STREET – KEY WEST, FL – NIGHT" let's the director know that the scene is outside (EXT), and that it happens on Duval Street in Key West, Florida.

TRACKING SHOT: This instruction refers to any shot that isn't from a fixed position and that follows the characters or subject being filmed.

V.O.: Short for voice over, this instruction lets the director know that the dialogue should be off camera, coming from an unseen actor (or perhaps from a character's inner monologue). It will usually occur next to a character's name speaking the dialogue.

Finally, as an example, consider this early script segment from The Hangover.

```
EXT. BEL AIR BAY CLUB -- PACIFIC PALISADES, CA -- MORNING

It's a beautiful spring morning in the Palisades. High
atop the cliffs, looking out over the Pacific Ocean, sits
the exclusive BEL AIR BAY CLUB. Workers bustle about the
lawn, setting up a high-end wedding.

A STRING QUARTET warms up. A team of FLORISTS arrange
centerpieces. CATERERS set the white linen tables...

INT. BRIDAL SUITE -- DAY

A simple, classic wedding dress hangs on a closet door
in this sun-drenched bridal suite. Sitting at the makeup
table, surrounded by her bridesmaids, is the beautiful
bride, TRACY TURNER, 20's. She's busy doing her makeup.

Just then, Tracy's rich, stern FATHER, 50's, blows in.

MR. TURNER

                    Any word from Doug?

The way he spits out "Doug" tells us all we need to know
about how Mr. Turner feels about his future son-in-law.

TRACY

                    No, but I'm sure he's--

Just then, Tracy's CELLPHONE rings. She quickly answers
it.
```

TRACY (CONT'D)

                    Hello?

INTERCUT WITH:

EXT. MOJAVE DESERT -- MORNING

Heat-waves rise off the Mojave. Standing at a lone, dust covered pay phone in the middle of the desert is

VICK LENNON

He's in his late 20's, tall, rugged—and currently a mess. His shirt is ripped open, his aviator sunglasses are bent, his lip is bloodied, and he clearly hasn't slept in days.

VICK

                    Tracy, it's Vick.

Parked on the dirt road behind Vick is his near-totalled 1967 Cadillac Deville convertible; it's scratched, dented, filthy -- and missing its passenger side door.

Slouched inside are TWO OTHER GUYS, also looking like hell.

TRACY

                    Hey Vick!

VICK

Listen, honey...The bachelor party got a little out of control and, well...we lost Doug.

TRACY

                    (her jaw dropping)
                    What?! But we're getting married
                    in like four hours!

Vick squints at the rising sun.

VICK

                    Yeah, that's not gonna
happen.

```
CUT TO:

TITLE OVER BLACK: 40 HOURS EARLIER

CUT TO:

EXT. THE 10 FREEWAY -- DAY

The top down, The Who's "Baba O'Riley" blasting from the
stereo, Vick's pristine Cadillac convertible rockets down
Highway 10 towards Nevada.

At the wheel is Vick, looking as sharp as his Caddy in a
half open shirt and mint condition aviators.

Sitting shotgun is the groom, DOUG BILLINGS, late 20's,
handsome, barefoot, crunchy—an all around great guy.

Behind Vick sits ALAN MERVISH, late 20's, an anal tax
attorney from Connecticut, his Izod shirt tucked into
his khakis. He's currently applying sun screen to his
forehead.

Next to Alan is STU PRYCE, late 20's, former high school
linebacker and lovably dimwitted father of two. He drums
the back of the front seat to the music, totally pumped,
like this is his first time out of the house in years.
Because it is.
```

From this snippet, you might have noticed a few things. First, the script uses standard formatting and terminology (such as EXT), capitalizes the first occurrence of a character's name, notes the location of the shot, and other instructions discussed above. This part of the script also provides brief descriptions of the characters for the actors who play them, the costume designers who dress them, and the make up artists who need to add effects such as a bloody lip, not to mention set designers and whoever must procure the 1967 Cadillac Deville convertible.

However, these first few pages of the script clearly provide something even more important: the hook. Very quickly the audience understands the problem: there is a wedding planned to happen in four hours. Doug, the groom, is missing. Vick informs the bride that the marriage is "not gonna happen." The rest of the film shows the previous 40 hours and how the situation unfolded, how Vick, Alan, and Stu got in their mess, and make the audience wonder if Doug will actually get to his wedding.

When writing your own scripts, you don't need to include all of the elements of a Hollywood screenplay, but they provide important information to different audiences about different facets of a project's production. Most importantly, your script should provide the narrative of your visual text. However, other instructions help to inform those working with you (or even remind yourself) how certain scenes should be composed. Together, the narrative outline and technical instructions provide a blueprint for completing your project.

MAKING CONNECTIONS

AS A CLASS

Choose a movie, and find its script online. Before class, read the script, then watch the movie together. As you watch, note in the script where the screenplay and movie differ from each other or where they remain the same. How much did the film deviate from the script? Were such changes trivial, or did they significantly change the story being told?

IN A GROUP

Choose a short story, comic, or other story not already in movie or film form. Write a screenplay of this story as a film. How would you provide details about interior or exterior shots? How would you provide character descriptions? What would you want others to know who might be working on its production? What parts would you remove from the original story, and what parts would you add? Share your screenplay with the class and discuss the choices you made.

ON YOUR OWN

Write down your favorite five or ten movies. If you can, revisit the first ten to twenty minutes of each movie, and note when the hook occurs. What aspects of the hook make it compelling to keep watching the film? Why is it interesting? Do you feel it occurs too late, too early, or at an appropriate time? Answer these questions about each movie, as well as any other thoughts, and share your examples with the class.

Dialogue

According to the screenwriters in Figure 9.2, dialogue isn't the most important part of writing for a film. However, it still represents what the audience hears and plays a major role. When writing dialogue for your own project, there are several guidelines that you can follow to make it sound more authentic and believable.

Read: Find a variety of scripts that contain different kinds of dialogue, and read them. Note how the dialogue is written to mimic spoken language and what cues the screenwriter provides to the actors for guidance. The more scripts you read, the more familiar you'll become with how to write good dialogue. You can also use plays in addition to scripts.

Speak: In addition to reading the dialogue in the screenplays you find, try speaking the dialogue out loud. This will give you a sense of how the written word translates into a spoken performance. You might also watch clips of film as you follow along in the screenplay to hear how the lines of dialogue are delivered by actors.

Cause and effect: Typically, dialogue should follow a natural flow from one line to another, where the response spoken by a character makes sense based on the line that came before. In other words, dialogue should feed off itself. If a character's line states "Why did you burn the house down?" the following line might be something like "It's the only way I could stop the infestation of the alien virus," not "I need to get some bread." The lines should be logically connected.

Don't infodump: Often in science fiction books and films, at some point the author has to explain the new word she is introducing or explain how some piece of technology works. This technique is called an "infodump" because the author is dumping a lot of information through dialogue that is often forced, clunky, and unnatural. Of course, this can also occur with places or situations you are familiar with, where the director might find it necessary to bring the reader up to speed on some aspect of the story. However, instead of including this information through dialogue, try to use actions, props, or other visual elements to convey the information rather than dialogue that doesn't ring true. Let the audience pick up on the visual cues and subtext of the film. Show them, don't tell them.

Motivate the dialogue: When characters speak, it's typically because they want something from another character. Dialogue should be motivated by these desires of the character. What is the character trying to accomplish in the scene, and how does speaking help them to do this? When writing narration for video that is expository, what is your motivation for the narration? What are you trying to point out with words that isn't evident in the images? How does narration help you make your point to the audience?

Perform: Once you've written your own dialogue, speak it, and have others speak it as well. As with any writing that provides instructions, you should user-test your material to make sure it does what you want. You should perform your writing even if that writing is voice-over narration.

Revise: After you've performed your dialogue, revise those areas that sound forced or unnatural. Perform the new lines, and revise again as needed.

These are just a few tips to help you craft dialogue in your projects. They apply to both fictional narratives as well as nonfiction, expository works. Study carefully how other writers craft scripts, not just those for the traditional Hollywood film but also for television, documentaries, nature shows, or other kinds of programs. Finally, consider looking at genre-specific scripts such as horror, suspense, mystery, romance, or science fiction if you have narrowed your interests to a precise genre.

MAKING CONNECTIONS

AS A CLASS

Bring in scripts from different types of movies and highlight the sections that contain heavy dialogue. In small groups—with the rest of the class as the audience—take turns performing some of these scenes. As you either watch or perform, note how the dialogue sounds when said aloud, if the dialogue sounds correct or authentic, and if there are changes that you'd make to the dialogue. Discuss the scene, not necessarily for the performance, but for how the dialogue captures (or doesn't) actual speech. Is the dialogue motivated? Does it exclude unnecessary information? Does one line trigger the next?

IN A GROUP

Craft a short scene between two characters that primarily features dialogue. Follow the guidelines above, making sure that the dialogue helps the characters to achieve some goal and that dialogue from one character feeds into the following line of the other character. When you've completed the script, perform it before the class, and get their feedback on the quality of your dialogue.

ON YOUR OWN

Because of each panel's limited space, comic books require sparse use of dialogue, relying on dialogue that is tightly crafted and highly motivated. Bring in a comic book or graphic novel and study the dialogue. Compare this dialogue to what you might find in a film, play, or novel. Do you notice any differences? Similarities? Does the dialogue serve other functions that it doesn't in other genres? Draft a short report with your findings and share them with the class.

Narration

Unlike dialogue, voice-over narration isn't meant to sound like "natural" speech, so your goals for producing this kind of writing are very different.

Rather than just telling a fictional story, narration might be used to try and sell something (advertising), inform (public service announcement), explain (nature documentary), or persuade (social or political documentary). Just like any piece of writing, you should understand your purpose for the narration as well as your audience.

- Are you writing to a general audience in which you should choose basic diction so that people from a wide range of educational backgrounds can understand it?

- Are you writing for children, so that you must discuss complex concepts in simple ways?

- Are you writing narration for other specialists in which they might expect disciplinary language?

Each of these audiences come with their own constraints and expectations and will determine how you should script your narration. However, narration should sound more like natural speech than the essays you compose in other writing classes.

While timing is important when delivering dialogue, it's extremely important when crafting narration. Not only do you have a limited amount of time into which you must fit all that you'd like to say, you must also decide when to include narration. You must decide when visuals might need some sort of narration to enhance the viewer's understanding and when it might be better to include silence, letting the power of the image speak for itself, allowing the audience's imagination to work without other input. Remember that images can evoke powerful emotional responses in your audience. You will most likely find that using images to elicit emotional reactions will be more effective than using narration to tell the audience what to feel in a particular scene.

Narration shouldn't be used to tell the story but rather to comment on the visual aspects of the story. Action should be shown, not told about. However, some narration can be used to comment on the action of the scene that might be unclear to viewers. This technique is common in nature documentaries, where the camera may show some activity performed by an animal, with the narrator explaining exactly what the animal is doing (building a nest, courting a mate, or ambushing prey) (Figure 9.11).

In cases in which this activity is obvious, the narrator might indicate how the activity is happening or some other biological fact about the creature. For instance, in a scene showing two cuttlefish courting each other, the narration might explain the purpose of their complex color changes or how these changes occur biologically.

For fiction, voice-over narration should not be a device that suddenly appears in a film but a particular style that permeates the film as a whole, as in *The*

Assassination of Jesse James (Figure 9.12). Narration shouldn't happen once, but occur regularly throughout the movie, as in *Fight Club,* where the main, nameless character played by Edward Norton continually narrates events and his thoughts to the audience.

Credit: BBC

Credit: ©Warner Brothers/Courtesy Everett Collection

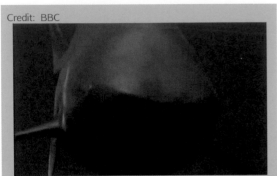

Figure 9.11
The BBC series *Planet Earth* uses narration to describe the various creatures and landscapes. To what extent do you also think the narration contributes toward storytelling?
http://www.youtube.com/watch?v=3-uA8t7-msY

Figure 9.12
The opening scene from *The Assassination of Jesse James by the Coward Robert Ford* uses voice-over narration to provide information about the main character.
http://www.youtube.com/watch?v=r2gY_e1ZKD8

Bad examples of narration occur when directors use it to fill in plot holes due to a poorly written script. While this is true of fictional narratives, it can also be true of nonfiction, expository scripts as well. Make sure your original script for any kind of video is complete and provides a thorough blueprint that expresses your point even if narration is removed.

Just as you should read other scripts to better write your own scripts, and read other dialogue to better write your own dialogue, you should read and listen to other examples of voice-over narration to help you better write narration. Listen to many different kinds of narration and to specific instances that align with your particular goals. If you're creating an advertisement, seek out these examples. If you're producing your own nature documentary, turn on the Discovery Channel and pay attention to how the network's programs craft their narration. Learn from the examples of others.

Also, just as with dialogue, user-test your narration. Let others read your narration as well as listen to you speak it aloud. You can also ask others to read it aloud so that you can hear it yourself. If you're casting someone else to narrate, let this person read over it a few times, and if possible, adjust the language or sentence structure to better suit their speaking style. You might also include cues for how you want certain lines or words to be delivered, such as cues for emphasis, volume, or tone.

Edit the script to make sure the narration is consistent for speech style, including tone of voice, use of first, second, or third person, and the use of contractions. Make sure that the narration at the beginning of the script has the same style as the narration at the end of the script.

Finally, pay attention to your transitions so that each sentence logically flows into the next and so the narration makes sense with what occurs onscreen. You don't want the narration to detract from the visual elements, only to reinforce or add to them. When you feel the written narration is polished, record it and listen to it through your sound editor so you can hear how it will sound when outputted through speakers, experiencing it the way your audience will.

MAKING CONNECTIONS

AS A CLASS

Find and watch a short film, television program, or other video that uses narration. As you watch, note the function of narration in the film, as well as the instances that narration occurs. After you've discussed the program, watch it again, having your instructor mute those segments that use narration. With the narrator on mute, did the essential message change? Do you still understand the action, or does narration provide a critical role in making sense of the piece?

IN A GROUP

Find documentary footage that is re-narrated and placed on YouTube, such as the "Honey Badger" clip in Figure 9.13. Discuss the role that tone has when adding narration to image. How is this similar to anchorage? How would the same words, delivered differently, produce another interpretation of the clip? How would the voice of a particular actor influence how you receive the video? Take the raw footage from one of these clips, and write and record your own narration. Share your remixed video with the class, as well as the original, and discuss how narration plays a role in audience reception.

Figure 9.13
That Honey Badger is Nasty!
http://www.youtube.com/
watch?v=4r7wHMg5Yjg

Many commercials use voice-over narration delivered by famous celebrities, yet often these celebrities aren't given name credit. For example, Gene Hackman provides the narration for commercials for the hardware store Lowes, while Jeff Bridges narrates many commercials for the car company Hyundai. Although many viewers might recognize the voice, most probably cannot identify the voice by name. Why do you think companies would hire such celebrities for their voice alone, rather than use less expensive voice talent? What do they gain? Draft a short memo with your thoughts, and share them with the class.

Storyboards

Often, before shooting a film directly from the script, directors will create storyboards in order to provide a visual representation of the shots they hope to produce. Storyboards help make shooting go more smoothly, as they provide an intermediary translation of what a particular shot should look like before spending time and money on set with equipment and actors. A storyboard can also give the entire production staff a clearer idea about the overall process and final vision. Storyboarding can be a time-consuming process, but it is extremely important toward getting the final look that you're after. Consider the clip in Figure 9.14 of Stephen Spielberg discussing his storyboard process.

If you're creating a storyboard for a visual production such as video, start with your script. Although it provides general instructions for how to create the movie, it leaves a lot of room for the director and actors to insert their own creative ideas. The storyboard will help fill in these details and provide visual life to the words in the screenplay. Read through it, and try to break down each scene into individual shots (a shot consists of a segment of footage with no cuts), with each storyboard panel representing one shot. After reading through the script, you should have developed a shot list from which you can create the storyboard (as well as shoot the actual footage).

Credit: AFI

Figure 9.14
Steven Spielberg on storyboarding.
http://www.youtube.com/
watch?v=nBH89Y0Xj7c

As you read the script and evaluation each shot, consider the following suggestions to create your final list and the corresponding storyboard panels:

- Location for each shot
- Number of actors in the shot
- Important props or set pieces
- Important camera directions for the shot (aerial, close up, long zoom in)
- Movement of characters or objects
- Movement of camera (is it fixed or does it move with the action)
- Lighting needs
- Special effects

Although you'll have a more complete idea of your film if you storyboard every shot, this isn't always necessary. Sometimes you only need to consider the most important sequences or the general unfolding of a scene. Often, a basic sketch will give you enough clarity that you can set up the equipment, help the actors perform their roles, and start shooting. You can also improvise and go off-storyboard if you or other collaborative members have ideas on location. While you typically don't want to improvise the entire project, be flexible with your script and storyboard and revise when inspiration strikes. This can be especially important if uncontrollable elements interfere with your previous plans, such as changing weather conditions, other natural phenomena, or the general unforeseen occurrence.

Storyboards aren't restricted to video, however. They can be useful when designing websites in order to layout the site's design and flow from the home page to other pages. You can also use them for podcasts, helping you lay out when to include your own narration, when to include pre-existing clips, or as a way to add voice-over directions or other notes. If you were writing a print output, such as a novel, you can also use a storyboard to help you organize the plotline, figure out where to add subplots or character introductions, or other important elements to the story. Storyboards allow you to further rearrange all the pieces to easily experiment and see if other sequences might produce better results.

Credit: wiredfly.blogspot.com

Figure 9.15
Storyboards can easily take up a whole wall.
http://wiredfly.blogspot.com/2010_04_01_archive.html

Several techniques can be used to create your own storyboard, and like all writing activities, you'll discover the strategies that work best for you. When you think of storyboarding, you might think of hundreds of hand-drawn images posted onto a wall to lay out an entire sequence (Figure 9.15). While this is certainly one method, several software applications can help make the task easier and more transportable.

Graphic design programs such as Adobe Photoshop, Adobe Illustrator, or The Gimp can be used to digitally sketch the scenes and save them in a variety of image formats. If you decide to hand-draw your scenes, you might scan the sketches to send them to collaborators and insert them into programs such as Microsoft PowerPoint or Prezi to more easily arrange their order (Figure 9.16). In either case, consider using the slug lines from the script as the titles for each card so you clearly understand where and when each scene occurs.

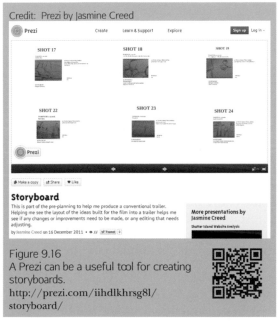

Once you have your rough sequence completed, you can use the storyboard as a checklist, making sure you capture each shot. A storyboard also makes it easier to shoot out of sequence and still ensure you capture all of the shots you need, as well as make sure you put them in the correct, final order. Finally, consider including any dialogue in the scene next to the appropriate images.

Figure 9.16
A Prezi can be a useful tool for creating storyboards.
http://prezi.com/iihdlkhrsg8l/storyboard/

This technique can help you better understand how the images flow together and might help you catch any images that are logically out of order.

If, like Spielberg, you're not good at drawing, you could find pre-existing images that represent what you're trying to convey in the final shot, or take photographs that mimic the description in the screenplay. As a worst-case scenario, you could also write textual descriptions of each scene that are more complete than the details in the script. However, a storyboard is important and should be drafted before shooting begins. Together with the instructions of the script, the storyboard can offer the best blueprint that assures you create a well-designed, quality production.

MAKING CONNECTIONS

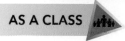

AS A CLASS

Develop a thirty-second commercial for your course. How would you sell the idea of this course to other students? How would you make it seem relevant to those who control funding? Create a basic script, and then develop the storyboards. You might divide the class into smaller breakout groups to work on specific parts of the design before coming together to revise.

IN A GROUP

Revisit the earlier prompt that asked you to create a short screenplay based on a short story, comic, or other story not already in movie form. Create a shot list and storyboard for your screenplay. In addition to images, consider including other direction and dialogue to help orient the viewer. Finally, place your storyboard in a digital format, such as Prezi, and share it with the class.

ON YOUR OWN

Create a storyboard for a traditional essay that you wrote for another class. How would you convey the information from this essay in images? How would you break up the essay into individual shots? Once you've finished, share both the storyboard and original essay with a peer or the class and get their feedback.

Captions

Not all new media projects you compose will consist of video, and so you'll need to learn writing for other kinds of visuals as well. Captions may be one of the more common kinds of genres you'll write since they should accompany many of the still images you might include. Whether you're writing brochures, reports, instructions, manuals, or other kinds of documents, illustrations (images, figures, maps, graphics, charts, diagrams) often require some sort of textual description to help the reader understand what they're looking at and why. Note, however, that a caption is not simply a label. In addition to identification, a caption also explains and establishes meaning within the context of the document in which it appears.

Captions might seem easy to write, given their general brevity. However, a few tips can make them more accessible to your audience and help you better integrate the visual with its surrounding text.

Determine your purpose: Consider the purpose for including the image, as well as the purpose for the document in which you include the image. Remember that text juxtaposed next to an image will influence how a reader responds to that image. As discussed in Chapter 4, text will anchor the meaning of an image for your audience, and it might then be difficult for them to see the image in other ways. If you keep this information in mind, you'll write a caption better rhetorically crafted to help you make your argument.

Identify important elements: While some objects in an image may seem self-apparent, you should make sure to identify the people in an image, as well as any important objects you want the audience to focus on. Again, what you identify is a rhetorical choice, shifting the audience's gaze to a certain element of the photo, implying that other parts are less important.

Reserve judgment: If you're composing a piece for a factual report or journalistic story, reserve judgment about the people or action occurring in the illustration. While a person may look "angry" or seem to be acting "stupidly," those are your own judgments about the image and may unduly influence your reader (or turn them off, affecting your *ethos*).

Keep it succinct: Although captions can be long or short, refine the sentences so that they're accurate, concise, and straightforward.

Add a location: If relevant, include the location where the photograph was taken.

Add dates: Often, dates aren't necessary for a caption. However, especially with historical photographs, dates can help situate viewers so that they better understand the event or action in a photograph.

Check facts: When informing or making an argument, you want your facts to be as accurate as possible. When you're identifying people or objects, or including other factual information such as dates or locations, make sure that these are factually correct.

Use active verbs: Since you want your captions to be as precise and clear as possible, write your captions in the active voice so that the events taking place in the illustration are easier to understand and less wordy.

Remember, not every image needs a caption, and sometimes you might purposefully leave an illustration "textless" in order to leave its interpretation more open to the audience. However, some writing situations call for captions, and how you compose those captions have serious effects on how your reader responds to those images and your document as a whole.

MAKING CONNECTIONS

AS A CLASS

Analyze captions from a variety of sources, including newspaper photographs, scientific illustrations, captions in this or other textbooks, magazines, websites, or other documents. How are the captions written differently for each outlet? How are they similar? Do you think any differences exist because of the medium in which they appear, because of the rhetorical goals of the author, or both? How does the purpose of each document influence the composition of the caption?

IN A GROUP

Find a famous photograph with an original caption. How well do you think this caption was written? Does it just label the image, or does it also explain the photograph? How would you rewrite the caption if it was intended to be used in:

1. an online news site;
2. an elementary textbook;
3. a high school textbook;
4. a college textbook;
5. a business report;
6. a book of famous photographs?

How would you consider the purpose and audience for each case? What kinds of explanations would you try to make to each audience? What would be your expectations for each audience, and how would you adjust the caption to meet those expectations? Share you photograph and captions with the class along with your rationale for each caption.

ON YOUR OWN

You might be familiar with tumblr.com sites, where users link preexisting images or short clips to an original caption, such as http://wheninclemson.tumblr.com. How do these new captions create meaning? What do you think is the author's intended purpose? Does the author attempt to convey information, provide detail, or tell a story? What is the audience for the particular site and images you've selected? Are the captions audience-specific? Finally, create your own tumblr post, writing an original caption for a preexisting image or meme.

SUPPORTING DOCUMENTS

In addition to screenplays, dialogue, narration, storyboards, and captions, a variety of other kinds of writing can help you plan, draft, and organize your project so that it comes together as you envision. Not all of these written documents will be necessary for every project, so use them at your discretion according to what helps you stay on track and complete the assignment.

Logline

A logline is a brief synopsis of a work, typically a film, usually 25-50 words or less. While the logline can tell an audience what a movie is about, it's also very useful for an author at the beginning of the writing process to keep her focused on the final goal of the film. In this way, the logline can be thought of as the main thesis statement of the film, helping the writer keep track of the story she wants to tell. For example, a logline for a movie about King Tut might state:

> *"As a boy ruler of Ancient Egypt, King Tutankhamen had to contend with conspiring advisors and jealous generals, one of which would take his life."*

This logline focuses the story on the mystery of who killed King Tut, making it a historical mystery film. One could redirect the intention of the film, and its thesis, toward a romance by restating the logline as:

> *"Despite falling deeply in love with a local slave girl, King Tut is advised to marry his half-sister Ankhesenamun for political reasons. He must decide between love and duty."*

Treatments

Before writing a full script, screenwriters or film producers will often write a film treatment that provides a comprehensive outline for the movie. A treatment is usually between 30-60 pages, and includes full descriptions for each scene. If a film script is not solicited by a studio, screenwriters will often write and distribute a presentation treatment to pique interest from potential collaborators rather than taking the time to draft a full screenplay. If you have an idea for a video production, a treatment can help you organize and provide detail for each scene before fleshing out camera directions and full dialogue.

Descriptions

One of the more common kinds of writing you'll probably compose includes descriptions. In order to work collaboratively, or even to provide reminders to yourself, you should write descriptions of characters, places, events, plotlines, scenery, props, special effects, music, or any other element that might be incorporated into your production (figure 9.17). Since it's typically cheaper to write these descriptions before trying to film them, they can save you time and money, and give others a sense of the visual aesthetic you're trying to achieve.

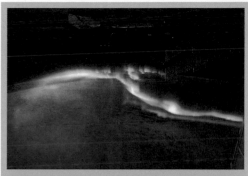

Figure 9.17
How would you describe your idea for a special effect to someone else?

When writing descriptions, try to use active verbs and precise language when possible. You want the reader to have a very clear understanding of your vision, so include concrete language with sensory details such as colors, textures, sounds, as well as comparisons with things the reader might already be familiar with. Finally besides physical details, also describe the mood that a character, setting, or scene evokes.

Lists

Although you've probably created many lists, it's important to remember this valuable writing genre. Lists can help organize complex information into either step-by-step guides, or simply provide a reminder of things to do. When composing new media projects, you should maintain many lists, including lists of:

- characters
- settings
- shots
- images
- sounds
- props
- permissions

As you can see, sometimes you need to create a list of lists to write. Determining these lists before you start composing—as well as keeping track of fine points such as permissions during the process—will help you be more efficient and ensure that you attend to all of the details.

Summaries

When working collaboratively, often you'll need to write information or task lists to other members of your team, describing what they need to know or what to accomplish. When describing parts of the product, you might need to compose summaries for these collaborators who may not need all the information you have, thereby making the information more digestible and more quickly accessible.

In addition, not all audiences need access to the same level of detail. While the actors might only need a general summary of the shooting locations, the set designer will need to know much more, including not only the details of the physical environment but also its history or other important information to make sure all of the elements such as trees, furniture, vehicles, animals, props, costumes, or other elements belong in the location and aren't out of place.

When conducting research for your project—whether video-based or not—you'll need to condense that research into basic, usable material for yourself as well. Summarizing will enable you to quickly recall information to mind and help you work more efficiently. Writing summaries of your research will also help you better master the material of your project.

When you compose summaries, you have to decide what to leave in, and what to leave out. When beginning your research, first make sure you understand the content of what you're reading. Then, edit the original piece by highlighting the key points and crossing out what you feel is superfluous information. You can always go back to the master document if you need to find these details. Rather than copying sentences from the original piece word-for-word, try to rewrite the information in your own words. You can further edit your own subsequent writings in the same way before distributing them to others.

Instructions

In addition to distributing summaries, you may also need to write instructions for others. This chapter has already looked at some standard camera instructions to be included in a screenplay. These instructions provide details to the director or other cast and crew members about how to film particular shots. Of course, the entire screenplay itself is much like a set of instructions for how to create the film as a whole. When writing instructions that don't require film-specific language, there are a few guidelines that can help.

Know your audience: Make sure you understand your audience and what you can expect them to already know about a subject. If you're writing for a particular, disciplinary audience, then you can expect them to be well-versed in specific jargon. If you're writing for a general audience, however, you'll need to explain terms or steps in more detail.

Be consistent: If you call an item by one term, use that term throughout the instructions. For instance, if you refer to a chromakey background as a "green screen," then use "green screen" throughout the document. Don't later refer to it as a "chromakey background" (figure 9.18).

Figure 9.18
When writing instructions, be consistent with your terms such as "green screen."

Include illustrations: Diagrams, charts, or other visual aids often make instructions much clearer than written descriptions (figure 9.19). If you want to instruct a collaborator about where to set up a camera in relation to the subject, an overhead diagram with distances is much more effective than writing it out in paragraph form.

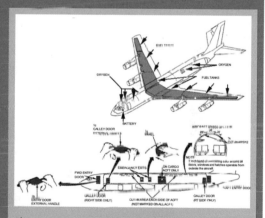

Figure 9.19
This illustration of a 707 aircraft helps to identify the exits and other elements in a much more efficient way than a written description.

Use action words: Always start your instruction with an active verb, such as "stand, hold, grab, press." Since instructions inform an audience how to "do" something, begin each instruction with a "doing" verb.

Be specific: Use specific language when writing your instructions. The audience should never be confused because of vague language. Action words will help make the exact action you want the audience to perform much clearer.

Include definitions: If you need to use terminology that you don't think your audience will know, make sure you include definitions of these terms as a note or in a glossary.

List tools or parts: Sometimes, the user will need specific tools, parts, or equipment to carry out the instructions. If this is the case, make sure you include a list of what they will need to finish the task.

Point out dangers: If the user might experience any kind of danger while performing the instructions, make sure you identify these dangers, as well as point out the severity of the danger. Common colors used to highlight dangers include:

Credit: SB_Johnny

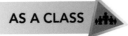

Figure 9.20
Warning labels are usually orange or red and indicate possible bodily harm or even death.

- Notes (any color but yellow/orange/red): Notes offer useful information that might help the reader better complete the task, but do not indicate any safety hazard.

- Cautions (yellow): This indicates that the audience should exercise caution, as damage to equipment might result if instructions are not followed properly.

- Warnings (orange/red): If injury or death might result from improperly following instructions, then a warning is included, usually with orange or red graphics (figure 9.20).

User-test: Whenever possible, read through your finished instructions and attempt to perform the task. Better yet, have someone else try to follow them.

MAKING CONNECTIONS

AS A CLASS

Write loglines for the most recent film you've seen, as well as your favorite film. Compose these without looking anything up about the film—use only what you remember. Share your loglines with the class, but also look up the official logline of the film (or check the Internet Movie Database: IMDB.com) for its version. How do your memories compare with the official logline version? Which do you like better? Which do you think better represents the film?

IN A GROUP

Create a set of instructions for some task that you've learned in this class, such as performing a certain image manipulation in a photo editor, working a digital camera, building a website, or other action not specifically covered in this text that you think your classmates would benefit from. Once you've completed a draft, swap them with another group, and user-test each other's instructions. Use the suggestions by your peers to further edit your instructions, and share the final version with the class.

ON YOUR OWN

Write summaries for each of the following texts and share them with the class:

- a film
- a print advertisement
- a television commercial
- a podcast
- a television news story
- a YouTube video

KEY TERMS		
script	storyboard	description
screenplay	caption	list
dialogue	logline	summary
narration	treatment	instructions

OUTPUT: PHOTO ESSAY

For this assignment, produce a photo essay that makes an argument or relates some story, either fictional or based on real events. A photo essay is an arrangement of images used to tell a story to an audience or express a real-life event. Often, the images provide an emotionally charged narrative that captures details that the written word cannot. These photographs are arranged in a specific order to tell this story, usually chronologically.

The guidelines below offer some considerations and a place to start. However, use your imagination and go beyond these suggestions. Of course, follow other instructions from your instructor who will provide details about length, topics, or specific requirements. Classes that don't have access to cameras can also complete this assignment with images found on the Web. For examples of other photo essays, check out www.thephotoessay.com (figure 9.21).

Credit: thephotoessay.com

Figure 9.21
This site offers many examples for you to model your own photo essay on.

As you script your photo essay and then finalize it in visual form, remember to reference the rhetorical tetrahedron and ask yourself questions about the essay's audience, message, and design (the medium and genre are, of course, video and essay). Also think about how you can use *logos*, *ethos*, *pathos*, and *kairos* in composing your essay.

***Choose a topic*:** A photo essay, like a written essay, first requires that you choose your topic, that you determine what you'd like to write about. As with other writing, find a topic that interests you, one that calls you to write. You can document the football or basketball team throughout their season (or just on game day), a local political race, the aftermath of a major weather event, an essay about the state of public schools, the production of an arts performance, conditions at the local animal shelter, or other numerous possibilities. If you plan on creating this photo essay by taking your own photographs, make sure you're able to get the shots you want.

Research: As with any writing assignment, much of the work comes before you start writing. If you're documenting your school's football team, try to interview players and coaches to get their perspective. Talk with the equipment managers and the other "unseen" personnel and elements of preparing a team that the public typically doesn't get to see.

Research where you'll take most of your photographs so you can ensure that you can bring the right equipment. Will you need a tripod? Extra lighting? Study how the environment will play a role, and plan accordingly.

Finally, consider how you will get to your locations. Unless your class has a large travel budget, you probably won't be able to take your own photographs of illegal fishing off the coast of South America. In addition, make sure you are safe when taking your own photographs, and ask for permission when shooting on private property or other locations that require it.

Find your angle: Since documenting a football team might be too general, try to find an angle or specific story within the story. Is the football team led by a beloved coach who is retiring at the end of the year? Does one of the players have some personal setback that they have had to overcome? In other words, what makes your particular essay interesting or unique? Good research will help reveal the angle (or several angles) that you might take.

Plan: Before you enter the field with your camera, or find your images online, try to plan the story you'd like to tell. What's the argument you plan to make? What story would you like to tell? Make a script, treatment, and storyboard of the essay, or make a list of the photos you need to shoot. Most of the writing genres in this chapter can be used for this assignment. Determine which best suits your purposes, and plan out your essay before you get too deep in production. Sometimes, however, you might compose your story after you have taken your photographs, using them to help find the story or narrative arc. If so, you can still organize and plan your essay using the above techniques, which can help you figure out how to arrange them into an argument.

Pinpoint the emotional tone: Determine what emotional tone you want to establish with your photographs. Are you trying to express joy, hate, fear, sadness, regret, or a range of emotions? In your essay, consider the emotional story you want to tell your audience through the photographs. Perhaps you want to show the change of emotions that a football team undergoes throughout a season. Discover whatever emotional angle you feel tells the best narrative and use photographs that convey those emotions to connect with your audience.

Take multiple photos: While you should have a shot list of specific photographs you'll need, take multiple shots of each of those items on the list. Sometimes the first shot will be out of focus, or include some undesirable element, so taking several shots of the same list item can ensure you have usable photographs when you begin to edit and arrange your essay.

Consider captions: Many photo essays include captions that help guide the reader through the essay. However, don't let captions take over and undercut the power that your photographs can provide on their own. Use the captions according to the advice in this chapter, such as pointing out important details the audience might miss, explaining the general events occurring in the photograph or expressing your particular focus. When including specific details, make sure you check that any factual information is correct.

Arrange: Once you have selected your photographs, determine the best arrangement that will express your argument (remember, arguments can be implicit). Does one photograph offer a "claim" or "conclusion" more than another? Does your essay have a narrative arc with a beginning, middle, and end? Order and reorder your photographs to try different arrangements before deciding on any particular order. You might also have a peer evaluate different arrangements to let you know which they find is the most effective.

Review and Revise: As with any essay, you should have a peer review your essay and give you feedback. If possible, compose a specific list of questions that you would like your reviewer to answer about your essay; this will make the review session more productive. After you have feedback, revise your photo essay.

Distribute: Once you have selected and arranged your photographs and have written any captions that you want to include, determine how you might best distribute the essay in its final form. You can certainly create a photo essay through a word processor, but you might consider integrating the photos into a website, blog, Prezi, PowerPoint, or even design your own booklet. Of course, the final delivery form should satisfy whatever audience you're trying to reach, as well as the requirements made by your instructor.

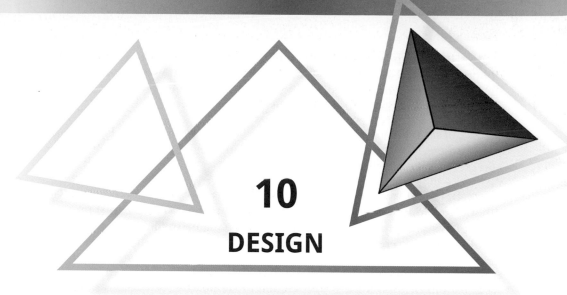

10
DESIGN

This chapter covers all of the design techniques that you'll need to complete your visuals, including basic strategies concerning color, typography, layout, perspective, balance, and other considerations. While this chapter will cover "how" to implement these design practices into your compositions, it will also explain "why" you should use certain design elements and techniques. In other words, the chapter discusses the rhetorical impact that a particular design element will have and how such an element might further your rhetorical goals for making a visual composition in the first place.

Given this chapter is called "design," it may seem clear how the rhetorical tetrahedron ties into its subject matter. However, you also have to think of design in relation to your audience, the text's message, and the medium and genre in which you actualize your design. Since a rhetorical situation is always shifting and in flux, you should think about how your design meets a particular moment (*kairos*) and interacts with the other parts of the rhetorical tetrahedron.

DESIGN BASICS

Color

While you might think that colors are "red" or "blue," the term "color" more accurately names totality of a color, which is made up of three parts: *hue*, *value*, and *saturation*. Red by itself is really a hue and not a color. As a starting point, consider the classic color (or hue) wheel developed by Sir Isaac Newton (Figure 10.1). This hue wheel is based on the primary hues of red, blue, and yellow, which combine to make other hues.

Figure 10.2 depicts hue wheels with the primary hues and the secondary hues of orange, purple, and green (left wheel). The primary hues mix to make these other hues. For instance, yellow and red make orange, red and blue make purple, and blue and yellow make green.

These hues can be mixed further as depicted by the right wheel in Figure 10.2, producing tertiary hues, so that yellow and orange make yellow-orange or blue and green make blue-green.

However, these three hues—red, blue, and yellow—are mainly used to create other colors when mixing paints. When designing and rendering final projects for print, you'll need to mix colors according to the colors cyan, magenta, yellow, and black, creating the acronym CMYK (Figure 10.3). It's important to make sure any work to be printed by professional printers is created based on this color scheme, as these are the ink hues used by their equipment to produce all the other hues.

Alternatively, colors produced by light, such as theater spotlights or computer monitors, do so according to the colors red, green, and blue (RGB) (Figure 10.4). You should produce work intended for online presentation in this color scheme. In most photo editors and other design software, you'll have the option of creating and saving your work as either a CMYK (print) or RGB (electronic) version.

Figure 10.1
This color wheel shows the basic hues of red, blue, and yellow.

Credit: Isaac Newton

Another important aspect of color is value, which refers to the lightness or darkness of a hue. Value can help emphasize or deemphasize objects within a design. Elements with similar value will tend to blend together, while those with contrasting values will separate and appear more striking in opposition to each other. This is especially true when using black and white.

Finally, the saturation of a color determines how dominant one of the primary hues is within the color. Look at the color cone in Figure 10.5. The primary hues are located around the outside of the chart, and any of these

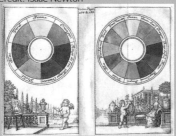

Figure 10.2
The color wheel developed by Isaac Newton has seven colors (left), which can then be mixed to produce even more (right).

Figure 10.3
Printing is usually done with cyan, magenta, yellow, and black inks.

Figure 10.4
Red, Green, and Blue color systems are used for electronic documents.

Figure 10.5
This inverted cone shows hue, value, and saturation.

colors are high in saturation. However, as you move more toward the center, toward white, the colors become desaturated, losing the dominant hue until no hue dominates the color. When adjusting saturation within a photo editor, you are increasing or decreasing the dominance of a particular hue within your design.

When using multiple hues in a design, one of the design goals is that of color harmony. Although this chapter will return to harmony later, especially concerning spatial arrangement, here are a few tips to strike color harmony when designing color palates.

When applying color, two primary methods involve choosing analogous hues or complementary hues. Analogous hues appear close together on the color wheel. For instance, yellow, yellow-orange, and orange are analogous hues. Together they create a color palate where all the hues are similar and blend well together. No one hue clashes with the other, creating a pleasing design.

Alternatively, complementary hues appear oppositely from each other on the color wheel. Most viewers often consider white and black as complementary or other combinations such as yellow and purple, red and green, or orange and blue. If you look at the colors of different sports teams, many of them use either analogous or complementary color schemes. The Green Bay Packers use green and yellow (analogous), while the Denver Broncos use orange and blue (complementary) (Figure 10.6).

Credit: Scott Boehm/Getty Images North America

Humans approach color differently, depending on cultural backgrounds and psychological associations, as well as "natural" associations. Colors are often considered natural when they appear universally in the natural world. For instance, most types of vegetation are green, and most oceans are blue (with varying shades, of course). You might expect most people who have seen vegetation or the ocean to agree about how green and blue associate with these elements.

Figure 10.6
The Denver Broncos use complementary colors, while the Green Bay Packers use analogous colors.

However, colors can mean different things to different groups and individuals. While the United States and many Western nations use the color red to symbolize danger, some Asian countries consider red to symbolize good luck or happiness. In Ireland, green is the color for good luck. The chart in Figure 10.7 analyzes some of the moods associated with different colors in ten cultural contexts.

Love, #53, is represented by red in Western/American, Japanese, and Eastern European countries, green in Hindu, yellow in Native American, and blue in African cultures. Such differences don't preclude you from using any particular color, but you should be attuned to your audience's perceptions and associations about colors when making your selections. Research how your primary and secondary audiences might respond to colors when considering your design choices.

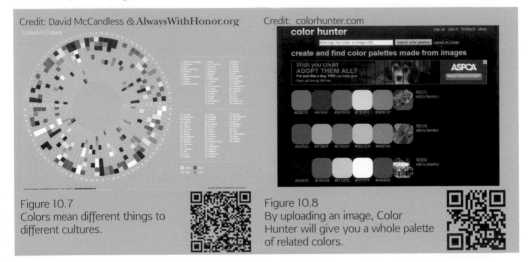

Credit: David McCandless & AlwaysWithHonor.org

Credit: colorhunter.com

Figure 10.7
Colors mean different things to different cultures.

Figure 10.8
By uploading an image, Color Hunter will give you a whole palette of related colors.

Beyond the color wheel, there are many online tools that you can use to help select color palates for making design choices. Some of these examples include websites such as colorhunter.com, which allows you to upload a picture and provides a color palate based on that image (Figure 10.8). If you happen to have an image that has the color aesthetics you like, this site will give you the colors and HTML codes that you can then use in an HTML or photo editor.

Although many ways to use color exist, the guidelines above are meant to suggest some basic color theory when selecting colors for the designs you create. Keep in mind that they are only guidelines and not intended to stifle your design choices; you should feel free to experiment with color. However, the theories above can give you practical reasons why you might choose a certain color scheme and help you to persuade an audience or client about a particular design you might produce for them.

MAKING CONNECTIONS

AS A CLASS

Browse through various advertisements online and analyze their color choices. Do these advertisements use colors similar to the product's color? Do they achieve color harmony? Do they use analogous or complementary colors? How do you think the colors in the ads would affect an international audience?

IN A GROUP

Choose four or five company brand marks. Analyze the colors in these brand marks and why you think the companies chose these particular colors. Then, import these images into a photo editor and manipulate the colors. How do such colors change the meaning of the brand mark? Produce alternative versions of these brand marks by changing their colors to create a new meaning, and share them with the rest of the class.

ON YOUR OWN

Choose your favorite color and using the chart in Figure 10.7 as a starting point, research as many meanings of this color from as many cultures as you can find. How does this research change your perception of this color? Compose a short report for your instructor that details your findings as well as a Prezi that depicts your report in a visual format and present this to your class.

Typography

Typography refers to how the individual letters are arranged in design, and the letter designs are called typefaces. Usually typefaces are created by professional type designers for specific purposes. The word sometimes substituted for typeface—font—refers to a larger complex that not only includes the typeface, but also variables such as bold, italic, or underlined; Garamond is a typeface, while Garamond-bold-italic is a font (Figure 10.9).

If you've ever used the font drop-down menu in a word editing program, you've noticed that you have hundreds of options when selecting a font. This section will provide some general guidelines to help you understand which fonts

Figure 10.9
Garamond

Figure 10.10
Typefaces such as Garamond and Times New Roman have serifs, which are indicated in this diagram.

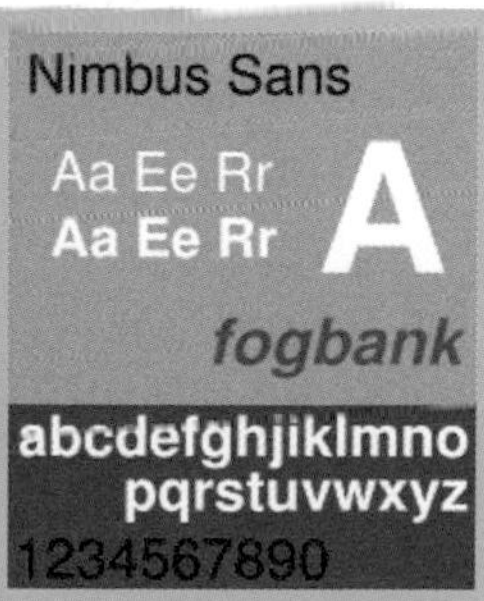

Figure 10.11
Nimbus Sans is an example of a typeface without serifs.

should be used in particular situations and allow you to filter through the many font options to select the one that's best for your particular project.

One of the basic differences between typefaces are those with serifs—which are the small lines that extend from letters (Figure 10.10) such as the ones in this font—and sans serif typefaces (without serif), which have no serifs, such as Arial or Nimbus Sans (Figure 10.11). In general, choose serif typefaces for most of your large blocks of texts since the serifs help the audience by making reading easier, blending one letter into the next.

Sans serif typefaces are better used for any text elements you want to stand out, such as headers or titles, since the letters are more distinct. These are just some guidelines, but when you do select a font, research the intended use for which it was designed. Some fonts display better on paper stock, while some are designed specifically for reading on a computer monitor. These details about a typeface may help confirm your choice or may give you pause to alter it. Either way, it will also provide some evidence if you have to justify your typeface choice to a client.

Point size simply refers to the size of the font, which is usually presented numerically, such as Arial 12, which indicates the typeface Arial at a 12 point size. For selecting a point size, consider how readable it will be for an audience and where it appears in a document. If the reader will be physically close to the document, such as a website or printed page, then 12-point font will probably be large enough. However, this same point size on a poster, or even something larger like a billboard, will probably be unreadable. For these genres, you should select a larger point size that can be read from a distance.

Point size should also change depending on the part of the document. While paragraphs of text can be set at 10-12 point, titles, headers, and other elements demand more emphasis; increasing the font size can make these features stand out from the rest of the page. Of course, other tools for emphasis, such as boldface and italics, can do this as well.

You might find that the typefaces loaded into your word editor or photo editor don't have the best options for your project. By entering "font" into an Internet search engine, you will find many sites that

Credit: fontstruct

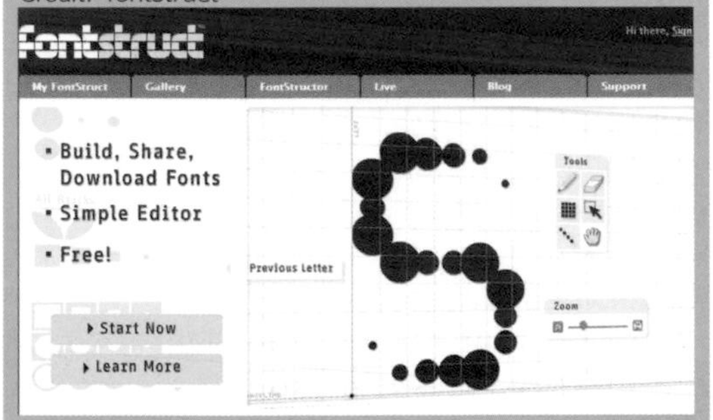

Figure 10.12
Websites such as Fontstruct allow you to make your own typefaces.

Figure 10.13
Black and white offer the greatest contrast.

offer free fonts, such as Dafont.com (Figure 10.12). Also, sites such as fontstruct.com allow you to design your own typeface for more custom applications.

MAKING CONNECTIONS

AS A CLASS

Scroll through the list of typefaces on a word processor, then analyze and discuss each font design. Consider what rhetorical situations might call for each typeface design.

IN A GROUP

Locate a series of advertisements that feature text. Analyze the typeface used on the advertisement and discuss whether you think the typeface is effective.

ON YOUR OWN

Choose a typeface design from the list of fonts on your word processor. Research the history of the typeface, noting why the typeface was designed in a particular way and for what purposes. Share your findings with the class.

Contrast

In the context of visual rhetoric, contrast is the technique used to separate a particular part of an image from its background and other objects within the image. While many methods may be used to create contrast, the most important design feature to achieve effective contrast is to make any differences obvious. For instance, using black and white will achieve a high level of contrast, but using white with a cream color probably won't (Figure 10.13).

Besides emphasizing some elements over others, contrast can help you direct your audience's attention, showing them how to read your document. If you use size to create contrast, you're encouraging your audience to read the largest element first since this element will usually grab their attention before the smaller elements. This is one reason why the title on a poster or flyer usually appears larger than other textual elements.

Contrast also emphasizes importance. On a movie poster, the title of the movie is usually more important than who stars in the movie, which is in turn more important (to a typical movie viewer) than the casting company, which probably appears in very small print at the bottom.

However, you can have too much contrast by making a particular element too large. While one key is to make the contrasting element sufficiently different, you should also try to achieve balance between the different objects in an image so that your rhetorical goals are achieved.

Scale

As indicated above, contrasting with scale is an easy way to emphasize some elements over others. Until one object appears next to another in a design, that object only has a size, some absolute value (which may be in millimeters, inches, feet, or miles). Only when another object is introduced can you compare the two in size, and this creates a scale between the objects. This difference (or similarity) in scale can be used to contrast the elements, which can be smaller and larger images, smaller and larger fonts, or a combination of text and images at different sizes.

Color

As discussed earlier in the chapter, juxtaposing colors can create contrast (Figure 10.14). Black and white is usually considered to produce the most striking contrast. However, many colors will contrast against these two colors, such as red and white, or yellow and black. In addition, *complementary colors* on the color wheel also contrast with each other while analogous colors may fail to achieve any meaningful contrast. It's also possible to use too much color. If every object in an image has a different color, then no single object gains emphasis. Instead, try to use color to achieve rhetorical emphasis—to guide your reader toward a particular interpretation. Consider your reason and specific purposes for using color and why you want to make a part of your visual stand out.

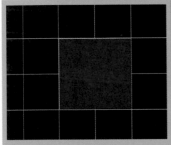

Figure 10.14
This image offers contrast through both the size of the squares and their colors.

Value

Also discussed in the section on color, value refers to the darkness or lightness of an image. When contrasting different images, the further apart in value—that is, a darker value juxtaposed with a lighter value—the more contrast you'll achieve.

Type

Typography can create contrast in all the ways discussed above. You might use different size fonts, different colors, use both serif or sans serif typefaces, or use bold and italics. However, just as with color, size, or any of the techniques already mentioned, choose only a few methods to create contrast, otherwise you may confuse your audience about what exactly you're trying to contrast.

You can apply numerous other techniques to images to create contrast. For example, you can add texture or filters to different objects within an image by using a photo editor equipped with these tools. You can also contrast information using shapes, such as a circle and square. You might also align objects differently by placing some in the center and others in a corner. Such placement can also create direction and movement that will guide your reader through the document in particular ways.

The contrast controls in photo editors work according to these principles as well. Increasing the contrast makes the individual colors (or gray scales) more distinct from each other. Decreasing the contrast washes the color from the photo, making the elements blend together. Often, you'll only need to adjust the contrast slightly, otherwise the image may become significantly distorted.

Consider the contrast in the movie poster (a kind of flyer) for *Transformers* (Figure 10.15). The designer has contrasted several elements here, beginning with the transformers Optimus Prime and Bumblebee appearing opposite of each other. In terms of color, Optimus Prime has blues and reds, while Bumblebee is depicted mostly with shades of yellow.

Regarding scale, viewers see the enormous size of the transformers which dwarf the size of the human characters. Finally, the text appears at the bottom with the first part of the title (which also happens to be the brand name) more prominent in size than the subtitle. This single poster uses numerous levels and techniques to create contrast.

Credit: ©Paramount/Courtesy EverettCollection

Figure 10.15
This poster for the movie *Transformers* uses many kinds of contrast.

MAKING CONNECTIONS

AS A CLASS

Visit sites that most students visit regularly, such as Facebook. Discuss how the site uses contrast in its design. What are the rhetorical reasons for creating contrast in these sites?

IN A GROUP

Locate a series of advertisements or flyers and analyze how the documents use contrast. Do they use scale, color, or type? Do they use contrast effectively? Why or why not? Discuss these questions and share your results with the class.

ON YOUR OWN

Open a photo in a photo editor and adjust the contrast. Note how the image changes as you make adjustments. What kinds of emphasis change as you adjust contrast? How does the meaning of the image change? Share the results of this experiment with the class.

Perspective

You may recognize the man in Figure 10.16 as the "Head Crusher" from the TV program *Kids in the Hall.* As you can see, his hobby is "crushing" the heads of people who pass him on the street. Try it yourself: Close one eye, and then place your fingers near the open eye. Notice that objects in the distance (like heads) appear much smaller than your fingers. Now "crush" them. You've probably noticed this phenomenon before; the closer something is to you, the larger it appears, and the further something is from you, the smaller it appears.

Credit: CBC Television

Figure 10.16
Head Crusher from *Kids in the Hall.*
http://www.youtube.com/
watch?v=8t4pmlHRokg

Most of you know that objects look larger or smaller depending on proximity, but this knowledge lets you do more than just crush the head of a passerby. Artists and designers can reproduce the effects of this phenomenon using linear perspective. The basic rules of linear perspective can help you to add a sense of depth and a touch of realism to your designs.

This section will introduce you to the concept of linear perspective and show you how you can use linear perspective when you create your own images. If you read this section carefully and work through the examples provided, you will be able to use scale and position to make images that appear to be three-dimensional.

Perspective refers to the position from which a viewer looks at an image. Perspective also relates to the sizes and positions of objects in relation to one another, as the Head Crusher has shown. The positions of objects (such as fingers and heads) and the position of the viewer (Head Crusher) can change the relative sizes of objects, making relatively small objects like fingers appear much larger than relatively large objects like heads. If you know how much the relative sizes of objects appear to change with proximity in real three-dimensional life, you can represent this change in size on a two-dimensional surface, like a computer screen. In other words, if you know how to use the rules of perspective, you can make a two-dimensional image appear three-dimensional.

When you create an image on a two-dimensional surface, you can often assume that the viewer will be positioned in front of the image, looking at the image as if looking through a window. Because you know the viewer's position, you can reproduce the viewer's perspective using the geometrical principles of linear perspective.

Linear perspective was first demonstrated during the Italian Renaissance by architect Filippo Brunelleschi (Figure 10.17). Renaissance painters were the first to think of the painting as a kind of window that the viewer looks through

Credit: Lorenzo di Pietro di Giovanni Vecchietta

Figure 10.17
This painting (*St Bernardino Preaching*) achieves perspective by placing the vanishing point on the cross in the background.

to see the image in the painting. The metaphor of a painting as a window is now commonplace, and it has been transferred to other visual media like photos, TVs, and computer screens. The metaphor has become such a part of the experience of visual media that the text you are reading right might appear in a computer "window."

While the idea of looking at visual media through a window is common now, it was revolutionary during the Renaissance because it led directly to the use of linear perspective in painting. Since painters knew the relative perspective of the viewer to the image, they could create realistic paintings from that perspective.

Because viewers approach visual media as windows looking into space, you can design images so that they approximate that perspective, creating realistic-looking depth in the images. The most common ways to create realistic depth are to use one-point perspective and two-point perspective. Other types of multipoint perspective, such as three-point perspective, can be tricky for beginners and can sometimes distort images so that they don't look as realistic. For those reasons, this section will focus on one-point and two-point perspective.

One-Point Perspective

Figure 10.18

Figure 10.19

Here's how one-point linear perspective works.

Just as the horizon is always at eye level when you look into the distance outside, a horizon line runs across the image at the eye level of the viewer. The horizon line may be obscured by other objects in an image, but images created with linear perspective at least start with a visible horizon line. The horizon line runs parallel to the page or screen and runs across it as a straight line.

Figure 10.20

Figure 10.21

All lines that are parallel to the surface of the window and the horizon will appear parallel to each other.

All lines that are perpendicular to the window appear to move closer together as they move further from the viewer. These perpendicular lines are called orthogonal lines. Orthogonals continue to look like they are closer together until they converge at a point on the horizon called the vanishing point.

Figure 10.18 demonstrates one-point perspective. In this photo, the railroad tracks run along parallel orthogonal lines that converge at a vanishing point at the horizon. Notice that the tracks look smaller as they recede into the distance. When drawing an image, making one part of an object larger than another part of that object is called foreshortening. In Figure 10.19, the horizon is marked by a blue line. You can now see that the horizon line runs across the image, parallel to the "window" of the photo.

In Figure 10.20, the orthogonal lines of the tracks are marked with green lines. You can see that the red lines along the tracks meet on the horizon. The point where they appear to meet is the vanishing point, marked as a red dot.

All orthogonals meet at the vanishing point, and all parallel lines share the same vanishing point. You can see in Figure 10.21 that all the lines parallel to the railroad tracks, such as the fences and the gravel road beside the tracks, also converge on the same vanishing point.

Using orthogonal lines that merge at a vanishing point, image-makers can create the sense that some objects in the image are closer to or farther away from the viewer.

Figure 10.20 of the railroad tracks is in one-point perspective because all parallel lines run toward a single vanishing point.

Two-Point Perspective

Another common use of linear perspective is two-point perspective. Like one-point perspective, two-point perspective starts with a horizon line but uses two sets of parallel orthogonal lines that merge into two different vanishing points.

Figure 10.22 shows a building in two-point perspective. You can see in this image that the horizon line is visible on the road and partially obscured by the building. In Figure 10.23, the horizon line is marked in yellow, and the two sets of orthogonals are marked in green and blue. Each set of parallel orthogonal lines runs toward a different vanishing point, marked in red.

If you know how to use orthogonals and vanishing points in one-point and two-point perspective, you can learn to scale and position the objects in your images so that they have realistic depth. The next two sections show you how to draw a simple geometrical figure, a box, to give you practice working with

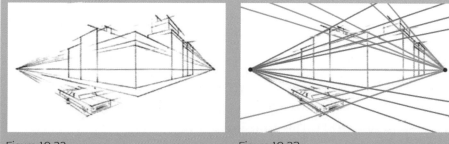

Figure 10.22   Figure 10.23

basic linear proportion. Follow these guides for drawing a box in one-point and two-point perspective and then practice using orthogonals to scale the objects in an image to create a scene with depth.

Drawing a Box in One-Point Perspective

First, draw a horizontal line across the page or screen, near the top. This will be the horizon line (Figure 10.24).

Next, place a vanishing point somewhere on the left half of the horizon line (Figure 10.25). If you are using paper, you may want to draw this point fairly lightly, so you can erase it later. If you are using a computer to draw, you will be able to erase the point later.

Draw a square near the bottom right corner of the screen (Figure 10.26).

Next draw light lines from the vanishing point to each of the three closest corners of the square (Figure 10.27). These are the orthogonal lines. You will erase the orthogonal lines after the boxes are drawn.

Draw a horizontal line between the two orthogonals to the right, and draw a vertical line between the two orthogonals to the left (Figure 10.28). The square is now becoming a box, and these lines are the sides and top of the box.

With the orthogonal lines in place, you can continue drawing boxes that appear to recede into the distance. When you have finished, you can erase the vanishing point and orthogonal lines (Figure 10.29).

When making an image with one-point perspective, use only a single vanishing point in the image. To draw other boxes in other locations in this image, draw another square, then draw orthogonals from that square to the same vanishing point used to make the first box (Figure 10.30).

Drawing a Box in Two-Point Perspective

Draw a horizontal line in the top one-third of your page or screen (Figure 10.31). This is the horizon line.

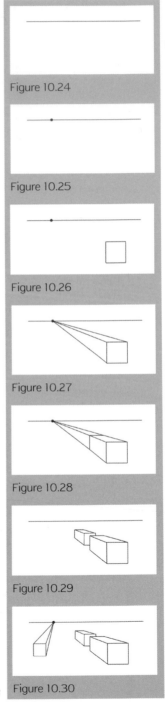

Figure 10.24

Figure 10.25

Figure 10.26

Figure 10.27

Figure 10.28

Figure 10.29

Figure 10.30

Place two vanishing points near the ends of your horizon line (Figure 10.32).

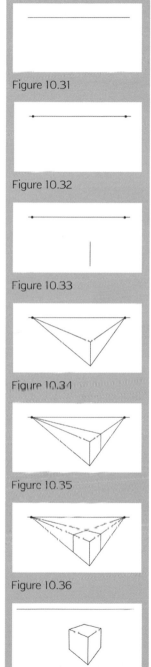

Figure 10.31

Figure 10.32

Figure 10.33

Figure 10.34

Figure 10.35

Figure 10.36

Figure 10.37

Place a vertical line near the bottom of the screen between the vanishing points. This line will be the front edge of the box (Figure 10.33).

Draw orthogonal lines from each vanishing point to both ends of the vertical line. If you are using paper, draw lightly, because you will erase all orthogonal lines when you are finished (Figure 10.34).

Draw a vertical line between the orthogonal lines to the right of the first vertical line (Figure 10.35). This will be the right edge of the box. Draw orthogonal lines from the left vanishing point to the top and bottom of the new vertical line.

Repeat the last step on the opposite side. Start with a vertical line between the original orthogonal lines to the left of the first vertical line. Then draw orthogonal lines from the vanishing point on the right side to the top and bottom of the newest vertical line (Figure 10.36).

Fill in the lines that make up the top and bottom edges of the box, and then erase the orthogonal lines and vanishing points, leaving you with a box in two-point perspective (Figure 10.37).

Creating a Scene in Perspective

With just a horizon line and three different images, you can see how to use vanishing points and orthogonal lines to create a sense of depth (Figure 10.38).

Decide which object should be in the foreground. Once that object is in scale and position, draw (or imagine) a square/rectangle around it (Figure 10.39). Draw orthogonal lines from the corners of the rectangle to a vanishing point. You can see now how large that object would be if it were moved away from the viewer, closer to the horizon line. This can help you decide the proper scale when trying to draw distance.

In Figure 10.40, you should assume that the two aliens are about the same size when standing side-by-side. In order to keep the purple alien in the foreground but move the other behind it, scale the image of the second alien until it fits within the orthogonal lines at the preferred distance.

Now you can move the second alien to the left or right, staying on the blue horizontal line that marks its distance from the purple alien (Figure 10.41).

Let's assume the alien tree is about twice the height of both aliens. You can place the tree in the orthogonals noting the point where the top orthogonal lines cross the tree (Figure 10.42).

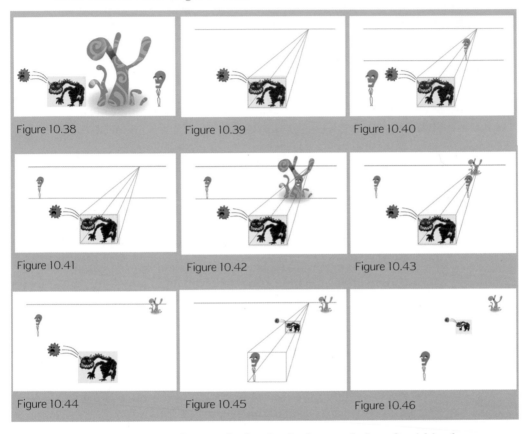

Figure 10.38

Figure 10.39

Figure 10.40

Figure 10.41

Figure 10.42

Figure 10.43

Figure 10.44

Figure 10.45

Figure 10.46

If you want to move the tree further back, then scale it to fit within the orthogonal lines, being sure that the top orthogonals cross the tree in the same spot noted in the last step (Figure 10.43).

Now you can move the tree horizontally, keeping it in the appropriate vertical position for its new scale (Figure 10.44).

Using the same principles, you could scale and position the images differently. The orthogonal lines in this image extend from the vanishing point past the image of the purple alien. Now you can scale the image of the green alien in order to make it appear closer to the viewer than the purple alien (figure 10.45).

The resulting scene now carries a different meaning, achieved only by scaling objects using the principles of linear perspective (Figure 10.46).

MAKING CONNECTIONS

AS A CLASS

Search online for the term "perspective" and locate images of showing the use of perspective. Which techniques do the images use to achieve perspective in their designs?

IN A GROUP

Locate other uses of perspective and analyze the rhetorical effect created by this technique. What does the design "argue" by using perspective in these particular ways?

ON YOUR OWN

Find three different images using an online search engine and save them to your computer. Resize the images and position them to create a scene using linear perspective. This assignment can also be done by cutting out images from different pages in a magazine and positioning them so that they appear to be in correct linear perspective. If you are using a computer, be sure to prepare two images, one with the orthogonals and vanishing point highlighted and one with those guiding lines erased. If using paper and magazine photos, lightly draw the orthogonals with a pencil and a ruler.

Emphasis

Often you need to direct the audience's attention to a particular visual element just as you might emphasize a particular word or phrase when speaking. Emphasizing a visual element within a larger composition creates a focal point, a point in the composition where you want a viewer to direct her or his gaze. The focal point is often the most important element in the design, and you should keep in mind the rhetorical reasons why you might include a particular focal point in your own compositions. Three main techniques can create emphasis: contrast, isolation, and placement.

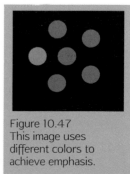

Figure 10.47
This image uses different colors to achieve emphasis.

Contrast

As discussed above, contrast distinguishes different parts of a design, separating elements so that the audience can better understand the various pieces and how they fit together. For emphasis, you can use any of the contrasting techniques already discussed. For instance, if you use a single element of color among black and white, then the colored element will draw the audience's attention and create the focal point (Figure 10.47). Also, a large element inserted amongst other small elements will draw attention as will a difference in shape.

Isolation

Figure 10.48
This image uses negative space to create emphasis through isolation.

You can also emphasize an object by isolating it from other objects in the composition's frame. Whitespace is one method to achieve this kind of isolation, or you could use borders or boxes. The illustration in Figure 10.48 uses a combination of techniques. Whitespace separates the dot from the other shapes, but the single dot draws the audience's gaze because it is isolated from a larger group and thus becomes a focal point.

Placement

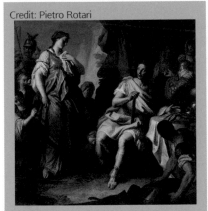

Credit: Pietro Rotari

Figure 10.49
This painting creates emphasis by making Roxanne (left) and Alexander the Great (right) the main focal points of the other figures (and each other).

Emphasis can also be created by placing an element in a particular location on a page. Often, this focal point is in the center of an image (even though that may break the "rule of thirds" discussed below). Returning to Figure 10.15, even though the larger transformers are in the foreground, the center of the image features the two humans. The poster also uses perspective, and the audience's eyes follow the lines of perspective toward this focal point.

If the object is placed at a location that's a focal point for other objects in the images, then the object can become a focal point for the viewer. For example, Alexander the Great and Roxanne in Figure 10.49 gain emphasis because most all of the other figures are looking at them, giving them attention.

MAKING CONNECTIONS

AS A CLASS

Emphasis is used in other visual media, such as video. As a class, watch a television show or film, and note examples that use one of the three techniques mentioned above. As a group, discuss how the technique is adapted for video.

IN A GROUP

Find natural designs, such as the wing of a butterfly, or the abdomen of a black widow. Discuss how you think these elements achieve emphasis. Share these findings with your class.

ON YOUR OWN

Find several examples of flyers around your campus or city. Analyze how they emphasize important details and which techniques they use to do so. Besides the three techniques mentioned in this section, do the examples use any other ways to achieve emphasis?

USE OF SPACE

Whitespace

You're probably already familiar with whitespace from writing your conventional academic papers. For example, you probably use one-inch margins on each page, place space between the title and the first paragraph, include space between major sections, or indent at each new paragraph. All of these features of a typed page create white space that helps separate the elements from each other so that the audience can more easily read the page.

In creating visuals, whitespace (also called negative space) achieves the same goals. Whitespace is not simply empty space but space that helps to organize, balance, direct, and create an aesthetic effect. Whitespace separates, groups, arranges, and emphasizes the individual elements in the overall visual composition. Whitespace can be divided into two subcategories, micro and macro whitespace.

Micro whitespace refers to the smaller uses of whitespace that you're probably most familiar with. Indenting a paragraph, inserting a break between a header and the section it identifies, the space between columns, and even the spaces in between individual words and letters all constitute micro levels of whitespace. Typically, this level of whitespace will determine how legible your text is to the reader. If letters and words are too close, then the text may be too hard to read. Alternatively, if the letters and words are spaced too far apart, then it may be difficult for the reader to easily scan the text, since large gaps between letters slow the pace of reading.

Micro whitespace may also include the whitespace within a group of elements separated by macro whitespace, such as an image and caption grouped together. Micro whitespace would be the amount of whitespace you use to separate the image and caption, or the title of image, such as the space used in the examples in this text. You can also use whitespace instead of gridlines when designing a chart, table, or other graphic displaying information in column and row format.

Macro whitespace is used to separate larger elements, such as complete blocks of text, images, and any object that needs separation from the rest of the image. Macro whitespace can be a clean and simple way of highlighting or emphasizing elements. While one option might be to place a box, circle, or some other outline around such elements, these can become repetitive and clutter the overall design of the composition.

Macro whitespace can also be used to show relationships between multiple elements. Smaller areas of whitespace indicate that one element should be read in relation to another, while larger areas of whitespace create more distance and separation, showing what information belongs closer together.

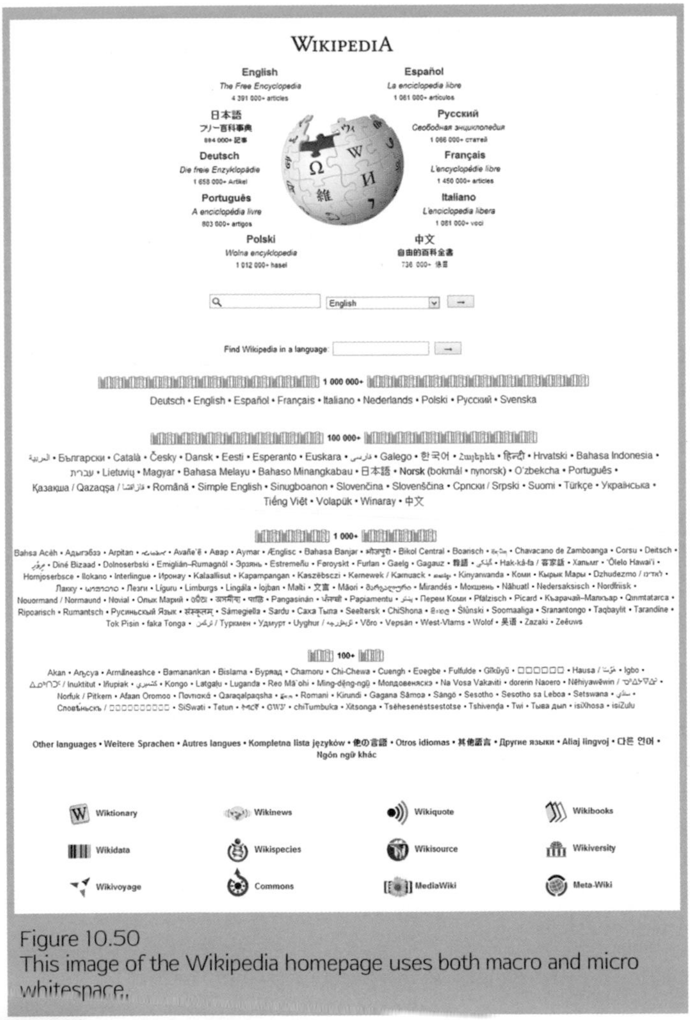

The homepage for Wikipedia (Figure 10.50) uses a mixture of micro and macro whitespace. As you might notice, the brand mark in the center is separated from the language options, while the text itself is separated by smaller, micro whitespace. The text also uses macro white space in between some of the more important sections and margins as well as the links at the bottom. The micro whitespace on the page is subtle but important so that like information is grouped together and separated from other kinds of information.

The medium you choose will dictate physical constraints that limit your overall design and therefore limit how

Figure 10.50
This image of the Wikipedia homepage uses both macro and micro whitespace.

much whitespace you can use. You can only fit so much information on a piece of paper, and even though a Web page can be limitless, you generally want a design to fit within typical monitor dimensions (typically 1280 x 768 pixels). In addition, you will have to include certain information on the medium, and doing so might take up every bit of space (consider a newspaper, for instance, which has much less white space compared with a magazine).

Finally, whitespace need not be "white" per se but any color devoid of text, images, or other information, and sometimes whitespace is referred to as "negative space," or any space that is empty. In the movie poster for *Transformers* (Figure 10.15), the negative space is black. This "blackspace" is used to separate and bookend the title, framing and separating it slightly from the image above. The black frame also creates the illusion that the transformers are stepping out of the picture, providing a faux 3D effect.

MAKING CONNECTIONS

AS A CLASS

Gather several documents, anything from books, CD or DVD liners, magazines, instruction manuals, product packaging, etc. Bring them into class, and together discuss how each uses whitespace differently. What rhetorical or design reasons do you think led to the decisions to use whitespace in these particular ways?

IN A GROUP

Choose a publication that has both print and online presences. How does this publication adjust their use of whitespace for each medium? Physical constraints aside, which do you find more enjoyable to read (which produces a better aesthetic experience)?

ON YOUR OWN

You might typically think of whitespace as a design element of printed publications. As an alternative, analyze how any videos that you watch use negative space to separate visual elements, create emphasis, or other effects. You will probably do well to think broadly about what counts as negative space in these videos. Share your examples with the class.

Proportion

Proportion names the relationship between different elements in a design, usually regarding the relative scale of those elements. Typically, a good design creates a harmony within this scale, thus creating good proportion.

Several relationships can be shown by varying scale. If two objects appear similar in scale, they're considered more equal than if one object were larger than the other. If you refer back to Figure 10.15, you can see varying relationships of scale. For instance, the two transformers are similar in scale (therefore more or less equal), as are the two humans.

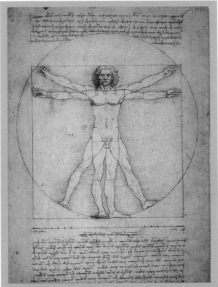

Figure 10.51
Leonardo da Vinci's Vitruvian Man was thought to depict the ideal human proportions.

Credit: ©Paramount/Courtesy Everett Collection

However, the transformer-to-human scale is much greater, showing more importance on the transformers. This poster creates dominance of the transformers over the humans but also offers of focal point by creating diagonals toward the humans, so that even though they are of less importance in terms of proportion, they're still important in the overall harmony of the design (as well as the narrative). The scale between the two sizes also creates a balance between large and small.

Part of this psychological effect comes from the viewer's experience of the human body, the figure from which viewers derive most of their expectations of proportion (Figure 10.51). Generally, if you see a head, you know roughly how big the body will be in relation. When you see Optimus Prime's and Bumblebee's giant heads without their body (Figure 10.52), you know that their body must be equally enormous. If somehow the foreground scene of the poster was removed and you saw tiny robot bodies attached to the heads, you would feel that the proportion was out of harmony and badly designed.

Viewers also react emotionally due to bad proportion. For instance, how would you feel if you opened a 16" pizza box but only found a 4" pizza inside? Or how do you think you would feel if the doorknobs to a house were the size of basketballs, making gripping them very difficult? Such proportions would be annoying if not dangerous for someone who needed to get out of the room immediately.

Figure 10.52
Based on our knowledge of the human body's proportions, Optimus Prime's body should be huge, even though he's a robot.

While viewers generally react negatively (or, at least, immediately notice) when something is out of proportion, especially human proportion, this kind of reaction may be your design goal, eliciting attention or reaction from the audience. A building with extremely high ceilings may create a sense of wonder by making one feel small. However, you also risk offending the aesthetic sense of your audience, which may turn them away from your ultimate rhetorical goals.

MAKING CONNECTIONS

AS A CLASS

Find a variety of cartoon characters that have proper and improper proportions. Which characters are in proportion, and which ones aren't? What are the different situations that might have led the artists to design the cartoon characters the way they did? For those characters drawn out of proportion, would the cartoon be as effective or entertaining if the characters had normal proportions? Why or why not?

IN A GROUP

Analyze news websites such as CNN or ESPN. How do these sites use proportion to suggest emphasis or importance? Which elements are largest? Which are smallest? Be sure to analyze not only the images, but other parts as well, such as navigation menus, social media updates, or font sizes.

ON YOUR OWN

Locate a flyer or print advertisement. How does it use proportion to make its point? Is this use of proportion effective, or could it be redesigned? How would you redesign it? Share your example and findings with the class.

Rule of Thirds

Typically, you might think that if you want to emphasize a subject, you should place it in the middle of your viewing frame if taking a picture or capturing video. However, asymmetrical designs are often more engaging and dynamic to viewers. When working with space in your designs, one technique you might consider is the "rule of thirds." This rule divides an image into nine segments by virtually dividing the image with two horizontal rules and two vertical rules (see Figure 10.53). Any major compositional elements should lie somewhere near one of the four intersections of these lines.

For instance, if you were taking a picture or shooting video, rather than aligning your main object in the center of the frame, you would align it on one of the four vertices. This alignment gives your picture a more dynamic feeling if you're depicting a moving object, or it provides a greater sense of depth and context if you're producing an image of a static object.

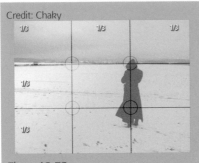

Credit: Chaky

Credit: Raiana Tomazini/

Credit: NBCUniversal

Figure 10.54
Fibonacci spiral.

Figure 10.55
Many interviews use the rule of thirds to arrange their shots.

Figure 10.53
The focal point of this image is emphasized through the rule of thirds.

The rule of thirds in some ways is a shortcut to creating designs with an aesthetic use of spatial arrangements. A more precise layout follows the "Golden Mean," displayed by the Fibonacci spiral (Figure 10.54). When overlayed on several photographs, notice how the major area of focus aligns with the spiral. Another shortcut to this Golden Mean, then, is to divide the composition into fifths rather than thirds and align your major point of interest along the two-fifths or three-fifths lines in any direction (portrait or landscape). However, the rule of thirds will generally produce good results, and many video cameras have a feature that simulates gridlines in your viewfinder allowing you to align your subject with one of the four intersect points.

You can usually notice the rule of thirds while watching television, specifically during interview scenes. For example, this still from *The Office* in Figure 10.55 uses the rule of thirds to position the interviewee's head in the upper right intersect point. If filming your own interviews, you should make use of these upper two points, positioning your subject's face in either of these two spots.

MAKING CONNECTIONS

AS A CLASS

Search for stock photographs on sites like corbisimages.com or gettyimages.com, and overlay the Fibonacci spiral onto a few images. How well do the major focal points align with the Golden Mean (or even the rule of thirds)? If not, do you think the image is still effective as those that do?

IN A GROUP

As discussed above, television shows such as *The Office* use the rule of thirds during their "interview" sequences. Locate other instances of television or films that use this technique, either fictional shows or news programs. Share your examples with the class.

ON YOUR OWN

Using a camera—either provided by your class or just a cell phone camera—practice taking photos of a variety of objects using the rule of thirds. However, also take a series of photos placing objects in other orientations. In a photo editor, overlay a rule-of-thirds grid onto the images, seeing how well your images align with this principle. Share your images with the class, and discuss which photos are more engaging and whether the rule of third improves the composition of your images.

Balance

This chapter has often referred to the need to "balance" certain design elements, such as balance in proportion, color, or whitespace. However, balance is itself a formal principle and has three main spatial arrangements that you should consider when implementing balance in a design: symmetrical balance, asymmetrical balance, and radial balance.

Credit: Dr F. Nemos

Figure 10.56
Butterflies exhibit symmetrical balance.

Symmetrical balance appears when two parts of the design are mirror images of each other when divided in half. This balance can be vertical or horizontal. If you draw a line down the middle of Figure 10.56, each side is nearly the same as the other. Symmetrical balance can be applied to the design of the entire document. If you were to fold in half the *Transformers* poster in Figure 10.15, each element would roughly correspond to a part of the other side.

Asymmetrical balance can be achieved by

Figure 10.57
Note how this ad creates balance through the text's placement.

Figure 10.58
Without the text and graphics, the image feels out of balance.

organizing objects through different combinations of "weight," just as if you were trying to balance a set of scales. The graphic in figure 10.57 uses asymmetrical balance. Although the single largest arrow appears on the left and dominates the overall design in terms of size, several smaller arrows on the right offset the weight of the larger arrow. If you were to remove these smaller arrows, as in figure 10.58, then the image might feel "left-heavy" as if it could tip to one side.

Figure 10.59
An orange displays radial balance when cut in half.

Radial balance occurs in images that can be divided in any direction and still produce mirror images of each other. Radial balance most commonly occurs in circular shapes, such as the orange in Figure 10.59. This kind of design creates balance and draws the eye to a central focal point no matter where on the design you first look.

MAKING CONNECTIONS

AS A CLASS

Search online for movie posters of the latest films coming out. Discuss how each poster tries to achieve balance using the above techniques. As an alternative, you might also analyze popular websites, noting how they arrange different elements to create balance.

IN A GROUP

Look through the halls or bulletin board spaces on your campus or community. Find examples that use symmetrical, asymmetrical, and radial balance in their designs. Share them with the class and discuss whether you think the use of balance in these documents is effective both aesthetically and rhetorically. If not, how would you change the design?

ON YOUR OWN

In a photo editor, create two designs, each using either symmetrical or asymmetrical balance. Use any objects you want, such as simple geometric shapes or images found online. However, use the same objects for each design and then compare how the meaning of the composition changes as you change the balance between the elements.

Harmony

Like balance, many techniques can be used to achieve harmony, which—when successful—shows the audience how all the different parts of a design complement each other. While unity (discussed below) uses the repetition of like elements, harmony blends different elements so they work together. As an illustration, you might consider something as simple as a bolt and a nut (Figure 10.60). Separately, each has a different shape, yet they fit together as a structural unit. Visually, they look dissimilar, but they also share the spiral shape (outside on the bolt, and inside of the nut). Harmony attempts to accentuate the tension between these differences and similarities so that their strengths emerge and, like the bolt and nut, hold together as a design.

Figure 10.60
A nut and bolt share the spiral shape of the threads.

Credit: Honza Groh

Another common object that achieves harmony is a typical die or a domino. Although the sides are square or rectangular, the dots are circular, and the different shapes balance each other (Figure 10.61).

You can achieve harmony in a variety of ways. For instance, you may link dissimilar objects together by using similar colors for each. A bolt and nut have different shapes, but are often both metallic. Alternatively, you may present different colors within the same shape. A rainbow is made up of different colors but ties together as an arch (Figure 10.62).

Figure 10.61
Domino's brand mark includes both squares and circles in harmony.

Figure 10.62
The different colors are harmonized through the shape of the arch or bow.

A design does not necessarily have to be harmonious. In fact, you might intentionally design a composition so that it is disharmonious in order to capture the audience's attention. Also, a design that has too much harmony may seem monotonous. Some contrast is good and will help keep your audience engaged.

MAKING CONNECTIONS

AS A CLASS

Develop a list of examples from the natural world that achieve harmony, as the rainbow example illustrates. You might also consider everyday objects—such as a fork and knife—that look different but work together in harmony.

IN A GROUP

Visit a variety of websites and analyze their various elements. How are they different? How are they similar? How do the elements integrate and complement the rest of the design? Share the website and your analysis with the class.

ON YOUR OWN

Look at the *Transformers* poster in Figure 10.15. In what ways does this poster use harmony in its design? Find other flyers or posters that make good (or bad) use of harmony, and share them with the class.

Proximity

Proximity places similar objects together within a design. For instance, if you look at most websites, all the links to other parts of the site are placed together in a menu so that users can easily navigate the site. Or, on a restaurant menu, appetizers are placed together, as are lunch items, drinks, and desserts. In this way, proximity helps to organize information. You can help create proximity by using boxed elements or whitespace to separate elements from each other and group the information that an audience would expect or find useful to be together as a unit.

The flyer in Figure 10.63 uses borders and images to reinforce proximity. The organization and title information for the flyer appear in a separate section away from the other details of the event. The other information is grouped and placed together using boxes so that the reader can quickly discern what kind of

Credit: Abhijith Jayanthi

Figure 10.63
This flyer uses proximity to group similar information. It also uses borders to help create separation.

Credit: crotonyachtclub.com/

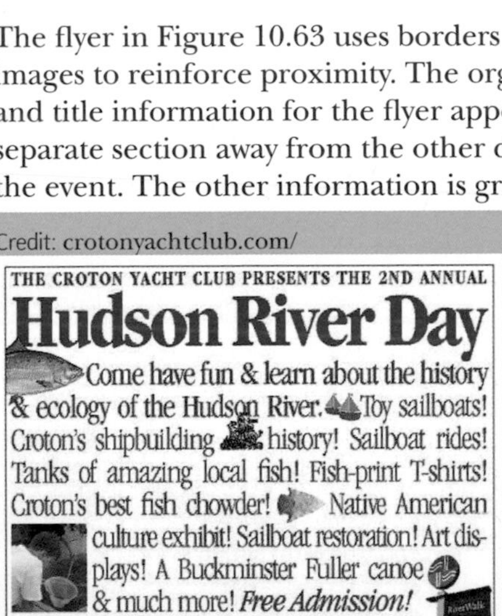

Figure 10.64
This flyer does not use proximity well.

information is located in a particular area. Finally, most of the images are grouped together along the right margin rather than scattered randomly.

Figure 10.64, however, demonstrates bad use of proximity. Even though the author attempts to separate some information through use of color, all the text and images run into one another. Even if the design was limited by the size constraints of the flyer, it could be tweaked at the level of font size, the arrangement of images, and more whitespace to help create visual separation and guide the reader.

By creating a three-dimensional perspective, the *Transformers* poster (Figure 10.15) places like objects in proximity. For instance, the humans are placed together in the center of the poster and "further back" from the two transformers. Optimus Prime and Bumblebee are placed together in the foreground, even though the horizontal space between them seems greater.

MAKING CONNECTIONS

AS A CLASS

Look at a Facebook page. How does the site use proximity to group different kinds of visuals and information? How might you rearrange the site to make similar items more proximate? You may also look at other websites and discuss how each site uses proximity in their designs.

IN A GROUP

Figure 10.64 attempts proximity but could be better designed. Analyze the way that the authors have attempted to place different kinds of information together and what could be improved. Next, sketch out your own design for a new poster that focuses on the proximity of like information. Share your designs, and discuss the choices you made with the class.

ON YOUR OWN

Watch one of the cable news stations, such as CNN, MSNBC, or Fox News. Analyze how each station uses proximity to organize the information the viewer sees. Compare this design with their respective Web pages, and write a brief report that explains how the television channels and websites differ in proximity and how they use it in similar ways.

Unity

Unity ties all the different parts of a design together so that the audience understands it as a single, cohesive image. While unity may seem a lot like harmony, unity focuses on creating a like pattern throughout with all objects, making sure the audience sees how this pattern works toward a single idea.

Figure 10.65, a flyer for an annual walking event, uses a variety of arrow shapes, but they're all tied together by the repetition of the arrow symbol. You might say that this image uses both harmony and unity, since each individual arrow complements others via its unique shape while the arrow points create unity.

Credit: hazencreative.com

Credit: Airforce357

Credit: The Everett Collection

Figure 10.65
The arrow shape helps to unify this design.

Figure 10.66
The circular frame of each image helps to unify them.

Figure 10.67
Unity in the *Harry Potter* poster.

In Figure 10.66, a series of images runs along the left of the page, but with another image in the upper right corner. One of the ways an audience knows that these images are connected is that they're all bound by a circular enclosure, creating unity among them.

You already use unity in alphabetic writing. Every sentence you write uses different words but ties together in a single, unified message. Likewise, sentences unite into paragraphs, which unite as an essay. A collection of essays can be thematically unified to create a book, and a collection of books can tie together to create a series. In visual design, unity is an attempt to create a single, coherent idea made up of all the different elements of the design.

In the *Harry Potter* poster (Figure 10.67), although Harry and Voldemort are opposed in the movie, within the poster they create unity, demonstrating—via their placement—that they both appear in the film and that there is tension between them. Within the film, the two are opposed; within the poster, their depictions create an overall unity to the design. This unity is a culmination of all the other principles this chapter has discussed already, such as balance, proximity, harmony, and proportion. If you've done well to make use of these principles, then your design will hopefully achieve unity.

Unity can play an important role in creating an overall design cohesion, especially with an image like a brand mark, which must be unified with other elements of an organization's brand identity (Figure 10.68). For example, if a brand mark contained geometric shapes, such as triangles, then you may consider using a triangle-based motif for other documents, such as Web pages, business cards, letterhead, flyers, or other professional materials that can double as marketing materials. Each type of document is clearly different, but the design of each should be similar enough to link them together.

Credit: M.Minderhoud

Figure 10.68
Although Unilever's brand mark is made up of many different objects—such as a palm tree, snow flake, spoon, bird, heart, and other shapes—it achieves unity within the shape of a "U" that holds them together.

MAKING CONNECTIONS

AS A CLASS

Look again at a popular website. Discuss how the different parts create a unified whole to the site, so that you know they all belong on this page. Consider not just the visual aspects of the site but also the language used in the textual elements. Are there any elements that you could remove that would not disrupt the unity of the site?

IN A GROUP

Analyze short, online videos produced by a single organization, such as Disney, National Geographic, or the National Football League (any source will do). Note how the videos create unity both within a single video but also among different videos. What visual elements help to link the videos and give them a coherent visual identity? Share your examples and findings with the rest of the class.

ON YOUR OWN

Choose your favorite sports team, and search online for a variety of documents, images, or objects produced by the organization. These examples should include uniforms, transportation, written documents, videos, etc. Analyze how the team creates an overall unity between all the documents, so a reader or viewer can clearly recognize that all are united.

MOVEMENT THROUGH SPACE

You can create a sense of movement in your design by using different spatial arrangements, even when the composition is still. When a viewer typically looks at an image, the eye scans to the upper left, then clockwise around the image, and then horizontally through the image. A viewer also typically looks from large objects to smaller ones, color to noncolor, or from the unusual to the familiar. By arranging elements to capture an audience's first glance, you can help guide how they view the rest of the design.

Repetition and Rhythm

Just as the repeated drumbeats of a song create rhythm and drive the music, keeping it moving along, repeated elements of a visual composition achieve the same effect. Nearly any element can create rhythm as long as it's repeated throughout the design. Repetition of shapes, colors, objects, or patterns can all create rhythm and guide the viewer's gaze. The eye will pick up on the pattern, follow it, and move along the design space.

Figure 10.69 features a poster for the band Iron & Wine. Notice the repeated use of matches from the match book in the upper-right corner diagonally to the lower-left corner. Typically, the eye will begin with the larger object, the matchbook, and follow the trail of matches. Notice how the designer inserted bits of information (styled in the same colors as the matches) along the trail so that the eye picks them up as it follows the repeated elements.

Also, the positioning of the source of the matches (the matchbook) creates a natural sense of movement since viewer's know that gravity will cause objects to fall and thus understand the matches as moving from the top of the page to the bottom.

You can also use repetition when writing with words. For instance, when you write a speech you may repeat the use of key words or phrases to make sure your audience receives the particular message you want conveyed. While you should typically try to vary some words in written texts to avoid monotony, you may repeat certain language that the audience identifies with. For instance, if you're writing a cover letter for a job, you may repeat certain phrases from the job advertisement so that your reader clearly sees how your skills connect with the company's needs.

Credit: hazencreative.com

Figure 10.69
The matches in this poster repeat and create a rhythm.

Repetition and rhythm can use alternating elements as well. A series of dots will guide a reader through a page, but if you alter these dots by changing their colors, the audience may become more interested as this alteration keeps the design from becoming too monotonous. Think about how these repeated elements should tie into the overall design, keeping in mind the principles of unity and harmony.

MAKING CONNECTIONS

AS A CLASS

Return to one of the websites you've already looked at. What elements repeat and create rhythm for the reader to follow? How do these elements relate back to the page's unity?

IN A GROUP

Look through a variety of magazines. How do these magazines create rhythm through repetition? Pay attention to color, fonts, and other elements. Do you think the use of these repeating elements makes the magazine, or individual articles, easier to read? Share your examples and findings with the class.

ON YOUR OWN

Revise your résumé (or write one) by creating rhythm through the repetition of certain elements. For instance, you may use color to highlight specific parts of the document, or you may change font sizes. Create at least three different versions and share them with your class.

Variety

Variety uses many variables—including color and contrast already discussed above—to create movement through a design's space by guiding the audience's gaze through the composition. Variety can also use repetition and rhythm as described in the previous section to guide a reader's eyes and keep a design from becoming too boring. The chief means to create variety include differences in size, color, or shape. However, you should usually only change one variable so that the design still maintains a sense of unity (Figure 10.70).

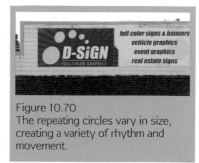

Figure 10.70
The repeating circles vary in size, creating a variety of rhythm and movement.

MAKING CONNECTIONS

AS A CLASS

Examine the advertisements for different Apple products. How do these ads make use of variety, both individually and as a collection? Why do you think Apple used variety in this way? Does variety, in this case, say something about Apple's *ethos* as a company?

IN A GROUP

Create a list of examples from nature that display variety in their visual designs. In these examples, why do you think variety is helpful? Make a list of your examples, and share them with the class.

ON YOUR OWN

Look back at the Iron & Wine poster in Figure 10.68. How does the artist use variety to make the poster more interesting? Do you think the artist uses enough variety? Too much? Record your thoughts and share them with the class.

Action

A variety of techniques can display action and thus movement. Some images can create movement simply by the positioning of the object (such as the Iron & Wine example in Figure 10.69). If positioned correctly in the composition, a bird in flight or a skydiver in free fall creates movement because the viewer understands the natural trajectory of their bodies. Such movement is sometimes referred to as anticipated movement, because the viewer anticipates that the figure would move in a particular way if it wasn't a still image.

Figure 10.71
The blurred wings of this hummingbird indicate that they were moving when the photo was taken.

Movement can also be communicated by giving an object fuzzy boundaries or indistinct outlines. If you've ever watched an object at high speed, such as a pitcher throwing a fastball, or water spraying from a hose, it's difficult to see the ball or water sharply. Instead, viewers experience fast moving objects as more blurry than stationary objects. In visual designs, blurring an image can help show the audience that a particular object is in motion, such as the wings of the hummingbird in Figure 10.71.

Diagonal lines, or objects posed at a diagonal, also create movement. The Heisman Trophy statue's pose creates a diagonal vector pointing toward the way he would move. Actual vectors, such as arrow shapes, also create movement as viewers have become conditioned to following them as movement indicators via traffic signs and other aids. Arrows direct attention, and so move the viewer's eyes along a design. However, the vector need not be an actual arrow. The arm of the Heisman Trophy creates a secondary vector that draws the eye toward the outstretched hand.

Even eye position—where a figure is looking—creates an invisible vector that directs the audience's attention to some other part of the image. A pathway, such as a road, trail, staircase, or aisle can also create movement, as these elements may be physically shaped as diagonals but are also places where one physically moves or where movement occurs.

Figure 10.72, the famous cover of the Beatles' album *Abbey Road*, displays many of these characteristics. The Beatles themselves are actually in movement from left to right, and their gaze straight ahead reinforces this direction. The cross walk provides an example of a path, yet the vanishing point created by the road they're crossing provides a secondary axis of movement, although dominated by the vector along which the main subjects walk.

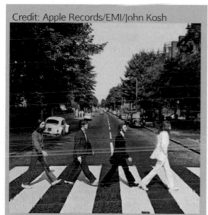

Credit: Apple Records/EMI/John Kosh

Figure 10.72
The cover art for *Abbey Road* conveys movement in several ways.

Credit: Urban Freeflow

Figure 10.73
This image superimposes several images into one in order to show movement.

Finally, multiple objects can be shown in a single image to convey movement. These objects might appear across several frames, like a comic or the person jumping in Figure 10.73. Here, several frames are overlaid to show the flow of movement, and the viewer understands the full motion of his action. Of course, a single shot of the figure in the air about to fall would also express this to the audience. However, this sequence lets the viewer know that he landed on the next building.

MAKING CONNECTIONS

AS A CLASS

Look at a variety of still advertisements for sporting products. Analyze which ads attempt to convey a sense of action and which ones do not. Which ads to you find more effective for the product they're advertising?

IN A GROUP

Look at several comic strips either online or in a newspaper. List all the various techniques that the artists use to visualize movement to the reader. Share your list with the class.

ON YOUR OWN

Collect brand marks and still advertisements for organizations that specialize in transport or delivery, such as moving, freight, or mail companies. Analyze if these brand marks or ads use action in their designs. If so, do you think these designs are effective at making a rhetorical point about their company? If the visuals don't use action, are they still effective, or would you suggest revisions? Share you findings with the class.

Sequence

Another way of creating movement within a still image is through sequence. While one method of sequence uses the techniques of comics, isolating individual steps through separate frames, you can also show a progression of movement within a single frame. Figure 10.74 depicts the classic evolution sequence that illustrates a movement through time. Figure 10.75 shows a sequence that demonstrates how to exercise by swinging a kettlebell. This image instructs the viewer how to move in a particular way, but does so by conveying a sense of movement.

Figure 10.76 shows a sequence of the word "UNITED" becoming the word "CHANGE." In this image, each letter "moves" until it has transformed into another. Note that one of the reasons this sequence is successful is that each

Credit: José-manuel Benitos

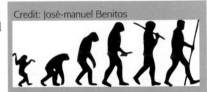

Figure 10.74
This image depicts evolution as a sequence.

Figure 10.75
This sequence informs the viewer how to perform this kettlebell exercise.

step introduces only small changes, allowing the viewer to see the transformation. However, the changes are large enough that the designer can fit the entire sequence on a single poster.

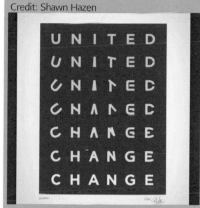

Credit: Shawn Hazen

If you are composing a sequence to show a particular movement, such as the kettlebell movement in Figure 10.75, then all the other elements of the image (such as the background) should remain as consistent as possible so that the focus is on what changes—the movement itself. Notice in this example, the background consists of a white backdrop so the reader doesn't become distracted.

Even within moving images, you can still break a scene into a sequence of camera angles to make the scene more dynamic. For instance, you can shoot a single scene from different angles and put them together to present the entire action in a more dynamic way. Changing angles can provide emphasis on different objects in the scene, thus offering

Figure 10.76
This poster "moves" the letters to change the word "UNITED" into "CHANGE."

rhetorical choices for the director, who might want the audience to identify with a particular character or point of view, or to move the plot in a specific direction.

MAKING CONNECTIONS

AS A CLASS

Watch an episode of a popular television sitcom or drama. As you watch, write down how the director distills different scenes into a smaller series of sequences. Note the important aspects of each shot. After the show is over, discuss what you noticed and how the director created sequences to change meaning or emphasis. How do these sequences help move the story along? If the show doesn't use sequences, discuss why you think this might be as well.

IN A GROUP

Choose a simple task that you perform every day and create a sequence of images depicting this task. You can do this with a still camera, taking photos as you perform the task, or you can use video, freezing the footage and taking screenshots. Try and distill the sequence to as few images as possible while still conveying everything that the audience might need to know to complete the action themselves.

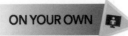

ON YOUR OWN

Look at your favorite comic book, or find one online that you can use. Analyze how the artist creates sequences between the panels. How do you know that each panel is related to the one before? If the scene changes, what indications does the artist give to let you know that the previous sequence has ended?

KEY TERMS		
action	isolation	sans serif
asymmetrical balance	perspective	saturation
balance	placement	sequence
CMYK	proportion	serif
color	proximity	symmetrical balance
complementary colors	radial balance	typography
contrast	repetition	unity
contrasting colors	RGB	value
emphasis	rhythm	variety
harmony	rule of thirds	whitespace
hue		

OUTPUT: FLYER

As you may have noticed, many of the examples used in this chapter are various forms of flyers. This section repeatedly referenced the *Transformers* poster (Figure 10.15) to illustrate many of the design techniques you can use to create your own visual documents. For this output, create your own flyer for an event, community organization, non-profit group, a neighbor that needs help, or other purpose designated by your instructor. Here are some suggestions:

1. Approach a community organization such as a homeless shelter, and create a flyer for an upcoming event.

2. Locate a problem, situation, or important event in your community; create a flyer making citizens aware of it.

3. Identify a neighbor or friend who needs help finding a lost pet or who needs advertising some other pressing need, and create an appropriate flyer to meet the exigency.

As you think though how you should design your flyer, you'll obviously consider design and genre (a flyer) from the rhetorical tetrahedron. You should also consider the medium on which that flyer will be placed. For instance, if the flyer is in a location where it might get wet, you should print it on waterproof paper. Of course, you must also consider your message and audience, and how *logos, ethos, pathos,* and *kairos* factor into your design and distribution.

Step by Step

To create your own flyer or poster, you must first consider some rhetorical questions applicable to all writing.

Exigency
What is the situation that demands this flyer? Is this the best kind of document to create for your situation?

Purpose
What is the goal of the flyer? To persuade? Inform? What do you want to accomplish with the flyer? What kind of flyer will be most effective?

Audience
Whom do you hope to reach with this flyer? Who is your primary audience? Can you identify secondary audiences? How will you design your flyer to accommodate all of these audiences?

Delivery

How will you distribute your flyer? On bulletin boards? Online? Through the mail? If you post the flyer in a public space, how will you place or design it so that it can compete for the attention of the audience amongst all other flyers and visuals? Where can you place the flyer so that it will most likely reach your intended audience?

Once you determine what kind of flyer you want to produce, you must also consider some of its physical properties.

Size

What size paper (or other material) will you print your flyer on? This is probably the first question to answer, since it will determine how you design the flyer.

Stock

What kind of paper will you use? Will you use basic printer paper or something more durable, such as glossy card stock?

Font

What kind of font will you use for the most important information? You need to grab the reader's attention, so a large sans serif font will usually work best, but paragraphs of information might be written in a serif font. Also, simple fonts that can be easily read usually work better than a complicated font that is too difficult to make out.

Color

How can you use color to emphasize important information? You want different elements in your flyer to contrast with each other so none becomes lost to the viewer. You might also use color thematically. For instance, if your flyer is about an environmental event, green becomes an obvious choice. If the flyer pertains to your college or university, then you might use the school's colors.

Layout

How will you layout the title, text, and images on the flyer to best organize the information to the viewer while still making it aesthetically pleasing?

Images

Remember, the flyer itself is an image, regardless of whether it contains images. However, is an image important to your argument? Is it ancillary, or the central component, such as a flyer for a missing child or pet?

After you have considered these questions, use the guidelines below to create the flyer.

1. Create a headline or title: This title should be short enough to be read quickly and grab the reader's attention. However, also think of key words that will help make it stand out. For example, using "Sublease Close to Campus" might be more appealing than just "Sublease," since it includes information that might be attractive to a student. Including the price in this title might also be effective. Anticipate and appeal to the reader's needs and wants. If the flyer is for a business, do not include the business name in the title; instead, include what you will do for the reader.

2. Use colorful and emphatic graphics: While your flyer shouldn't look too cluttered with information, it should use color and graphics to make your argument. Use graphics that will get your point across as well as color to help you highlight important information.

3. Focus on benefits/consequences: Ultimately, you need to appeal to the reader, and explain what the audience will get from the flyer's message. In other words, how does the information affect them? You may have lost a pet, but what information can you include to make the audience want to act? An appeal for their sympathy? A reward? If it is for an event, why should they want to attend? If fundraising for a charity, why should they donate? While you might not have space for all your claims, evidence, and reasons, you should at least include some reasons for them to act.

4. Organize boxed elements and contrasting colors: Placing important information into small boxes, using whitespace to separate elements or using colors can help call attention to the information.

5. Clearly identify your main points: In a one-page flyer, you don't have much room to make your argument, so try to stick to the most important information, which typically includes who, what, where, when, why, how. Don't go into too much detail, and make the most important information as clear as possible. As a whole, try to keep the flyer simple, so don't get too complicated.

6. Provide details: You should provide details that let your readers know how to act if they're persuaded by you message. Include contact information, dates, prices, important names, or other information they might need. You can also include URLs or quick reference codes that will take them to online information if necessary.

7. Use the back: Although flyers traditionally only have information on one side, especially if they're posted on a wall, there is no reason they

have to be one-sided. Consider if there is any specific or important information that would be useful to print on the backside of a flyer. Perhaps use the space for more images to better highlight or illustrate what you wish to communicate.

8. Proofread: A spelling or design inconsistency in a flyer can destroy an author's *ethos*, especially since it is such a short document. Remember, flyers are meant to be distributed to many people, so this effect is multiplied. You can never know who will really see this flyer, so make sure everything is correct. As with any document, let your peers review the flyer as well.

9. Delivery: Choose the right medium and placement for your flyer. The delivery medium does not just mean the kind of paper you use when printing but also the overall ecology of the flyer's distribution (as discussed in Chapter 5). To choose the best medium and location, you should screen the environment, taking note of how it will affect your text. Where can you place the flyer so it has the greatest chance of being seen, and thus, delivery to the audience?

Flyers are relatively cheap to produce, and you can easily make a large quantity of high quality flyers using glossy paper and a good color inkjet or laser printer. However, they can also contribute to pollution (Figure 10.77). If you're going to mass-produce a flyer, consider some following guidelines:

- Try to use post-consumer, recycled stock if possible.

- Consider using a stock that is biodegradable, especially for events that will pass and for which the flyer will become obsolete.

- Although an inconvenience, make sure you remove your flyers if you have posted them in a public area once you feel your message has been delivered (or, if for an event, after that event has taken place). Flyers often become detached from their surface and become litter in streets, drains, landfills, and contribute to pollution.

Credit: User:Ld

Figure 10.77
Flyers can litter the streets if not removed once they've served their purpose.

Also, remember that many flyers are exposed to the elements, and that weather, such as rain, can alter the message of a flyer if it causes the ink to bleed.

11

EDITING

One of the most important stages in the writing process is the step of editing. This step is important not only for alphabetic text, but also for documents composed through new media. Of course, editing for visual modes is much different than editing for spelling, grammar, and other issues you might typically think of when writing traditional papers. For example, once a film director has captured the raw footage via camera, an editor takes that footage and assembles it into a final format (Figure 11.1).

The editor is not concerned with comma splices or dangling participles but with the cuts, film splices, and transitions needed to create a coherent whole out of many hours of footage, often taken at different times and in different locations. During this process,

Credit: Andrew Toos

"No, go ahead and critique my mss. I'm always ok ... after the initial reaction."

Figure 11.2
If you're editing your peer's work, be tactful when offering criticism.

Credit: Starz Entertainment

CUT

Figure 11.1
Most directors will tell you that a good movie requires good editing.
http://www.youtube.com/watch?v=508M HvMGWEg&list=FLJtroKLbeSoVdiNCZT UL-lg&feature=mh_lolz

the editor looks through the footage for consistency between the shots, props, scenery, and other elements, and revises the work to make the film match the final vision shared by the director and producer.

This chapter will cover techniques that will help during the editing and revising process for image and video as well as traditional writing, since all of these media are intertwined during the production process. While new media require their own set of specific practices when editing, some basic underlying principles govern all types of revision, and here you'll learn both. While editing may not be pleasant, as Figure 11.2 indicates, it's an important and necessary process.

While "editing" doesn't appear on the rhetorical tetrahedron, you should still think through the tetrahedron as you edit. For example, you might ask how a particular change affects the message, how your various audiences will view the change, how that change affects the overall design, or how an edit will enhance or detract from *logos, ethos, pathos,* and *kairos.* In this way, you can use the rhetorical tetrahedron as a tool to think about how editing will affect your overall text.

KINDS OF EDITING

Although you might lump terms such as proofreading, editing, and revising into one group, the three activities are quite different and will be addressed separately throughout the rest of this chapter. As you work on editing and revising, keep in mind the different roles each play as well as the strategies and goals for this step in the writing process. Use the inverted triangle in Figure 11.3 as you follow the editing process, starting with the broader changes (revising), continuing with more detailed changes within smaller sections (editing), and finishing with corrections (proofreading).

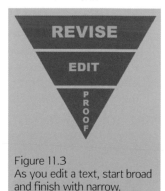

Figure 11.3
As you edit a text, start broad and finish with narrow.

Revising

When looking over your initial draft of a project—whether text, image, or video—you should first make changes on a large scale. *Revising* focuses on the whole document, making larger structural, design, and argumentative changes rather than picking apart the smaller details. While you'll eventually get to these

Figure 11.4
Revising entails working with the text as a whole.

smaller matters in editing and proofreading, you should start with the bigger picture. This is the work of revising (Figure 11.4).

Text

When revising your text—whether an essay, report, script, or proposal—start with the largest scale and work inward. For instance, if you're working on a traditional essay, you should revise your larger argument, check that all of the paragraphs within the document support that argument, and ensure that these paragraphs are grouped into sections that make sense. Once you have the general order figured out, you can then move down to individual sections, then to individual paragraphs, reordering them if necessary and deleting what you don't need. If you were to edit and proofread prior to this step, you might be proofreading paragraphs that you would later delete anyway, wasting much of your time. Always work from large to small, from the big picture to the details.

Not all of your work needs revision, and sometimes you might accidentally revise for the worse as you cut and paste, moving sections or paragraphs around trying to find the best fit. To help ensure that you don't lose this work forever by over-editing, save your work as you revise, but save it under a new file name from time to time. Sometimes you might want to revert back to a prior version that you think sounded better, and if you simply save over your existing file you'll lose that version forever. This advice also applies to writing with images or video: Save multiple versions as you progress through the revision process.

When you revise, you're literally "looking again" at your initial draft. Notice the gaps that need to be filled. Also notice the redundancies that you can remove. Although you can correct smaller errors as you revise, worry about them later. You first want to make sure the foundation and frame of your project is solid before worrying about what color to paint it.

You might find that you need to add an entire section to strengthen your argument, building on what you already have, or you may decide to remove an entire section that doesn't make sense. Make these large-scale changes to the paper now before you worry about individual words and sentences. However, during the revision process you should make the decision about the tone and voice you want to use, as this affects how every paragraph and sentence will be read and interpreted by the reader. Some general revision elements to consider include:

- **Reorganizing**: When you reorganize, group similar evidence together, or change the order of your points starting with the least important and moving toward most important, or vice versa.

- **Refining the main ideas**: As you can see, most of the revision process focuses on the ideas in the text rather than the text's mechanics. Decide if your thesis statement needs refocusing and revision, and check that each section and individual paragraph has a clear topic.

- **Improving the argument**: Although you probably have many reasons and much evidence to support your claim by the time you finish your first draft, you can always revise the argument by adding additional points. Particularly, add counterarguments that seem to disprove your claim, and then argue why these counterarguments are wrong by offering counter evidence as a rebuttal. By acknowledging these other voices in the final draft, you'll improve your goodwill with the audience and strengthen your argument.

- **Deleting the unnecessary**: Although it's often hard to delete large sections of text once you've composed them, sometimes a paragraph or entire pages don't add to your argument. Be honest about text that should stay in and text that needs to be deleted. If you save multiple copies during your revision process, you can always reclaim them if you change your mind (Figure 11.5).

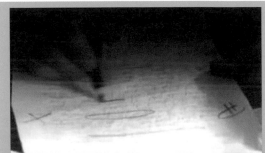

Figure 11.5
Editing often requires the writer to cut much of what you've already written.
http://www.youtube.com/watch?v=4php_B1LQiM

- **Determining tone**: Although your tone may seem like a small element of your writing, it affects the work on a large scale, and inconsistencies across the document can confuse or annoy the reader. Read through your document, and make sure that your tone and voice seem consistent throughout the piece. This revision step is especially true if you collaborate on a document, and each partner writes separate sections. During revision, you should make the tone of voice consistent throughout so that the document seems as if it were written by a single person.

Once you've covered these large, global issues in your text you can then proceed to editing and proofreading. Working in this order will save you time and help you revise with more efficiency and focus.

Image

Like a textual document, you should revise an image by starting with the "bigger picture." Before you touch up the details of the photo, consider what large-scale changes you might need to make. Some of the revisions include:

- **Flipping:** Would the photo work better if it was flipped horizontally or vertically?

- **Rotating:** Sometimes, an image needs to be rotated in order to best orient it onto a design. Most photo editors can rotate an image a full 360 degrees so that you can angle it at any degree needed.

- **Cropping:** Even if you captured your subject perfectly in a photograph, the background might contain too much information, cluttering the photo and drawing your audience's attention away from the focal point. Consider cropping out sections of the photo, or cropping it to a particular size to fit the larger document in which you plan to insert it.

- **Resizing/Scaling:** Your image may be too large or too small for the final document in which you plan to use it. Decreasing an image size is easy without losing too much detail. However, increasing an image's size often results in pixelation or fuzziness. Most online images have 72 dots per inch (dpi), and you can't increase them without significant pixelation. However, you can often scan hard copy images at a high resolution and enlarge them for other purposes.

- **Artistic manipulations:** Most photo editors have a wide array of filters or other ways to manipulate and customize an image. For instance, you might remove color information, turning an image to black and white. You might make a photograph appear to be a watercolor (Figure 11.6) Research what options your photo editor has—or research how to perform the effect you want—and revise your image so that it best fits the goals of your project.

Figure 11.6
The "watercolor" filter in Adobe Photoshop was used to edit this photo.

Like text, it's best to perform these revisions before you start with other details, such as removing red eye or adjusting colors, as these steps may be completely unnecessary depending on the large-scale changes you make.

Video

Before you worry about editing individual cuts, you should revise your video as a whole. Ideally, you wrote an excellent script that was relatively free of plot holes or gaps in argument and provided a clear blueprint for producing your project. From this footage, you should assemble the rough cut of the video, stitching the shots together into a complete draft. However, once you capture the script on film, you might be surprised that a certain scene or shot doesn't look as expected. Some scenes might even need to be re-shot. Here are a few steps you might take when revising video:

- Assemble: In a video editor (Figure 11.7), assemble a complete version of your video.

- View: Once you have a complete rough cut, watch the draft and take notes, paying attention to the large-scale issues that you see. Do some scenes seem out of place? Does the order of the shots seem logical? Do you notice any gaps in argument or narrative that would confuse the audience? Does the hook appear close enough to the beginning? You may also want to have a peer view the rough cut with you.

- Reassemble: Revise your video based on your notes, and reassemble the shots into a new version.

- Review: Watch this new version, repeating the process.

Most of your video revision strategy should focus on arranging these parts into a whole. Once you assemble the pieces according to your script and storyboard, you can better judge if a particular order doesn't make sense or would be more effective if altered. Much like a written text, you may decide that you want to reorder the scenes to present a more persuasive story or narrative. If you're not happy with what you see, don't be afraid to completely alter the video from your original script or idea. You may find that playing with the footage in the video editor, such as dragging and dropping scenes into new arrangements, can help you think visually about your project and help you come up with new ideas for revision.

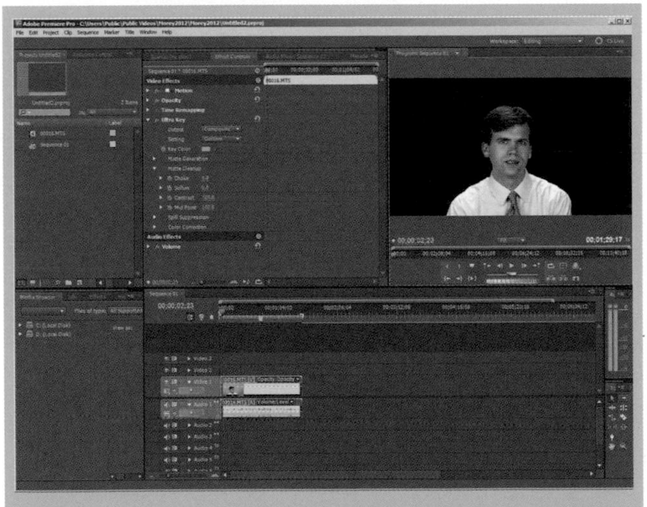

Figure 11.7
A video editor allows you to combine individual clips to create larger sequences.

MAKING CONNECTIONS

AS A CLASS

Choose a famous image that has been heavily remixed by artists and advertisers such as the Uncle Sam "I Want You" poster originally displayed during World War I (Figure 11.8). Search for as many remixed versions as you can, and then discuss the revisions that were made. Are the revisions simple, such as cropping, flipping, or resizing, or are they more complex? What do you think such revisions accomplish? What was the exigency that prompted the revision? Who was the artist's intended audience?

Figure 11.8

From Darth Vader to zombies, this recruitment poster has been remixed into many new contexts. This poster was itself adapted from another poster. Can you figure out which one?

IN A GROUP

Select several video clips and assemble at least three different rough cuts by changing the sequence of the clips. How does each arrangement differ from each other? Do they all make sense in their own way, or does one particular order seem most effective? Share your three versions with the class and get their opinion as well.

ON YOUR OWN

Locate an essay that you have written for another class. If you were going to make a video based on this essay, how would you revise the essay to make it better fit a visual medium? Would you change the order of its major points? Would you change when you present your major thesis? Write a short report that lists the changes and explains your rationale behind them, and share them with the class.

Editing

While revision deals with the global structure of the document, editing usually addresses the next step down, the details and technical aspects (Figure 11.9). Since *editing* is usually performed once a draft is already finished, this step is usually given the least amount of attention due to time constraints or general neglect. However, thoroughly editing your text can make it much more professional and acceptable to audiences. Many readers or viewers love to find a misspelled word, a misplaced comma, or a poorly edited image and chide the author for his or her carelessness. As an author, such mistakes harm your *ethos*, so don't give audiences a chance to find these errors.

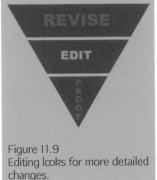

Figure 11.9
Editing looks for more detailed changes.

Text

When editing text—rather than revising or proofreading—your goal is to improve the quality and flow of the writing. You may rewrite sentences for clarity, cohesiveness, grammatical correctness, or change entire paragraphs to meet these goals. When editing, you should also check for consistency. Do you use the same formatting throughout? Do you write out all numbers, or use numerals? Are abbreviations consistent throughout? Does the document use a single style format, such as MLA or APA?

For the most part, editing and *proofreading* occur at the surface level of writing. But while simple proofreading only checks if a word is spelled correctly, editing requires that you make decisions about the appropriateness and placement of words. When editing, you're making decisions about what to leave in and what to leave out. Does one word best fit the argument you're trying to make, or would another work better? Would a word receive more emphasis if it was placed at the end of the sentence rather than the beginning? These are important questions to tackle before moving on to proofreading. In general, editing requires that you consider:

- the placement of individual words
- deleting unnecessary words
- revising awkward or grammatically incorrect phrasing
- moving sentences or paragraphs
- editing transitional words between sentences
- punctuation choices
- formatting choices, such as paragraph form versus a bulleted list
- adjusting the tone to make sure it's consistent
- checking that any references or citations are correct

Image

When editing an image or composition that uses visuals, you should consider many of the elements you would for a written text. If you're creating an information graphic about the price of gasoline, you should check that you use only one term—gasoline or gas—within the visual, otherwise you may confuse your readers. If you're using various colors in this information graphic to represent different suppliers of gasoline, editing ensures that those colors are consistent.

You might also consider technical aspects of editing within a *photo editor*. For example, you could find it beneficial for an audience if you were to adjust the contrast, brightness, hues, or sharpness of an image so that it's easier to read and understand. You might blur out individuals' faces to protect their identity (Figure 11.10). You might remove dust or other blemishes from an image so that it's clearer.

Figure 11.10
The blur tool can be used to protect a subject's identity.

However, if you're using a photograph for journalistic purposes, there is only so much photo editing that you should perform while still maintaining factual, journalistic integrity. For example, check out the recommended photo editor adjustments suggested by the news agency, Reuters (see QR code).

When shooting photographs for Reuters, the organization only permits a certain amount of post-production done to the photos so that the original content is not substantially changed. However, if you intend to use your photograph for rhetorical purposes, to persuade rather than to present facts, then you should feel more free to manipulate images to express your argument (without, of course, outright lying to your readers through an image; they should understand and recognize your attempt at purposeful editing).

You should also edit across text and image. Make sure that figure numbers for each image correspond to what you've indicated in the body of the text. Check that any textual descriptions in the text match the image to which it refers, and make sure the captions reflect the context for why you included the image.

Finally, save the image in the correct format. If you're using the image for the Web, you can save it as a JPG, PNG, or GIF at 72 dots per inch (dpi) and in RGB color. If you're using the image for print, then save it as an EPS, TIFF, or even PDF at 300 dpi or higher and in CMYK color. Although file formats might not seem like image editing, selecting the right format is an important part of ensuring your image will appear the way you intend it to.

Video

After revising and before proofreading, the step of editing video becomes one of the most important parts of the post-production process. While revising leads to a rough cut and concerns the larger story or argument you're trying to make, and while proofing removes the smaller blemishes, editing removes the traces that it was ever edited at all. This may sound paradoxical, but good editing appears seamless. In other words, the best editors make their work disappear so that the audience focuses on the story rather than transitions.

When editing, you should focus on the transitions between shots and scenes. These transitions—such as cuts, wipes, or dissolves—should appear at points where the audience should expect some sort of change (Figure 11.11). Use the following guidelines when editing your own video at the level of transitions:

- **Motivate your transitions:** When you make a cut, you should have some reason for doing so and that reason should be apparent to the audience. If one character reaches out his hand to offer money to someone, you might then transition to a shot of the outstretched hand holding the money. However, the cut should only happen after the character has outstretched his hand so that the audience sees this important movement. Other actions that can motivate a cut include a glance made by an onscreen character, a noise that causes a character to react, a prop that is introduced into the scene, or a character that walks into the camera frame. All of these events can provide reasonable motivation to transition into shots that focus on these events.

Figure 11.11
Brandon Pinard, from *Videomaker* magazine, discusses some common transitions.
http://www.youtube.com/watch?v=iCEdSGeFCCA

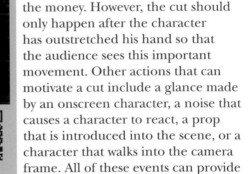

- **Cut during action:** Since you want to make edits as seamless as possible, onscreen action can capture the audience's attention so that they focus less on the cuts from scene to scene. If the camera focuses on a car moving down the street, you should cut in the middle of that movement; the audience doesn't need to see the car traveling the whole distance. The scene may then cut to the interior of the car, or perhaps someone on the street watching the car. The audience should then become engaged in the movement from one action to another rather than the actual transitions.

- **Cut between rooms:** You can transition between shots as characters move from one room to another, or from inside to outside and vice versa. Cut the shot based on the main character's eyes. End the preceding shot as the character's eyes move through the doorway, but start the next shot just before that character's eyes enter the new room or exterior. This extra time gives the audience a moment to adjust to the transition and pick up the character's eyes again before too much has occurred in the new shot.

- **Use close-ups:** Although the advent of HDTV has increased detail for all shots, video does best as a medium when it uses close-ups of characters, objects, or other points of interest. Use establishing shots to give the audience a sense of location or context, but transition to close-ups to show better detail. If close-ups don't seem right for the particular project, consider using medium-shots instead. Close-ups are very dramatic, and may not be appropriate for lighter situations.

- **Transition after your visual statement:** Since each shot should be motivated, it shows some statement that you intend to make. Once that goal has been accomplished, any remaining action in the shot serves little purpose and you can then cut away. Transition quickly after you reach the goal for each shot and move on to the next one. Quick transitions after your statement will keep the scene moving and keep your audience interested and engaged.

- **Old and New:** When writing a traditional essay, textbooks often teach to move from old information to new information. In other words, you should orient your reader at the beginning of a sentence with information they already know before moving on to new information. This practice helps the audience to not get lost in unfamiliar information.

A similar technique can be used when editing video. For objects, places, or characters that may already be familiar, you only need to dedicate a few seconds before transitioning to another shot. For instance, an audience has probably already seen the Eiffel Tower, so you don't need a ten-second shot before moving on; a few seconds will do. However, if you're presenting something the audience hasn't seen before, such as an alien spaceship, they might require more time to study and take it in (Figure 11.12). If the information isn't necessarily important, or if the shot only presents familiar, everyday objects, you don't need to spend a lot of screen time showing them (also, see the section on montage in Chapter 4).

Credit: ©Paramount/Courtesy Everett Collection

Figure 11.12
In the movie *Star Trek*, the audience sees a long fly-by glimpse of the new U.S.S. Enterprise at the same time the main characters do.
http://www.youtube.com/watch?v=O9Rj-r25OTk

- **_Base tempo on context:_** The timing of your transitions should match the tone or mood of your scene. A quiet picnic by a lake should probably have longer shots than a fast-paced action scene, which will probably make use of short, quick cuts to heighten its intensity and suspense. However, you should vary the tempo throughout the piece as a whole, as the fast-paced action sequence will wear the audience out, and a constant slow-pace will bore them.

- **_Include B-roll:_** When watching an interview between two people, you might notice that the scene includes shots besides the interviewer and interviewee. This footage is known as B-roll, and may include images relevant to the topic being discussed. Adding B-roll can make the scene more interesting or provide valuable information that enhances the verbal conversation.

  For instance, if you were watching a video tutorial on how to repair a car engine, rather than just focusing on the head and face of the mechanic explaining the repair, you might also include shots of necessary tools, parts, or other equipment. If the video depicts a fictional story, B-roll might include other shots besides the main characters that can help tell the story or make the scene more engaging to viewers. When editing your video, think about where such shots can be added.

- **_Cut it out:_** Although most of the guidelines above instruct you to add materials into your video project, you should also be equally willing to remove shots from the final cut. If you think any added footage or B-roll detracts from the message you're trying to communicate, use your instinct and remove it. Just because you can add an image, shot, or special effect doesn't mean you should. Try to make sure that any shots you include add something to the final piece, either logically or emotionally. Otherwise, cut them out.

These guidelines only apply to continuity editing, when you are attempting to tell a linear story and make the audience forget about the medium that they are viewing. Sometimes, you may want the audience to be aware that they're watching a video, so you may use more jarring cuts to get their attention or make a statement about video itself. When editing video and selecting appropriate transitions, you're making rhetorical choices that affect how an audience receives your argument. Even though all of your footage has been shot, some of the most important parts of the video writing process occur when the camera is turned off.

MAKING CONNECTIONS

AS A CLASS

Choose a film or video clip and analyze the kinds of cuts the editor used to transition from scene to scene. Do these transitions occur between physical spaces? With movement? With dialogue? Or does the editor or director use some other technique to move from shot to shot, scene to scene? Do you find these cuts effective, distracting, or both? Would altering the kinds of transitions used significantly change the experience of watching the video? Why or why not?

IN A GROUP

Choose a short video clip from YouTube or another video source. Using a *video editor*, change the transitions in the clip to any kind other than what is currently used. Show both the original version and new version to your peers and discuss how the same footage with new transitions changes (or doesn't).

ON YOUR OWN

Locate a famous example of a journalistic photograph that was manipulated prior to its printing. For instance, Figure 11.13 shows a photo from the 1970 Kent State University shootings in which a sign post was removed. Write a report that examines the context of the photo's manipulation, including why and how it was manipulated, the reaction by the public when the manipulation was discovered, and how the journalistic community reacted to the ethics of the manipulation. Share the example and your findings with the class.

© 1970 Valley News-Dispatch and John Filo

Figure 11.13
This famous photograph from the 1970 Kent State shootings was altered by removing the post above the woman's head.

Proofreading

While the steps of editing and revising usually are applied to the larger work as a whole, proofreading looks for the smaller mistakes (Figure 11.14). With traditional, alphabetic writing, such mistakes usually occur at the level of spelling, punctuation, misuse of words, alignment, format, or other errors of consistency.

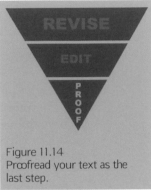

Figure 11.14
Proofread your text as the last step.

Text

You've most likely proofread a text document, either your own or a peer's. Some general strategies can help ensure you proofread more efficiently and accurately. These tips apply equally to a traditional term paper or the captions you might write for an image.

- *Forget your writing.* The best way to catch errors in your own writing is to forget what you wrote, making it less familiar. Often, when you read your own work, you know it so well that you gloss over the sentences because you've already read them so many times. When you've finished drafting a piece, put it away for as long as you can; a week or more would be ideal, but even a day or a few hours will help. The more you can forget what you wrote, the better.

- *Find a proofreader.* Because of your familiarity with your own work, you can easily miss errors when proofreading your own document. As an alternative, try finding a proofreader unfamiliar with your work who can help identify errors or other issues with your writing.

- *Proofread backwards.* Another method to defamiliarize your writing is to read backwards. This helps break the flow of normal reading, forcing you to slow down and pay attention to details. You can read backwards at three different levels: 1) word by word, which helps you pay attention to spelling errors; 2) sentence by sentence, which helps you identify problems with sentence structure; and 3) paragraph by paragraph, which helps you ensure that each paragraph coheres as a whole and that you use correct punctuation.

- *Read aloud.* You can also try reading your work aloud. This technique not only slows down your reading so that you don't skip over errors, but it also helps you catch mistakes by hearing them, making yourself more conscious of sentence structure and wordiness.

Image

Before printing a final diagram, illustration, photograph, or other visual design, you should proof the final draft to ensure it will look as you intend. When you proof a visual, you are checking to see how it will appear on the final medium you have chosen, whether it's a book, poster, flyer, television, or computer screen. If you were designing a brochure, you should have a proof printed to ensure that colors, fonts, arrangement, alignment, and other elements appear correctly. If they don't, you can go back and correct these errors before ordering a large quantity from a printing vendor. The following checklist offers some suggestions of elements to look for, and can apply to print documents as well.

- Does the image need to be touched up for errors or blemishes, such as red eye, skin tones, or color correction? For example, Figure 11.15 shows a photograph of a politician on a political mailer. In the left image, you can see that the camera lighting is reflected in the candidate's eyes. The right image has been edited to remove most of the lights.

- Does the image need to be cropped in order to remove unwanted elements or to focus in on a particular feature?

Figure 11.15
This photo was edited to remove the camera lights from the subject's eyes (photo on the right).

- Does the image appear in the correct place within a larger document? If a figure, does it appear near the text that refers to it?

- Does the image need a caption? If so, is the caption's text free of errors?

- If a text is made up of many images, are all the images present? Are these images labeled correctly and appear in the right order?

- For more complex visual documents such as brochures, manuals, or visual essays, are all the sections or pages present? Do they appear in the proper order? Do they have (or require) page numbers?

- Are all the elements of the design aligned correctly? Are the margins consistent on each page or section?

- Are all the fonts of the document correct and consistent, including both typefaces and font sizes?

While this list isn't exhaustive of all the aspects you might proof, it will help you check the major details of the image and any document in which the image occurs. As always, ask a peer to review these details for anything you might overlook. In addition, consider printing out your documents and proofing them in hard copy. When a reader views text on a screen, he or she tends to skip over words more often and therefore miss more errors. Reading a draft on paper will help you, or your reviewer, catch more mistakes.

If the final version isn't digital, the last production step is printing, which usually requires a significant financial investment. You should proof the final version two or three times, with as many eyes as possible, to notice any mistakes before the printing press starts.

Video

Once the main sequence of the video is assembled and you've cleaned up the rough cut, you can then carefully analyze and proof the footage to notice any details that might have been missed.

Sometimes, errors occur on the part of the editor. As you know from *The Empire Strikes Back*, Darth Vader cuts off Luke's right hand during their lightsaber battle. Luke later gains a mechanical hand, covered by a black glove (Figure 11.16).

Credit: Lucasfilm

Credit: Lucasfilm

Figure 11.16
Most of you know that Luke Skywalker lost his right hand in a lightsaber duel with Darth Vader.

Figure 11.17
This shot of Luke reverses the image and disrupts continuity, making it appear that Luke's glove has disappeared.

However, during the speeder scene on Endor in the sequel *Return of the Jedi*, Luke's glove switches from his right hand, to his left hand, and then back to his right hand (Figure 11.17). This error is most likely due to a shot that was horizontally reversed by the editor to make it look like the camera angle was changed.

Sometimes *continuity errors* can be the fault of the actors or the crew. In the film *Prometheus*, the character Shaw isn't wearing gloves in a scene on the planet's surface. The scene cuts away to another shot, but when it returns to Shaw, she is suddenly wearing gloves. In other cases, the error occurs because of factually incorrect information in a script. Again, in *Prometheus*, the ship travels 35 light years to reach the alien planet (205.8 trillion miles). However, in one scene, Charlize Theron's character states that they are half a billion miles from Earth. Since the distance from Earth to Saturn is a little more than 755 million miles (more than half a billion), the ship wouldn't have made it out of the solar system, much less to an alien planet, according to her estimate (Figure 11.18).

When proofing your own video, check for the following errors. While some errors might be difficult to change—such as errors in the original footage—you can usually use transitions to cut away from any major problems or expand the size of the screen outside of the viewable margins so that errors on the periphery disappear.

Figure 11.18
Astrophysicist Neil deGrasse Tyson called out *Prometheus's* factual error on Twitter.

- **Continuity error:** These errors occur when some aspect of the scene— such as the character's clothing, props, or position are inconsistent from one shot to the next. The glove examples above are errors of continuity. If you were filming an instructional video about how to change a light bulb but took several days to film this action, you might make sure the talent wears the same shirt each day to make it look like the action all occurred in a single day, therefore maintaining continuity. Sometimes you can change these errors in post-production either through digital effects or by simply cropping undesirable elements from the shot.

- **Factual error:** These errors occur when some image, prop, line of dialogue, or scene presents information that is factually incorrect or historically inaccurate. For example, a *factual error* would occur if characters in a Revolutionary War movie were wearing boots worn during the Civil War.

- **Plot hole:** This error occurs when some part of the film doesn't make sense given what the audience already knows to be true, thus creating a logical error in the plot. Sometimes plot holes are caused by editing that is out of order and a simple re-ordering of scenes is necessary. Other times, however, plot holes result from a poorly written script and should have been caught before shooting commenced. Of course, if you're not creating a fictional-based video, you can look for gaps in a logical argument rather than plot.

- **Revealing:** this type of error appears when some part of the wardrobe, props, or set is meant to be hidden but is accidentally revealed to the audience, usually at the edge of the shot. In the movie *Snow White and the Huntsman*, Snow White rides a horse bareback through the forest, without the aid of saddle or reigns. However, in a few of the shots where the horse is trapped in the mud, the audience can see a thin set of reigns used by the actor to help control the horse (Figure 11.19).

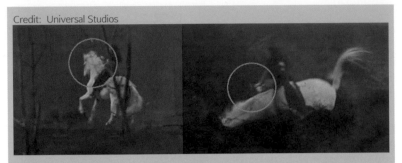

Credit: Universal Studios

Figure 11.19
While most shots show Snow White riding a horse without reigns, this shot accidently reveals them.

- *Visible crew/equipment*: Sometimes, a piece of equipment, such as an overhead microphone, drops into the picture frame. This can destroy the suspension of disbelief and call attention to itself as a movie. Sometimes, such mistakes can be cropped out of the frame. These errors also occur if something reflective in the scene reveals the camera and crew or if crew members happen to be on the set (Figure 11.20).

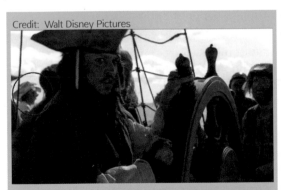

Credit: Walt Disney Pictures

Figure 11.20
A crew member accidently appears in this shot from *Pirates of the Caribbean: Curse of the Black Pearl.*

Like proofreading a written document, you can also proof video by watching each shot or scene in reverse sequence. This will prevent you from getting distracted by the unfolding story and help you focus on catching mistakes just as reading your own work backwards helps to make it less familiar.

Another technique used for proofreading written text is to look for only one kind of error at a time. In this technique, you would make one pass looking for punctuation mistakes, and another pass looking for spelling mistakes. Similarly, when proofing an image, you might look for only one kind of error, such as visible equipment, before moving on to continuity errors.

MAKING CONNECTIONS

AS A CLASS

Visit the site www.moviemistakes.com. Without looking at the mistakes found by the website, view one of the movies with many mistakes and keep notes of all the mistakes you notice. After you've viewed the movie, compare the mistakes found by the class with those listed on the site. Did you find them all? Did you find others? Did the mistakes detract from watching the film, or were they minor errors that didn't make much difference?

IN A GROUP

Look back at Figure 11.13, which shows the woman present at the Kent State shootings. Assume that were given the task of removing the fence post above her head. Research how you might remove the fence post in a photo editor. What options do you have? Which technique do you think is best? If you have access to a photo editor, locate the image online and try removing the post using all of the options. Show the class your final, edited image and discuss which technique worked best.

ON YOUR OWN

Find a digital image of yourself or a friend. Through an online search engine, research how to remove blemishes or red eye from a photograph. With a photo editor, edit your image using these techniques. Then create your own set of instructions informing someone else how to perform these edits. Allow a peer to user-test these instructions on their own image.

KEY TERMS

continuity error	*photo editor*
editing	*plot hole*
factual error	*revealing error*
revising	*video editor*
proofreading	*visible crew/equipment error*

OUTPUT: VIDEO ESSAY

For this output, create a video essay that makes a claim and supports it with reasons and evidence. Remember (as discussed in Chapter 8) that an argument can be explicit or implicit, and much of your supporting evidence may offer examples that make your point implicitly based on metaphor or analogy, appealing to *pathos* rather than *logos*. Of course, you can construct an explicit argument through video as well (Figure 11.21).

Although your instructor will provide you with more specific guidelines for your video essay, the overall project should:

- last 3-5 minutes in length
- provide a thesis or claim with reasons and evidence
- include a short research report
- include a script
- include a rough cut prior to revising, editing, and proofing

Figure 11.21
This essay about the pencil was produced by students trying to make an explicit argument (through the persona of Nicholas Cage).
http://www.youtube.com/watch?v=3BEc5CDju_k

- include a 1-page memo detailing what changes were made during the revision process

As you've already learned from the previous chapters, much alphabetic writing will go into this project before the video is even shot. Rather than just cobbling a video together, take serious care during the prewriting phase of this project to make sure that it comes together in a clear, coherent, and professional manner. While the quality of the video and audio will depend on the available resources you have in your class or on campus, the quality of the video's content depends on the amount of time and effort you put into its research and preparation. As a general process, consider using the following steps when completing your video essay.

Choose a topic: A video essay, like a written essay or photo essay, first requires that you choose your topic, that you determine what you'd like to produce your video about. As with other kinds of writing, find a topic that interests you, one that calls you to write. You might compose a short argument based on an environmental problem in your community, or an evaluative argument discussing why you feel one energy source is better than another. However, you might choose a topic on which you can easily find sources of video online or shoot your own video footage with your own camera.

Research your topic: As with any writing assignment, much of the work comes before you start writing. If you're focusing on a local environmental issue, research not only the perspectives of the local players involved in the conversations, but also the context and history of the environmental problem. If the issue concerns drilling for oil offshore, you should research the history of oil drilling, its problems and benefits, so you have a better understanding of the issue as a whole.

You should also plan, as you think about your script, what kinds of footage you're capable of shooting and what video already exists for you to incorporate. As with the photo essay, unless your class has a large travel budget, you probably won't be able to take your own video of oil rigs off the coast of Texas. In addition, make sure you are safe when taking your own video, and ask for permission when shooting on private property or other locations that require it.

Plan and draft: Before picking up the camera, plan your initial components and the structure of your argument. This plan can include writing an essay first—making sure you have a claim, reasons, and evidence—or it can offer a more basic outline of the argument and the major scenes and visuals you hope to include. Once you clarify the main points for yourself, you can start to think more visually, developing a script that will depict the scenes you hope to show as well as any audio you might use, including any voice-over narration. As discussed in Chapter 9, this step can be the most important and may determine if your project fails or succeeds.

Create a storyboard: Once you've completed a script, create a storyboard that depicts each shot. The storyboard will be invaluable as both a conceptual tool—helping you to see your video before you actually assemble and edit it— as well as an organizational tool, providing a framework for visually arranging your script and making sure you account for all the shots you might need.

Create a shot list and gather footage: Once you have a script, you can create a shot list. This list will provide an important resource to ensure that you gather all of the video footage you'll need. You might also develop a coding system for this shot list, noting which footage you plan to shoot yourself and which footage you plan to use from other archival sources. Dividing your list this way can help you manage your time since the footage that you shoot yourself will probably take longer to gather than archival footage. When producing video, try to gather this footage as early as possible, as editing will be more time-consuming than you may realize and is often the longest part of the process.

Add narration: Although your project may not require it, you may want to add voice over narration to your video to comment on the footage or to maintain the argumentative arc. If you've adequately planned for your film, you have already written this narration in your script. Like your shooting list, create a list of sounds you plan to use, including narration, and create these audio files before starting the revision process.

Create a rough cut: After you have gathered your footage and recorded any narration you'll need, use your storyboards as a guide to assemble your clips into a single rough cut of your video essay. Try to complete as much of the video as possible so you will have a better idea of how you might revise the piece.

Revise, edit, proof: Once you have a rough cut, you can begin revising. As discussed in this chapter, start with the large-scale changes first. Notice where the gaps in argument occur, which shots and scenes look bad, and which look bad when sequenced together. Once you've accomplished the revision, you can begin to edit transitions and other elements before performing a final proof. Remember, ask peers to review your work as well, since they can offer input on problems you might not notice.

Save and distribute: As you work, save your video file often. Once you've finished, consider what file format you'll need to distribute it in. You might plan to burn the file onto a DVD. If so, you can consider large-format files such as high definition (HD) formats. If you're distributing the video online, you might consider MPEG, AVI, MOV, or other formats that use less memory. However, sites such as YouTube can accept a wide away of video file formats including HD formats. Whatever distribution method you plan, research what file formats are acceptable and research the specifics of those file formats. While your video might look good in the video editor, it can look lousy if you save it in the wrong format.

12
DELIVERY

The ancient Greek orator Demosthenes (Figure 12.1) once claimed that *delivery* was the most important aspect of rhetoric. You might laboriously struggle though researching a project, crafting a script, drawing storyboards, shooting film, creating images, revising, editing, proofreading, and all other steps in the process; however, if you don't effectively deliver your final project, then you won't reach your intended audience, and your message will go unheard.

You might stay up all night writing that final paper, but if your alarm fails you in the morning, or your e-mail attachment doesn't go through, your instructor will never receive your work, and you won't receive credit.

Credit: Sting

Figure 12.1
Demosthenes was considered by many ancient rhetoricians as the greatest of orators.

Without effective delivery, your audience may be unaware that you have attempted to get their attention at all. However, delivery not only affects the physical reception of communication but also whether an audience accepts the premise of your message. How you say something can be as important as what you say, and this chapter explains different considerations for how to deliver your new media texts, whether those considerations are as simple as where to post a flyer in the community, different websites to upload videos for particular audiences, or even something as complex as search engine optimization for blogs so that audiences can more easily find them

For Demosthenes and classical Greeks, delivery had several components, most of which involved the orator's physical presence in front of the Greek assembly. The most important aspect was probably vocal projection and verbal articulation. Orators had to be able to send out their voice and fill the space but also know how to alternate between loud and soft volumes to draw in their audience.

Two famous anecdotes tell how Demosthenes would practice his speeches at the seashore, shouting above the volume of the surf (Figure 12.2); he would also put pebbles in his mouth, trying to articulate his words despite the stony impediments.

These stories show that delivery happens well before one is actually ready to deliver a work. Although you don't need to practice speaking with pebbles in your mouth in order to deliver a video online, you might think of what a digital situation requires. For instance, your message might be better received if you already have a positive *ethos* as an author. Or, if you were disseminating new media projects through your website, then your website should look the part as well, showing your audience what kind of aesthetic design or quality to expect.

Credit: Jean-Jules-Antoine Lecomte du Nouÿ

Figure 12.2
The Ancient Greek orator, Demosthenes, used to deliver to the roaring ocean.

Credit: Gilbert Austin

Figure 12.3
These are a few gestures that used to be taught to students of delivery.

Credit: John Robert Charlton

Figure 12.4
Lady Gaga makes careful use of clothing in all her public appearances.

Besides the voice, classical delivery also included attention to the rest of the body. Orators would have to be aware of their posture, their facial expressions, when and how they walked, and their arm and hand gestures (Figure 12.3). Roman teachers of rhetoric also emphasized that students should pay attention to clothing, jewelry, and grooming as well and when it was acceptable to remove one's outer garments (Figure 12.4).

You might associate many of these guidelines with acting in a scene, either in a play or on a movie set. An actor must not only remember her lines and how to stress each word but also her physical acting beyond the voice. An actor can say much without saying a word, and so she must be fully aware how she moves her body at all times. In these ways, an orator and an actor do not differ much in the techniques they use to either persuade or entertain. In fact, the Greek word for delivery, *hypokrisis*, became synonymous with acting. The Latin word for delivery, *actio*, speaks for itself.

Like "editing," the term "delivery" doesn't appear on the rhetorical tetrahedron. However, perhaps more than other rhetorical elements, delivery affects—and is affected by—each of the terms along the rhetorical tetrahedron. You must understand your audience to deliver well, and you must deliver well to help your audience understand your message. Your own *ethos* as a writer can affect your delivery as well as the genre and medium you choose. Your design can also make the audience more —or less—receptive to your message, also affecting delivery. If you've ever watched a good or bad standup comedy routine, you know timing (*kairos*) significantly affects delivery. Make sure you keep the rhetorical tetrahedron in mind when thinking about how to deliver your text, for all the elements affect each other.

DELIVERY ON PAPER, THROUGH PRINT

While delivery, either through acting on camera or on stage, has clear connections with visual media, you should first consider delivery's role in print. When communication occurs face-to-face, in your audience's presence, then the body is important for communicating.

However, once you write down your message on some medium and send it across the city, state, country, world, or solar system, your body stays with you, not with your message, and the two become separated. In print culture, a piece of paper serves as your "body," which is still divided according to a human physiology with the "header" at the top of the page, the "footer" at the bottom of the page, and the "body" in the middle. Of course, a piece of paper can't make facial expressions, pace across the stage, or gesture to a crowd. For the most part, it remains passive and does not "act." However, print documents, especially legal documents such as laws, determine how one should act (Figure 12.5).

Figure 12.5
The act of signing can often determine how others will act.

How then, might a static piece of paper "act"? Your favorite book obviously moves you in some way, creating an emotional response and connection. This appeal to emotion is one of the principle functions of delivery. Aristotle bemoaned the ability of orators to use delivery in place of logic when persuading an audience. Aristotle felt that the best argument was the most reasoned, logical one, not the one best delivered.

However, as you read in Chapter 1, humans don't only think with the logical parts of their left brain hemisphere and must address the whole brain when making an appeal, especially with visual media. Such visual media include physical bodies (just watch any physical comedian), but also the media you use when you can't be present, including paper.

Credit: Nathan Beach

Figure 12.6
High-quality paper can increase your writing's delivery.

For instance, if you submitted your résumé to your employer printed on clean, high-quality resume paper and another printed on thin, standard copy paper, which do you think would most impress the employer? All other factors being equal (i.e., the same resume, the same type of job), the resume printed on high-quality paper will probably look (and feel) more professional and persuade this potential employer that you care about getting this job and that you will hopefully bring this same attention to detail to the workplace (Figure 12.6).

Figure 12.7
Marshall McLuhan famously wrote "the medium is the message."

Your choice of medium—even if simply choosing one kind of paper over another—affects how the audience responds to the message and becomes an important factor in delivering that message. As Marshall McLuhan (Figure 12.7) wrote, "the medium is the message" and reaches the audience at a level beyond the actual content (7). What kind of message do you want to send with your medium?

Typography, layout, use of color, and other textual features can also change how the audience receives a message. While you might think of these features as elements of style, you can also think of them as choices of delivery. Just as an orator has a variety of hand gestures, writers have a variety of fonts, and changing a font can affect how an audience interprets one's writing.

For example, look at the text in Figure 12.8. This text is the same as in the previous paragraph, except that it appears in the typeface **Comic Sans MS**. While the rest of this book is written in Times New Roman, a very standard typeface used for professional applications, **Comic Sans MS** doesn't exude the same mood or expectations, and so you would not expect to read a business report that used this typeface.

Typography, layout, use of color, and other textual features can also change how the audience receives a message. While you might think of these features as elements of style, you can also think of them as choices of delivery. Just as an orator has a variety of hand gestures, writers have a variety of fonts, and changing a font can affect how an audience interprets one's writing.

Figure 12.8
Comic Sans can make any text more "comical."

In 2010, LeBron James (Figure 12.9), a professional basketball player for the Cleveland Cavaliers, announced that he was signing with the Miami Heat. The Cavaliers' majority owner, Dan Gilbert, wrote a letter to Cavalier fans about the decision and placed it on his team's website. Rather than use the standard font of the website, he chose to post the letter in the typeface Comic Sans MS, a typeface generally considered to have only limited applications and not intended for widespread use (Figure 12.10). A major reaction to Gilbert's

Credit: Keith Allison

Figure 12.9
Lebron James as a member of the
Cleveland Cavaliers.

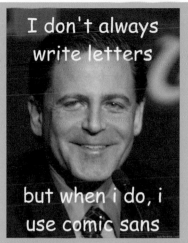

I don't always
write letters

but when i do, i
use comic sans

Figure 12.10
Perhaps Comic Sans isn't the best
typeface choice for a CEO?

letter came not necessarily from the content of his message (although, certainly, some critics focused on this), but how he delivered his message. Consider Robert Quigley's take on Gilbert's font "decision":

Cavaliers Owner Dan Gilbert Addresses Cleveland in Comic Sans: Why We Facepalm

In case you haven't heard, the only news in the world today is that LeBron James decided that he is going to play basketball for the Miami Heat instead of the New York Knicks or the Cleveland Cavaliers. This has made some people in Cleveland very sad, including the team's owner, Dan Gilbert

Dan Gilbert was so upset, in fact, that he wrote a very angry open letter to Cleveland fans, laden with surprising capitalizations and lines like "The self-declared former "King" will be taking the "curse" with him down south. And until he does "right" by Cleveland and Ohio, James (and the town where he plays) will unfortunately own this dreaded spell and bad karma," and "'I PERSONALLY GUARANTEE THAT THE CLEVELAND CAVALIERS WILL WIN AN NBA CHAMPIONSHIP BEFORE THE SELF-TITLED FORMER 'KING' WINS ONE' You can take it to the bank."

We will leave it to our sporting brethren at *SportsGrid* to parse the meaning and sporty implications of all of this to the world of people who care about sports. For our part, the most important thing to note about Dan Gilbert's letter is that it was written in Comic Sans. Comic Sans.

As you may be aware, Comic Sans is a Vincent Connare-designed font with promising enough origins—Connare was partly inspired by John Costanza's lettering for *The Dark Knight Returns* and Dave Gibbons' lettering for *Watchmen*—but it has since blossomed into a long history of infamy, thanks in large measure to its inclusion in Windows 95. While Connare says the font was never intended for widespread use, the lighthearted, readable font has since been inappropriately used the world over, for things like, say, composing office memos, or announcing one's feelings to millions about the star basketball player on their franchise departing in a cold attempt to woo the Chinese market.

Comic Sans is widely hated by designers primarily for the inappropriate uses to which people turn it, Gilbert's letter being a prime example. But there are deeper, more design-specific reasons: Gibbons, *The Watchmen* letterer whose work partly inspired the font, blasted it in an interview with The Guardian:

"It's just a shame they couldn't have used just the original font, because it's a real mess. I think it's a particularly ugly letter form," he says. "The other thing that really bugs me is that they've used an upper case 'I' with bars on it: it looks completely wrong to the comic eye. And when you see store fronts done in it, it's horrible."

Another major Comic Sans complaint concerns the font's kerning, or spacing between letters: By default, there's some odd and uneven spacing which breaks the flow of reading. There's even a designer-led movement to ban Comic Sans. From afar, all of the Comic Sans hate might sound a little heavy in response to a font which was originally "only intended for Microsoft's cartoon dog, Rover." But when a billionaire sports team owner makes a heavy, angry, somewhat crazy announcement to be read by millions in a zany, unbalanced font, it all sort of makes sense.

Figure 12.11
Although "toy" and Comic Sans might go together, Comic Sans and the subject of weapons probably don't.

According to Quigley, you can assume that any use of Comic Sans will instantly destroy your *ethos* as a designer and thus your delivery. You might find a use for the typeface from time to time, but you would need to use it with extreme caution. Just as certain gestures or facial expressions might be used at appropriate moments to deliver a speech, fonts and other typographical elements can provide tools for expressing aesthetic and emotional content, such as Gilbert's attempt to "shout" by writing some of his sentences in ALL CAPS. Each typeface has specific uses—whether for body text, headers, footnotes, indexes, title pages, advertisements, Web pages, or other situations and contexts. As Figure 12.11 demonstrates, individual typefaces each have their own message to deliver, and choosing the wrong typeface can be counterproductive to your rhetorical goals.

Color, of course, also becomes an important tool when trying to deliver a message through print. As discussed in Chapters 9 and 10, an audience often associates certain colors with particular meanings and emotions. For instance, white and black are often used to signify themes of good and evil (Figure 12.12). The colors green and brown depict earthy, naturalistic feelings, while blue can be melancholic.

Although print doesn't typically use colors in these ways, it can still use colors rhetorically to help organize material for the reader, highlight important information, or emphasize a particular word, paragraph, or other graphical element. Just as an orator can change his

Figure 12.12
Sony Playstation uses color to create a sense of good vs. evil. Do you see any problems with the use of color in this ad? Many consider the ad racist.

or her tone, volume, or pitch when pronouncing a word, a writer—especially one using a computer's word processor—can think of the available graphical options as choices of delivery, choices for how one can augment the body of the page so that it best captures and holds the reader's attention.

In some ways, Dan Gilbert's choice to use Comic Sans was rhetorically brilliant since it delivered his message to a much wider audience. Even if Gilbert wasn't taken seriously, his letter achieved a higher degree of circulation than it otherwise would, and with delivery, getting your audience's attention is half the battle.

These visual features in print can help you organize a document, which helps you deliver by creating a positive design that affects your readers emotionally. Your audience would still be able to read your writing if you don't include line breaks between paragraphs, margins, pages numbers, good choice of fonts, helpful use of color, boldface, italics, bulleted lists, and other textual choices.

However, will they *want* to read such a document? In an oral context, if a particular speaker or actor is bad, the audience may stand up and leave. Likewise, even if an audience starts a text, they won't necessarily want to finish it if reading becomes too difficult. Even though the text's content might be stellar, what you deliver in the text may be undercut by how you deliver it.

MAKING CONNECTIONS

AS A CLASS

Discuss how you consume media. Do you prefer to read documents, watch video versions of those documents, listen to audio versions, or consume information in other ways? Does the type of information determine if you prefer to read, view, or listen? Is this preference based on enjoyment, efficiency, or some other quality? How does this choice of medium affect its delivery and how you respond?

IN A GROUP

Find several official memos or other documents from the White House, your college or university, or other institution. Create different versions of the documents by altering their typography. Use a variety of fonts and colors to provide a range of changes. How do the new versions compare with the originals? Show the new documents to your class. Ask them how they respond to the documents. Do they take them less seriously, even though the documents are from serious, government, and professional institutions and the content remains the same? As an alternative, find a funny, humorous piece of writing and put it in a very serious typeface. Do you notice the opposite effect? Share your examples with the class.

ON YOUR OWN

In order for paper to "deliver," it has to travel from person to person. Research the history of letter transport, from human runners, the pony express, to modern day transit. Write a report on your findings, and share them with the class, discussing what you and your peers discovered.

DELIVERY THROUGH VISUALS

Despite the typographical and layout changes you can make with print, the technology is still fairly limited in terms of delivery. Even when print becomes highly circulated through the Internet, no longer limited to the "delivery" of postal mail, the actual document doesn't do much once you start reading it. Other media, especially electronic media, offer other possibilities for delivery not available with print. In general, learning to write with these media is the goal of this book so that you're not limited to expression through alphabetic text alone.

Although they're also static, still images can offer the emotional component of delivery in a way much different from print. You have already learned how visuals attempt to evoke emotional responses from an audience by tapping into evocative images, using connotation to create associations, creating visual metaphors to suggest connections, or developing puncepts to suggest new ways of thinking. Still images can also show poses, gestures, facial expressions, and other features of a human body that print can only abstractly mimic. An image can make the human body visible again, offering a seemingly more direct connection with the author even though they may be thousands of miles away (or even deceased).

An image can also deliver content much more quickly than print. Consider some of the billboards you examined in Chapter 5. This text has already discussed the placement of billboards and how the environment in which you place a visual text affects how the audience views it. However, a typical billboard also needs to deliver information quickly and efficiently. If these billboards presented their information in print alone, it would be much more difficult to read while driving down the road than a billboard with an image and some text for anchorage.

Credit: Mercy for Animals

Figure 12.13
This billboard argues that the audience should treat pigs and dogs equally.

For example, Figure 12.13 shows a billboard promoting vegetarianism. The billboard juxtaposes a piglet and a puppy, suggesting equality between the species. The text offers a rhetorical question: "Why choose one over the other?" with the main claim presented as "Choose Vegetarian." The image of the piglet and puppy provides a visual representation of the implicit argument of the animals' equality, and no other words are needed. The image also creates an emotional connection, portraying the two animals with "puppy dog eyes" that make a plea to the viewer.

However, an alternative, text-based billboard would need more commentary in addition to the existing text, such as: "You should consider a pig and a dog to have equal worth. Both are cute animals, too cute to slaughter." Obviously, an image makes more impact emotionally and also delivers that information much more quickly, allowing a passing motorist to absorb the image and text and make the connection the billboard is arguing for. As the cliché goes, an image is worth a thousand words; only a few words are provided above, and you could probably come up with many more to describe the picture and its message. But even if the billboard was filled with a thousand words, such text would be rhetorically ineffective compared with a well-designed image, and delivery would fail.

When using video, sound, or both, many more aspects of the body become prevalent again. This fact became apparent in 1960 when Richard Nixon and John F. Kennedy appeared in the first presidential debate broadcasted on television (Figure 12.14). As Erica Tyner Allen explains:

Figure 12.14
John F. Kennedy and Richard Nixon appeared in the first televised presidential debate.
http://www.youtube.com/watch?v=C6Xn4ipHiwE

The Kennedy-Nixon Presidential Debates, 1960

On 26 September 1960, 70 million U.S. viewers tuned in to watch Senator John Kennedy of Massachusetts and Vice President Richard Nixon in the first-ever televised presidential debate. It was the first of four televised "Great Debates" between Kennedy and Nixon. The first debate centered on domestic issues. The high point of the second debate, on 7 October, was disagreement over U.S. involvement in two small islands off the coast of China, and on 13 October, Nixon and Kennedy continued this dispute. On 21 October, the final debate, the candidates focused on American relations with Cuba.

The Great Debates marked television's grand entrance into presidential politics. They afforded the first real opportunity for voters to see their candidates in competition, and the visual contrast was dramatic. In August, Nixon had seriously injured his knee and spent two weeks in the hospital. By the time of the first debate he was still twenty pounds underweight, his pallor still poor. He arrived at the debate in an ill-fitting shirt, and refused make-up to improve his color and lighten his perpetual "5:00 o'clock shadow." Kennedy, by contrast, had spent early September campaigning in California. He was tan and confident and well-rested. "I had never seen him looking so fit," Nixon later wrote.

In substance, the candidates were much more evenly matched. Indeed, those who heard the first debate on the radio pronounced Nixon the winner. But the 70 million who watched television saw a candidate still sickly and obviously discomforted by Kennedy's smooth delivery and charisma. Those television viewers focused on what they saw, not what they heard. Studies of the audience indicated that, among television viewers, Kennedy was perceived the winner of the first debate by a very large margin.

The televised Great Debates had a significant impact on voters in 1960, on national elections since, and, indeed, on our concerns for democracy itself. The impact on the election of 1960 was significant, albeit subtle. Commentators broadly agree that the first debate accelerated Democratic support for Kennedy. In hindsight, however, it seems the debates were not, as once thought, the turning-point in the election. Rather than encouraging viewers to change their vote, the debates appear to have simply solidified prior allegiances. In short, many would argue that Kennedy would have won the election with or without the Great Debates.

Yet voters in 1960 did vote with the Great Debates in mind. At election time, more than half of all voters reported that the Great Debates had influenced their opinion; 6% reported that their vote was the result of the debates alone. Regardless of whether the debates changed the election result, voters pointed to the debates as a significant reason for electing Kennedy.

The Great Debates had a significant impact beyond the election of 1960, as well. They served as precedent around the world: Soon after the debates, Germany, Sweden, Finland, Italy, and Japan established debates between contenders to national office. Moreover, the Great Debates created a precedent in American presidential politics. Federal laws requiring that all candidates receive equal air-time stymied debates for the next three elections, as did Nixon's refusal to debate in 1968 and 1972. Yet by 1976, the law and the candidates had both changed, and ever since, presidential debates, in one form or another, have been a fixture of U.S. presidential politics.

Perhaps most important, the Great Debates forced citizens to rethink how democracy would work in a television era. To what extent does television change debate, indeed, change campaigning altogether? What is the difference between a debate that "just happens" to be broadcast and one specifically crafted for television? What is lost in the latter? Do televised debates really help us to evaluate the relative competencies of the candidates, to evaluate policy options, to increase voter participation and intellectual engagement, to strengthen national unity? Fundamentally, such events lead to worries that television emphasizes the visual, when visual attributes seem not the best, nor most reliable, indicators of a great leader. Yet other views express confidence that televised presidential debates remain one of the most effective means to operate a direct democracy. The issue then becomes one of improved form rather than changed forum.

The Nixon-Kennedy debates of 1960 brought these questions to the floor. Perhaps as no other single event, the Great Debates forced us to ponder the role of television in democratic life.

From Kennedy's tan and fitness level to Nixon's pale complexion and rehabilitating physique, the body suddenly becomes much more important to anyone on television.

As discussed in Chapter 9, alphabetic writing is still important in producing new media, but video and audio require physical and vocal skill to pull off whatever narration, dialogue, or scene descriptions are written. If you use live talent in your project—short of taking acting classes—you don't have much control over this aspect.

However, you can direct other facets of delivery. If you think of typographical and layout choices in print as decisions about delivery, similar choices can affect how audiences receive video. Many of the editing techniques for video mentioned in Chapters 4 and 11 can be thought of in terms of delivery. Although a match cut transition in a film isn't the same as a raised eyebrow by an orator giving a speech, the two offer aesthetic selections that affect how the audience interprets the content. To the extent that these choices draw in an audience, make them pay attention, and hopefully act in some desired way, stylistic choices are also delivery choices.

You could also make a similar argument about arrangement and delivery. Often, a document meant to be read live will include repetitive signposts that help the reader remember previous points, as well as cues to let the listeners know what the orator will speak about as a whole, what they are speaking about in the moment, and what they have just spoken about. Since a live audience member can't simply flip back to a previous page and re-read what was just said, these reminders help orient listeners and keep them on-track with the speaker.

The arrangement of these cues becomes not just a delivery aid for the speaker—helping him or her navigate a speech—but also the audience members, so they can remember what has been said, where they are now, and where the orator will lead them. If these cues are improperly arranged, the audience may lose track of the argument, resulting in an ineffective delivery.

For example, consider Figure 12.15, a transition to commercial (or between major segments if watching on DVD) in the series 24. In this transition, you should hear the beeping of a clock counting toward the end of the

Credit: Fox Studios

Figure 12.15
The television show 24 arranges multiple viewpoints to help create suspense and enhance delivery.
http://www.youtube.com/watch?v=7Frl4Bw2kec

24 hours, the length of time that a season of the series spans. During this transition, you also see several scenes simultaneously juxtaposed, arranged so that you can see real-time action happening at once. This transition is a reminder of the various plot lines but also creates suspense as you see all the characters struggling to achieve their disparate goals. If the show simply faded to black from one of these many plot lines, you would not be as immersed in the real-time device of the show, and you would not be as aware of the time-sensitive nature under which the characters act. The show would not be as suspenseful, or as engaging. This arrangement affects the delivery of the show's emotional content to viewers.

MAKING CONNECTIONS

AS A CLASS

Divide the class into two groups. One group will watch a recent debate through video; the other will close their eyes and only listen to the audio. After you've seen or heard the debate, discuss who you thought won. Are your opinions the same or different? In either case, why do you think you reached a particular result? If you heard the debate, what details did you notice? If you watched the debate, what persuaded you to choose one candidate over the other?

IN A GROUP

Think of the more memorable theme songs from television shows. Often, these songs create a connection between the viewer and the show, whetting their emotional appetite and preparing them for the rest of the program. Recall theme songs without lyrics, and—with a video editor—swap songs between show openings, many of which can be found online. How does changing the theme song alter how you respond to the introduction? How do you think these theme songs function in delivering the show to the audience? Where else might the theme song be used besides the beginning of the show? How does this increase the show's delivery to an audience?

ON YOUR OWN

Research a particular photographic or film technique, such as a wipe transition, montage, use of a fish-eye lens, etc. Why was this technique invented? What is its primary purpose? How can this technique be thought of as rhetorical, and how can it help delivery? Write a report of your findings and share them with the class.

DISTRIBUTION

You can also think of delivery in terms of *distribution*. Once a movie is finished, the film distributor must consider the best outlets for disseminating the film. The kind of distribution you're probably most familiar with is a theatrical release. This kind of distribution usually receives the most media attention and promotion.

However, if a film isn't likely to do well in the theatre, the distributor might consider delivering the film through video, simply called "straight-to-video" release (or now, straight-to-DVD). In some cases, the distributor may use both options at once, called a simultaneous release. The film may be distributed through television, either through network or cable channels, or video-on-demand. Some filmmakers don't have the backing of a large-scale distributor and may deliver their films online.

Since you probably don't have a large-scale distributor, you will have to distribute your work in other ways. Text documents, images, and smaller files can easily be e-mailed directly or posted to the Web. From there, you can link the document to Facebook or Twitter. You might even place the documents on a website and optimize the site's content and descriptions for intermediary audiences such as search engine robots. As you can probably see, delivering to audiences you know is not a problem; delivering to those you don't can be more challenging. Use nonhuman audiences such as Web robots to help disseminate your documents to those audiences you don't know but might benefit somehow from seeing your texts. For advice on how to reach Web robots and better deliver your texts on the Web, return to the section on search engine optimization in Chapter 6.

For delivering video, you most likely know about YouTube and Vimeo. Each of these sites can affect delivery differently. YouTube has much more traffic than Vimeo, so, in theory, you have a better chance of someone finding your video. However, more videos also mean more competition during a search, so your audience might not find your video. Vimeo has less visitors but offers more customization, including the ability to place your own brand mark on your video and cleaner, higher-quality uploaded videos. However, Vimeo charges a small fee for some of its services, while YouTube is completely free. You should research the pros and cons of any site that you're considering as a delivery platform, and determine how your audience will respond when viewing the video on a particular site.

But distribution can also be thought of in other terms. Aspects such as the *genre* and *format* of the document, greatly affect how a reader responds.

Genre:

The term "genre" can cover a range of meanings. For instance, in a written essay, itself a genre, you might choose subgenres such as satire, parody, or opinion.

You could select a range of technical writing genres such as letters, memos, reports, manuals, or other kinds of documents. For example, letters are often used in more formal situations with audiences outside of your organization, while memos are used for more informal, internal situations.

Film, as this text has already discussed, has a wide array of genres and subgenres as well, including documentary, comedy, drama, romance, suspense, fantasy, or science fiction.

Your photographs might fall under the genres of fashion, advertising, still life, fine art, nature, travel, architectural, portrait, or photojournalism. As you plan your project, consider how the audience will react to the genre you choose. This reaction affects the document's overall delivery.

Format:

When you think of format, you might think of the formal aspects of a document, such as the page size, margins, layout, or spacing. While this type of format certainly affects an audience (such as your teachers, who might demand 1" margins), other kinds of formats are important for writing in new media, particularly file formats.

If you want to deliver to a wide audience, you should select formats that are more universal. While Microsoft Word documents can be opened by many computers, Adobe PDFs are more accessible, and the PDF reader can be downloaded for free.

While your video might look better in a high definition format, this format might not be easily viewable if the intended audience doesn't have a fast download connection to the Internet.

When preparing a document, research which file formats are most accessible, and consider what technological capabilities your audience will have. If you know they can view an HD video, then upload the larger file. However, if you're not sure, use a lower quality version or provide the option for either. If your audience can't download or view your file format, then your delivery will fail, and moreover, you'll probably frustrate your reader.

Of course, not all of the documents you deliver will be online. As discussed earlier in this text, a flyer for a lost dog will probably be distributed in hard copy around the neighborhood. In addition to aspects such as typography, layout, or color, how and where you place your document matters. Chapter 5 offers extensive guidance on how and where to place your documents in an environment.

MAKING CONNECTIONS

AS A CLASS

Everyone should suggest a movie title. Next, research who distributed each movie. Does the distributor affect how you view the movie? Does it have any effect? Research the background for each distributor. How does this information, if at all, influence how you might receive future movies released by the distributor?

IN A GROUP

Select three online sites that allow you to upload, store, and share photos. What are the differences between these sites? What are the pros and cons of each? What are the different audiences for each site (e.g., personal vs. business use)? How do you think each site would affect a photo's delivery differently? Write a report that outlines your findings and share them with the class.

ON YOUR OWN

Create a list of the different file formats in which an image can be saved. Research each format, noting the intended purpose and use of the format type. How might these formats influence a file's delivery? How does each format affect the image's viewing and dissemination differently? How does this information influence how you think about saving your own images in the future? Draft a report, and share your results with the class.

ENVIRONMENT

Figure 12.16
Auditoriums are specially designed to maximize sound acoustics

The *environment* and location also play a part in delivery. Auditoriums are designed to maximize an orator's volume and carry his or her voice to the back row (Figure 12.16). They're also designed so that every seated audience member can see the speaker on stage. Recording studios are soundproofed so that noises from the outside environment don't disturb the vocal talent or dilute the recording process. Likewise, the environment in which you place your text will play a huge part in how that message is delivered and received.

This text already discussed how the design and arrangement of a billboard affect the way its message is delivered, but where and how it's placed in its environment also play a role. In Chapter 5 you looked at several examples of billboards, considering how the overall environment influenced the way that an audience viewed and interacted with the genre.

For example, this text discussed how the American Atheists attempted to place their billboard (Figure 5.7) in a heavily Jewish community so that they could best reach their intended audience. Such a decision not only shows a savvy awareness of using the environment rhetorically but also how such rhetoric extends to an awareness of delivery.

The billboard in Figure 12.17 depicts a fishing lure from the fishing goods company Rapala. One of these billboards is placed at the Florida Turnpike exit ramp for the Florida Keys. A few environmental factors make the placement of this billboard rhetorically effective: 1) many people coming to the Keys do so to fish; 2) the exit bends past the sign, making it hard to miss; 3) traffic slows down to 35 mph so that the driver should have plenty of time to see it. While their lure gets "more hits than Google," the ad probably gets more hits than a Google ad over the course of a year.

Credit: Steve Baird

Figure 12.17
Rapala is hoping that fish aren't the only species that take their bait.

When considering delivery and environment, you might use the ecological concept of *niche* as a way to think about your audience. In the field of ecology, a niche is a specific role or category that a species occupies within an environment. That role is defined, in part, by its relation to the niches of other plants or animals.

In general, each species specializes in a particular way of surviving and living within this niche helps to ensure that it has resources other animals can't use. When thinking about delivery, you might ask several questions about niche and delivery. For example: do you have a product or argument that no one else has? If so, you might choose language that explains how it's unique. On the other hand, you might have a product that many people can use, but you want to target a specific group of people who best fit your intended audience. In advertising, each of these groups would be examples of a "niche market."

Depending on the kind of college or university you're attending, apartments close to campus are often the most desirable to students so that they can walk to campus. This kind of property is the equivalent of beachfront property on the coasts. Companies that own such apartments have a desirable, niche product, and should focus their marketing on this fact (Figure 12.18). Of course, these companies also have a specific, niche audience: university students, staff, and faculty.

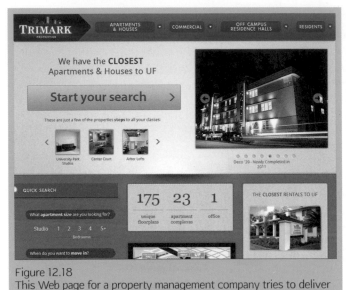

Figure 12.18
This Web page for a property management company tries to deliver a niche product (apartments close to campus) to niche consumers (students).

To most effectively deliver their message, the company most likely will target their marketing to these three populations. Although anyone who lives in the same town could be a potential tenant, the most likely viewer to respond to such advertisements would be someone connected to the school. For this example, then, the location of the product—as well as the specific niche it inhabits among the kinds of apartments available—affects how the marketing director would attempt to reach her audience, ultimately affecting how the message becomes delivered.

Chapter 5 extensively discusses environment, and all of the information in that chapter is pertinent to understanding and executing delivery. Failure to thoughtfully consider the environment in which you place a text can cause viewers to miss it, or even cause the text's destruction. For a few quick guidelines toward better delivery in a particular environment, consider the following:

- Where is best location to reach your intended audience?
- What will your audience be doing in this location?
- How can you best integrate your text into the environment?
- How might an electronic environment affect your text?
- How might a natural environment affect your text?

These guidelines will help ensure that—once placed in a particular environment—your text has the best chance of reaching your audience and optimizing delivery.

MAKING CONNECTIONS

AS A CLASS

Bring in advertisements for the apartment or rental house in which you live. How do these rental companies integrate the location of the building into their advertisements? How does this portrayal (or lack thereof) affect the delivery of their message? How would you change their ads to better reach their intended audience?

IN A GROUP

Walk through your campus, paying attention to where visuals appear. Create a list of niches into which these visuals might fall. Once you have noticed all the niches in use, see if you can identify niches that aren't being occupied by a particular visual. How might these unused spaces be rhetorically effective or enacted? How might it aid a text's delivery? Share your list and results with the class.

ON YOUR OWN

Often, a university's auditorium or coliseum can be rearranged into a variety of configurations depending on the event being held. For example, event personnel will arrange the venue for a graduation ceremony differently than for a musical concert. Research the different options available for your local venue and the different purposes for each arrangement. How do you think each formation affects delivery differently? Can you think of alternative arrangements that would be more effective? Write a report based on your findings, and share them with the class.

KEY TERMS

delivery

distribution

environment

format

niche

OUTPUT: IREPORT/PUBLIC SERVICE ANNOUNCEMENT

While most anyone can post a message on the Web, delivery entails that someone else actually receives that message. Video search engines such as YouTube allow you to gain followers, tag videos, and share them with others. These tools enhance delivery.

Figure 12.19
CNN iReport allows you to upload your own news reports. They also give out assignments, such as this one looking for "mom" tattoos.

For the past few years, the news organization CNN has encouraged the average citizen to record newsworthy events and upload them to the CNN Web page as an "iReport" (Figure 12.19). This kind of dissemination—should the video be accepted by CNN's editors—has enormous potential for delivery as the videos are sometimes also shown on CNN's cable channel.

For this output, you will compose your own CNN iReport. Although you are not required to actually gain CNN's acceptance of the video, think about what kind of report will best attract notice from an editor. As an alternative, you can also create your own public service announcement, informing your audience of some important topic in your community. Use the guidelines below as you craft your videos.

iReport Guidelines

View other iReports: To get an idea of the genre of iReports, visit CNN's iReport Web page (ireport.cnn.com) and view some of the iReports they've already published. You can also view the current assignments that ask for specific iReports if you can't think of a topic that's important to your own community. This page also offers further tips and advice for creating an iReport.

Conduct research: Make sure you understand the basics of your story, such as who or what this video is about, and where, when, and why it occurred. You should also follow the suggestions for researching found in Chapter 7.

Script a story: Using the advice in Chapter 9, create a script for your report that tells a clear story of the event or topic you're covering. Consider focusing on a single individual as your protagonist, providing a central character for your audience to identify with. Your story should also have an introduction, middle, and conclusion. Check that each scene flows into the next so that the audience isn't surprised and confused by the sequence of shots.

Make it significant: Make sure your audience understands WHY your story is important to them. Does it involve their community? Who is affected by the story? Why should they care and keep watching? You must connect with your audience at this basic level.

Make it emotional: As discussed throughout this text, images offer an emotional connection more potent than print. Use what you have learned about *ethos* and visuals to make an emotional connection with the audience, keeping them engaged and invested in your report.

Use basic narration: Since CNN has millions of visits each day, the editors have to make sure that the language is appropriate for a diverse audience. When writing your narration, choose words that are clear, accurate, and understandable by a general audience. In other words, tell the story like a normal person and not an expert. Only include jargon or complex language when you must, and then make sure to explain these terms to the viewer.

Review and revise: Once you have a rough cut you can begin revising. As discussed in Chapter 11, start with the large-scale changes first. Notice where the gaps in argument or story occur, which shots and scenes look poor, and which look poor when sequenced together. Once you've accomplished the revision, you can begin to edit transitions and other elements before performing a final proof. Remember, ask peers to review your work as well since they can offer input on problems you might not notice.

Submit: After you've revised, upload your iReport to CNN's website, or to other video sites such as YouTube or Vimeo. Tag your video with relevant keywords so that your audience can best find it.

PSA Guidelines

While an iReport focuses on a real-life, fact-based story, a public service announcement can take more creative license in appealing to a viewer. The topic you choose may have real-life ramifications, but you can create a fictional story to explain, inform, or persuade your audience about that topic. Many of the guidelines below mimic those for the video essay, so you can return to that assignment to brainstorm ideas for your PSA.

View other PSAs: To better understand the genre of PSAs, view some examples online. Note how PSAs typically make their argument in less than a minute. Note their use of analogy, comparison and contrast, and other rhetorical techniques discussed in other chapters. Consider modeling your own PSA on one of these examples.

Choose a topic: Like your video essay, you should choose a topic that interests you, one that calls you to write. You might compose a short argument based on an environmental problem in your community or an evaluative argument discussing why you feel one energy source is better than another. However, you might choose a topic on which you can easily find sources of video online, or which you can shoot with your own camera. Remember, PSAs are short, so your topic should be focused.

Research your topic: As with any writing assignment, much of the work comes before you start writing. If you're focusing on a local environmental issue, research not only the perspectives of the local players involved in the conversations, but also the context and history of the environmental problem. During this research, try to narrow down the topic to one aspect of this larger issue since you don't have much time to make a broad, complex argument. Also plan what kinds of footage you're capable of shooting and what video already exists for you to incorporate. In addition, make sure you are safe when taking your own video and ask for permission when shooting on private property or other locations that require it.

Plan and draft: Before picking up the camera, plan your initial components and structure of your argument. This plan can include writing a short essay first, which includes a claim, reasons, and evidence, or it can provide a more basic outline of the argument and the major scenes and visuals. Once you clarify the main points for yourself, you can start to think more visually, developing a script that will depict the scenes you hope to include as well as audio, such as voice-over narration or background music. As discussed in Chapter 9, this step can be the most important, determining if your project fails or succeeds. However, because of the short length of a PSA, you probably only have time to include one reason and one piece of evidence; therefore, you should select whatever evidence you feel is the most powerful.

Grab your audience: Since a PSA is so short, you don't have a lot of time to hook your audience and keep them watching. Quickly use a shocking fact, a question, a joke, or some other means to get their attention. Also consider using emotionally charged images, but don't use anything so offensive or grotesque that your audience turns away. Remember, as you saw in Chapter 2, many memes have been created making fun of how emotionally disturbing the ASPCA commercials can be.

Create a storyboard: Once you've completed a script, create a storyboard that depicts each shot. The storyboard will be invaluable as both a conceptual tool—helping you to see your video before you actually assemble and edit it—

as well as an organizational tool, providing a framework for visually arranging your script and making sure you account for all the shots you might need.

Create a shot list and gather footage: Once you've written your script, use it as a blueprint to create a shot list. This list will provide an important resource to ensure that you gather all of the video footage you'll need. You might also develop a coding system for this shot list, noting which footage you plan to shoot yourself, and which footage you plan to use from other archival sources. Dividing your list this way can help you manage your time since the footage that you shoot will probably take longer to gather than archival footage. When producing video, try to acquire this footage as early as possible, since editing will be more time consuming than you may realize and is often the longest part of the process.

Add narration: Although your project may not require it, you may want to add voice-over narration to comment on the video footage or to maintain the argumentative arc. If you've adequately planned for your PSA, you have already written this narration in your script. Like your shooting list, create a list of sounds you plan to use, including narration, and create these files before starting the revision process.

Create a rough cut: After you have gathered your footage and recorded any necessary narration, use your storyboards as a guide to assemble your clips into a single rough cut of your PSA. Try to complete as much of the PSA as possible so you will have a better idea of how to revise the piece.

Revise, edit, proof: Once you have a rough cut, you can begin revising. As discussed in Chapter 11, start with the large-scale changes first. Notice where the gaps in argument occur, which shots and scenes look poor, and which look poor when sequenced together. Once you've revised, you can begin to edit transitions and other elements before performing a final proof. Remember, ask peers to review your work as well since they can offer input on problems you might not notice.

Save and distribute: As you work, save your video file often. Once you've finished, consider what file format you'll need to distribute it in. You might plan to burn the file onto a DVD. If so, you can consider large-format files such as high definition (HD) formats. If you're distributing the video online, you might consider MPEG, AVI, MOV, or other formats that use less memory. However, sites such as YouTube can accept a wide away of video file formats including HD formats. Whatever distribution method you plan, research what file formats are acceptable and research the specifics of those file formats. While your video might look good in the video editor, it can look lousy if you save it in the wrong format.

VIDEO LINKS

Chapter 1

Figure 1.3

Which way do you see the dancer twirl?

http://www.youtube.com/watch?v=nwsGDfzDEOA

Figure 1.5

Right vs. left brain test: what did you see?

http://www.youtube.com/watch?v=ffUm9ZxxLaHM

Figure 1.6

Right vs. left brain test: did you see the color "blue"?

http://www.youtube.com/watch?v=arbT8ZqXnwk

Figure 1.7

Sir Ken Robinson argues that teachers must change education.

http://www.youtube.com/watch?v=iG9CE55wbtY

Figure 1.18

Remember to "think before you post" images or other documents to the Internet, because once you hit send, it's "out of your hands."

http://www.youtube.com/watch?v=cBkZkf2Vmdw

Chapter 2

Figure 2.1

A defense of rhetoric.

http://www.youtube.com/watch?v=BYMUCz9bHAs

Figure 2.8

New Team Jordan Signature Shoes: celebrities and designers add their credibility to Nike's discussion of these shoes.

http://www.youtube.com/watch?v=grGSpZoGaRg

Figure 2.12

This public service announcement uses a song to elicit *pathos*, and a celebrity to create *ethos*.

http://www.youtube.com/watch?v=YliPZ0p0SNQ

Figure 2.19

Testimonies from former smokers are effective, but are they too effective?

http://www.youtube.com/watch?v=EyVLKHEqTu0

Figure 2.22

The unfortunate shooting at Sandy Hook Elementary School provided a kairotic moment to discuss gun control.

http://www.youtube.com/watch?v=gAmr-A-F8K8

Figure 2.24

This AT&T ad shows how writing technologies can work together to solve problems more quickly.

http://www.youtube.com/watch?v=cZwEIKBxgtU

Chapter 3

Figure 3.4

The Federal Emergency Management Agency would like to help keep small business owners from going underwater.

http://www.fema.gov/medialibrary/media_records/12398

Figure 3.13

Note how this ad uses *pathos* to convince you to wear a helmet.

http://www.10ad.org/wear-a-helmet-and-protect-your-life/

Figure 3.14

This AT&T ad makes an appeal to social privilege.

http://www.youtube.com/watch?v=VZv_duAByDI

Figure 3.15

This Old Spice ad uses improbable transitions to appeal to the viewer.

http://www.youtube.com/watch?v=owGykVbfgUE

Figure 3.16

The Forest Service appeals to a sense of adventure.

http://www.discovertheforest.org/about

Figure 3.22

Governor Bob McDonnell uses a kairotic moment to discuss the role of women in the military.

http://www.youtube.com/watch?v=Hx9bKObcoPo

Figure 3.25

General Electric taps into the kairotic moment of environmental conversations.

http://www.youtube.com/watch?v=MCH-T8kMh7A

Chapter 4

Figure 4.5

Pacific Life has been "breathing" for 140 years.

http://www.youtube.com/watch?v=i2-wtfR98Kg

Figure 4.6

Pacific Life continues to "guide" its customers.

> http://www.youtube.com/watch?v=rR4WBVrfYCA&feature=youtu.be

Figure 4.7

Pacific Life "listens" and adapts when necessary.

> http://www.youtube.com/watch?v=ELYjfrsNxpU

Figure 4.8

Allstate commercials often personify "mayhem" to create an analogy.

> http://www.youtube.com/watch?v=6QIxySt3e-g

Figure 4.13

If you're not you when you're hungry, are you like Betty White?

> http://www.youtube.com/watch?v=UbMN7wvIw_s&feature=youtu.be

Figure 4.16

Do woodchucks chuck wood? If so, then Geico can save you money on your car insurance, according to the enthymeme they construct.

> http://www.youtube.com/watch?v=4faBo4PdFpU&feature=youtu.be

Figure 4.24

Quint tells Hooper and Brody of the night the USS Indianapolis sunk.

> http://www.youtube.com/watch?v=u9S41Kplsbs

Figure 4.31

This Corona commercial juxtaposes different scenes to create a mood.

> http://www.youtube.com/watch?v=ETPxQu1TQcA

Figure 4.36

Literal version of "Rainbow Connection."

> http://www.youtube.com/watch?v=Ywvwp0aQz-o&feature=youtu.be

Figure 4.39

This music video attempts to tell a story to make an argument.

> http://www.youtube.com/watch?v=aMfSGt6rHos

Figure 4.44

Team America shows how to make a montage.

> http://www.youtube.com/watch?v=oJc0PxeikfA&feature=youtu.be

Figure 4.49

The *Rocky* movies make frequent use of montage scenes.

> http://www.youtube.com/watch?v=rV7rjT_dGbY&feature=youtu.be

Figure 4.55

You should always "think before you post" online.

> http://www.youtube.com/watch?v=KhbxOxftr-U

Figure 4.64

History of the CBS brand mark.

> http://www.youtube.com/watch?v=wB63odkphhg

Chapter 6

Figure 6.1

This was a successful screen test for Henry Thomas for the movie E.T.

> http://www.youtube.com/watch?v=t0Cinb1j5-s

Figure 6.24

This Volkswagen commercial was widely shared.

> http://www.youtube.com/watch?v=R55e-uHQna0

Figure 6.25

Will it blend? This question has made it a popular meme.

> http://www.youtube.com/watch?v=lAl28d6tbko

Figure 6.28

Kevin Slavin explains how algorithms shape the world.

> http://www.youtube.com/watch?v=TDaFwnOiKVE

Figure 6.30

Barney Stinson has a very imaginative video résumé.

> http://www.barneysvideoresume.com/

Figure 6.31

Matthew Epstein eventually landed his dream job with this video résumé.

> http://www.youtube.com/watch?v=HRHFEDyHIsc

Chapter 7

Figure 7.11

Kirby Ferguson explains that "everything" is a remix.

> http://www.youtube.com/watch?v=Z-HuenDPZw0

Figure 7.21

Keep America Beautiful's commercial featuring "The Crying Indian."

> http://www.youtube.com/watch?v=j7OHG7tHrNM

Chapter 8

Figure 8.5

Dwight D. Eisenhower argues that voting for his opponent will result in "high prices."

> http://www.livingroomcandidate.org/commercials/1952/high-prices

Figure 8.6

Ronald Reagan told a positive story about his presidency.

> http://www.youtube.com/watch?v=EU-IBF8nwSY

Figure 8.16

When depicted with the music of Psy, Zombies aren't so scary (just stylish).

> http://www.youtube.com/watch?v=B4hv0-FPDxc

Figure 817

The Lion King opens with what's commonly interpreted as African sounds and rhythms.

> http://www.youtube.com/watch?v=JQ89RTVJB4c

Figure 8.18

U2 argues against the violence in Northern Ireland through their song "Sunday, Bloody Sunday."

> http://www.youtube.com/watch?v=Q59HvK2HM2c

Figure 8.19

Bruce Springsteen's "Born in the U.S.A." implicitly argues against how returning soldiers have been treated.

> http://www.youtube.com/watch?v=EPhWR4d3FJQ

Figure 8.20

Lupe Fiasco's song "Words I Never Said" (featuring Skylar Grey) makes an implicit argument through its lyrics (and the images in the music video).

> http://www.youtube.com/watch?v=22l1sf5JZD0

Figure 8.21

The documentary *The Corporation* makes a very explicit argument.

> http://www.youtube.com/watch?v=s5hEiANG4Uk&feature=relmfu

Figure 8.24

This trailer remixes scenes from the comedy *Dumb and Dumber* to make it seem like a dramatic thriller.

> http://www.youtube.com/watch?v=zLDx-BPgxxA

Chapter 9

Figure 9.2

There are some misconceptions about being a screenwriter.

> http://www.oscars.org/video/watch/screenwriters_misconception.html

Figure 9.6

This transition dissolves one image into another.

> http://commons.wikimedia.org/wiki/File:A2o_dissolve.ogg

Figure 9.7

This scene from *Breathless* makes heavy use of jump cuts.

> http://www.youtube.com/watch?v=OwLH6-bDhuE&list=PLOToExFaWoNJnJE6y3V3St 32gtnmz9Cr8

Figure 9.8

This aerial shot from *The Shawshank Redemption* also establishes the new location of the prison.

> http://www.youtube.com/watch?v=wyDifF2_ Csk&list=PLOToExFaWoNJnJE6y3V3St32gtnmz9Cr8

Figure 9.9

This match cut from *2001: A Space Odyssey* is perhaps one of the most famous.

> http://www.youtube.com/watch?v=mI3s5fA7Zhk&list= PLOToExFaWoNJnJE6y3V3St32gtnmz9Cr8

Figure 9.10

This reverse angle reveals Tim to the viewer, but not the velociraptor.

> http://www.youtube.com/watch?v=dnRxQ3dcaQk

Figure 9.11

The BBC series *Planet Earth* uses narration to describe the various creatures and landscapes. To what extent do you also think the narration contributes toward storytelling?

> http://www.youtube.com/watch?v=3-uA8t7-msY

Figure 9.12

The opening scene from *The Assassination of Jesse James by the Coward Robert Ford* uses voice over narration to provide information about the main character.

> http://www.youtube.com/watch?v=r2gY_e1ZKD8

Figure 9.13

That Honey Badger is Nasty!

> http://www.youtube.com/watch?v=4r7wHMg5Yjg

Figure 9.14

Steven Spielberg on storyboarding.

> http://www.youtube.com/watch?v=nBH89Y0Xj7c

Figure 9.15

Storyboards can easily take up a whole wall.

> http://wiredfly.blogspot.com/2010_04_01_archive.html

Figure 9.16

A Prezi can be a useful tool for creating storyboards.

> http://prezi.com/iihdlkhrsg8l/storyboard/

Chapter 10

Figure 10.16

Head Crusher from *Kids in the Hall.*

> http://www.youtube.com/watch?v=8t4pmlHRokg

Chapter 11

Figure 11.1

Most directors will tell you that a good movie requires good editing.

> http://www.youtube.com/watch?v=508MHvMGWEg&list=FLJtroKLbeSoVdiNCZTUL-lg&feature=mh_lolz

Figure 11.5

Editing often requires the writer to cut much of what you've already written.

> http://www.youtube.com/watch?v=4php_B1LQiM

Figure 11.11

Brandon Pinard, from *Videomaker* magazine, discusses some common transitions.

> http://www.youtube.com/watch?v=iCEdSGeFCCA

Figure 11.12

In the movie *Star Trek*, the audience sees a long fly-by glimpse of the new U.S.S. Enterprise at the same time the main characters do.

> http://www.youtube.com/watch?v=O9Rj-r25OTk

Figure 11.21

This essay about the pencil was produced by students trying to make an explicit argument (through the persona of Nicholas Cage).

> http://www.youtube.com/watch?v=3BEc5CDju_k

Chapter 12

Figure 12.14

John F. Kennedy and Richard Nixon appeared in the first televised Presidential Debate.

> http://www.youtube.com/watch?v=C6Xn4ipHiwE

Figure 12.15

The television show *24* arranges multiple viewpoints to help create suspense and enhance delivery.

> http://www.youtube.com/watch?v=ZFrl4Bw2kec

REFERENCES

Abramowitz, Rachel. "Johnny Depp Explains How He Picked his Poison with the Mad Hatter." *Los Angeles Times*. 24 Dec. 2009. Web.

Allen, Erika Tyner. "The Kennedy-Nixon Presidential Debates, 1960." *The Museum of Broadcast Communications*. N.d.

Barthes, Roland. *Image, Music, Text*. Tran. Stephen Heath. New York: Hill and Wang, 1978. Print.

Bolter, David Jay and Richard Grusin. *Remediation: Understanding New Media*. Cambridge, MA: MIT Press, 2000. Print.

Branson, Matthew. "How to Effectively Market with Memes (Without Forcing It)," *blueglassarchive*.com. 23 February NO YEAR. Web.

Brownlee, Jim. "Building a Better Radiation Warning Symbol." wired.com. 20 Feb. 2007. Web.

Dobrin, Sidney I. and Christian R. Weisser. *Natural Discourse: Toward Ecocomposition*. Albany: State University of New York Press, 2002. Print.

Ferguson, Kirby. "Everything is a Remix Part 2." *Vimeo*. 1 Feb 2011. Web.

Forer, Ben and Olivia Katrandjian. "Soft Drink Industry Fights Back, Depicting Bloomberg as Nanny." *ABC News.* 2 Jun 2012. Web.

Gusky, Bill. "Damien Hirst: Shark Killer." *Artblog Comments.* 1 October 2006. Web.

Hall, Jonathan C. "Marketing That Makes the Product Better." *Creative Distraction.* 4 August 2009. Web.

Hoffman, Maxwell. "Creating a New Language for Nutrition: McDonald's Universal Icons for 109 Countries." *TC World.* Sept-Oct 2007: 22-25. Web.

Homer. *The Iliad.* Trans. Stanley Lombardo. Indianapolis: Hackett Publishing, 1997. Print.

Homer. *The Odyssey.* Trans. Ian Johnston. Arlington, VA: Richer Resources Publishing, 2006. Print.

Hoyle, Ben. "Movie's Blue-skinned Aliens Aim to Open Our Eyes to War on Terror". *The Times.* 11 Dec. 2009. Print.

Isaacson, Andy. "Are You Following a Bot?" *The Atlantic.* 2 April 2011. Web.

Krech, Shepard III. *The Ecological Indian: Myth and History.* New York: W. W. Norton, 1999. Print.

Kilburn, Kevin J. "Eric Burgess: Manchester's First Rocket Man." *Astronomy in the UK.* 11 Sept 2007. Web.

King, Jr., Martin Luther. "I Have a Dream." Lincoln Memorial, Washington, D.C. 28 Aug. 1963. Address.

Merica, Dan. "*Atheist Group Targets Muslims and Jews with 'Myth' Billboards in Arabic and Hebrew.*" *CNN Belief Blog.* 1 March 2012. Web.

McLuhan, McLuhan. *Understanding Media: The Extensions of Man.* Cambridge, MA: MIT Press, 1994. Print.

McCoy, Stuart. "Rhetoric: What Are Some Examples of Kairos in Web Design?" *Quora.* 11 Feb 2011. Web.

"The Misconceptions of Being a Screenwriter." *The Academy of Motion Picture Arts and Sciences.* N.d. Web.

Mitchell, W. J. T. *Picture Theory.* Chicago, IL: University of Chicago Press, 1995. Print.

Murray, Peter. "51 Percent of Total Online Traffic Is Non-Human." *Singularityhub.com.* 23 Mar. 2012. Web.

Postman, Neil. "The Reformed English Curriculum." in A.C. Eurich, ed., *High School 1980: The Shape of the Future in American Secondary Education* (1970). Print.

Quigley, Robert. "Cavaliers Owner Dan Gilbert Addresses Cleveland in Comic Sans: Why We Facepalm." *Geekosystem.com.* 9 July 2010. Web.

Ridolfo, Jim and Dànielle Nicole DeVoss. "Composing for Recomposition: Rhetorical Velocity and Delivery." *Kairos: A Journal of Rhetoric, Technology, and Pedagogy* 13.2 (2009). Print.

Santorum, Rick. "Santorum concerned about women in combat." Interview with John King. CNN. *YouTube.* 10 February 2012. Web.

Schaper, David. "Gang Signs And A Sticker: Chicago Pulls Teen's Design." *NPR News.* 9 February 2012. Web.

Shute, Nancy. "Why Drug Companies Are Shy About Sharing On Facebook." *NPR News.* 22 August 2011. Web.

Smith, Roberta. "Just When You Thought It Was Safe." *The New York Times.* 16 October 2007. Web.

Ulmer, Gregory L. *Internet Invention.* New York: Longman, 2003. Print.

Wikner, Martin. "How to Cast a Movie and Choose the Actors." *Martinwikner.com.* 25
　　Mar. 2011. Web.

Zelizer, Julian. "How Political Ads Can Elect a President." CNN.com. 29 May 2012. Web.

INDEX